JAPAN'S ROAD
to the PACIFIC WAR

THE FINAL
CONFRONTATION

Studies of the East Asian Institute • Columbia University

The East Asian Institute of Columbia University

The East Asian Institute is Columbia University's center for research, publication, and teaching on modern East Asia. The Studies of the East Asian Institute were inaugurated in 1962 to bring to a wider public the results of significant new research on Japan, China, and Korea.

JAPAN'S ROAD
to the PACIFIC WAR

THE FINAL
CONFRONTATION

JAPAN'S NEGOTIATIONS
with the UNITED STATES,
1941

JAMES WILLIAM MORLEY, *editor*
DAVID A. TITUS, *translator*

Columbia University Press • New York

Columbia University Press
New York   Chichester, West Sussex
Copyright © 1994 Columbia University Press
All rights reserved

Library of Congress Cataloging-in-Publication Data

Taiheiyō sensō e no michi. English. Selections.
    The final confrontation : Japan's negotiations with the United States,
    1941 / James William Morley, editor; David A. Titus, translator.
        p.   cm.—(Japan's Road to the Pacific War)
    Translation of selected portions from Taiheiyō Sensō e no michi.
Cf. Pref.
        Includes bibliographical references and index.
        ISBN 0-231-08024-7
        1. World War, 1939–1945—Diplomatic history. 2. Japan—Foreign
    relations—1912–1945.   3. United States—Foreign relations—1933–
    1945.   4. Foreign relations—United States.   5. United States—For-
    eign relations—Japan.   6. World War, 1939–1945—Causes. I. Mor-
    ley, James William, 1921–   . II. Title. III. Series.
    D753.T352513   1994   94-1392
    940.53′2—dc20   CIP

Printed in the United States of America
c 10 9 8 7 6 5 4 3

To the Memory of
Shumpei Okamoto

Contents

This is the fifth and final volume of the series *Japan's Road to the Pacific War*, a translation with scholarly introductions of selected portions of *Taiheiyō sensō e no michi*. This remarkable collection of essays by Japanese scholars was undertaken over thirty years ago under the direction of Kamikawa Hikomatsu for the Japan Association on International Relations (Nihon Kokusai Seiji Gakkai) and published in seven volumes by the Asahi Shimbunsha in 1962–63.

The authors were given access to a wide range of primary materials, including not only those of the International Military Tribunal for the Far East but also a mass of hitherto unavailable documents from the former imperial army and navy, the Justice Ministry, and the Foreign Ministry. The private papers of Prime Ministers Konoe Fumimaro and Okada Keisuke, General Ugaki Kazushige, Colonel Ishiwara Kanji, and others were opened. A number of leading participants in the events made themselves available for interview.

The result is the most richly documented account of the Japanese story of these extraordinary events that we have—so useful to Japanese that the entire series was republished in 1987, and so useful to non-Japanese scholars as to have formed one of the essential sources for nearly every study of the origins of the Pacific War since. Its translation into English for a wider audience, therefore, seemed imperative.

It had been hoped when this project was begun that the translations could be produced more expeditiously than has been possible. In the intervening years much new research has been done and scholars on both sides of the Pacific have offered additional interpretations of these critical years. But the extraordinary richness of the factual data presented in the Japanese scholarship translated here has not been superseded.

In addition, this final volume has a special interest. When Kamikawa died, Tsunoda Jun, then a professor of diplomatic history at Kokugakuin University, was invited to take over direction of the entire project. He was a man of a different stripe from the other participants. In the years leading up to Pearl Harbor, he had been looked on as one of "the best and the brightest" of his generation. A graduate of Tokyo Imperial University, an executive secretary in the Shōwa Juku, a training school for the Great East Asia Co-Prosperity Sphere, and an aide to Prince Konoe, he had had an up-front view of the events the scholars were examining. He knew many of the participants and had strong opinions about where to lay the principal blame for what was obviously a disaster: on the navy and Kido on the Japanese side, and on Hornbeck and Hull on the American side.

The project was too far along for Tsunoda to be able to influence the views of the other participants, but his personal research assignment gave him an opportunity to vent his spleen. The reader can not help but find Tsunoda's interpretations provocative. He or she will also find in David Titus's introduction a pointed critique of some of the more problematic issues raised.

As the project is completed, I wish here to thank the Japan Association on International Relations for sponsoring the original study, the Japanese and American scholars who have persevered so long to complete it, the Asahi Shimbunsha for giving its permission to publish a partial translation, and Columbia University Press for keeping the faith.

On a more personal level, I want to thank three individuals in particular: Dale K. A. Finlayson, who has performed a Herculean task of clarifying meaning, polishing style, and standardizing usages—of names of persons, places, documents, and incidents for all volumes in the series; the late Shumpei Okamoto; and David Titus.

I first came to know Shumpei Okamoto when he came to Columbia as a student in Japanese politics and history. Driven by financial pressure to work throughout his graduate studies, he completed a brilliant doctoral dissertation, published as *The Japanese Oligarchy and the Russo-Japanese War* (1970), and took up a teaching position at Temple University in Philadelphia. He had earlier begun helping me with the *Road to the Pacific War* project, checking all translations against the originals for absolute accuracy, and when several translators had finally thrown up their hands at the Tsunoda volume, he volunteered to take it on. His untimely death prevented its completion, but his mark is upon it as it is upon all this series—and upon the lives of all who knew him.

And my special thanks to David Titus, who picked up this translation when his friend, Shumpei, was forced to lay it down and whose assiduity, linguistic skills, and acumen show on every page.

A note of technical explanation. Throughout the series, the principle of selection has been to include those essays or portions of essays that focus primarily on the policy of Japan rather than other countries and that use unusual and important materials. In each case as faithful a translation as possible has been rendered, but translation is not a mechanical process. With languages and cultures as different as the Japanese and the Americans, minor omissions, revisions, or insertions have occasionally been made to make the translated version more readily intelligible. In addition, for the convenience of researchers, footnotes have been clarified and occasionally changed, for example, to indicate the published location of sources originally used archivally. An effort also has been made to standardize spellings and identifications of the names of persons and institutions and the titles of documents. While each essay stands on its own authority, its value has been greatly enhanced by a brief introduction by its scholar-translator.

Place names are spelled according to the current usage of the National Geographic Society. Except for widely recognized romanizations, such as Nanking or Canton, Chinese and Mongolian place-names are romanized according to the modified Wade-Giles system, retaining only essential aspirants. Personal names are rendered in the romanized form preferred by their users insofar as we have been able to ascertain them; otherwise, standard orthographical principles have been followed: modified Wade-Giles for Chinese, modified Hepburn for Japanese, and modified Library of Congress for Russian.

The complete set of five volumes in the series *Japan's Road to the Pacific War* includes:

Japan Erupts: The London Naval Conference and the Manchurian Incident, 1928–1932 (1984)

The China Quagmire: Japan's Expansion on the Asian Continent, 1933–1941 (1983)

Deterrent Diplomacy: Japan, Germany, and the U.S.S.R., 1935–1941 (1976)

The Fateful Choice: Japan's Advance into Southeast Asia, 1939–1941 (1980)

The Final Confrontation: Japan's Negotiations with the United States, 1941 (1994)

J.W.M.

Acknowledgments

The completion of this long overdue final volume of selected translations from *Taiheiyō sensō e no michi: kaisen no gaikō shi* (The Road to the Pacific War: A Diplomatic History of the Origins of the War) has involved a great deal of time and a great number of people. The late Shumpei Okamoto had been working on the volume for over five years before his untimely death in December 1985, and it is an enormous loss to the quality of the present volume that he was unable to bring his expertise to its completion. His corrections to the text and footnotes in the margins of the Japanese original, as well as his rough translation of the first 110 pages, were invaluable to me in completing the translation. Asada Sadao of Dōshisha University contributed generously of his time in translating a portion of this volume, checking my translation, and assisting with the footnotes. I am also grateful to Michael Cutler for his assistance in translating a substantial section of the concluding chapter. Hatano Sumio of Tsukuba University updated the footnotes and references while he was researcher/archivist in the National Institute for Defense Studies of the Defense Agency. Dale Finlayson worked not only with me but also the late Shumpei Okamoto in bringing the volume into readable prose; she contributed greatly in clearing up ambiguities and inconsistencies in the translation deriving from the original Japanese text as well as my own inadequacies as a translator and scholar of Japanese diplomatic history.

Throughout the translating and research I have benefitted from the support of my colleagues at Wesleyan, in particular William Barber, Anthony Chambers, John Frazer, Giulio Gallarotti, William Johnston, Peter Kilby, David Morgan, Yoshiko Yokochi Samuel, and Ellen Widmer. Wesleyan's generous sabbatical policy and research support also facilitated the completion of this volume. Special appreciation is due to Wesleyan's expert and willing library staff: Documents Librarian Erhard Konerding; Reference Librarians Joan Jurale, Alan Nathanson, and Edmund Rubacha; and Steven Lebergott, Head of Interlibrary Loan. They not only tracked down obscure

xiv ACKNOWLEDGMENTS

references but also provided instant responses to innumerable requests, including those for interlibrary loan sources in both English and Japanese. Above all, I am deeply grateful to Fran Warren, whose virtuosity with the computer and patience over the past six years quite literally made this volume possible.

Theodore Cook and Carol Gruber of William Patterson College organized a conference on "The Pacific War and Modern Memory: War, Culture, and Society" held on December 6 and 7, 1991, on the occasion of the fiftieth anniversary of the attack on Pearl Harbor. Intellectual perspectives and personal reminiscences presented at the conference were most helpful in preparing the introduction to this volume. Joe Devlin of Bellows Falls, Vermont, provided several sources on the Pearl Harbor attack that would not otherwise have come to my attention.

James Crowley of Yale University was unstinting in his intellectual and moral support over the past six years. Hideo Kaneko and his staff at Yale's East Asian Collection of the University Library were most helpful in locating Japanese sources that enabled me to verify facts and identify persons as well as check citations to Japanese sources in the original Japanese text.

To my late friend of thirty-seven years, Michael Harwood, and to his widow Mary I owe a debt of gratitude beyond measure.

Finally, I owe an apology to the editor, James William Morley, not only for the inordinate time it has taken me to complete this last volume in the series but also for the deficiencies that nonetheless remain.

David A. Titus
Kyoto, Japan
April, 1993

A Note on the Translation

The present volume is a translation of chapters 3 through 5 of volume 7 in the series *Taiheiyō sensō e no michi: kaisen no gaikō shi* (The Road to the Pacific War: A diplomatic History of the Origins of the War) published in 1962–63 and reissued in 1987–88. Volume 7 is the last volume of essays in the series, to which was added a volume of documents. Volume 7 concludes with an essay by Fukuda Shigeo, "Amerika no taiNichi sansen" (America's Entrance into the War against Japan), which is not translated here. Chapters 3–5, as well as chapters 1–2, were written by the late Tsunoda Jun. The translation here should be read as a continuation of Tsunoda's first two chapters, the key portions of which are translated in James William Morley, ed., *Japan's Road to the Pacific War: The Fateful Choice—Japan's Advance into Southeast Asia, 1939–1941* (New York: Columbia University Press, 1980), chapter 5. That chapter sets forth Tsunoda's basic thesis about the Japanese navy's initiative in promoting and provoking Japan's advance into southeast Asia, a theme that recurs in this volume, most notably in chapter 2.

Unless otherwise noted, all material in brackets has been supplied by the author. All material in parentheses is in the original source cited by the author. For the sake of clarity, brackets appearing in the original source cited by the author have been changed to parentheses by the translator.

Japanese names are given in the Japanese order: surname followed by given name. In many English sources the prime minister, Konoe Fumimaro, is referred to as Konoye, and the special envoy to the United States, Ikawa Tadao, is referred to as Wikawa.

Contributors

JAMES WILLIAM MORLEY is Ruggles Professor Emeritus of Political Science at Columbia University. Born in 1921, he received his B.A. from Harvard College in 1943 and his PhD from Columbia University in 1954. A former director of the East Asian Institute, Columbia University, chairman of the University's Department of Political Science, and President of the Association for Asian Studies, he has, in addition to editing and contributing to the present series, written estensively on Japanese foreign policy and international politics in the Asia-Pacific region. He has most recently edited and contributed to *The Pacific Basin: New Challenges for the United States* (1986), *Security Independence in the Asia-Pacific Region* (1986), and *Driven by Growth: Political Change in the Asia-Pacific Region* (1993); he has authored *Japan and the Asia-Pacific: Defining a New Role* (1993).

DAVID A. TITUS is Professor of Government at Wesleyan University, where he has taught since 1966. A graduate of Harvard College in 1956, he received his PhD in political science from Columbia University in 1970. At Wesleyan he has chaired the College of Social Social Studies, the Department of Government, and the East Asian Studies Program. He has also served as Resident Director of the Associated Kyoto Program in Japan, 1975–76 and 1984–85. He is author of *Palace and Politics in Prewar Japan* (Columbia University Press, 1974), "The Making of the 'Symbol Emperor System' in Postwar Japan" (*Modern Asian Studies*, October 1980), and "Accesssing the World: Palace and Foreign Policy in Post Occupation Japan" in Gerald Curtis, ed., *Japanese Foreign Policy After the Cold War: Coping with Change* (M.E. Sharpe, 1993).

TSUNODA JUN (1910–1990) graduated from Tokyo Imperial University in 1933, and in the years leading up to the Pacific War served as an aide to Prince Konoe and an executive secretary of the Shōwa Juku, an important training center devoted to Japan's mission in Asia. In the postwar years, while remaining close to Japan's wartime

leaders, Tsunoda became Professor of Diplomatic History at Kokugakuin University in Tokyo, head of the Shidehara Peace Collection of
the National Diet Library, and managing director of the Japan Strategic Studies Center. He wrote extensively. Some of his works include
Taiheiyō ni okeru Eiteikoku no suibō (The Decline and Fall of the British
Empire in the Pacific) (Tokyo: Chūō Kōronsha, 1942), *Bōrudouin,
Cheimubarin, to Hitoraa* (Baldwin, Chamberlain, and Hitler) (Tokyo:
Ochanomizu Shobō, 1958), and *Manshū mondai to kokubō hōshin: Meiji
kōki ni okeru kokubō kankyō no hendō* (The Manchurian Question and
National Defense Policy: Changes in the National Defense Environment in the Late Meiji Period) (Tokyo: Hara Shobō, 1967). Upon the
death of Kamikawa Hikomatsu, Tsunoda became chairman of the
research team that produced this series and, in addition to the present volume, contributed the essays translated as chapter 5 in *Japan's
Road to the Pacific War: The Fateful Choice—Japan's Advance into Southeast Asia, 1939–1941* (1980).

Introduction

DAVID A. TITUS

It is now more than fifty years since the Japanese attack on Pearl Harbor. It is also thirty years since the *Taiheiyō sensō e no michi* series was first published—long enough to attempt to evaluate its place, and particularly that of the work translated here, in the broad stream of scholarship on Japan's entry into World War II.[1]

Hatano Sumio, historian of war and diplomacy at Tsukuba University, has pointed out that although the fourteen scholars who participated in the series did not always share the same interpretive perspective, there was "a basic agreement among all the contributors to adhere strictly to the orthodox approach to diplomatic and military history"; that is, "to focus on the diplomatic and military activities of the top and middle-ranking officers and officials" without placing those activities in a broad theoretical or interpretive framework. The basic editorial policy of the series was in reaction to what the contributors generally felt were deficiencies in Marxist historiography, which dominated so much of Japanese scholarship at the time.[2]

It is not surprising, therefore, that the Marxists, and others as well, attacked the approach taken in the series:

> They were dissatisfied with what they construed as the series' insufficient attention to the all-important China question. They made a valid point that the succession of Japanese aggressions following the Manchurian Incident are treated largely within the narrow framework of the origins of the Japanese-American war. In the eyes of these critics, the series gave undue emphasis to the "inevitable" confrontation between Japanese and American "imperialism," while neglecting the conflict between Chinese nationalism and the "imperialist powers." This slant, the leftist critics asserted, obscured the real causes of and responsibility for the Pacific War. In short, they charged hyperbolically that the series represented an "imperialistic view of history."[3]

Hatano is perhaps overly generous to Marxist criticism of the series, the focal point of which is, after all, the Pacific War—largely a Japanese-American conflict, however disproportionately Australia, New Zealand, and the countries and colonies occupied by Japan suffered. Neither the "China question" nor "Chinese nationalism" is ignored, although quite naturally both are dealt with as key developments leading to the Pacific War. Chinese nationalism figured prominently in the escalation of the Marco Polo Bridge Incident of July 7, 1937, into a full-scale but undeclared war.[4] The Japanese army's desperate efforts to "resolve" the "China question" figure prominently in the volume translated here. For example, the army's special envoy to the informal Japanese-American talks in Washington that produced the Draft Japanese-American Understanding of April 16, 1941, was able initially to enlist army support for the Draft precisely because the Draft went right to the army's "sore spot" (p. 61) by holding forth some promise of resolving the China Incident, which the army had been unable to settle for almost four years "through its own efforts— military, political, or cunning" (p. 60). It was United States intransigence over Japan's withdrawing its troops from China, particularly Secretary of State Cordell Hull's November 26, 1941, "ultimatum," that made war "inevitable" (pp. 301–20). Earlier in the series Hata Ikuhiko had pointed out that 48 percent of the supplies reaching China from abroad arrived across the French Indochina border;[5] sealing off that major supply route was a major objective in Japan's September 1940 occupation of northern French Indochina, which in turn became the first stage in Japan's advance southward—an advance the army had been planning throughout 1940.[6] If the navy's primary objective in advancing south was to secure oil and other natural resources, an objective made even more imperative in its eyes when the United States froze Japanese assets in the United States and instituted a total embargo on oil and other critical resources between July 25 and August 1, 1941, that objective dovetailed with the army's need to close off supplies to China and to acquire resources for the successful prosecution of the China Incident.

Nor does the series argue that the China Incident and war between Japan and the United States were inevitable. Quite the contrary. The army initially hoped to contain and defuse the Marco Polo Bridge Incident which, unlike the premeditated and collusive Manchurian Incident of September 18, 1931, might not have expanded had the navy not insisted on sending forces to Shanghai. The navy's success triggered further advances by the army and finally full-scale war from December 1937 on.[7] There was, in short, nothing inevitable about the China Incident, however *likely* it was to occur. Because the series "revealed, as fully as documentation allowed, the complex realities of the 1930s, which could not be neatly explained in terms of the Marxists' schematic framework,"[8] "inevitability" is hardly a term that could be applied either to the China Incident or to war with the United States. Tsunoda's account of the final confrontation between Japan and the United States discusses a number of opportunities to avoid war that were missed by both countries, although the reader may find his evaluations of those opportunities less than convincing. Tsunoda describes the vectors toward war and their growing weight and convergence. From mid-1940 on, chances to avoid war decreased markedly as northern French Indochina was occupied, United States embargoes increased, Japan's war preparations gathered almost irreversible momentum, Japan occupied southern French Indochina, America's actions became increasingly harsh and its negotiating stance more and more rigid, and Japan's willingness to make concessions, never that great to begin with, virtually vanished. For Tsunoda, however, war became "inevitable" only with Hull's November 26, 1941, "ultimatum." If anything, Tsunoda's presentation makes war less "inevitable" than it was.[9]

A more serious criticism of the series was leveled by the outspoken liberal historian, Ienaga Saburō:

> It is deplorable when scholars substitute tendentious analysis for objectivity. *Taiheiyō sensō e no michi* (The Road to the Pacific War), a collaborative research project headed by Tsunoda Jun, and published in 1962–63, is an example. Not all of the contributors shared Tsunoda's point of view. Nevertheless, Kamikawa Hikomatsu's plan to reassess the war because excessive emphasis on war responsibility "would produce a guilt-ridden nation," coupled with Tsunoda's ideological preferences, gives the whole study a certain thrust and tone. There is an unmistakable effort to shift war responsibility away from Japan. Although the series is well-documented with new materials and facts, its basic approach is seriously flawed.[10]

The previously translated portions of the series, however, reveal that this is not an entirely objective criticism of the series as a whole. A detailed examination of Japan's involvement in China need not obscure the responsibility of those involved in doing the involvement, and in fact the detailed analyses of the 1931 Manchurian Incident and the 1937 China Incident reveal precisely who did what and when, insofar as documentation and oral histories allowed. They also show how different the two incidents were in terms of who the responsible actors were.[11]

The detailed description of the complex events and the actions of persons involved in those events does tend, however, to obscure the larger questions of why Japanese forces were in Manchuria and then China proper in the first place, and why both Tokyo and the forces in the field were unable or unwilling to rest content with Manchukuo, with its three provinces of Manchuria and one in Mongolia comprising well over twice the territory of Japan's home islands. But even this larger question is addressed by authors such as Seki Hiroharu, who points to the visionary and apocalyptic view of world history and Japan's destiny therein held by many Japanese. Ishiwara Kanji, for example, posited a final confrontation between a Japan dominant in the East and a United States dominant in the West.[12] Ishiwara's revised "History of War" (1931) "left no doubt about his expectation that it would require war with the United States, the Soviet Union, China, and Great Britain to achieve a final solution of the problems of Manchuria and Mongolia."[13]

Ishiwara, as Seki indicates, was well networked with other officers, right-wing groups, civilian bureaucrats, and business leaders. And he was not alone in his visionary view. For example, General Utsunomiya Tarō on his deathbed in February 1922 called in members of his group and "gave them as his benediction a glorious vision of expansion." Pointing to a world map, he said, "That must all become Japan's!" "The area he claimed in his final testament included all of Siberia, China, India, and Southeast Asia as far as Australia and New Zealand."[14]

At the International Military Tribunal for the Far East in Tokyo, which began its deliberations on May 3, 1946, "Ishiwara Kanji attacked the American prosecuting attorney in these terms":

> Haven't you ever heard of Perry? Don't you know anything about your country's history? . . . Tokugawa Japan believed in isolation; it didn't want to have anything to do with other countries and had its doors locked tightly. Then along came Perry from your country [in 1853] in his black ships to open those doors; he aimed his big guns at Japan and warned, "If you don't deal with us, look out for these; open your doors, and negotiate with other countries too." And then when Japan did open its doors and tried dealing with other countries, it learned that all those countries were a fearfully aggressive lot. And so for its own defense it took your country as its teacher and set about learning how to be aggressive. You might say we became your disciples. Why don't you subpoena Perry from the other world and try *him* as a war criminal?[15]

Here was an activist officer confronting the United States for provoking Japanese aggression, and giving an explanation of why Japan
had been in Manchuria and China and of why, ultimately, Japan had
gone to war with the United States.

It is this larger context of Japanese resentments and responses
against the dominant western powers, particularly the United States,
that is largely absent from Tsunoda's account of Japan's confrontation with the United States in 1940–41. As Ienaga points out, "The
diversity of ignorance [in Tokugawa Japan] was replaced by the con-
formity of state-approved knowledge" after 1900,[16] and education
was "militarized" during the Russo-Japanese War of 1904–1905. Beginning from as far back as the Sino-Japanese War of 1894–95,
China was held in contempt by Japanese leaders and the public.[17]
Indoctrination and thought control made the Japanese public more
jingoistic than Japan's top leaders from 1931 to 1941.[18] At a 1932
Asahi Gurafu-sponsored roundtable discussion among "fifth- and
sixth-grade boys and girls from the Taimei Elementary School in
Tokyo," one student said: "Americans are so arrogant. I'd like to
show them a thing or two." And another chimed in: "They act so big
all the time, they need a good beating. I'd annihilate them." [19]

That "popular" attitude would become more pronounced as the
public lined up virtually to a person in support of the 1937 China
Incident and against the United States in 1941. Crisis mongering
and the glorification of war and war heroes was endemic.[20] The
representatives of "the people" in the Japanese House of Representatives were no less chauvinistic than the public at large. After the
Manchurian Incident, for example, "despite distressing financial conditions, the Diet never rejected or reduced the vastly expanded military allocations." [21] In February 1940 Representative Saitō Takao was
expelled from the Diet for criticizing Japan's New Order in East Asia:
"his remarks constituted 'blasphemy against the holy war' . . . " [22]

Ogata Sadako notes that liberal groups in Japan were also disillu-
sioned by United States responses to the Manchurian and China
incidents, that they were increasingly chauvinistic as well as censored
after 1937.[23] Nor did the conclusion of the Tripartite Pact on September 27, 1940, "produce any sense of fear or shock among Japanese
liberals." There was "little indication that liberals were at all apprehensive that the pact might have a provocative effect." [24]

Tsunoda quotes former Prime Minister Wakatsuki Reijirō at the
conference of Senior Statesmen on November 29, 1941: "Even
though we don't have to worry about the spiritual strength of our

people, there is a need to study carefully whether or not they can endure a protracted war [with the United States and its allies] from the standpoint of commodities" (p. 325). Tsunoda gives no indication of how that "spiritual strength" was created and, in fact, the constraints that such "spiritual strength" placed upon Japan's leaders in terms of *not* going to war with the United States.

The activist side of such spiritual strength manifested itself in assassinations and threats of assassination from the fatal wounding of Prime Minister Hamaguchi Osachi in 1930 to the coup attempt (and assassination of Privy Seal Saitō Makoto among others) in the February 26 Incident in 1936. Such threats continued up to the Pearl Harbor attack. Tsunoda marginalizes this atmosphere of intimidation and crisis in his discussion of Privy Seal Kido Kōichi's unwillingness to recommend Prince Higashikuni Naruhiko as Prime Minister in October 1941. Tsunoda intimates that Higashikuni would have been able to control the explosive and revolutionary situation that would have arisen had Japan decided not to go to war with the United States under any circumstances (p. 235). Tsunoda later notes:

> Suzuki Teiichi, the person most frequently in touch with Kido from the 13th to the 16th [of October 1941], later recalled that Kido opposed Tōjō's plan [for a Higashikuni cabinet] first because of his habitual concern to constrain the emperor from speaking out, and second out of concern for his own personal safety in the event of the domestic disturbances he feared (p. 243).

Because Tsunoda pays little attention to the crisis atmosphere, the state of public opinion, and the enormous intimidation of Japan's moderate leaders during 1940–41, Kido appears to be a coward as well as an obstructionist. But Kido's actions cannot be understood in the virtual vacuum in which Tsunoda places them. And perhaps it is this absence of the larger context and larger issues that is a key factor in Marxist and liberal criticisms of the series; if those criticisms of the series as a whole are misplaced, as I have suggested above, they are, I think, particularly applicable to Tsunoda's description of the events and actions that led to war in 1941.

Is there an "unmistakable effort to shift war responsibility away from Japan" in Tsunoda's presentation? I think the answer is yes. In his frequent references to the collisions between United States Ambassador Grew in Tokyo and the State Department Far Eastern Division's Stanley Hornbeck in Washington over how best to deal with Japanese aggression, militarism, and expansionism (about which they were agreed), Tsunoda implies that had Grew's advice only been heeded war might have been avoided (e.g., pp. 92–95). There is no question that as the United States stepped up its embargoes, Japan stepped up its preparations for a southern advance and became more determined to go to war. Hornbeck's argument that increasing economic pressure would deter Japanese aggression produced precisely the opposite effect.[25]

Grew's empathy for Japan and the Japanese and Hornbeck's antipathy, contempt, and condescension are well documented and presented by Tsunoda. However, Tsunoda does not deal with the question of whether any policy, Grew's conciliatory policies or Hornbeck's policies of embargo and other forceful measures short of direct military action, would have deterred Japan. If Hornbeck's hard-line policies (and those adopted by the United States from July 1941 on) ultimately provoked Japan, would not Grew's policies, based on unrealistic optimism over the resurgence of liberal leadership in Japan, simply have allowed Japan to pursue its course of aggression at a more leisurely and less costly pace? Without addressing that question frontally Tsunoda cannot justifiably suggest that the United States missed opportunities to settle differences and avoid war by not adopting Grew's advice.

In his discussion of the failure of Konoe's proposal for a summit meeting, first proposed via Ambassador Nomura between August 7 and August 9, 1941, and rejected by Roosevelt on September 2, Tsunoda approvingly cites Grew's support for the proposal, censures Hornbeck's opposition, and then shows strong army opposition to the proposal and Nomura's accurate reading that the United States would not back down or agree to a summit unless Japan stopped pursuing its policy of armed force (pp. 179–97). Tsunoda's ambiguous weighing of all these factors obscures the basic fact that Japan was not about to give up the exercise of armed force, much less withdraw its forces even from southern French Indochina, regardless of whether Grew's endorsement of a summit talk had been accepted. By August 18 Ambassador Nomura had given up on the idea of a summit meeting and had told Tokyo there was no hope for such a meeting. But "Nomura's recommendation for a change in Japanese policy posed difficulties for Konoe" (p. 191), because the Imperial Conference decisions of July 2 and September 6 had sanctioned the southern advance and, however much they were "exercises in semantics," they simply could not be ignored by holding a summit meeting. As will be discussed below, the real difficulty was army and navy intransigence over any change in Japan's policies, and it is astonishing that Tsunoda could even suggest, as he does throughout his narrative, that such decisions were merely exercises in semantics or nothing more than rhetoric.

The United States (including the bigoted Hornbeck) appears to have had a much better reading on the actual state of affairs in Japan at the time than did Tsunoda writing in 1962–63. Tsunoda notes that Roosevelt told Nomura on August 28 that he was concerned "whether an invasion of Thailand could be expected during the conversations with Prince Konoe just as the invasion of Indochina occurred during Secretary Hull's conversations with Your Excellency" (p. 196). On October 16 Nomura cabled his government what Navy War Plans Director Captain Richmond Kelly Turner told Terasaki Hidenari, first secretary to the Japanese embassy in Washington: "it is doubtful that . . . the present Japanese cabinet . . . has the support of the Army, and if the Military finds itself at variance with the opinions of the cabinet, the cabinet might be overthrown at any time. Therefore, the United States cannot help feeling a little trepidation in broaching any negotiations with the Japanese Government under these circumstances" (p. 197).

This was written on the eve of Konoe's resignation as prime minister because of army opposition, primarily that of his army minister General Tōjō Hideki, to Konoe's plans to continue negotiations with the United States. Such opposition was based on fears that Konoe might make concessions on anything Japan had done, was doing, or planned to do. Tsunoda himself points out that the army was working diligently to undermine a summit meeting (pp. 195–96). At this juncture the United States was quite rightly convinced that nothing it did short of war would deter Japanese aggression.

Tsunoda's discussion of why the assault on Pearl Harbor became a surprise attack is problematic to say the very least. On December 2 (Japan time) the two chiefs of staff reported to the emperor on the plan to attack Pearl Harbor. They "put the emphasis on a surprise attack by the task force," "Sunday being a day of rest and recreation" at Pearl Harbor with "relatively high numbers of warships . . . berthed" in the harbor (p. 323). Having cited this report at length, Tsunoda then goes on to argue that the attack became a surprise attack because of negligence and unconcern in Hawaii and in Washington, as well as because of the dereliction of duty by Japan's embassy staff in Washington (pp. 329–39).[26] And in praising Admiral Yamamoto Isoroku for his wisdom and restraint, his honesty and integrity, Tsunoda wobbles badly on whether Yamamoto, the architect of the Pearl Harbor attack, was for a straightforward or surprise attack (pp. 332–33). Here the United States and Japan are equally to blame for what Japan planned as a surprise attack in the first place. The United States was certainly asleep at the switch, but that was precisely what Japan hoped for regardless of Tsunoda's tortured reasoning.[27]

Not only does Tsunoda "shift war responsibility away from Japan" in his discussion of the attack on Pearl Harbor; he also shifts blame away from government and military leaders who were collectively responsible for the decision to go to war with the United States, Britain, and Holland onto Lord Keeper of the Privy Seal Kido Kōichi, a palace official who served as the emperor's key political adviser from 1940 to 1945 (pp. 230–46, passim). Kido refused to recommend Higashikuni Naruhiko, an imperial prince, to succeed Prime Minister Konoe Fumimaro, who had resigned on October 16, 1941. Instead, Kido recommended Konoe's army minister, Tōjō Hideki, who was largely responsible for the collapse of the Konoe cabinet (pp. 226–31). In so doing, Tsunoda argues, Kido violated his role as privy seal, blocked the emperor's wishes, lost an opportunity to reverse Japan's course toward war with the United States, and recommended as the new prime minister a person who, though dedicated, intelligent, honest, and completely loyal to the emperor, was simply unsuited to be Japan's prime minister at the critical juncture between war and peace with the United States.

Moreover, Kido then failed to follow through on the emperor's wishes by not making certain that Tōjō made a thoroughgoing reexamination of the decision to go to war with the United States if and when it became clear that there were no prospects for success in the Japanese-United States negotiations (pp. 243–45, 249, 258–59, 290–91). That Kido was a patriot, even "an opportunistic advocate of a military advance to the south" (p. 236), and committed to Japan's mission in Asia and its quest for international power and status, is not the issue. The issue is Tsunoda's misrepresentation of Kido's role as the emperor's chief political adviser (pp. 236–43). Even before the death in 1940 of Japan's last Elder Statesman (Genrō), Prince Saionji Kimmochi, the privy seal had become the key official responsible for orchestrating the process of selecting a new prime minister when a cabinet resigned and for recommending the nominee so selected to the Throne for appointment as prime minister (see n. 51, chapter III). In doing so, the privy seal was basically concerned with preserving the integrity and impartiality of the Throne, the transcendental role of the emperor in Japanese politics as the fount of all political authority.[28]

As Tsunoda himself suggests (pp. 242–43), Kido's opposition to Tōjō's strong recommendation that Higashikuni be appointed Konoe's successor was grounded on precisely such considerations. However, Tsunoda does not follow through on that suggestion but rather suggests that by not following Tōjō's recommendation Kido lost an opportunity to avoid war. If an imperial prince had been appointed, and if Japan had gone to war, despite the efforts Tsunoda alleges he would have made to avoid war no matter what the consequences, and had suffered the ultimate disaster that actually occurred, then the emperor and imperial institution would have been placed in even greater jeopardy than they were in 1945–46. Tsunoda's criticisms of Kido's judgment in October 1941 are questionable at best, and they seriously overestimate Japan's capacity to avoid war at this late juncture.

What were the chances of avoiding war in October 1941, with or without a cabinet under Prince Higashikuni? Tsunoda insists, at least ambiguously, that there were such chances despite his own evidence suggesting that there were virtually none. On the American side, Tsunoda documents America's adherence to the Four Principles from April 16 (pp. 53–54) on, the shifting hard and soft lines pursued by Secretary of State Hull and others from Hull's June 21 counterproposal, which made Japan feel as if "it had been betrayed by the United States" (p. 59), and the effects of the July 26-August 1 freezing of assets and complete embargo on oil (pp. 159ff). On the Japanese side, war preparations, plans for the southern advance, and a virtually absolute commitment to creating a "New Order in East Asia" by military means were all in place long before October 1941. The mentality that gripped Japan and its leaders was given eloquent testimony by Tōjō at the cabinet meeting of October 14, 1941, two days before Konoe resigned, and it revealed the tenacity of Japan's military in never backing down from any of its conquests and projects:

... the army regards the issue of withdrawing troops to be of great moment. To submit to the contentions of the United States in their entirety will annihilate the gains from the China Incident and by extension threaten the existence of Manchukuo, even affecting Japanese rule over Korea and Taiwan.

Since the Incident started, Japan has had hundreds of thousands of war casualties—dead, wounded, and sick—and has cared for bereaved families several times that number. Several million troops and one hundred million civilians have fought against hardships on and off the battlefield, and billions have already been expended from the national treasury. Yet Japan has adopted a policy of nonannexation and no compensation, an attitude of generosity unexampled among the Great Powers. Japan is merely securing the gains of the Incident by stationing troops. There is no need whatever to defer to the world. There is no need to submit to ingenious pressures from the United States.

If we are reluctant to take an immovable position on north China and Mongolia, the foundation on which Manchuria has been built will be endangered, bequeathing to the future a great source of trouble that will take another war to recoup. Of course, if we want to go back to the little Japan of pre-Manchurian Incident days there's nothing else to be said, is there?

You say we will make good the stationing of troops under the rubric of withdrawing troops, but withdrawal is retreat and armed forces that have lost their morale are the same as no armed forces at all. It is necessary to stipulate clearly that we will station troops. However, we ought to station troops only in essential areas, and military forces other than these ought to be withdrawn in good time.

Stationing troops is the heart of our demands. We must insist on what we ought to insist on. Is it necessary to make one concession after another and then beyond that yield further, to the point of endangering our very life? What is a foreign policy that yields this far? It is submission. Because it will embolden the United States more and more, I don't know where it will end. If you are saying that you are confident of success only by yielding, that I cannot accept (p. 227).

In criticizing the stipulations in Hull's reply of October 2, 1941, moreover, Tsunoda argues that Japan's acceptance of Hull's conditions would mean that "in the Sino-Japanese War Japan accept its own defeat and China's victory, totally abandoning any and all standing it had gained thus far in Manchuria, China, and Indochina as well as all future prospects" (p. 198). For both Tōjō and Tsunoda, conceding on the issue of stationing troops would have been to acknowledge defeat for Japan, for Japan's mission in Asia.

Tsunoda does not discuss whether the United States might have been willing to concede on Manchuria (Manchukuo), allowing it to remain a puppet state under Japanese control. By October 1941, of course, there was little possibility that the United States would have conceded on anything. But in the informal negotiations between Japan and the United States during 1941, withdrawal of Japanese forces from China and French Indochina was stressed, and Manchukuo's status was left ambiguous. The October 2, 1941, reply[29] and the November 26, 1941 "ultimatum"[30] mentioned withdrawal of armed forces from China and Indochina; the status of Manchukuo was not raised. Back in 1931, Hugh Byas of the *New York Times* and R.O. Matheson of the *Chicago Tribune* had questioned "whether Manchuria could properly be considered Chinese territory,"[31] and in 1933 Rōyama Masamichi, a professor of public administration at Tokyo Imperial University, "made a distinction between Japan's policy toward Manchuria and toward China and, with all the power at his command, urged that Japan's 'special position' be restricted to Manchuria."[32] At the same time, "Rōyama fully recognized the cultural identity of Manchuria and China. . . . if Manchuria were to be effectively divided from China, it must be through the establishment there of an "efficient and just government, one with no corruption."[33] There are, in short, some grounds, however slender, for arguing that withdrawing armed forces from China and French Indochina would not have threatened Japanese hegemony in Manchukuo, contrary to both Tōjō's and Tsunoda's assertions, and however unwilling the United States was to accord formal recognition to Manchukuo.

More important, Tōjō's statement reveals a profound problem in the attitude of Japan's military leaders, as well as many civilians—a "mentality" issue that Tsunoda supports rather than questions. As Hosoya Chihiro notes:

> The value structure of the military leaders is also in part accountable for their decision. The military people had been thoroughly imbued with such values as moving forward with bravery and according high regard for honor, besides many others, in the course of their training and education. The most abhorrent thing for them was to retreat or give in. They were supposed to choose death rather than surrender or suffer humiliation of any sort.
>
> . . . when they were confronted with the three alternative responses to the oil embargo, they immediately ruled out the first choice, that is, substantial concessions on the part of Japan. When the choice was narrowed down to submission or war, the latter appeared as the only alternative in their view, no matter how much risk was involved nor how high the odds. In their view, Japan had no alternative but to go to war while it still had the power to do so. It might lose, but defeat was better than humiliation and submission. It is well known that War Minister Tōjō told Premier Konoe that "Sometimes a man has to jump from the veranda of Kiyomizu Temple with his eyes closed."[34]

Such a "value structure" allows no concessions: what has been acquired by aggression cannot be conceded because of all the blood and treasure invested in it. When Tōjō undertook the reexamination of state policy in late October 1941, he told his navy minister, Shimada

Shigetarō: "The two hundred thousand souls who died in the China Incident would never forgive me if I were to turn back now. And yet, if it comes to war between Japan and the United States, great numbers of officers and men will have to be sacrificed" (p. 250). Here the only concern is the sacrifices Japan had made and would have to continue to make; there is no thought whatever of the sacrifices Japan had imposed on others, and would continue to impose.

The mentality of Japan's military was actually even more problematic than this. Tsunoda quotes Army Chief of Staff Sugiyama Gen as telling Tōjō early in the morning before the marathon Liaison Conference of November 1, 1941:

> If the negotiations go well it will mean removing the troops [from the southern regions] that have been put in readiness. This will be a problem. We have dispatched 200,000 troops from Japan, and troops from China as well. It will affect morale if, having sent troops to the South Seas, we pull them out without their having done battle (p. 256).

Not only must troops remain in areas they had conquered, sacrificing Japan's blood and treasure; they had to remain in areas into which they had been sent without doing battle, because not doing battle would impair their morale. This is not the kind of logic that leads to compromise or concessions.

This military ethos is severely marginalized by Tsunoda, who places responsibility largely on Privy Seal Kido for Tōjō's failure to reverse Japan's course from October 18 to November 1, 1941. Kido failed to have the emperor's message to "wipe the slate clean" transmitted to the army and navy high commands; not having been "notified officially of that policy," the Supreme Command was "thus not bound by it" (p. 243). "Kido was hesitant to take decisive, revolutionary action" (p. 244). "Kido considered the issue of 'wiping the slate clean' as largely a formalistic process" (p. 244). "Because Kido had never formally conveyed the emperor's clean slate message to the high command, however, the military were not bound by it in any way" (p. 249). In the reexamination of state policy conducted by Tōjō, "Kido had already foreclosed the option of a literal and thorough-going policy of enduring hardship and privation when he transmitted his 'wipe the slate clean' policy to Tōjō in the first place" (p. 259). "[T]he Tōjō cabinet . . . was confined by a Kido-style 'wipe the slate clean' policy. . . ." (p. 291).

Given the military mentality described above and the irreversible direction of its policies, it is hard to blame Kido for the outcome of

Tōjō's reexamination of state policy. What prevented *Tōjō* from telling the high command to "wipe the slate clean"? The emperor's chief military adviser and liaison with the high command, moreover, was the chief aide-de-camp, not the privy seal: during the whole of 1941 Privy Seal Kido met with the chief aide-de-camp, General Hasunuma Shigeru, eighty-two times; he had only five meetings with the two chiefs of staff, which "took place at the palace and at the initiative of the Chiefs of Staff."[35] Why did the chief aide-de-camp not transmit the emperor's wishes to the high command? Or Kido ask the chief aide to do so? In any case, the high command had actually been made clearly aware of the emperor's opposition to war with the United States in audience with the emperor on September 5, 1941, and at the following day's "stormy" Imperial Conference (pp. 173–77).

Tōjō knew full well what the emperor's wishes were. In order to change the September 6 Imperial Conference decision, "Tōjō pointed out [on October 13] that bringing new personnel into both the government and the high command was the *sine qua non* for starting all over again" (p. 231). "From October 7 on, Tōjō had become more and more firmly determined to rescind the Imperial Conference decision and turn the situation around by bringing new personnel into the government; for this purpose he was convinced that no one but Prince Higashikuni could be the new prime minister" (p. 235). Why did he not follow through when he, not Higashikuni, was made prime minister? Was it because only Prince Higashikuni could do that? That seems unlikely. Tsunoda credits Tōjō with an honest effort to wipe the slate clean, but army and navy intransigence, not Kido, was responsible for the reexamination of state policy reconfirming the fateful September 6 Imperial Conference decision shortly after midnight on November 1.

Although Tsunoda criticizes Ambassador Nomura for misleading his government on the meaning of the April 16 Draft Japanese-American Understanding (pp. 55–59), why did Tokyo ignore his accurate warnings about the position of the United States and his suggestions for some change in Japanese policy that would indicate Japan's good faith from late July on (pp. 189–191)? What prevented Foreign Minister Toyoda and Foreign Minister Tōgō from adopting Nomura's suggestions? Tsunoda tries to make the case that United States intransigence was very much to blame, but there was enormous intransigence on the part of the Japanese military and their allies as well. Toyoda's conciliatory policies up to Konoe's resignation on October 16 did nothing but intensify distrust in Konoe on the part of both the army and the United States, as Tsunoda notes (pp. 195–97).

For the army in particular that "distrust" was based on fears that Toyoda and Konoe would "gut" the September 6 Imperial Conference decision by making reasonable concessions that would indicate good faith on Japan's part, as Ambassador Nomura had advised Tokyo to do.

If "Tsunoda's presentation is often ambiguous, uneven in coverage, and scattered with questionable value judgments,"[36] his presentation of American miscalculations and underestimation of Japan, especially on the part of Stanley Hornbeck, and his description of the hubris, miscalculations, wishful thinking, and narrow reasoning (particularly in chapter I part 1 and chapter III parts 3 and 4) on Japan's part can be read with profit. The parallel ineffectiveness of American Ambassador Grew and Japanese Ambassador Nomura reflects the opposite directions their governments were pursuing: Japan's do-or-die opportunism in creating its Greater East Asia Coprosperity Sphere, first announced by Prime Minister Konoe on November 3, 1938, and America's increasingly rigid opposition to Japan's actions in the context of its concern for the war in Europe and its efforts to aid Britain and defeat Germany. Matsuoka Yōsuke's brash arrogance, which ultimately forced him out of the cabinet in July 1941, was as counterproductive in adjusting Japanese-American relations as were the American embargoes advocated by Hornbeck and others.

Although the reader may find Tsunoda's argument that the army was "induced" by the navy to determine on going to war with the United States unconvincing (chapter II part 1), given the army's longstanding commitment to a southern advance, Tsunoda shows clearly how much the army was indulging in wishful thinking about avoiding war with the United States and being able to take advantage of German victories in pursuing its expansionist policies. Tsunoda's criticisms of Navy Chief of Staff Nagano Osami for his utter neglect of preparations for protracted war in terms of island fortifications and convoying reveal clearly the "blind spots" in the navy's narrow rationality of risk during 1941. Against Nagano's rash and fatalistic arguments for war Tsunoda cites Admiral Inoue Shigeyoshi's brilliant forecast about what a war with the United States in the Pacific would look like and the critical priorities, all of which were ignored by the navy high command, that Inoue advocated based on that forecast (pp. 280–81). Inoue's forecast and evaluation were remarkably presentient about the American navy's War Plan Orange against Japan that had first been developed in 1907 and took its final island-hopping form as Rainbow Five in 1940.[37] In short, Tsunoda does reveal the thoughts, attitudes, and behavior of Japanese elites at a frantic and desperate juncture in Japanese history. And he reveals the inactions and actions of American elites as they despaired of bringing a Japan, which they greatly underestimated, under control.

Born in 1910, Tsunoda was a young participant-observer in the events, decisions, and actions he describes. He became an aide to Prince Konoe from 1938 to 1941 as well as an activist in the Shōwa Kenkyūkai, a brain-trust organization of journalists, scholars, politicians, and business leaders built around Konoe. Formed in 1933 by the politician Gotō Ryūnosuke, a close friend of Konoe, it had great diversity in terms of the backgrounds and policy preferences of its members, but it was united as an organization in its dedication to Japan's mission in Asia and to the quest for a political restructuring of Japan that would overcome the perceived defects of liberal democracy. One organization among its complex of organizations was the Shōwa Juku; established in September 1938 and disbanded in November 1941, it focused ideologically on Japan's mission and renovation. Its teachers included political scientist Rōyama Masamichi (president of the Shōwa Kenkyūkai), Satomi Kishio, Miki Kiyoshi, Matsumoto Shigeharu, and Ozaki Hotsumi. Typical of the Shōwa Kenkyūkai in general, the school's teachers embraced a wide range of views and perspectives, from right-wing obscurantist (Satomi) to Marxist and Communist spy (Ozaki), from philosopher (Miki) to liberal journalist (Matsumoto). Tsunoda was one of five executive secretaries of the school, as was Ozaki Hotsumi.[38]

This was the heady environment in which Tsunoda worked from the age of 28 to 31 and may well account for the "ideological preferences" that Ienaga noted and the "questionable value judgments" noted by Asada. For example, there is nothing Tsunoda offers by way of criticism of Japan's mission in Asia, an objective embraced by the Shōwa Kenkyūkai. Tsunoda's remark that "American sympathy for China was . . . born of a curious compound of sentimentality, idealism, ignorance, and self-interest" (p. 4) fails to see the same elements in Japan's attitudes toward China, attitudes with far more serious consequences for China than "American sympathy." His criticism of Hornbeck for having "virtually no sensitivity to or perception of the ever-changing power balance in the Far East among Japan, the Chinese Nationalist government, Chinese Communist political power, and the Soviet Union" (pp. 94–95) ignores the fact that that "ever-changing power balance" was largely the product of Japanese aggression into a vast area rent by warlord politics and enormous instability, even after Chiang Kai-shek's successful Northern Expedition of 1926–28 had in theory united the country. The best one can say about Japan's China policies from the murder of Manchurian warlord Chang Tso-lin in 1928 to the outbreak of the Pacific War is that they were based on a combination of idealism and do-or-die opportunism, which also characterized Japan's decision for war against the United States, Britain, and Holland in 1941 (as Tsunoda suggests).

By the time Tsunoda takes up his narrative I think it is much too late to blame the Pacific War on anyone but Japan. However, if the immediate cause of the war was Japan's attack on Pearl Harbor, for which Japan was clearly responsible regardless of United States embargoes and whether or not President Roosevelt or other key American leaders knew that the attack was imminent, the deeper responsibility for the war is certainly borne by the United States and the other status quo western powers. Japan was admitted to Great Power status after defeating Imperial Russia in 1904–1905. It then joined the victorious Allies in 1914–1918. But it was never fully accepted as an equal. In his soliloquy in March and April 1946, the late Shōwa Emperor pointed to the "deep" causes of the Pacific War:

> When we look for the causes of the Greater East Asia War, they lie in the past, in the peace treaty after World War I. The proposal on racial equality put forth by Japan was not something the Allies would accept. Discrimination between yellow and white continued as before, as in California's prohibition against immigration, and this was more than enough to cause resentment among the Japanese people. This applies to our having been forced to return Tsingtao as well. With such popular resentment in the background, it was no easy task to bring the military to heel once it came to the fore.[39]

Japan was the first nation of color to become a Great Power, but its people were denied racial equality. If Japan was a "respected member of the community of advanced powers" in the 1920s,[40] it was not "respected" as were the other members of that community. Japan's accomplishments, domestically and internationally, up through 1922 "drew special attention and consideration to the Japanese from Europeans and Americans, even murmurs of admiration; but they did not bring genuine respect."[41]

This was all the harder for Japan to accept given its goal of standing tall in the world as a great nation, a goal that emerged with the 1868 Meiji Restoration. "From the commencement of the Meiji Restoration to the conclusion of the Pacific War, Japan pursued the status of a great power through expansion abroad and reform at home."[42] Ishiwara's defiance of the American prosecutor at the 1946 Tokyo war crimes trials cited above gives some indication of the feelings of many Japanese leaders and the people at large as Japan struggled in a hostile world to accomplish those goals. The legacy of resentment against western racialism, of the aggressive international competition Japan felt itself pitted against, and of the somewhat equal but still separate treatment by the western great powers as they blocked Japanese ambitions is given testimony as late as September 1941. Tsunoda notes that in preparation for the September 6 Imperial Conference, the Army General Staff drew up a set of questions and answers, among which was the following statement: " . . . United States policy toward Japan rests on a status quo world view that would obstruct the Empire's rise and expansion in East Asia in order to dominate the world and defend democracy. The policy of Japan is in fundamental opposition to this" (p. 170). As this statement reveals, by September 1941, and contrary to Tsunoda's ambiguous arguments about opportunities to avoid war, that legacy was carved in stone. Expansion abroad and reform at home, begun more than 70 years earlier, were not to be denied. The cost proved enormous both at home and abroad.

By 1940–41 the Japanese were no longer divided over *how* to accomplish Japan's goals of reform at home and expansion abroad. They were to be accomplished by military means, not by diplomacy and economic policies as in the early 1920s.

None in Japan, whether Marxist revolutionary or radical Japanist, enlightened cosmopolitan or military bureaucrat, whether a Japanese of 1868 or one of 1941, had ever doubted that Japan was deserving of international equality with the world's great nations. The crucial issue facing Japan, particularly after its victory over Imperial Russia in 1905, "was the question of the economic expansion of Japan."[43] "The nation's army and navy were considered necessary tools of economic expansion, and forceful territorial acquisitions were often considered desirable to accomplish the goal."[44] During the decade following World War I, cosmopolitan Japanese leaders believed that Japan could secure its all but universally agreed upon goal of expansion by employing economic and diplomatic means in alliance with Britain and the United States. That conviction required them to persuade other leaders and the public that an "economistic foreign policy" "would in fact pay and would not be incompatible with other objectives such as security, prestige, and national identity." The period from 1919 to 1931 "witnessed the fruition of economistic thinking" and was "the time when the Japanese were willing to try to integrate themselves into the liberal international order and to avow that they belonged to the world, that they were world citizens as well as Japanese subjects."[45]

Count Makino Nobuaki, the protégé of cosmopolitan statesman Prince Saionji Kimmochi and Japan's plenipotentiary to the Paris peace talks in 1919, endorsed those internationalist values. Back in Japan, however, Prime Minister Hara Takashi and Foreign Minister Uchida Yasuya were hardpressed to convince other Japanese leaders to go along with what Makino, and Saionji, had accepted at Versailles,[46] indicating that while the liberal economistic and internationalist position was ascendant it was only tenuously so. If "the decade of the twenties seems like a golden interlude, bracketed by decades of war and depression,"[47] it was also the high point of leadership by those since the Meiji Restoration who "continued," in John Dower's brutal terms, "to indulge in the 'Caucasianization' of themselves."[48]

While this is true of Japan's ingestion of western civilization and technology, it did not mean that the most enlightened and cosmopolitan Japanese renounced their being Japanese. Prince Saionji, for example, believed in joining what was best in Japan with what was best in the world at large, particularly western civilization. He was greatly concerned about Japanese atavism and chauvinism throughout his long political career. As far back as February 1895, before becoming foreign minister in June that year, Saionji censured Japanese reactions to Japan's 1895 victory over China: "There is great insistence on 'Japanism' and 'an aggressive fighting spirit,' but behind these are lies and greed. There will be no end to the misery which arose without warning from victory in war, unless we develop adequate countermeasures."[49]

In the 1930 controversy over the London Naval Treaty Saionji argued that by insisting on a 70 percent ratio in naval ships, Japan would "throw away its grip on the handle" of genuine international power and prestige and "join the ranks of France and Italy."[50] Saionji's argument was that cooperation and compromise with Britain and the United States were the sure ways to secure Japan's eminence in the "community of advanced powers." He was as concerned with Japan's international prestige and strength as were all other Japanese leaders. He differed profoundly with the military and right-wing leaders over how that prestige and power were to be sustained and nurtured.

With the Manchurian Incident, and the wave of assassinations that began in 1930–32, advocates of a liberal economistic foreign policy retreated into the background, if they did not lose their lives. After 1930 Prince Saionji and his allies attempted to keep what they could of their waning influence by retreating into the imperial palace, where they could exert some influence over the emperor's appointment of prime ministers and cabinet ministers. It was this group on whom Ambassador Grew primarily relied, and on whom he pinned his hopes until the very end. The result, contrary to Tsunoda's interpretation, is that "Grew's misinterpretations of Japanese realities encouraged his superiors to adopt a negative policy toward Japan."[51] Even Tsunoda's presentation, in all its ambiguity, reveals that by 1940–41 liberal foreign policy advocates had not even the slightest chance of regaining power, a power that was tenuous even at its height in the 1920s. Between 1931 and the coup attempt of February 26, 1936, power gravitated securely into the hands of military and bureaucratic leaders, backed by a jingoistic public and imperial legislature. The "Fundamentals of National Policy" adopted by the Five Ministers Conference on August 7, 1936, articulated the navy's "defend the north, advance to the south" priorities, and Britain, Holland, and the United States were clearly identified as the enemy.[52] "The belligerence of the navy leadership is the most remarkable aspect of these [1936] decisions," and the navy's policies of 1936–37 led ultimately to war with the United States.[53]

Japanese military preparations and aggression escalated steadily thereafter. In February 1939 the navy occupied Hainan island off the coast of southern China, its territory only slightly smaller than Taiwan's. By the end of 1939 there were 850,000 Japanese troops in China.[54] Back on April 1, 1938, Japan enacted a National General Mobilization Law.[55] It is difficult to argue that any actions on the part of either Japan's moderate leaders or the United States could have had any effect in halting this momentum by 1940–41. The momentum toward war was actually stepped up by Japanese and American actions during those years, and it is no wonder that the Japanese-United States negotiations in 1941 failed.

For the almost 90-year build up to that confrontation the United States bears serious responsibility up until 1931; thereafter, it is difficult not to place the responsibility squarely on Japan's shoulders. The final confrontation was, in fact, the fulfillment of Ishiwara Kanji's vision that he had set forth in 1927–31.

The *Taiheiyō sensō e no michi* series has been highly influential in English language scholarship on the Pacific War. The volume here translated has been judiciously used by Barnhart, Borg and Okamoto, Iriye, and Pelz, to name only a few. These works provide a larger context for evaluating Tsunoda's presentation, and qualify or correct the questionable value judgments and ambiguous, even contradictory, interpretations he provides.

JAPAN'S ROAD
to the PACIFIC WAR

THE FINAL
CONFRONTATION

ONE

Confusion Arising from a Draft Understanding Between Japan and the United States

1 Matsuoka's Policy Toward the United States

The United States Departs from a Neutral Position

In August 1940 the destroyers-for-bases deal was arranged between Great Britain and the United States and immediately implemented. With this the United States clearly departed from a position of neutrality in the traditional sense of that term, and thereafter American claims of neutrality were little more than rhetoric. Even U.S. officials regarded this action on the part of the United States as a clear violation of international law.[1]

That deal gave international expression to the fact that the United States had begun to contemplate military intervention against Germany in Europe. For Germany it now became even more a matter of concern that Britain be defeated—before the United States amassed its national strength in support of Britain. On the other hand, it was anticipated that the war between Britain and Germany would reach a stalemate in September. With these points in mind, Germany came increasingly to regard Japan as playing a vital role in constraining the United States to revert to a position of neutrality and cease its nonbelligerent aid to Britain. From this perspective, the Tripartite Pact arose in part from causes originating with the United States. But Foreign Minister Matsuoka Yōsuke, who hoped to intimidate the United States through this alliance, only infuriated President Franklin D. Roosevelt and his secretary of state, Cordell Hull, whose global policy was by now aimed at the defeat of Germany. The beginning of September, just before Adolf Hitler ordered the indefinite postponement of the planned invasion of Britain, marked the height of the air war between Britain and Germany, the outcome of which Hull was watching carefully before determining his policy toward Japan.

Within the State Department, as early as August 15, i.e., prior to the conclusion of the Tripartite Pact, Stanley K. Hornbeck, who as special adviser to the department's Division of Far Eastern Affairs exercised more real power than the chief of that division, replied to a query by Treasury Secretary Henry Morgenthau, Jr., that Japan was

> in no position deliberately to challenge us; . . . I have all along believed that her policy and action with regard to a possible attack upon the Netherlands East Indies will be on the side of caution pending clarification of the situation in Europe; . . . not desperately needing petroleum at this time, she would not proceed toward seizure of the Netherlands East Indies, with the exposure of her naval position that would be required, merely because of an embargo by this country nor would she act drastically against us.[2]

Hornbeck was also convinced that, if Japan advanced southward, "they would do so [over land] in a series of steps designed to safeguard their flank."[3] On September 19 Hull told the British ambassador to Washington, Lord Lothian, that "the Japanese would not, in the light of [U.S.] naval disposals prevailing in the Pacific, be likely to embark upon a campaign against the Netherlands East Indies if they had reason to believe that such a campaign would require the sending of a large naval force and substantial landing forces."[4] Hull thus accepted Hornbeck's estimate and, while he was in fact itching to adopt strong measures, he refrained for the time being from resorting to any political or military action that might directly provoke Japan.

On October 14 the Department of State wrote U. S. Ambassador to Tokyo Joseph C. Grew:

> Japan does not seek "appeasement." If Great Britain falls, they can get appeasement, and more. If Germany falls, no provisional settlement by way of appeasement will stand. . . . If our continued supply of arms enables Britain to stand and ultimately to win, we shall be able to have an accounting in the Far East under such terms and at such a time as we may choose.[5]

This note characterized American policy toward Japan at the time, blending anger, observations on the future of the war in Europe, and restraint from concrete measures against Japan. Then, on January 21, 1941, after concluding that Germany would not invade Britain, Roosevelt sent a message to Grew describing in further detail U.S. policy toward Japan. This letter was in reply to a letter from Grew dated December 14, 1940, and was drafted by Hornbeck[6] in response to Roosevelt's request of January 3.[7] Since it did little more than paraphrase a December 31, 1940, letter to Philippines High Commissioner Francis B. Sayre, which may have been authorized by Roosevelt himself, the letter to Grew may well have expressed the president's own ideas.[8]

> I believe that the fundamental proposition is that we must recognize that the hostilities in Europe, in Africa, and in Asia are all parts of a single world conflict. . . . Our strategy of self-defense must be a global strategy which takes account of every front and takes advantage of every opportunity to contribute to our total security.
>
> You suggest as one of the chief factors in the problem of our attitude toward Japan the question whether our getting into war with Japan would so handicap our help to Britain in Europe as to make the difference to Britain between victory and defeat. In this connection it seems to me that we must consider whether, if Japan should gain possession of the region of the Netherlands East Indies and the Malay Peninsula, the chances of England's winning in her struggle with Germany would not be decreased thereby. . . . Our strategy of giving them assistance toward ensuring our own security must envisage both sending of supplies to England and helping to prevent a closing of channels of communication to and from various parts of the world, so that other important sources of supply will not be denied to the British and be added to the assets of the other side.
>
> . . . . I firmly believe, as I have recently declared publicly, that the British, with our help, will be victorious in this conflict. The conflict may well be long and we must bear in mind that when England is victorious she may not have left the strength that would be needed to bring about a rearrangement of such territorial changes in the western and southern Pacific as might occur during the course of the conflict if Japan is not kept within bounds.[9]

In short, U.S. policy toward Japan during the half year between the signing of the Tripartite Pact and Matsuoka's return to Japan was to check Japan's southern advance while avoiding war with Japan, and this policy evolved slowly but surely through numerous oblique measures.

Will the United States Harden or Soften?
A Fifty-fifty Chance?

On September 16, 1940, with no knowledge that the Tripartite Pact was being concluded, Secretary Hull told British Ambassador Lord Lothian and Australian Minister Richard G. Casey that the U.S. government's chief acts and utterances vis-à-vis Japan were "part of the well-known history of our disturbed relations with Japan during recent years, including oral protests, protests in writing, protests in public statements and various moral embargoes, as well as the discontinuance of our commercial treaty and the stationing of our Navy at Hawaii . . . that in these circumstances, this Government has gone almost to the limit of resisting step by step Japanese aggression without the very serious danger of a military clash."[10] On the 30th, following the conclusion of the Tripartite Pact, Hull reiterated to Lord Lothian the "definite and somewhat progressive line of acts and utterances" the United States had taken against "Japanese aggression and treaty violations during recent years." These included: "repeated aid to China, successive moral . . . [and] actual embargoes under law, abandonment of the commercial treaty, the sending of our Navy to Hawaii, together with appropriate statements and notes of strong remonstrance against Japanese steps of aggression."[11]

Hull had touched on the issue of avoiding a military clash as early as June 28, when he asserted to Lord Lothian that [the United States was doing everything possible—trans.] "short of a serious risk of actual military hostilities."[12] On October 5 he repeated to Lord Lothian that [the United States was doing everything possible—trans.] "short of intending to become engaged in war in the East."[13]

American sympathy for China had been virtually a national tradition from the beginning, and Roosevelt himself was strongly pro-Chinese. By the spring of 1940, therefore, the policy of aiding the Nationalist government was well established. American sympathy for China was, however, born of a curious compound of sentimentality, idealism, ignorance, and self-interest.[14] China's supporters entertained, to say the least, an erroneous picture of China that did not help to promote realistic thinking about the Chinese situation,[15] and it was against this background that the policy of support for China was developed. On September 25, immediately after Japanese troops were stationed in northern French Indochina, $25 million was loaned to China. On November 30, the day the conclusion of a treaty between Japan and the Wang Ching-wei regime was announced, Roosevelt himself declared that his government was considering a $100 million loan to China.

As far as embargoes against Japan were concerned, the two restrictions enforced during the Yonai cabinet were continued. Then on July 26, 1940, as a precaution against extensive stockpiling through accelerated and special imports initiated in the closing days of that cabinet, an export licensing system was laid out for aviation fuel and lubricants, tetraethyl lead, and high-grade scrap iron. On September 26 a comprehensive licensing system was established for all iron, steel, and pig iron scrap; this was put into effect on October 16, two days after Prime Minister Konoe Fumimaro's provocative speech in Kyoto. The aim of this embargo was to avoid provoking Japan while bringing more and more pressure to bear, not only to impede Japan's war production, but also to haunt it with the constant threat that more severe measures might be applied. A State Department memorandum of April 14, 1941, stated: "This Government's policy has had as one of its effective purposes the attrition of Japan's energies and resources by steps undertaken gradually on a basis designed to obviate creating the impression that they were in the nature of overt acts directed primarily at Japan." [16]

On the Japanese side, Wakamatsu Tadakazu. chief of the Army General Staff's Intelligence Division, complained openly in mid-February 1941 to an assistant military attaché of the British embassy in Tokyo:

> Japanese military opinion is still divided on the question of a southward advance. . . .
>
> This division of opinion is due in part to the fact that while the United States during the past year or more has progressively restricted the export of certain important military materials to Japan, these restrictions have not been made simultaneously effective at any time. This step by-step policy has made it difficult for Japanese opinion to crystallize and conservative Japanese circles are able to point out that, despite restrictions, trade with America is still continuing. Had the United States at the beginning ceased all exports to Japan it would have facilitated a definite Japanese decision as to the best course of action. [17]

At the heart of the American protests against Japan were, needless to say, Hull and Undersecretary of State Sumner Welles. On September 20, 1940, for example, Welles told Japanese Ambassador Horinouchi Kensuke that, with respect to the negotiations then in progress in Hanoi to reach a local agreement between Japan and French Indochina, he "would be lacking in candor if I did not make it clear to the Ambassador that, consistent with its policy with regard to Great Britain, the United States would likewise feel it necessary to furnish such means of assistance in the way of supplies, munitions, et cetera, for these victims of aggression in the Pacific area as might be required." [18] And when Horinouchi protested against the September 26 embargo, Hull retorted that "it was unheard of for one country engaged in aggression and seizure of another country, contrary to all law and treaty provisions, to turn to a third peacefully disposed nation and seriously insist that it would be guilty of an unfriendly act if it should not cheerfully provide some of the necessary implements of war to aid the aggressor nation in carrying out its policy of invasion."[19]

Finally, there was the question of the U.S. fleet remaining at Hawaii. Admiral James O. Richardson, commander-in-chief of the fleet, was opposed to this. Summoned to Washington, he arrived on October 7 and conferred with Roosevelt and Chief of Naval Operations Admiral Harold R. Stark on the 8th. During their meeting Roosevelt took the position that even though the presence of the fleet at Hawaii might not serve as an effective deterrent to Japan, its withdrawal to the West Coast would have strong political implications. In a letter to Navy Secretary Frank Knox on September 1, Richardson had previously proffered objections to the fleet's remaining at Hawaii. But Roosevelt, in full knowledge of this, had decided that the fleet was to remain there for political reasons. On October 24 Roosevelt told Chiang Kai-shek through the American ambassador to China, Nelson T. Johnson, that while the danger of a Japanese attack on Singapore did indeed exist, it did not seem imminent; the Japanese, he continued, must realize the difficulties of such an operation and "would not lightly embark upon such a venture while Great Britain is still strong in Europe and the American fleet is at Hawaii."[20] Thus Roosevelt's decision was quickly put to use as an asset in diplomacy.

During the Imperial Conference deliberations over the draft of the Tripartite Pact on September 19, 1940, Matsuoka had expressed the opinion that, although signing the pact might cause the United States to "stiffen temporarily, it is likely to make a level-headed calculation of its interests and recover a level headed attitude; of course, the chances are fifty-fifty as to whether it will stiffen more and more, leading to a more critical situation, or reflect on the matter with a level head."

Were the four kinds of overt measures taken by the United States as described above, which the Japanese could not help but take cognizance of, a "temporary stiffening" after which the United States would recover a "level-headed attitude?" Or had the United States advanced to the point where it would "stiffen more and more, leading to a more critical situation"? In a Columbus Day speech during his campaign for a third term, Roosevelt declaimed:

No combination of dictator countries of Europe and Asia will halt us in the path we see ahead for ourselves and for democracy. No combination of dictator countries of Europe and Asia will stop the help we are giving to almost the last free people now fighting to hold them at bay.[21]

On December 29 he appealed to the entire nation in a fireside chat:

> . . . a nation can have peace with the Nazis only at the price of total surrender. . . .
> Such a dictated peace would be no peace at all.
> . . . all of us in the Americas would be living at the point of a gun—a gun loaded with explosive bullets, economic as well as military.[22]

Given Roosevelt's attitude, there was little basis for judging that U.S. measures against Japan represented merely a "temporary stiffening." Matsuoka nonetheless seemed to believe, throughout the half year or so between the conclusion of the Tripartite Pact in September 1940 and his return to Japan from his European tour in April 1941, that the chances were still fifty-fifty as to whether U.S. policy would stiffen or ease up.

Matsuoka's Basic Policy Toward the United States

At a farewell party for Ambassador Nomura Kichisaburō given by the America-Japan Society on December 19, 1940, Matsuoka asserted:

> I owe it to candor to admit that the relations between our two countries are severely strained at this moment. Now, the causes that have brought about the present unfortunate deterioration are, of course, many and manifold, but the fundamental cause, let me be frank, is American misapprehension of Japan's aims and aspirations. . . . our political efforts had better be restricted to only those spheres in which we are vitally interested, and not be extended to other people's domains. If regional peace is effectively secured through regional understanding [between Japan and China], the world will, by its aggregation, be able to enjoy a universal peace. . . . We only desire, on the one hand, to be left alone, so that we may carry on our constructive work unhindered, and on the other hand, to see the trouble in China and the war in Europe brought speedily to an end, without adding more participants, particularly such a powerful one as America. . . . After all, the fate of China is largely a question of sentiment to the Americans, but to us it constitutes a truly vital issue affecting, as it does, the very existence of our Empire.[23]

On January 15, 1941, in a statement to the House Foreign Affairs Committee, Hull for the first time publicly named Japan and criticized its aggressive policy. In response to this Matsuoka made a foreign policy speech on the 21st that was even more forthright than that at the America-Japan Society:

> The United States has evinced no adequate understanding of the fact that the establishment of the Greater East Asia Coprosperity Sphere is a life-or-death requirement for Japan. The United States takes the position that its own first line of defense on the east lies along the mid-Atlantic and on the west lies not only along the eastern Pacific but as far as China and the South Seas. Then it ventures to criticize Japan's dominion in just the western Pacific as grasping ambition, which is excessively self-serving and hence does nothing toward the promotion of world peace.[24]

In a reply given at a plenary session of the House of Representatives Budget Committee on January 26, Matsuoka stated:

> Although some Americans understand, for some reason, however hard we try to explain, those in positions of leadership in the present American government do not want to understand. . . . For us there is no recourse but to maintain in our dealings with the United States that we cannot change our convictions to accommodate the American viewpoint. I wish to declare that if the United States does not understand Japan's rightful claims and actions, there is not the slightest hope for an improvement in Japanese-American relations.
>
> Although they may not expect Japan to abandon its continental and southern policies, the precondition [for the United States], to put it plainly, is for Japan to retreat by about half. . . . It is no go unless we pay the price of either suspending or curtailing our state policies by half. And although they claim that they have striven for friendly relations, they have made it no go from the outset.
>
> I shall continue to try to enlighten the United States. I think the only ray of hope is to persuade them with Japan's firm resolution, and not proceed with coquetry. But I shall still not give up on that ray of hope. I am convinced that this is the only way for Japan to proceed.[25]

In these two statements Matsuoka essentially reiterated the arguments he had made during the September deliberations on the Tripartite Pact draft, showing that since then his policy toward the United States had remained fundamentally unchanged despite the actions taken in the meantime by the United States.

Matsuoka's written instructions to Nomura on January 22, immediately before the ambassador's departure for the United States, were unequivocal and high-handed:

(1) Unless we drastically change our national policy, it will be totally impossible to reach an understanding . . . and cooperate with the United States. (2) Furthermore, if the present situation persists, there is no guarantee that the United States will not enter the European war or start a war with Japan. . . . (4) If there is no way to achieve understanding and cooperation between Japan and the United States, . . . we must prevent the United States, if necessary by means of pressure and intimidation, from going to war with Japan or entering the war in Europe. . . . (7) Should the three contracting parties recognize that "an attack by a third power" has taken place, as stipulated in Article 3 of the Tripartite Pact, Japan will of course be faithful to the alliance. There should not exist the slightest doubt on this point.[26]

Shortly after Nomura's arrival in Washington, Matsuoka amplified on this, stressing Japan's obligation to go to war under the Tripartite Pact:

Japan is firmly and unshakably resolved to march forward in accordance with its established state policy. (Dispatch of February 7)[27]

I fully appreciate that you, Mr. Ambassador, have acted with particular caution. However, on the question of whether Japan would go to war if the United States should attack Germany, I have already answered affirmatively on such occasions as the plenary session of the House of Representatives Budget Committee. I request you to respond likewise should a similar question arise in the future. (Dispatch of March 4)[28]

Matsuoka's policy of preventing the United States from going to war against Japan or entering the war in Europe, even if Japan had to pursue it through pressure and intimidation, was feasible only if there were "a fifty-fifty chance" of success through such means. This Matsuoka admitted frankly to Hitler in Berlin on April 4:

. . . in his own country he had always declared that if Japan continued in the same fashion as at present, a war with the United States sooner or later would be unavoidable. In his view this conflict might better occur sooner than later. Accordingly . . . should not Japan decide to act with determination at the proper moment and take the risk of a war against America? Exactly by such means the war might perhaps be postponed for generations, especially if Japan secured domination in the South Seas. . . . if Japan proceeded further along the present course she would some day have to fight and . . . this might happen under more unfavorable circumstances than at present.[29]

On March 4, immediately before his departure for Europe, Matsuoka had told General Hata Shunroku:

> (1) I have no intention of starting something with the United States now. We should do that after gaining a foothold in the South Seas. I am leery about being dragged along [by Germany] and the like. . . . (5) I judge that the United States has no will to fight [Japan?].[30]

Adding this remark into the equation, Matsuoka's Berlin statement could be interpreted to mean that "the chances were fifty-fifty" if, once the south were occupied, the United States could be prevented from going to war with Japan and entering the war in Europe through pressure and intimidation, even though this risked the danger of war with the United States. At the same time, his scheme for the occupation of the south was closely linked with his assessment of trends in the war between Britain and Germany.

Matsuoka Sees Landing Operations Against Britain as Inevitable

At Konoe's farewell party for Ambassadors Nomura and Ōshima Hiroshi on January 15, Matsuoka stirred up a hornet's nest by asserting: "Germany *will* land on the British Isles."[31] And during the Liaison Conference of February 3, he stated that "it would be best for me to go to Europe before Germany attacks Britain,"[32] clearly presuming that Germany would carry out an attack on Britain. Ōshima arrived shortly in Germany, and on March 2 he reported Hitler's official statement dissembling about the order the fuehrer had handed down in September 1940 postponing operations indefinitely:

> Yesterday I conferred with Fuehrer Hitler for about one hour after presenting my credentials. . . . Regarding the attack on Britain, he said that Germany would deal Britain a severe blow by means of submarine operations, which were to commence, depending on weather conditions, between the end of March and the end of April. . . . With regard to the air force, he said that Germany intends to launch air attacks on a vast scale, but this also depends greatly on weather. Landing operations will also depend on the condition of the seas. Operations against Britain, Hitler stated, are no longer a question of strategy but of tactics, which have to be determined by weather, meteorology, and marine conditions. He explained that although Germany is determined to carry out these operations their timing would be difficult to predict.[33]

Hitler's statement appeared to give official confirmation to Matsuoka's previous assessment. On March 24, when he arrived in Moscow
on his outbound trip and before he had a chance to see for himself
the actual situation in Germany, Matsuoka met with Axis diplomats
and set forth that assessment. On the same day the gist of this was
reported to U.S. Ambassador to Moscow Lawrence A. Steinhardt by
the Romanian minister:

> According to his [Matsuoka's] information, the United States could not
> "increase its production substantially before June" and could not give
> "decisive help" to England before the end of 1941. By then England
> would be beaten although, of course, an empire as big as the British
> could not collapse "in a day or two."
>
> After the collapse of the British Isles, the United States would "not
> continue the struggle" but would withdraw and "think of its own inter-
> ests and affairs." [Matsuoka] said that the continuance of the war by
> the United States aided by the British fleet . . . was a "chimera." [34]

Arriving in Berlin, Matsuoka repeated this view to German Foreign
Minister Joachim von Ribbentrop on March 28: "When England was
crushed, the United States in his opinion would not continue to
support the British Empire." Whereupon Matsuoka "expressed himself as personally very strongly in favor" of Ribbentrop's "line of
reasoning" when the latter asserted that "in his opinion Roosevelt
would not let it come to war since he was well aware of the impossibil-
ity of any action against Japan. . . . If Japan captured Singapore, the
greater part of the world would have come under the control of the
Tripartite Powers, and America would find herself in an isolated
position." [35] Having sounded out Hitler in addition to Ribbentrop,
Matsuoka apparently felt that his assessment of the course of the war
between Britain and Germany prior to his visit to Europe had now
been directly confirmed. Lunching with Steinhardt on April 8 in
Moscow, which he revisited en route home, Matsuoka reported that
"Hitler firmly believed he could reduce Britain by submarine and
aerial warfare this spring and summer and that an invasion would
not be necessary but that all preparations had been made for it and
that it would be attempted should it become necessary." [36]

Matsuoka Plans a Junket to America

Pursuing the line of reasoning in the above statements, we might at
this point summarize the logic of Matsuoka's policy toward the
United States over the two months or so starting with his instructions

to Nomura and his statement in the House of Representatives in late January and ending with his conversations with Hitler and Ribbentrop in late March and early April: 1) The war between Britain and Germany would end with British surrender in the spring or summer of 1941; 2) American aid to Britain would not prevent this eventuality; 3) Japan would take advantage of Britain's defeat to launch a surprise attack and occupy the south; 4) thereupon, Japan would apply pressure and intimidation against the United States, even at the risk of war with America; but 5) the likelihood of avoiding a war with the United States as a result of this policy was only 50 percent.

Moreover, in order to increase the prospects of avoiding war with the United States, which he considered only 50 percent, to 100 percent, Matsuoka might have believed that individual skill above and beyond diplomatic measures was now necessary, and he may also have fancied that he himself was truly the one person able to take charge of the situation. In his December 19 speech to the America-Japan Society he had proclaimed: "The world is now in a state of upheaval. The era of debating small and petty problems has been rendered a thing of the past. It has become an era when everything must be conducted on a grand scale."[37] On the eve of his trip to Europe he revealed what was on his mind to Foreign Ministry Counselor Saitō Yoshie: "I intend to wind up my visit to Europe quickly and then go immediately to the United States." He added that "if I were to go and explain fully Japan's true intentions and express our sincerity wholeheartedly, no matter how difficult it may be, it would not be impossible to have the United States change its mind."[38] In any case, for Matsuoka "the United States was without doubt his second home," and it was "apparently his child-like ambition to dance on the grand stage of Washington D.C., Japan's delegate and a world-class prodigy to boot."[39]

When Matsuoka recalled Horinouchi Kensuke as ambassador to Washington, he first approached the journalist Matsumoto Shigeharu, then Admiral Nomura, with no policy in mind in making the selection. This was because he expected almost nothing from Horinouchi's successor as far as coping with Japanese-American relations was concerned; rather, the important point for him was to keep Japanese-American relations just as they were until he himself visited the United States.[40] Bishop James E. Walsh and Father James M. Drought had called on Matsuoka in December 1940, and at their meeting on the 5th or 23rd he had declared to the two priests "that if he could only see the President for an hour he felt sure that he could bring about an improvement in relations."[41]

Evidently keeping his plan to visit the United States to himself, the first move Matsuoka contemplated was to sound out Roosevelt about mediating a peace between Japan and China, and he approached Ambassador Steinhardt about this, Steinhardt happening to be in Moscow when Matsuoka stopped there en route to and from Berlin. Steinhardt reported what Matsuoka said on these occasions:

> ... Chiang Kai-shek was relying upon American help and ... the President was in a position to bring the Japanese-Chinese conflict to an end at any time on terms satisfactory to all concerned if he would use his influence in this direction with Chiang Kai-shek. ... the present was the time "for statesmen to take decisive action" and that "what matters are the big things and not the little ones." ... the President has a splendid opportunity "to clear up the entire situation in the Far East" by discussing with Nomura the terms on which the war with China could be terminated. (March 24)[42]
> ... the President could accomplish this by intimating to Chiang Kai-shek that the United States would withhold any further assistance to China if Chiang Kai-shek refused to accept "fair and reasonable terms."
> ... if the President and Mr. Hull would "trust him" and assist him in bringing about peace in China everything in the Far East would be cleared up to their satisfaction. (April 8)[43]
> ... he had expressed a desire that the President and Mr. Hull trust him. ... he amplified ... that peace between Japan and China could only result from direct negotiation between the two countries as the Japanese public would not accept an intermediary. (As confirmed by Steinhardt with Matsuoka on April 11)[44]

Subsequently, Matsuoka informed Ōshima of the substance of these conversations: "While in Moscow I had U.S. Ambassador Steinhardt (whom I personally know very well) inform Roosevelt and Hull of my desire that Roosevelt should trust Japan and this Minister of State, advise Chiang Kai-shek to enter into direct peace negotiations with Japan, and inform Chiang that if he should fail to follow the president's advice, the United States would immediately terminate all aid to China."[45] And from Moscow on April 9 he conveyed his thinking that, "In view of Steinhardt's words and attitude at our conversation today, and considering other factors including Roy Howard's recent suggestion [that Matsuoka return home via America], I have the feeling that in the near future Roosevelt may take some kind of action in concert with this Minister of State."[46] Returning to Japan via the Trans-Siberian Railway, he received a brief telegram from Steinhardt before reaching Manchouli indicating that Roosevelt was interested in Matsuoka's idea. Apparently he began to contemplate his next move, and when, on arriving at Dairen on April 20, he received a telephone call from Konoe urging him to return to Tokyo without delay to discuss a draft Japanese-American understanding, Matsuoka was overjoyed, believing that his conversations with Steinhardt had born fruit. "Now begins my real work," he told his private secretary, Kase Toshikazu, who had taken Konoe's call.[47]

Matsuoka had been unusually diligent in reporting to and consulting with Konoe and Konoe alone, and the two had been in close touch. That this would have continued to be the case up to this point as well could have been surmised from the following statement by Konoe concerning the United States, comments the same as but even more sanguine than those of Matsuoka:

1. Great Britain and the United States assert that the China problem should be solved on the basis of the Nine Power Treaty or a similar new treaty. There is, however, no hope for solving the problem by a mere readjustment of rights and interests in China. This is the reason why Japan opposes Britain and the United States through the Tripartite Pact. To abandon our continental policy would endanger our nation's grand hundred-year program.
2. German victory [over Britain] is a matter of time.
3. We have instructed Ambassador Nomura to keep in mind in his negotiations with the United States the following three points, which our nation must maintain: a) Japan firmly abides by the Tripartite Pact; b) Japan will not abandon its continental policy; c) if the United States recognizes Japan's position, we also desire friendly relations with the United States. (Conversations in the Privy Council Lounge, January 29, 1941)[48]

2 Nomura and Ikawa: Emissaries to the United States

Nomura Mistrusts the Diplomacy of Konoe and Matsuoka

On August 24, 1940, Matsuoka asked the former foreign minister, Admiral Nomura Kichisaburō, to return to Tokyo from his summer retreat. Two days later Matsuoka called on Nomura, urging him to accept the post of ambassador to the United States and adding that Navy Minister Yoshida Zengo concurred completely in this. Later that day Nomura showed Yoshida his personal "memorandum" on

Japanese-American relations and discussed it with him; as a result, Nomura, with Yoshida's approval, refused to enter into negotiations over the appointment. On the 29th Matsuoka visited Nomura in a further attempt to persuade him but Nomura firmly refused. With that, the matter lapsed. Then, on October 2, Vice Navy Minister Toyoda Teijirō appeared on the scene to persuade Nomura, alleging that he conveyed the wishes of the new navy minister, Oikawa Koshirō. Because Toyoda stressed that, unlike in the days of Yoshida, this time "the navy really desires that you accept," Nomura began to feel cornered.

Meanwhile, Nomura had revealed to Harada Kumao his utter lack of trust in the policies of Konoe and Matsuoka toward the United States:

> My conscience does not allow me to serve as ambassador to a country toward which our government maintains a policy totally contrary to my own views. (August 31)[49] Our government has no defined policy toward the United States. (October 23)[50] A person like Matsuoka who only sees matters superficially can hardly be depended upon; to take seriously anything such a person says is out of the question. (October 8)[51]

During his August 26 meeting with Yoshida, Nomura had shown the navy minister his memorandum in which he asked: "How on earth can my understanding of the situation be reconciled with the present government's shift in diplomacy (to strengthening the Axis with Germany and Italy)?"[52] "In my view," the memorandum amplified, "it is utterly out of the question to try to improve Japanese-American relations while attempting to strengthen the Tripartite Alliance. Because it is impossible to rectify diplomatic relations between Japan and the United States by trying to juggle both Germany and the United States at the same time, I could not accomplish any purpose were I to go to the United States."[53]

Despite having expressed such strongly critical views, Nomura had suddenly been backed into a corner by Toyoda's forceful arguments, and finally he conveyed his informal consent to Oikawa around the 6th of November: "My ties to the navy make it impossible for me to refuse. Worth it or not, succeed or fail, . . . I feel I have to go."[54] Calling on Prime Minister Konoe on the 7th, he presented his "memorandum" and asked Konoe's endorsement, which was given enthusiastically.[55] On the 9th Commander-in-Chief of the Navy General Staff Prince Fushimi Hiroyasu declared that he "was of the same opinion as Nomura" and confirmed Toyoda's position.[56] And so, suppressing the lack of trust and the critical views he had held since August, Nomura at last resolved to accept the appointment to the United States in order to carry through his own policy.

Nomura had prepared three memoranda all told: the first, dated August 26, was to Yoshida;[57] the second, dated November 7, was to Konoe;[58] and the third, dated December 16, was written after he had resolved to accept the appointment.[59] On the basis of these memoranda, the key points of Nomura's policy toward the United States may be summarized as follows:

1) The inseparability of Great Britain and the United States: "The relationship of the two countries is to be acknowledged as virtually inseparable. A British war is clearly an American war, and the only question remaining now is that of formal participation in the [European] war."

2) No war with the United States: "The China Incident has already lasted over three years, greatly reducing Japan's strength. . . . A war [between Japan and the United States] would inevitably be a protracted one, pushing Japan into a drastically disadvantageous situation. Thus, there are natural limits on our taking a hard line against the United States. This in my view is the key factor to be borne in mind from the standpoint of political and military strategy."

3) It is a mistake to jump on Germany's bandwagon: "Germany will by no means do as Japan says. Nor should we think there is any chance of adjusting relations with the United States while Japan and Germany are working hand in hand. The Japanese navy should on no account enter into hostilities with the United States at this time just to make Germany happy."

4) It would be a mistake to advance south by force: "How far Japan advances south and by what means will determine whether there will be a war with the United States. I see [the chance of that happening] as about fifty-fifty. If the United States stays out of the war [in Europe] war between Japan and the United States is more likely to be avoided by self-restraint and self control on Japan's part. Japan must be careful about how it advances south and endeavor not to give the United States a pretext [for going to war—trans.]."

5) Prudent use of the Tripartite Pact: "It is highly probable that the United States will enter the war in Europe. How should Japan respond under the terms of the Tripartite Pact in that event? While its position must be determined in accordance with the state of the nation at that time, the utmost in prudent deliberation on Japan's part will be required."

These five points were utterly contrary to the "Main Principles for Coping with the Changing World Situation" and to the Tripartite Pact, state policies that Konoe had decided upon after forming his cabinet and that he had been putting into effect up until November 7. Moreover, Nomura had deliberately made sure of his position by concluding his memorandum to Konoe with the statement that "I hear that in the past some of our ambassadors were called liars by the U.S. secretary of state; it is essential that he be able to trust the words [of the ambassador]."[60] Despite all this, Konoe emphatically endorsed Nomura's policies *in toto* at their November 7 meeting, a blatantly inconsistent action that formed the effective cause for the gap that would arise between Konoe and Nomura in terms of the policies Nomura would carry out after he arrived at his post in Washington.

On the 6th Nomura had conveyed to Harada that "the situation was such that when I asked Matsuoka if the government had a policy toward the United States, he said no."[61] It may very well have been that Matsuoka had intentionally concealed from Nomura his policies toward the United States, plotting to postpone carrying out those policies until that day in the near future when he himself would go to the United States; being the kind of person who would be well received by U.S. officials, Nomura was to be dispatched primarily to work at easing tensions until that future day. And it may also have been that Konoe, who at the time was in virtual synchronization with Matsuoka on foreign policy, had merely given lip service to Nomura's policy pronouncements—as Matsuoka had told him to.

Toyoda's Purpose in Stringing Nomura Along

The navy was equally suspect. Having twice failed to persuade Nomura in August, Matsuoka had all but given up on him as a lost cause. It was the navy, and Vice Minister Toyoda in particular, who then took up the matter and relentlessly pressured Nomura to the point of informally accepting. In mid-September Toyoda had given the navy's de facto assent to the draft Tripartite Pact, and soon after that he met Matsuoka to discuss a successor as Japanese ambassador to the United States. Toyoda stated that "the only thing to do is to send Nomura." Having secured Matsuoka's support, Toyoda called on Nomura on October 2 and obtained his informal consent. When Toyoda conveyed this to Matsuoka he got Matsuoka to assent once again: "You have my whole-hearted concurrence on Nomura."[62] On July 18, 1941, after Toyoda was appointed foreign minister, Nomura himself told Undersecretary of State Sumner Welles that "Admiral

Toyoda was a close personal friend, and that as it was upon the insistence of Toyoda that Nomura had agreed to come here as Ambassador, Toyoda was under personal obligation to Nomura."[63] A few days earlier, on July 10, Nomura had telegraphed Oikawa and Navy Chief of Staff Nagano Osami: "I finally accepted my present post because of the navy's extremely ardent urging, although I had steadfastly turned down Foreign Minister Matsuoka."[64] Nomura again acknowledged the navy connection at a later date when he stated: "It was chiefly because the navy wanted me to go; I would not have gone if the Foreign Ministry had told me to."[65]

There was a reason for Toyoda's hustle and bustle. Because the opposition of Yonai Mitsumasa and others to the arbitrary manner in which he had agreed to the Tripartite Pact had been far fiercer than he had anticipated, he had been forced to change the way he behaved after agreeing to the treaty. He could not suppress the feeling that he had botched it, but he suddenly hit upon an easy way out: put Nomura to use. When he got his way with the perplexed Nomura by using the term "consensus of the navy," Toyoda recovered his usual élan.[66] At a later date even Nomura ventured the understanding that he had been induced to accept the post because it appeared to him that Oikawa was somehow uneasy after the Tripartite Pact had been concluded.[67] However, Toyoda's hustle was essentially nothing but a convenient bureaucratic way to extricate himself and Oikawa from the predicament into which they had fallen. He seemed almost blithely indifferent to the fundamental inconsistency between Nomura's policies and the general trend of logic that had begun operating within the navy from August—which Toyoda himself went along with but which was completely incompatible with the policies that Nomura had been promoting, also since August. That logic was: Japan's use of force against French Indochina would lead to a tightening of the U.S. embargo against Japan, which in turn would lead to Japan's seizure of the Dutch East Indies, then to a readiness to go to war with the United States, and finally to pushing forward preparations for war.

Although the words of Prince Fushimi ("I am of the same opinion as Nomura") resembled those of Toyoda in their irresponsibility, they did amount to a strong endorsement of Nomura's policies by the most senior naval officer on active duty as well as one endowed with the authority of the imperial family. Having given in to the pleas of navy leaders and then taken up his post in Washington, it was only natural that Nomura would set about carrying out his policies—given that he had obtained the approval of both Toyoda and Prince

Fushimi. Upon hearing of Nomura's appointment, members of the naval attaché's office at the Japanese embassy in Washington imagined that Nomura had assumed the post because he had received word from the navy leaders who had approved the Tripartite Pact to play down that treaty to some extent. However, this issue was later to become a primary cause for the cleavage in policy toward the United States, and for this the stances of Toyoda and Prince Fushimi were largely responsible.

Soon after he had made up his mind to take on the post Nomura visited Yonai. When he told Yonai that the navy "well understands my views and has promised to set me to work along those lines," Yonai warned him: "Be careful; if you do that, the gang around today are the kind who won't hesitate to pull the ladder out from under you once they've got you to climb up it."[68] Admiral Yamamoto Isoroku shared Yonai's worries:

[Toyoda] has played a key role in stringing Ambassador Nomura along, and I hope he will not put the admiral in an awkward position in the future. Admiral Nomura has no illusions about his chances for success. And the way things now stand it really is too much to ask him to straighten out relations [between Japan and the United States] or the like.[69]

Nomura subsequently commented: "Afterwards there were times when Yonai's words really struck home."[70] And on December 7, 1940, Ambassador Grew had recorded in his diary that "it would be futile to hope that the new Ambassador could undertake any revolutionary move to meet the views of the United States."[71]

Nomura requested Generals Anami Korechika and Sugiyama Gen to send to Washington an able special envoy who was well acquainted with the state of the Sino-Japanese War, which constituted a focal point in Japanese-American relations. And having himself conducted a tour of inspection in Manchuria and China, Nomura left for the United States on January 23, 1941.

At Honolulu Nomura was welcomed by two American destroyers. An aide, a lieutenant-commander on active duty, was delegated to greet him, after which the Pacific fleet commander himself, Admiral Husband E. Kimmel, paid his respects. In San Franciso two destroyers again sailed out in welcome, firing a formal nineteen-gun salute, and both the army and navy district commanders paid courtesy calls. The courtesies paid the admiral by the American military were most civil. But when Nomura arrived in Washington on February 11, the

Department of State sent only its chief of protocol to greet him. No top-ranking officials put in an appearance, and the State Department, in contrast to the military, appeared to be making a show of indifference. On the other hand, President Roosevelt said at a press conference that same day, "Nomura is an old friend of mine." And on his first trip to New York, major financial and media figures, as well as army and navy leaders from the eastern United States, attended a reception for Nomura, giving some indication of the expectations and hopes they had in him. For Matsuoka's purposes the selection of Nomura seemed to be working right into his hands.

With such an atmosphere prevailing in the United States, Nomura awaited an opportunity to embark on improving Japanese-American relations, calmly anticipating that it would take several months to achieve this. The issue of diplomatic negotiations, however, suddenly sprang up, and from an unexpected quarter, through the maneuvering of two individuals: Ikawa Tadao, an acquaintance of Konoe, and Colonel Iwakuro Hideo, who had been chosen to be the special envoy Nomura requested.

Catholics in U.S. Political Circles Make Their Move

On November 29, three weeks after the Nomura-Konoe meeting, Father James M. Drought, Vicar General of the Roman Catholic Foreign Mission Society of America at Maryknoll in New York, sent a letter to Ikawa Tadao, a director of the Industrial Federation Central Bank, asking for an interview. Father Drought, who was then in Japan, enclosed in his letter an introduction from Lewis L. Strauss, private secretary to former President Herbert Hoover. Following this, Father Drought and Bishop James E. Walsh, Superior General of the Maryknoll order, called on Ikawa.

As a result of this meeting Ikawa "felt that the clergymen were covertly sounding out possibilities for improving Japanese-American relations, above all in the area of economic cooperation." He therefore thought he might "in a private capacity hear what the clerics had in mind after consulting confidentially" with Military Affairs Bureau Chief Mutō Akira and Military Section Chief Iwakuro among others.

Drought revealed to Ikawa that "he had also met with Foreign Minister Matsuoka, but that was no more than a courtesy call. As Strauss had advised him to do, Drought wished to discuss vital issues with me [Ikawa]." Ikawa "thought that the meeting might amount to nothing, but it could be of some use should it provide an opportunity to sound out the intentions toward Japan of [Kuhn, Loeb and Company], which is as influential as [the House of Morgan] in American financial circles; so I have ventured to offer my services." However, when he raised the question of what kind of understanding there was between the American government and the important Kuhn, Loeb of which the introducer Strauss was a partner, the clerics responded in effect, "Don't ask too many questions." This Ikawa "found highly suggestive." When he wrote to Konoe about this on December 7, Ikawa added "I ask that you kindly wait patiently for the time being."[72]

On December 11 Ikawa called on the Maryknoll fathers at their lodgings and the next day reported privately to Konoe on the meeting. Then on the 14th Ikawa received a long memorandum from Drought, which he immediately sent to Konoe, adding his own evaluation of the document: "Although I was told that Drought had drafted it as if he were in the position of a Japanese, the fact that the memorandum deliberately reveals such delicate matters as the American president's true intentions, to which I confidentially referred at the outset of my previous letter to you, and the fact that the document is full of technical terms which should be foreign to a man of the cloth, lead me to suspect that the memorandum was not written by Drought alone and has considerable backing."[73] Drought's lengthy memorandum, entitled "Working Analysis of Our (Japanese) Position & Policy in the Far East, With Particular Reference to the United States," is extremely significant. Ikawa believed that it set down "the fundamental ideas for a Japanese-American draft understanding." Because it is a long document, I will not trouble the reader with its entirety. Suffice it to say that Drought's ideas can be boiled down to three points: isolationism, anticommunism, and a Japanese-American peace agreement in the Pacific. Its isolationism was expressed in its opposition to European imperialism and colonialism in Southeast Asia and its defiant contempt of the State Department for going forward with noncombatant aid to Great Britain. Its anticommunism could have originated in the Vatican, for Iwakuro was subsequently to suggest to Mutō that "an immediate expression of appreciation to the Vatican . . . will be in order, . . . if the draft agreement materializes."[74]

Walsh, Drought, and Postmaster General Frank C. Walker, who was soon to emerge through Strauss's good offices as the man behind the memorandum, were all Irish Catholics, and it was perfectly natural for them to express anticommunist and anti-British isolationist thinking. In early April, just prior to the completion of the Japanese-American Draft Understanding, Drought and Iwakuro were engaged in revising the text. While they were working, Drought excused himself from the room momentarily and contacted Walker directly. When he returned, he asserted that it would be fine to insert the provision: "If Japan were to withdraw from the Tripartite Pact, the United States would aid Japan in the event of war between Japan and the Soviet Union."[75] That provision too might well have been connected to this thinking. Not only did Walker play a role like that of secretary general for the Democratic Party as Roosevelt's campaign chairman; he was also a member of the finance committee of the Catholic Church of America and therefore a prominent figure who could sway on a substantial scale the sizable Catholic vote in a presidential election; even Roosevelt would find it difficult to reject his counsel outright. Based on such thinking and political backing, the straightforward purpose of Drought's memorandum was to attempt the consummation by "a single diplomatic stroke" of a Japanese-American agreement on peace in the Pacific through conversations between the leaders of the two countries—without the State Department. Subsequently, Hornbeck called this "a U.S.-Japan control of the Pacific," "a proposed Japan-United States 'non-aggression' agreement."[76] State Department officials called it "a joint overlordship by Japan and the United States," and more specifically a "provision" for spheres of influence in the Pacific for Japanese and American naval forces.[77] All these were apt understandings of the situation so far as they went.

Ikawa Goes Into Action

Matsuoka, who had met with the clerics, as well as Vice Foreign Minister Ōhashi Chūichi and others, reacted with coolness to their plan. Even Konoe, who evinced comparatively strong interest and some hope in the plan, warned Ikawa to make sure about what the army's intentions were beforehand. Ikawa therefore first approached Iwakuro and through Iwakuro's introduction had the clergymen meet with Mutō on December 27; that done, he and Iwakuro then called on Konoe. Mutō had responded in broad generalities, saying that he and his army colleagues were united in their desire to work toward a peace agreement between Japan and the United States and that he was prepared to do his utmost in helping to advance that effort. With that, Walsh and Drought believed that their goal of sounding out the Japanese side had been achieved, and they started home on December 28.

It is most odd that the memorandum made no reference to concrete matters such as the Tripartite Pact, mediation in the Sino-Japanese War, the withdrawal of Japanese troops from China, or confidential conditions for settling the Sino-Japanese War. Takagi Sōkichi, chief of the Navy Ministry's Research Section who served as a political antenna for the navy at the time, heard from Ikawa that the situation was such that "neither cleric had raised the two issues" of the Tripartite Pact and the withdrawal of troops, "and although Konoe was eager, he wondered if the United States government would really consider a summit meeting."[78] Nevertheless, Walsh later testified that during his stay in Japan, he

> heard from Japanese officials and spokesmen that their government was proposing the following provisions as the basis for a Japanese-American agreement: 1) a guarantee to nullify the Tripartite Pact, by a certain definite measure, which, if short of an explicit termination of the pact, would at the least amount effectively to a complete repudiation, 2) a guarantee to withdraw all the troops from China and to restore the geographical and political integrity of China. Of the Japanese government representatives, Ikawa was most enthusiastic. We regarded him as Konoe's unofficial representative.[79]

In fact, Walsh reiterated these two provisions in a memorandum he prepared immediately upon returning from Japan. Neither Konoe nor Iwakuro met with the priests. Mutō responded to them only in broad generalities. Naval Affairs Bureau Chief Oka Takazumi did not meet them. Matsuoka went no further than declaring his own views to them. Their meetings with the elder statesman Wakatsuki Reijirō and with Nomura wound up in superficialities. Yet right after their return from Japan the two clerics immediately voiced these two basic provisions as if they were from the Japanese government. Was this primarily the outcome of their discussions with Ikawa? And on this occasion was Ikawa speaking as a representative of the Japanese government or as an unofficial representative of Konoe? The facts are still utterly unclear. It should be noted here, however, that Ikawa was not fully trustworthy. Iwakuro was aware that Ikawa had a poor reputation in the Finance Ministry where he had once worked, while Matsuoka went so far as to castigate him as "so unreliable a person that he has had a long-standing reputation for being the kind of person he is."[80]

In any case, just before returning home the two clerics made arrangements to keep in touch with Ikawa. They agreed upon four words to encode their readings of the U.S. government's reactions:

"difficult" (no prospect for negotiations), "good" (smooth progress in all quarters), "satisfactory" (the president is considering it), and "complete" (preparations all set). That done, during January 1941 the two priests sent Ikawa one telegram after another: "good" (January 20); "satisfactory" (January 21); in plain language, "Hopeful progress as result of visit with president—expect developments" (January 25); "Last night consulted the boss [Roosevelt] again—extremely hopeful" (January 28).[81] Ikawa reported each of these telegrams to Konoe, Matsuoka, and Mutō. Prior to this, on the 11th, Konoe had met with Ikawa for the first time since this whole affair got underway; but after receiving these telegrams he instantly agreed to Ikawa's going to the United States and also became extremely well-disposed toward him. Ōhashi and other Foreign Ministry officials, on the other hand, had viewed the two clerics with suspicion right from the beginning. And they did not trust Ikawa as a person. Because they were cool, or even opposed to his trip to the United States, Iwakuro, who was in substantial agreement with Ikawa's aims, assisted him in his trip, using his own good offices to raise travel money. On February 13 Ikawa set out for the United States. The morning before he had called on Konoe. That Konoe had entrusted him with sounding out American intentions can be gathered from Matsuoka's telegram on March 17: "The prime minister expects Ikawa to maintain contact with those close to the president and to report from time to time on their intentions."[82]

3 Ikawa and the Draft Agreement in Principle

The Clerics and Ikawa: Divorced from Reality

On January 23 the two returned clerics talked for two hours with Roosevelt, Hull, and Walker. Roosevelt said he appreciated their efforts and that he would consider the matter carefully. It was agreed that the Maryknoll fathers would maintain their informal contact with the Japanese embassy and, through Walker, with Hull.[83] A comparison of the memorandum the clerics presented at that meeting (B)[84] with Drought's December 14 memorandum to Ikawa (A) makes concrete for the first time the following differences:

1) Regarding the so-called Japanese provisions: "We [Japan] must aim . . . to establish and strengthen our position in Indo-China, Thailand, Malaya (?) and the Dutch East Indies" in (A) was changed in (B) into " . . . the Japanese-American guarantee to check any third power attempting to alter the political status of the Philippine Islands, Hong

Kong, Singapore or Malaya, and the establishment of autonomous
Governments in Indo-China and the Dutch East Indies, in order to
remove these areas as potential war spoils [for the victors in Europe]
and in order to forestall the demand of Japanese Extremists for
forcible action." On the basis of these two measures, memorandum
(B) advocated a "recognition of a Far Eastern Monroe Doctrine."

2) Regarding the Tripartite Pact: In contrast to (A), which made
no specific reference to the pact, (B) stated, "The Japanese Government could maintain that as they accepted the Axis Alliance to maintain world peace by restricting the European war vis-à-vis the United
States. . . . they could apply the same principle to Germany and
threaten Germany with Japanese involvement if she extends the War
beyond its present confines."

3) Regarding settlement of the Sino-Japanese War: (A) contained
no specific reference to the issue, whereas (B) advocated "acceptance
of the cooperation of the United States in a settlement of the China
War on the basis of the secret Truce Terms offered last October by
Chiang Kai Check [sic]. [Perhaps a reference to the Matsuoka-Ch'ien
Yung-ming negotiations—trans.]. With some guarantee of politic-
economic order in China, and the removal of China as an immediate
military menace, or a political menace through a European 'sell-out,'
China and Japan could then unite to fight Communism in China and
in the Far East," there would be "no territorial aggrandizement in
China proper," and "Japan would grant a complete Open Door provided she received similar treatment from other Far Eastern countries."

4) On trade relations: While (A) had contained no reference to
such relations at all, (B) proclaimed that Japan "would write a Recip-
rocal Trade Treaty with the United States allowing free entry of
certain basic commodities, heavy machinery, etc."

The analytical portion preceding these points in memorandum B
was distinctive in that it probably originated in utterances made by
Ikawa. Its underlying tone, divorced as it was from reality, was bound
to become more pronounced after Ikawa's arrival in the United
States. On January 27 Walsh presented Walker a memorandum
which stated: "Today we received word by cable that the . . . [Japa-
nese] Government are now ready to send a trusted representative to
discuss the terms of a projected agreement."[85] The cable had probably been sent by Ikawa, the date of transmission being immediately
after the receipt of Walsh's January 25 telegram which said, "Hopeful
progress as result of visit with president—expect developments." Or
perhaps in its content it reflected the spirit of the meeting when

Ikawa visited Konoe on January 11. On board the *Hikawa Maru,* which sailed from Yokohama on February 13, he happened to meet U.S. commercial attaché Donald W. Smith, who was departing on home leave, and revealed that "he was the unofficial representative of a group of influential persons in Japan. . . . Iwakuro . . . one of 'the driving forces of the Army' . . . is scheduled to leave Japan during the early part of March and Mr. Wikawa expects to meet him in San Francisco on March 20, and accompany him to Washington."[86] Ikawa gave the impression that he was in some way laying the groundwork for Iwakuro's visit to the United States. He also hinted that the army would not take decisive action toward the execution of its policy of advancing into Southeast Asia until Iwakuro had had an opportunity to visit Washington. Smith also reported that the mission of Ikawa and Iwakuro appeared to have the sanction and blessing of the Japanese government, and Ikawa appeared extremely optimistic over the possibility of settling all difficulties between Japan and the United States.[87]

On February 27 Ikawa arrived in New York and again met Walsh and Drought. Accompanied by the two clerics he immediately visited Walker, the person in the background, at his private residence. Walker encouraged his visitors: "I will do anything I can as a man behind the scenes to put you in contact with Roosevelt and Hull, so I really hope that putting your heads together you three will come up with a way to normalize Japanese-American relations." Ikawa called on Nomura on the 28th. What he reported on how things stood can be inferred from Nomura's telegram of March 1:

> On February 28, Ikawa, a director of the Central Bank, came to see me and told me in detail of his connections with Walsh and Drought and their efforts to bring about a general conference between Japan and the United States through direct contact with the U.S. president. In order to facilitate my future dealings with Ikawa, I should like to be informed confidentially about what contact he has with Your Excellency and what the relationship is that he claims to have with Prime Minister Konoe and with army and navy authorities.[88]

Ikawa's Draft Agreement

True to his word, Walker cheerfully set about his liaison role. As early as February 28 he visited the White House and presented Roosevelt with the following memorandum:

A Plenipotentiary Representative of the Japanese Government is here in Washington. He is empowered to negotiate concrete terms for a settlement of all outstanding Far Eastern questions vis-à-vis the United States.

For such a settlement, the Japanese are prepared:

a) To invite the President of the United States personally to initiate mediation of the China-Japan conflict;
b) To nullify the Japanese participation in the Axis alliance, by a refusal to send any supplies to Germany and by the assumption of an obligation to keep the Germans out of the Far East, by military force, if necessary;
c) To freeze the Pacific nations *in statu quo*, by the recognition of autonomous governments comparable to the political units in the Americas;
d) To pledge, formally, their government against any further political and military aggression in the Far East;
e) By an economic-financial agreement to coordinate action that will assure continuance of amicable relations.

It is suggested that a representative of the President be appointed immediately, to work out, privately, with the Japanese Plenipotentiary, a draft of agreement. The Japanese Government would then indicate its official approval of the terms. Whereupon the President of the United States could call a public conference (preferably at Tokyo) to ratify this agreement which in fact had really been consummated previously.[89]

The content of this so-called Japanese proposal followed closely that of the January 23 Walsh memorandum, indicating that Ikawa after his arrival in the United States had reconfirmed the intentions of the Japanese government as the two clerics had come to understand them. The second half of the memorandum was particularly noteworthy for its suggestion of steps to be taken in the future.

On March 5 Walker visited Hull. Two days later, in a memorandum to the secretary of state, he called attention to the fact that the agreement envisioned in the proposal had not

... been communicated to Admiral Nomura or his Minister [Wakasugi Kaname],

As the Japanese Embassy (but not the Army) is totally unaware of the agenda agreed to in our memorandum; ...

It would be imperiling, as well as useless, to project, at this time, progressive diplomatic conversations with members of the Japanese Embassy. . . .

if, when Admiral Nomura, acting in his official capacity states . . . [tomorrow, the 8th] that his Government "would be pleased to consider actively the possibility of the reassumption of traditional cordial relations with the United States,["] Mr. Hull were simply, and cautiously, to indicate that the United States would entertain such a prospect.[90]

It was Walker who arranged for a secret meeting between Nomura and Hull with the aim of promoting this so-called Japanese proposal though a frank exchange of opinions. When informed of Walker's plan by Ikawa, Nomura overrode Wakasugi's objections and had his first private meeting with Hull on the morning of March 8 as specified. It took place in the study of Hull's apartment in the Carlton Hotel, to which the ambassador repaired via a back staircase. Walker, the two clerics, and Ikawa may have inferred from this that now not only Nomura but also Hull had begun to fall in line with their plan.

In any event, around March 10 Walker sent a memorandum to Hull, probably drafted by Drought, which stated, "We have already begun the preparation of the draft agreement," with the notation [at the top of the document, apparently by Drought—trans.] that "Wikawa has read, and agreed to, this memo with the stipulation that it must remain *absolutely confidential* to yourself [Walker?] and the *two other* persons [Roosevelt and Hull?] thus far concerned."[91] On March 13 Walker likewise sent Hull a memorandum, drafted by Walsh, at the end of which he pressed for an indication of the State Department's views:

I consider that we have reached a point in our conversations at which I really need to know, unofficially yet definitely, what objectives are of critical concern to the United States. I am working on the following:

1. Removal of Japan from the Axis Alliance;
2. Guarantee of Pacific peace;
3. Open Door in China;
4. Political integrity of China;
5. No further military or political aggression [by Japan];
6. Economic and financial treaty;
7. Use of Japanese merchant shipping;
8. Stoppage of all supplies to Germany [by Japan];
9. Obstruction to the spread of communism;

10.   An agreement with Japan based on certain principles as enunciated by Mr. Roosevelt and Mr. Hull.[92]

But it was too much for Walsh, Drought, and Ikawa to wait for the
cautious and deeply suspicious State Department to indicate its views,
and they began to prepare a draft agreement. On March 16 Walker
sent Hull the following memorandum, probably written by Walsh:

A preliminary draft of the "agreement in principle" is already drawn in
rather extended form. Certain points are so important and critical that
they should reach you, in summary form, at once.
. . . . an "agreement in principle" . . . provides:—
a. diplomatic, political, economic and financial instruments for the
dissolution of the German-Japanese partnership and the complete ces-
sation of all trade with Germany:
b. the release of a considerable tonnage of Japanese merchant ships
to be chartered to Americans without restriction as to cargo or destina-
tion, with the single exception of direct discharge in England or
Scotland:
c. formula by which the United States during the next three years
may request the cooperation of Japan's naval forces:
d. secret [Japanese] terms confided exclusively to the United States
for the settlement of the China War and provision for the intermedia-
tion of President Roosevelt if such terms meet with his confidential approval:
e. a recommendation for the formation of certain autonomous states
in the south western Pacific to forestall the pawning or seizure of such
states as war spoils:
f. guarantee of Philippine independence and conditional aid in the
event of unprovoked aggression by any third power:
g. Japanese pledge against military or political seizure of any territory within the Far Eastern region as defined and stabilized by a joint
American-Japanese declaration of a Far Eastern Monroe Doctrine to be
interpreted and applied, after consultation [between the two countries],
in a manner exactly paralleling the functioning of the Monroe Doctrine
in the Western Hemisphere.
h. the inauguration of vast economic opportunity for the United
States in the Far East (1) by economic treaty (2) by method of gold
credit allocation (but not physical transfer) which would make it impossible for the present Germany to trade in the Far East and, at the same
time, render Japan amicably, but so deeply, subservient to the United
States that political antagonism would be suicidal:
i. a conference at Honolulu, to be called as soon as practicable, to
specify the economics and limitations of the "agreement in principle"

and to signalize by appropriate circumstances (notably the attendance of President Roosevelt and Prince Konoye) the inauguration of a new era of Peace in the Pacific (and the end of the Axis Alliance! Alleluia!)

In the beginning of the memorandum it was noted that, "Incredible as it may seem, Mr. Wikawa has substantially approved. . . . " And toward the end it was noted that, "After consultation with Col. Iwakuro, Mr. Wikawa asserts that some modification but no substantial change will be made on the above-mentioned points of agreement."[93] This tells us that Ikawa had departed in one leap from the posture of waiting for Iwakuro that he had taken up to this point.

On the 17th Walker submitted to Hull yet another memorandum, probably written by Drought:

> The draft of our agreement establishes the basis not only of cooperative action by the United States [toward Japan] but inaugurates a revolution of "ideology" in Japan. What Mr. Wikawa has called the "180° change" cannot be produced in Japan without the greatest secrecy of preparation where public opinion . . . carries great weight. . . .
> N.B. 3.—As the complete reversal of the Axis policy for Japan can only be accomplished effectively by a *coup de main*, and as a thorough solution of "the Japan question" is desired as soon as possible by the United States, the Japanese will move with great rapidity and cable to their Embassy at Washington their formulation of our "agreement in principle" for official presentation by Admiral Nomura immediately upon my assurance that I have well-founded knowledge that it would prove substantially acceptable [to the United States also]. . . .
> P.S.—It cannot be too strongly emphasized that Prince Konoye, Count Arima [Yoriyasu—trans.] and Marquis Kido [Kōichi—trans.] (Lord Keeper of Privy Seal) are endangering their lives by these negotiations. Obviously, they will not confide in the Japanese Embassy at Washington until they are certain of substantial agreement with the two persons [Roosevelt and Hull?].[94]

On the same day the draft agreement in principle itself was completed. Compared to the memorandum the two priests had presented to Roosevelt on January 23, the new provisions that appeared in this draft agreement in principle, with Ikawa's consent, were largely as follows:

1. It referred directly to the Tripartite Pact for the first time:

> "The Japanese Government declares that its purpose and aim in affirming the Axis Alliance was a purpose of legitimate self-protection and an aim of distributive peace. . . .

If such an Alliance was conceived by others, or constricted by subsequent events, as a military manoeuvre initiated against the United States, the Japanese Government not only renounces such an event but reaffirms that it never contracted to such a consequence.

The Government of the United States cordially confirms its confident acceptance of the pacific assurances of the Japanese Government and reasserts that it has entered into no alliance, and will renounce any interpretation of existing political associations, as designed for military aggression against the people of Japan. . . .

The Governments of Japan and of the United States agree not to enter upon any political or military alliance with third Powers directed against the other."

2. It enumerated in concrete terms the secret provisions for settling the Sino-Japanese War. Six points therein that the Japanese were to guarantee were:

"(a) complete political independence of China:

(b) withdrawal of Japanese troops in accordance with a concerted [Japanese-American] plan agreed to by the Chinese:

(c) no . . . indemnities:

(d) no acquisition of Chinese territory, with the geographical definition thereof to be mutually agreed upon by the Chinese and Japanese. (It is implied that if, under such definition, the Chinese concede the recognition of Manchukuo, the United States Government subsequently would accept the Chinese decision and accord de facto recognition by sending an official representative to the Manchukuo Government.):

(e) resumption of the Open Door, with agreement to construct jointly (at some future, convenient time) a comprehensive interpretation of the political and economic meaning of that phrase as based on existing diplomatic exchanges and related to our new mutual understanding:

(f) no large-scale or concentrated immigration of Japanese into Chinese territory."

The six points that the Japanese were to request of the Chinese were:

"(a) no boycott or trade discrimination against Japan:

(b) adequate police control particularly in the northeastern area:

(c) civil action to discourage the spread of communism and cooperative suppressive action against military and organized political communism in China.

(d) effective use of present Chinese military forces acting, *without* assistance of Japan, to suppress the traditional widespread banditry in China:

(e) civil rights and protection for all foreign invested interests:

(f) the establishment of a unified Chinese Government . . . to retain, if the Chinese desire, Mr. Lin [Sen] . . . Chief Executive [of the Government] . . . , and to coalesce the present Governments of Chiang-Kai-Shek and Wang Ching Wei."

The following was also noted: " . . . the Japanese would pledge these terms secretly to the United States Government with complete confidence that Mr. Roosevelt would not disclose them to the Chinese or to any third Power."

3. In his memorandum of January 23 Walsh had expressed for the first time the unilateral hope for "such an agreement as would . . . put within the power of President Roosevelt the opportunity to immunize the Pacific [from the Japanese navy] for at least three years." The draft agreement in principle stipulated that "the United States and Japan agree to entertain, during the ensuing three years and thereafter by formally renewed mutual consent, a unilateral request for cooperation of their naval forces when either government judges that a national emergency requires such cooperation. . . . "

4. With regard to the summit meeting it was stipulated for the first time that "the agenda of the Conference would not include a reconsideration of the 'agreement in principle' but would direct its efforts to the specification of the pre-arranged agenda and the drafting of instruments to effectuate the 'Agreement.' "[95]

Ikawa Is Isolated and Helpless

By now the memorandum of December 14, modified in the January 23 version, had reached yet another stage. With Ikawa's concurrence, it had evolved into the March 17 draft agreement in principle. Revisions having been made by Iwakuro, it became in form and substance the Japanese-American Draft Understanding of April 16. That the essentials of the Draft Understanding had come into existence with the March 17 draft agreement is plain to see.

On March 18 Drought wrote that "a copy . . . was forwarded today to Prince Konoye—(unknown to Japanese Embassy)."[96] But it was not until March 22, when Ikawa reached San Francisco and met Iwakuro, that he sent a copy to Konoe by the home-bound *Tatsuta Maru*. And it was around April 11 or 12, only a week or so before the Draft Understanding would reach him by cable, that Konoe received it. Having received the Japanese-American Draft Understanding shortly after the draft agreement and without having examined the latter sufficiently, Konoe concluded that "although there are some differences" between them "the general line of reasoning is the same."[97]

To establish that he was authorized to act as the Japanese plenipotentiary, Ikawa cabled Konoe directly in uncoded language on March 5 at 8:15 p.m. from RCA Washington, and again on March 9 at 8:00 p.m. via Western Union; around the 10th he sent Konoe a lengthy telegram in code. Representations were made one after another: that it was most indiscreet for the Japanese embassy to talk with the journalist Roy Howard; that Konoe should propose a conference in Honolulu in the event Roosevelt agreed; that Konoe should instruct the embassy in Washington to request no further official talks pending advice from Ikawa; that Konoe should take over the Foreign Ministry portfolio immediately after Matsuoka left for Europe and instruct the Japanese embassy not to propose to the U.S. State Department that Matsuoka visit the United States; that every effort should be made to conclude a basic agreement in principle before the end of March; that Konoe "personally should prepare a draft of 'spiritual' principles affecting human freedom and rights."[98]

Ikawa openly voiced criticisms of Matsuoka, saying that the highest Japanese authorities had no confidence in their Foreign Ministry, that they planned to replace the foreign minister once an agreement was reached with the United States, that Matsuoka's journey to Europe should be seen as a stratagem to get him out of Japan so as to make it easier for Konoe himself to be able to exercise more direct control when it came to holding consultations with the United States.[99] On March 27 Ikawa a bit tardily told Joseph W. Ballantine of the State Department's Division of Far Eastern Affairs, "probably the officers of the Embassy would be disappointed that they were not in on negotiations, but . . . such negotiations should be in the hands of more experienced persons than the Japanese career diplomats. . . . [they were] out of touch with Japanese politics, and . . . he did not have any confidence in them."[100] Ikawa also asked Ballantine not to divulge anything he said to members of the Japanese embassy.

Ikawa's antipathy toward Matsuoka and the career diplomats might well have intensified the Foreign Ministry's strong distrust of Ikawa that had existed since Drought and Walsh were in Japan. On March 6, responding to Nomura's March 1 telegram of inquiry discussed above, Matsuoka replied that "as for the various rumors about Ikawa I have been hearing lately . . . I ask you to guide him using due caution."[101] Starting with that, Matsuoka sent Nomura other telegrams of instruction:

March 15:

> We continue to hear from various quarters highly distasteful reports concerning Ikawa. . . . Prime Minister Konoe wishes you to advise him not to proceed any further with talks.

March 17:

> Ikawa has cabled the prime minister seeking various kinds of support. This is outrageous. At this juncture it is absolutely forbidden on our part in terms of our foreign policy to give Roosevelt and others the impression, through any person or quarter, that we plan jointly with the United States to act as mediators in the European war. This would also be a betrayal of our allies, Germany and Italy. Accordingly, I ask you to admonish Ikawa thoroughly and give him strict orders not to overstep himself under any circumstances.[102]

On March 17, Finance Minister Kawada Isao cabled the following to Nishiyama Tsutomu, the financial attaché in New York:

> This is what I learned from the prime minister and others: the prime minister, the home minister, and members of the army and navy ministries all met with Ikawa before his departure and expressed their desire to avert war with the United States by every means; none of them, however, requested Ikawa in any way to conduct concrete negotiations; in view of our relations with Germany and for other reasons, it is most undesirable for him to give the impression that he was sent as the representative of the prime minister to carry out all kinds of negotiations; at least while Foreign Minister Matsuoka is in Europe, they want him to do nothing more than sound out American intentions and that is all.[103]

Matsuoka ignored Ikawa's reports to Konoe as unauthorized and outrageous. In light of his conversations in the Privy Council Lounge on January 29, cited above, it is hard to come up with evidence that Konoe on his part gave serious consideration to these telegrams from Ikawa, even though he had been quite interested and somewhat hopeful with regard to the clerics' plan when he received the Drought memorandum of December 14, and that he had been favorably inclined to Ikawa's going to the United States and had asked him to sound out American intentions. It appears that Ikawa's numerous proposals essentially went nowhere. In his cabled inquiry of March 1 Nomura had referred to "a lengthy draft telegram addressed to Your Excellency from Ikawa which I will deal with after receiving your reply to this telegram." In light of the cabled responses, the embassy in Washington refused to let Ikawa use the diplomatic code, and he was forced to send his coded telegrams to Konoe through the finance minister via financial attaché Nishiyama Tsutomu in New York.

As if in retaliation against Ikawa's lack of trust, embassy officials, from Minister Wakasugi on down, were ill-disposed, even obstructive toward Ikawa from the outset. Following Nomura's Carlton Hotel meeting with Hull, which Walker and Ikawa had successfully arranged, Nomura's confidence in Ikawa soared. Conversely, resentful from the start at the monopoly an amateur outside the diplomatic corps had over negotiating channels, and at the success he was having, embassy officials grew even more hostile toward Ikawa. The scramble for influence and status among the embassy secretaries, as well as their devil-may-care attitude toward the prospects for adjusting diplomatic relations,[104] may well have compounded matters. When on April 20 the embassy received from the ministry a secret fund of $50,000, Wakasugi and others urged Iwakuro to send Ikawa home, arguing that, with talks having begun through formal diplomatic channels, Ikawa's participation was no longer appropriate.[105] Because Nomura would not consent to this, however, no action was taken.

In view of such conditions as these on the Japanese side, and despite his protestations to Walsh, Drought, and others that he was a plenipotentiary representative, Ikawa was essentially isolated and helpless with respect both to his nation and to Washington until Iwakuro arrived in the United States. A resolution of the situation awaited Iwakuro's appearance in Washington.

4 Iwakuro and the Draft Understanding

Special Envoy Iwakuro: The Inside Story

On February 5, in response to Nomura's request that the government send as special envoy someone thoroughly familiar with the Sino-Japanese War, Army Minister Tōjō Hideki selected Colonel Iwakuro Hideo. Starting from February 1939, about six months before Mutō Akira became chief of the Military Affairs Bureau, Iwakuro had served a full two years as chief of the Military Section. During that period the section had been buffeted about by his overbearing ways.

Tōjō and Mutō felt that Iwakuro was undependable and difficult to work with. Rather than selecting him because he was right for Nomura's purposes, therefore, they used this personnel matter as an opportunity to transfer him out.

Iwakuro had had some notion about what was going on ever since Ikawa had consulted him about his proposed negotiations, but his appointment had no connection with Ikawa's aspirations to go to the United States. That his appointment came just before Ikawa's departure was purely coincidental, but because of this he was given further time to discuss with Ikawa how matters should be handled thereafter, and what Ikawa's policies should be until Iwakuro arrived in Washington.

On February 27 Iwakuro paid Ambassador Grew a courtesy call to inform him of his impending mission to the United States. According to Grew, Iwakuro announced "that he . . . did not believe that American-Japanese problems could be permanently resolved at this time but that he hoped to contribute toward maintaining an equilibrium [between the two nations] until prospects appeared of a basic solution being found."[106] This conformed at least with the logic of the Japanese-American Pacific peace agreement sought by the two clerics and probably reflected what Iwakuro had gathered from consultations with Ikawa. But before he left, Iwakuro spoke with no one in Japan, either within or outside the army, about the proposed negotiations; nor did he seek written, much less oral instructions. He thus had no consultations whatever with army leaders on how to coordinate the coming negotiations with the army's official policy toward the United States embodied in the "Main Principles for Coping with the Changing World Situation," whose influential advocates included Iwakuro himself.[107] In short, he left for the United States on March 6 keeping his ideas completely to himself. And upon sailing, Iwakuro quickly began his campaign with a cable to Ikawa: "Don't worry. Bringing detailed instructions Axis formula."[108]

Upon receiving this telegram, Ikawa asked the two priests not to take any further action until he had a chance to confer with Iwakuro. On March 27, having met Iwakuro at San Francisco and returned to Washington alone, Ikawa informed Ballantine that "Iwakuro was the driving force in the army . . . and was well thought of among all factions in the army, as well as in civilian circles. He had the complete confidence of General Tōjō . . . and General Mutō. . . ."[109] Grew also stated in his report on his meeting with Iwakuro that "Colonel Iwakuro, according to a reliable source, is one of the most important leaders of the young officers' group and has the complete confidence of the Minister of War [Tōjō]."[110] The American side consequently surmised that Iwakuro was a spokesman for the Japanese army, and they also clearly believed that he was bringing the most recent instructions from Tokyo.[111] Various courtesies were extended to him. Upon his arrival at San Francisco on March 20, for example, the local army district commander called on him informally. Immediately after he reached Washington on the 31st, Ballantine paid him a courtesy call "on Hull's orders."

Meanwhile, the draft agreement in principle had been completed and sent in secret to Hull. And then on March 18, with Iwakuro's arrival imminent, Walker submitted to the secretary of state the following memorandum, possibly written by Walsh:

1. Dangers of Delay.
(a) The Draft Document is a proclamation of a revolution in Japanese "ideology" and policy as well as a proof of the complete success of American statesmanship. Therefore, Konoye-Arima-Kido-etc., can not manage it piece-meal.
(b) The Japanese leaders will possibly be assassinated [if it is delayed]. Mr. Wikawa and Col. Iwakuro expect assassination in any event.
(c) Delay may be misinterpreted in Japan and so fortify the "fifth columnists" (Shiratori, etc.) to cement the Axis Alliance through Matsuoka [who is soon to be] at Berlin.
2. Immediate procedure suggested.
Complete review by the two or three persons [Roosevelt, Hull, and Walker?] and substantial change introduced or substantial approval given—so that Tokyo can immediately instruct its Embassy to submit the Draft officially—upon which both Governments can announce an "Agreement in Principle," publicly indicating some of the general points. In Japan, this announcement would have the Emperor's approval.
3. Proof of Japanese sincerity.
If an authoritative approval of substance is privately, but categorically, given to me by the two persons, we will request the Japanese leaders to instruct (within two weeks) Admiral Nomura to present personally to Mr. Hull the Draft of the "Agreement in Principle."
If this is not done, we can properly doubt the sincerity of the Japanese. . . .
5. Possibility of personally going over the material this week?[112]

Iwakuro Makes Revisions

When Iwakuro arrived in San Francisco on March 20 he met again with Ikawa, who had come to greet him. Explaining what had transpired while he was in the United States, Ikawa showed him the draft agreement in principle. Ikawa had earlier asserted to the two clerics, when he had agreed to the preliminary draft agreement, that "consultation with Col. Iwakuro . . . will not cause any substantial change," but Iwakuro's reaction evidently caused him to vacillate, and he prefaced the draft agreement in principle he sent to Konoe from San Francisco on the 22nd with the following:

> On the evening of March 18, a close associate of the president sent me a copy of what might be termed a draft proposal of basic principles concerning the maintenance of peace in the Pacific. . . . It is my understanding that the document was drafted in the view that a "personal conversation"[113] [between the two leaders] would be facilitated if there were some prepared topics of discussion. It seems that the president . . . is personally examining the draft proposal. I am sure it contains considerable room for revision. Together with Colonel Iwakuro and others I shall scrutinize the document without delay. Keeping this in mind, will Your Excellency kindly instruct us in strict secrecy on any points you will have noted upon your perusal. . . . I question if it is wise to show this document to our officials in charge, because by the time it reaches you it will have undergone considerable revision. . . . [114]

Iwakuro arrived in New York on the 30th and the following day began discussions with the two clerics. At the outset of their meeting, the colonel nailed down the point that "Japan cannot betray the Tripartite Pact currently in existence; should the United States fail to recognize this basic position of Japan and aim at alienating Japan from the pact, there is no possibility for entering into negotiations."[115] Iwakuro, forceful and self-assured as if representing both the army and Ambassador Nomura, thus convinced the two clerics that any modification of the Tripartite Pact was taboo. From the night of April 2 until the 5th Iwakuro made concrete revisions in the draft agreement in principle in consultation with Drought. On the 6th he personally handed the completed revised draft to Ambassador Nomura, making clear to Nomura for the first time what had taken place since last December. The ambassador examined the draft with Wakasugi, Second Secretary Matsudaira Kōtō, Army Attaché Isoda Saburō, and Navy Attaché Yokoyama Ichirō. By the evening of April 8 their work was completed, leaving Iwakuro's revised draft essentially unchanged. The draft presented to the U.S. government by Drought through Walker on April 9 could therefore be termed the Iwakuro draft.

On April 4, when Iwakuro and Drought were still engaged in their revisions, Walker sent Hull the following memorandum, probably drafted by Drought:

> . . . Colonel Iwakuro came to New York and gave his "unofficial" consent to every substantial point—viz:
>
> 1. No military action [by Japan] against the U.S., if our Government decides on "protective defensive action against Germany";
> 2. Mediation of President Roosevelt for China-Japan peace on basis offered to, and accepted by President Roosevelt, as just and prudent;
> 3. Acceptance of U.S. credit that would involve Japanese business in a substantial dependent alliance with the U.S.;
> 4. Release of high percentage of Japanese merchant marine;
> 5. Mutual pledge of Pacific peace and appropriate [Japanese and American] Naval placements;
> 6. Conference at Honolulu opened by President Roosevelt.
>
> Colonel Iwakuro feels that it will be impossible *politically* to effect a 180 degree change unless he can present some substantial benefits [to his government] (1) Economically—and as respecting Japanese ownership of some Dutch-East Indian oil and some rubber and tin; (2) Politically— and as respecting removal of Hong-Kong and Singapore as doorways to further political encroachment by the British in the Far East. . . .
> The Japanese desire to have their draft shown unofficially to Mr. Hull in the expectation that Mr. Hull will unofficially inform a third party, whether such a draft would be acceptable or rejected substantially.
>
> If acceptable, it would be presented immediately to Mr. Hull by Admiral Nomura.[116]

Among the Konoe papers, however, are two brief items, evidently telegrams, in English, neither dated nor signed, with a notation in Konoe's hand: "This from the Christians: report difficulties in the negotiations." The first reads: "Are they still genuinely sincere? Is there any way to restore the views of God and angels [to whom this refers is unknown] to their original state? Wonder what should be done next." The second: "Disappointed; Paul's [Ikawa's] friends have made excessive revisions." Presuming that they were sent around this time, they suggest that, for Walsh (?) at least, Iwakuro's revisions might have been disappointing in that they revealed little understanding of his original thinking. The State Department's Division of Far Eastern Affairs also judged the April 9 draft less promising in several respects from the point of view of the principles and policies of the United States than the draft agreement in principle.[117]

By comparing it to the draft agreement in principle of March 17 (A), the principle revisions made by Iwakuro in the April 9 draft (B) can be enumerated as follows:

(1) Concerning the South Pacific. Deleting from (A) "a joint American-Japanese declaration of a Far Eastern Monroe Doctrine," (B) made two additions: "On the pledged basis of guarantee that Japanese activities in the southwestern Pacific area shall be carried on by peaceful means, . . . American cooperation and support shall be given in the production and procurement of natural resources (such as oil, rubber, tin, nickel) which Japan needs"; and "The Government of Japan requests the friendly and diplomatic assistance of the Government of the United States for the removal of Hongkong and Singapore as doorways to further political encroachment by the British in the Far East."

(2) Concerning the Tripartite Pact. In place of the agreement in (A) not to enter into a hostile alliance, (B) proclaimed: "The Government of the United States maintains that its attitude toward the European War is, and will continue to be, determined by no aggressive alliance aimed to assist one nation against another. The United States maintains that . . . its attitude toward the European War is, and will continue to be, determined solely and exclusively by considerations of the protective defense of its own national welfare and security."

(3) Concerning the Sino-Japanese war. (B) added the demand for Chinese "recognition of Manchukuo." Where (A) had stated that President Roosevelt would publicly invite the two countries to peace negotiations and "publicly express his satisfaction that the Japanese would make a just peace with China," (B) stipulated, "The President of the United States, if the following terms are approved by His Excellency and guaranteed by the Government of Japan, might request the Chiang-Kai-Chek [sic—trans.] regime to negotiate peace with Japan. . . . Should the Chiang-Kai-Chek regime reject the request of President Roosevelt, the United States Government shall discontinue assistance to the Chinese."[118]

A memorandum Drought sent Hull directly on the same day, April 9, enlarged upon the implications of this:

(1) . . . "the general terms within the framework of which the Japanese Government will propose the [direct] negotiation of a peaceful settlement with the Chinese Government [are] to be in harmony with the Konoe principles regarding neighborly friendship and mutual respect

of sovereignties and territories and with the practical application of those principles, . . ."

(2) "Cooperation between Japan and China for the purposes of (a) preventing Communistic activities which may constitute a menace to the security of both countries; (b) maintaining for a limited required duration public order and safety in specified areas . . . restricted to North China and inner Mongolia, in accordance with a separate agreement between Japan and China."

(3) "Withdrawal of Japanese troops from China upon the resumption of peaceful relations and within a period of two years."

(4) "The Japanese forces at present stationed. . . [in Northern French Indochina] will be withdrawn as soon as the China Affair is settled or an equitable peace is established in East Asia.

The Government of Japan will not make any armed advancement, using French Indo-China as a base, to any adjacent areas thereof (excluding China), . . ."[119]

The Draft Japanese-American Understanding

Judging from what they had ascertained from the U.S. government via Walker, the two clerics were of the understanding that with the deletion from the Iwakuro revisions of only two points—concerning Hong Kong and Singapore and regarding the termination of aid in the event Chiang Kai-shek refused to negotiate a settlement— everything else was generally acceptable to the U.S. government as in the April 9 draft. They reported this to Iwakuro, and by the morning of April 16 the two had completed the final draft, the so-called Draft Japanese-American Understanding.

Ikawa was thoroughly intoxicated by the historic significance of the Draft Understanding, which ultimately hinged on swallowing whole what the two clerics thought it to mean. On April 9 he wrote Konoe:

While being tortured from within by the petty schemes of our interfering Foreign Ministry underlings, externally I had been struggling for weeks with the world champion sumo wrestler who is my negotiating counterpart. Then Mr. Iwakuro arrived and gave me support equal to that of one million friendly troops. The ambassador also came to place complete confidence in the two of us, and finally the staff of the embassy came to support wholeheartedly proposals they had once laughed at as "too good to believe." On the other hand, thanks to the absolute trust placed in me by President Roosevelt, Secretary of State Hull, Postmaster General Walker, and others and the immense respect they have for you, Prince Konoe, we have at last reached a point where, within a day or two, the foundation stone will be set in place for a great event that deserves special mention in the chronicles of world history. . . . It has already been confirmed that there will be a Japanese-American conference, for which President Roosevelt himself will travel to Honolulu. Consequently, it is the president's hope that the Japanese side do everything possible to have Your Excellency attend and that you and he make the opening ceremony an historic event. It seems that at the conference he intends to put in place the keystone necessary for the future maintenance of peace in the Pacific by issuing a Konoe-Roosevelt declaration which might even be termed a Pacific Monroe Doctrine.[120]

Iwakuro's attitude, however, was calmer and more complex. Since the night of April 2, when as virtually the sole representative of Japan he had worked continuously with Drought in making the revisions, he had unwittingly shifted his goal of securing a provisional peace agreement in the Pacific between Japan and the United States, his greatest hope as expressed to Grew before leaving for America, to that of bringing a halt to the Sino-Japanese War and achieving the recognition of Manchukuo, issues that had vexed the army for years. In the draft revision, therefore, Iwakuro focused his concern primarily on the question of what Japan would be prepared to yield to the United States in order to achieve these two objectives, which had been of only secondary importance in Drought's thinking.

Out of concern that the issue of Japanese-American mediation in the war between Britain and Germany might be construed as a Japanese-German peace offensive vis-à-vis the United States, Iwakuro agreed from the start not to raise it, it being a taboo to the American side. Nor was the Tripartite Pact, or anything to do with it, to be taken up, it being a taboo to the Japanese side. On Japan's obligations under Article 3 of the Tripartite Pact, Iwakuro furthermore acquiesced in a broad interpretation of the U.S. right of self-defense and of actions taken in self-defense. In return, he had the American side make it clear that it had no objection to the two main objectives which he had pursued since his arrival in the United States—U.S. recognition of Manchukuo and mediation between China and Japan to settle the Sino-Japanese War. However, it was basic U.S. policy not to allow Japanese troops to be stationed in China once the war was over. Consequently, aside from what might be settled through separate Sino-Japanese negotiations, Iwakuro failed to have that matter specified in the Draft Understanding as one of its provisions.[121]

Being a born schemer, from the time of his arrival in the United

States Iwakuro believed that activity on America's part, ostensibly based on the two clerics since the end of 1940, was itself a plot. Thinking he had no choice but to counter plot with plot, he responded initially with a wary approach. But gradually coming to believe that there was considerable substance in the American course of action, he concluded that Japanese-American relations could be improved, with unexpected ease, through this Draft Understanding.[122] In Iwakuro's judgment, the Draft Understanding was like a proposal a matchmaker might have concocted after listening to and fathoming the feelings of both sides. With both Japan and America adopting unofficially and simultaneously what this matchmaker proposed, he anticipated that by proceeding with an examination of that proposal through informal negotiations the way would be cleared for an adjustment of diplomatic relations.[123]

5 Distortions of the Draft Understanding

Nomura and Iwakuro Report

On April 14 Nomura met for the second time with Secretary of State Hull; one month had elapsed since their first meeting. Two days later he brought the just-completed Draft Understanding to Hull and discussed it with him. He sent Tokyo a complete text of the Draft immediately and in a separate telegram added the following explanation:

Today, April 16, I met with the secretary of state at his private residence. Hull said it would be all right to proceed with negotiations on the basis of Telegram No. 234 and asked me to obtain instructions from our government. (We call the document tentatively a Draft Understanding between our two nations. For some time now we have conducted clandestine maneuvers regarding this Draft Understanding and have "sounded out" the American government for its approval. Having confirmed that Secretary Hull had no objections to it for the most part, I myself secretly participated and had various negotiations carried out. The result is this Draft Understanding.) The secretary of state said that he wanted to do this because the United States government would be put in an awkward position if Tokyo should repudiate it after he and I had moved forward in our discussions. For some time I have studied this matter carefully with the embassy staff, the army and navy attachés, Colonel Iwakuro, and others. All of us have cooperated closely with one another. We have given due consideration to the situation both inside and outside Japan and have endeavored to turn this Draft Understanding to our advantage. Of course, it does not cover every aspect of our two nations' relations. There may be imperfections in the content of individual items. But it is our opinion that to reach an understanding along these lines at this time (1) would not be contrary to the imperial edict issued upon the conclusion of the Tripartite Pact, and we might, with due trepidation, presume further that it would be in accordance with His Majesty's wishes, (2) would by no means be contrary to our obligations under the Tripartite Pact, (3) would be the first step toward maintaining peace in the Pacific, which is our government's fundamental policy, and (4) would lay a foundation on which Japan and the United States might someday cooperate to restore peace in Europe. At this juncture, accordingly, we earnestly desire that for the sake of the larger picture you give us return instructions on how to correct imperfections in detail at our meetings and that you please authorize us to proceed with negotiations along the lines of the Draft Understanding.[124]

On the 17th Iwakuro dispatched separate but identical explanatory telegrams to Tōjō, Mutō, and Tanaka Shin'ichi, chief of the Army General Staff Operations Division. He wrote:

I. The prevailing atmosphere in the United States is one of preparation for war. There is momentum toward convoying merchant vessels and entering into the European war. I also believe there is a strong possibility that war will suddenly break out between Japan and the United States, triggered by a Japanese military advance southward or by American participation in the larger war. This atmosphere is fostered by government officials, young people, soldiers, and the press, and the general public is in accord with it. The real creators of this atmosphere are, however, the government authorities, starting with President Roosevelt. This political nucleus decides on its course of action by closely tracking public opinion. Thus, if the aggravated situation at present gets worse, I think it is not overstating matters to say that the way things are going the inevitable result will be American participation in the European war, the outbreak of war between Japan and the United States, etc. Even so, we must not overlook the following factors that still trouble the United States:

1. While ordinary Americans have blind faith that Britain will be victorious, the key leaders fear the British may be defeated and are worried about what measures should be taken in that eventuality.
2. The United States fervently hopes to avoid a two-front war.
3. It will be difficult for the United States to activate its defense plans

with full efficiency until after the autumn of next year at the earliest. *Until then, it will be close to impossible for the United States to
carry out operations in both the Pacific and the Atlantic.* (Author's emphasis)

4. A war with Germany, and certainly a war with Japan, would become greatly protracted, their outcomes uncertain, and their cost
stupendous. . . .

II. Steps taken up to completing the concrete draft cabled to the Foreign Ministry:

Since arriving here the ambassador has searched over and over
again for ways of improving relations between Japan and the United
States. Having decided to draw up a full-fledged rough draft, he has
scrutinized it every day since early April, with army, navy and Foreign
Ministry staff united around him. Certain principles have been established as a result, including the following:

1. A solution to the conflicts between Japan and the United States will
   not be possible unless resolute action is taken, across the board and
   in one concerted effort.
2. It must cover such issues as the China Incident, the trade embargo,
   Japan's southern problem, and the deployment of Japanese and
   American naval and air forces.
3. Not only must it not contradict our obligations under the Tripartite
   Pact, it must also steer the United States toward adhering to peace.
4. It would be most appropriate if reached while the outcome of the
   war between Germany and Britain is unclear.
5. The means adopted to achieve a solution must be on a grand scale.

While giving further thought to our own concrete demands based on
these principles, we also needed to know how far the United States on
its part would be prepared to go in accepting them. Therefore we first
proceeded with clandestine maneuvers (via the pipeline that has been
open since last December, namely "Drought-Walsh-Walker," which
Iwakuro and Ikawa made use of), and it has been decided to confirm
the results of those maneuvers by moving to unofficial talks between
the ambassador and Hull.

· · ·

III. This being the background of the second draft plan, I believe it
especially necessary at this point for the government to take a broad
perspective and decide on its policy toward this plan, without revision
if possible and as quickly as possible (by April 22–23 at the latest).
Finally, while U.S. agreement to this draft plan has been greatly influ-

enced by current conditions in the United States as described in item I above, at the same time it is also the result of pressure from the Axis alliance and of the progress in our military preparations for a southern advance. This is clear evidence of the great success that the empire's diplomacy has achieved thus far.[125]

...

We might ask, however, whether the Draft Understanding itself, as well as the elaborate explanations in the Nomura and Iwakuro telegrams, really embodied an accurate grasp of the actual situation in American government circles. Is it possible at least to assert that these were textually consistent with the Tripartite Pact? One could argue that the Japanese-American Draft Understanding, both in content and in how it was interpreted, contained serious distortions of reality from the very start.

The Draft Understanding and the Tripartite Pact

Under the terms of the Tripartite Pact it was clear that, if consultations based on the independent judgment of each of the three signatories concluded that one of them had been attacked, the others would be automatically obligated to go to war. It has been noted above that Matsuoka had officially affirmed such an interpretation. Nomura, however, believed that both Konoe and the leaders of the navy had agreed to a policy in which no war between Japan and the United States "was a fundamental fact of strategy, politically and militarily," for Japan. In a memorandum dated January 13, ten days before he left for the United States, Nomura declared: "It goes without saying that, [in the event the United States enters the war in Europe, Japan's participation] is to be decided only after exhaustive and careful deliberations based on our own national concerns. Our country is by no means obligated automatically to participate the minute the United States enters the war."[126] Thus, Nomura left Japan for his new assignment entertaining an interpretation of the Tripartite Pact considerably different in meaning from that affirmed by Matsuoka. At a press conference in the United States, Nomura replied that Japan's obligation to go to war under the pact "is a question of treaty interpretation which I do not want to go into."[127] As we have seen, that provoked Matsuoka on March 4 to dispatch a telegram of admonition. Nonetheless, Nomura let it be known at the new naval attachés' office: "If I had thought that Japan and the United States could not be reconciled, I simply would not have allowed myself to take on the responsibility for doing so here. Only because I truly believe they can be reconciled have I undertaken that responsibility."[128]

On the other hand, getting Japan to withdraw from the Tripartite Pact was central in the thinking of the two clerics, as reflected in such phrases as "nullify" the Tripartite Pact (Walker's February 28 memorandum), "the removal of Japan from the Axis alliance" (same of March 13), the "dissolution" of the Axis alliance (same of March 16), "the complete reversal of the Axis policy" (same of March 17), and a pledge not to conclude a hostile alliance (draft agreement in principle). And Iwakuro perceived this as soon as he arrived in the United States. Overcoming the displeasure of the two clerics, he got them to assent to setting the Tripartite Pact aside as "taboo" to Japan. In return, he conceded to the United States a broad interpretation of the right of self-defense in conflicts between the United States and Germany on the high seas. Bargains such as this made possible the Draft Japanese-American Understanding.

In the light of such delicate handling of the Tripartite Pact in the Draft Understanding, how on earth could Nomura go so far as to declare, in his item-by-item explanatory cable of April 18, that:

a) On the one hand the Draft Understanding makes it clear that there are no changes whatever in the obligations borne by the empire under the Tripartite Pact,

b) while on the other hand it most powerfully deters the United States from entering the European war and fully activates the spirit of Article 3 of the Tripartite Pact; in addition,

c) it averts a cataclysm between Japan and the United States and fulfills our objectives in concluding the Tripartite Pact. [129]

And again, in his April 21 response to inquiries, he stated:

a) Even after the Draft Understanding becomes reality the empire's obligations under Article 3 of the Tripartite Pact will continue in full force, and the danger of war between Japan and the United States as the result of the Axis alliance will be the same as at present. In consequence, it will not result in securing the rear of the United States to say nothing of Britain. As I see it, except for those forces needed for the war in the Atlantic, the United States will not pull out of the Pacific. This is analogous to our not being able to withdraw our troops from Manchuria despite having concluded a neutrality treaty with the Soviet Union.

b) I believe the Draft Understanding will reduce the danger of war be-

tween Japan and the United States, and by extension war between
the United States and Germany, arising from actions by either Japan or the United States. While on the one hand the United States
may increase its aid to Britain after this Understanding becomes reality, the empire will be able through this Understanding to deter
the United States from aggressive participation in the European
war. This coincides with Germany's having no desire to have a major confrontation with the United States, and it will give life to the
spirit of the Tripartite Pact as well. . . . The Draft Understanding
will make it clear that America's attitude toward the European war
"will be determined by the firm hate of war and considerations of
the protective defense of its own national welfare and security."
One is therefore justified in concluding that in the Draft Understanding the United States has by and large expressed its intention
not to participate aggressively in the war by attacking Germany to
save Britain, unless provoked by Germany. It goes without saying
that should the United States disregard the Draft Understanding
and enter the war, our empire will also be able to take independent
action in accordance with the Tripartite Pact. . . .

   In conclusion, I should like to point out in particular that this
Understanding should be regarded, like the Japanese-Soviet Neutrality Treaty, as a logical extension of the Axis alliance, the keynote of the empire's policies, and will have no influence whatever
on the efficacy of Article 3 of the Tripartite Pact, the foundation of
the Axis Alliance. . . .[130]

If a broad interpretation of America's right of self-defense were
taken, whether or not an attack had occurred under Article 3 of the
Tripartite Pact in the event of a conflict between the United States
and Germany would be decided primarily by how the United States
defined the scope of its right of self-defense. Conversely, Japan's
autonomy when such a decision was made would be restricted in
advance by what was advantageous to the United States. Furthermore, Matsuoka's policy toward the United States of preventing its
entry into the European war would be undone, based as it was on
intimidating the U.S. with the possibility that Japan might activate its
obligation to enter the war. Not only that. Nomura's aim as expressed
in his cabled response of the 21st—namely, to "be able through this
Understanding to deter the United States from aggressive participation in the European war"—would also self-destruct.

   Even then, it would still be the case that "even after the Draft
Understanding becomes reality . . . the danger of war between Japan
and the United States as the result of the Axis alliance will be the

same as at present." By its very nature the Draft Understanding could not eliminate confrontations between Japan and the United States in the Pacific. On the contrary, it implied that a new policy detached from Matsuoka's was needed to make those confrontations less critical. Rather than being "a logical extension of the Axis alliance," this Draft Understanding was therefore a product of subtle compromises flavored in Washington in their several peculiar aspects by, among other things, Matsuoka's handwritten instructions of January 22, the policy consistently pursued by Nomura, the thinking of the two clerics, and the bargains struck by Iwakuro. In this respect the Draft Understanding was to cause even greater confusion over Japan's obligation to go to war under the Tripartite Pact, an obligation that had never been clearly defined in the first place, and to advance the cancer afflicting the exploratory efforts between Japan and the United States thereafter.

The Two Clerics: A One-sided Understanding

Prior to participating directly himself, Nomura had explained that "for some time now we have conducted clandestine maneuvers and 'sounded out' the American government regarding its approval of the Draft Understanding. [I have] confirmed that Secretary Hull has no objections to it for the most part. . . ." And Iwakuro had also explained that "because the United States appears to have no objections for the most part, I propose that we move to discussing it between Ambassador Nomura and Hull . . . it is quite certain that the Draft has been approved by Roosevelt." In all probability these observations derived from deductions Iwakuro had made during his negotiations with the two clerics[131] and from what Nomura had concluded from talks with Hull on April 14 and 16.

Drought's original memorandum of December 14 had been deeply colored by his distrust of the State Department. Drought, the more able of the two clerics, prided himself in being clearheaded and gave the appearance of holding State Department officials in contempt— from Hull on down.[132] Consequently, after the two clerics had asked Walker to set the table for the first secret meeting between Nomura and Hull on March 8, they took a high-handed attitude the day before that meeting in transmitting to Hull through Walker specific desires that Hull was to express to Nomura. Moreover, in the Walker memoranda to Hull of March 18 and April 4, which the two clerics had been involved in drafting, they went ahead and asked that examination of the text of the draft be restricted to Roosevelt, Hull, and Walker, then proposed that substantive responses for and against the Draft and requests for revisions be confined to only these three persons, and finally suggested steps to be taken thereafter.

What the two clerics, who had already reached an agreement with Ikawa, the self-appointed representative of Japan, aimed at with the United States was a procedure for handling matters through high-level political decisions, excluding State Department staff. After April 10 when Walker, who from the outset had been insensitive to the actual situation between Hull and the State Department staff, returned the Iwakuro draft that both Roosevelt and Hull had finished reading (both desiring deletion only of the two points concerning Hong Kong and Singapore and the termination of aid to Chiang Kai-shek), the two clerics failed to perceive Roosevelt's dual stance of not closing the door to either Hull or Walker. Rather, they seemed to have understood, simply and unilaterally, that they had just hit the bull's eye, with the three persons having accepted the draft on the basis of a high-level political decision which excluded State Department staff, and that the next step was simply for Nomura to propose it officially. Even on May 2, about half a month later, Iwakuro cabled home:

> The Draft has been discussed by the above four persons [Roosevelt, Harry Hopkins, Walker, and Hull] plus Knox. It is certain that starting with the leading anti-Japanese figure, Henry L. Stimson, all other cabinet members and officials have been excluded. Up to now, it has often been the tendency for U.S. Far Eastern policy to be decided in accordance with the views of such people as Hornbeck and [Maxwell M.—trans.] Hamilton (both China experts and anti-Japanese) because Roosevelt, Hull, and other top leaders lacked knowledge about the Far East. But in view of its great significance, this Draft, which will restore Japanese-American relations, has received Roosevelt's personal approval. It appears that the other day Hull went so far as to tell State Department officers that the Draft for the adjustment of Japanese-American relations was to be decided by top level leaders and that if there were those who were unhappy about this he would like them to resign.[133]

A few days later Nomura sent a telegram along the same lines.[134] Behind both telegrams the one-sided understanding of the two clerics is strongly suggested.

America Takes a Dual Stance: Hard-line and Soft-line

The actual relationship between Hull and State Department officials was quite the opposite. For more than two months since January 23, when the Walker memorandum was presented to Roosevelt, State Department officials had painstakingly examined each memorandum the two clerics sent via Walker, severely criticizing each one and imploring Hull to reject them. Roosevelt himself, while keeping open the lines of communication via Walker, had from the very beginning entrusted Hull with the task of examining the proposals and meeting with Nomura about them. In light of the actual way in which matters were handled, the hustle and bustle of the two clerics was in fact little more than idle scurrying around.

Insofar as these proceedings were concerned, Hull's responses to Roosevelt's inquiries were essentially the opinions of leading members of the Far Eastern Division, notably those of Hornbeck. For more than two months Hornbeck had submitted to Hull numerous memoranda that we may infer had no small influence in shaping the attitudes of Roosevelt and Hull toward the matter at hand. Hornbeck's views may be summarized in his own words, first in regard to the international context:

With the world situation what it is, with the problems of this country both in the Atlantic and in the Pacific—and at home—what they are, with our relationship to Great Britain and our attitude toward China . . . and other countries that are resisting aggression what they are, it may well be doubted whether a conference . . . between representatives of the United States and of Japan would be likely to serve a useful purpose. . . . The effects of the making of such an announcement at this time would be those of a super-colossal political bombshell: tremendous repercussions in all directions. I can think of nothing that would produce immediately more of a shock—a shock which would not be to the advantage of this country and would not be to the advantage of Great Britain. (April 5) [135]
It must be remembered . . . that the Japanese-Chinese conflict . . . has become part of a world conflict; the Japanese-Chinese conflict cannot be dealt with as an isolated phenomenon and without relation to other parts of the world conflict of which it is a part. . . . that so long as and while Japan remains a member of the tripartite alliance, it would not be in the interest of the United States or in the interest of Great Britain that the Japanese-Chinese hostilities be brought to an end by any process which leaves Japan's military machine undefeated (undis-

credited) and intact. . . . The world situation being what it is, the world conflict and its problems being what they are, Japan's present involvement in China is to the advantage of the United States and Great Britain. . . . (April 7)[136]

. . . Nothing that might be agreed upon between the American and the Japanese Governments within the next few days or weeks will substantially alter the world situation in its material aspects; a negotiation between Japan and the United States might have some effect as regards deliberation and discussion between and among the various Japanese factions, but it would not enable any group not now in control of Japan's affairs to oust those who are in control and gain control for itself; the decision of Japanese leaders whether to move or not to move southward will be made in the light of the physical situation in Europe as they view it and the physical situation in the Pacific as they view it. . . . (April 11)[137]

The objective . . . should be not to drive the Japanese into a war of desperation, but rather to demonstrate to them the dangers of the activist program. . . . If by the end of the year the prospects of an early German victory should have faded, Japan might think twice before plunging into a long and potentially disastrous struggle. Japan might even voluntarily abandon its connection with the Axis. (Division of Far Eastern Affairs memorandum, April 17)[138]

Second, he was critical of the two clerics' memorandum:

In my opinion, the fundamental weakness of the proposal made in this memorandum arises out of . . . the fact that . . .[it does] not take realistic account of Japan's present policies and current practices. . . . The procedure [it proposes] . . . is not adapted to the facts of the situation. (March 1)[139]

Third, he advised Hull on how to respond:

. . . adopt and maintain the role of listener and . . . draw the Ambassador out while avoiding as far as possible any indication of perplexity, uneasiness, apprehension or eagerness on the part of your Government and any disclosure of your position, favorable or unfavorable, regarding any concrete proposals or suggestions for action which the Ambassador may put forward. . . .

Our immediate problems are, it seems to us, that of (1) keeping the Japanese in a state of hoping and yet having to guess and (2) finding out all that we possibly can regarding their thoughts and their actual or possible intentions. (March 7)[140]

If and when a draft is presented to the Japanese, it would be well, in my opinion, for us to include in such a draft less than we would be willing to agree to. . . . The Japanese have put into their draft a good deal more than they expect to agree to. We, if we give them a draft, should put ourselves in a position for bargaining. (April 11)[141]

. . . the Ambassador might be informed that, if the Ambassador will consult his Government and present proposals under authorization, the Secretary would be prepared to study the draft sympathetically.

If the Ambassador says that before asking his Government for instructions he would like to know whether this Government would be prepared to give favorable consideration to the proposal, the Secretary might say that we consider that the proposals as a whole offer a starting point for discussion, and that we feel optimistic that on the basis of mutual good will our differences can be adjusted and reconciled. (April 15)[142]

In fact, Hull's attitude toward Nomura took the form of a dual stance, both hard-line and soft-line, based on these memoranda. On the one hand he buoyed up Nomura's spirits, as at the start of their clandestine meeting on March 8: " . . . I was not absolutely certain whether . . .[you] would come; that at all times most countries have some responsible, fine, and capable citizens who are seeking earnestly and patriotically to make their respective contributions to better understanding and other desirable relations between their own and other governments; that in the instant situation I deeply appreciate their purposes and their efforts and have sent word to them to that effect."[143] And in a memorandum he sent to Roosevelt just before Roosevelt met with Nomura on March 14, Hull suggested that at the meeting " . . . you may care to say—as I did to the Ambassador on March 8—that you very much appreciate the purpose of the Ambassador's compatriots. . . ."[144]

On the other hand, Hull pointedly brought up his so-called "Four Principles" when, on April 16, Nomura presented the completed Draft Japanese-American Understanding as Hull had suggested he do two days earlier. According to Hull's memorandum:

I . . . remarked that the one paramount preliminary question about which my Government is concerned is a definite assurance in advance that the Japanese Government has the willingness and ability to go forward with a plan along the lines of the document we have referred to and the points brought up in our conversation in relation to the problems of a settlement; to abandon its present doctrine of military conquest by force . . . together with the use of force as an instrument of policy; and to adopt the principles which this Government has been proclaiming and practicing as embodying the foundation on which all relations between nations should properly rest.

I said:

"I will, therefore, hand to you as the basis for my preliminary question, the following four points on a blank piece of paper: [respect for territorial integrity and sovereignty, noninterference in internal affairs, equality of opportunity, maintenance of the status quo in the Pacific]. . . ."

. . .

I added that, if his Government should make up its mind to abandon its present policies of force and invasion, et cetera, and to adopt a peaceful course with worthwhile international relationships, it could find no objection to these four points reasonably applied. . . .

. . . that if his Government is in real earnest about changing its course, I could see no good reason why ways could not be found to reach a fairly mutually satisfactory settlement. . . .[145]

Having abruptly brought up all the basic premises for preliminary talks in this fashion, Hull entered into how the Draft Understanding should be handled. His statement was businesslike, precise, and indicated neither approval nor disapproval:

. . . we both agree that we have in no sense reached the stage of negotiations; that we are only exploring in a purely preliminary and unofficial way what action might pave the way for negotiations later.

. . . the document . . . contained numerous proposals with which my Government could readily agree; on the other hand, however, there were others that would require modification, expansion, or entire elimination, and, in addition, there would naturally be some new and separate suggestions by this Government for consideration [by Japan]. . . .

. . . [and] counter-proposals . . . and . . . independent proposals. . . .

[Your submission of the document to your government] does not imply any commitment whatever on the part of this Government with respect to the provisions of the document in case it should be approved by your Government.

. . . if I should thus out of turn agree to a number of important proposals in the document and these proposals should be sent to Japan and the military or extremist groups should ignore them, I and my Government would be very much embarrassed.

I do . . . recognize individually that . . . if the Japanese Government should approve this document and instruct the Ambassador here to propose it to the United States Government, it would afford a basis for the institution of negotiations. . . .[146]

On May 7, 11, and 12 he reiterated to Nomura statements to the same effect.

Nomura and Iwakuro Mislead Their Government

In light of Hull's basic attitude about carrying through on principles and his precise but noncommital policy for handling matters, what Nomura reported to Tokyo immediately after his April 16 meeting with Hull, as cited at the outset of this section, was partially accurate but gave a wrong impression of the meeting as a whole and the procedures to be followed for the deliberations. Iwakuro's cabled report in particular was grossly in error in judging that "barring major changes in the situation, the principal features of the Draft will certainly be settled within a day or two, as soon as the Japanese government indicates its intentions." On April 28 Walker told Nomura in private:

> Although Hull is slow to make up his mind, once he has done so he does not change it easily. And given Hull's relation to his superior there is also great danger that the matter will be dropped should fundamental revisions be made in the American proposal [Draft Understanding].[147]

From this example it would appear that Nomura was strongly influenced by the mistaken judgments of Walker and the two clerics on this point as well.

In their telegrams of April 17 Nomura and Iwakuro omitted reference to Hull's basic attitude about carrying through on the Four Principles. In Nomura's telegram of May 8 he at last mentioned in passing that, "In the actual discussions of the Draft Understanding the American side tenaciously advocated [the Four Principles], but I put a stop to this by proposing that neither side should go too deeply into arguments over principle."[148] And that was the extent of it. But the one-sided and farfetched understanding of the two clerics as to how matters were being handled within the United States government had penetrated deeply into Nomura's mind via Iwakuro and Ikawa. Did this predisposition have a powerful influence on his acceptance or rejection of what Hull had to say? Perhaps such a farfetched predisposition on the one hand and Hull's strategy, previously discussed, for sounding out Japan on the other caused Nomura and Iwakuro to be greatly mistaken in their grasp of Hull's basic attitude and how he proposed to handle matters when they held their conversations with him.

Iwakuro had regarded the Draft Understanding as a matchmaker's proposal to be examined unofficially by both sides in the course of informal negotiations. Nonetheless, in his report he clearly stated that "the main points in the Draft Understanding derive from Hull's proposals," judging that this would be expedient in securing a consensus within the Japanese government.[149] This was no innocent mistake but a stratagem directed at the government in Tokyo that was to lead to decisive mistakes in judgment on the part of the Japanese government from that point on. Furthermore, the government could not have failed to detect that the Japanese text of the Draft Understanding first sent to Tokyo on April 17 differed on several crucial points from the English original. For example, in the Japanese text the last sentence of the Preamble reads: "The Draft Understanding will require the final and official decision of the Japanese government *after* modification by the United States government" (author's emphasis). The English original, to which Iwakuro, Walsh and Drought, Nomura, and others consented, says: "mutual understanding subject, of course, to modifications by the United States Government and subject to the official and final decision of the Government of Japan." The Japanese version thus caused misunderstanding concerning the sequence of modifications by the two governments. In addition, what the Japanese text rendered as "acknowledge," "declare," "should recommend," and "a conference should be held," were, in the English original, "might acknowledge," "might declare," "might suggest," and "it is suggested that a conference . . . be held."

Some three months later, as he was about to resign as foreign minister, Matsuoka lashed out against Nomura, saying that from the very start the ambassador "had prepared a Japanese translation that differed on vital points from the English original. . . . When we compared [the English original] with the Japanese text that we first received, the sloppiness was astonishing—nay, we discovered that on numerous occasions we were given no choice but to think that bogus translations of points disadvantageous to our side were deliberately made in order to facilitate compliance on our part."[150] Although Matsuoka may have gone too far in his conjecturing, it can be inferred that Ikawa and Iwakuro did embellish the translation of the Japanese text first cabled to Japan, and it is certain that this was yet another factor in misleading the Japanese government.

Moreover, regarding the matter of mediation in the Sino-Japanese War, the draft agreement in principle and the memoranda of the two clerics up to this point all stated expressly that this depended on mediation by Roosevelt. The Draft Understanding also stated unequivocally that Roosevelt, "if the following terms are approved . . .

and guaranteed by the Government of Japan, might request the Chiang-Kai-Chek regime to negotiate peace," and made clear the premise that in advising peace Roosevelt could indeed approve the Japanese terms. With mediation being of such a nature, how on earth could it be affirmed, as in Nomura's explanatory telegram, that, "it being our purpose to prevent the United States from starting to meddle in the China Incident, Roosevelt will go no further than act as a peace mediator (*bons offices*)"? Some embellishments can be detected here as well.

In any case, having received the Japanese text of the Draft Understanding, Nomura's cabled report, and his item-by-item explanatory telegram, all on April 18, the Japanese government [was confused about the U.S. position on the Draft Understanding—trans.]:

1. It thought that the Draft was an official proposal by the United States government, even though Hull had given Nomura no such assurances.

2. It therefore thought that the United States would not retreat from the content of the Draft and would reach an agreement along its basic lines as soon as Japan presented a counterproposal, so long as Japan did not "repudiate" the draft or "kick it out"—although Hull had reserved to some future day the right to expand, eliminate, reject, make separate suggestions, present counterproposals, or make independent proposals.

3. It consequently thought that future talks between Nomura and Hull were to be characterized as formal diplomatic negotiations with the sole purpose of reaching official agreement on the Draft Understanding.

4. Moreover, it was given not the slightest clue as to Hull's basic attitude on the so-called Hull Four Principles, whose acceptance was the basic premise for commencing talks between Nomura and Hull, and which amounted to a demand that Japan abandon totally, concretely and even retroactively, the national policies it had pursued from the outbreak of the Sino-Japanese War up to and including the occupation of northern French Indochina.

5. It was forced to speculate about what the Draft meant in terms of U.S. intentions concerning the Tripartite Pact, because nothing of Iwakuro's bargain had been reported back to Tokyo, that bargain being a broad interpretation of America's right of self-defense in return for not bringing up the Tripartite Pact, which was taboo for Japan, and thereby a deviation from Matsuoka's policy toward the United States.

On May 7 Nomura accurately reported for the first time that Hull "had told me that he found in the Draft Understanding several points whose modification would benefit both nations."[151] And on June 3 Iwakuro finally sent Mutō the following very candid telegram, stressing that his aim in the Draft Understanding was different from that of Matsuoka as well as from that of the two priests in that it lay in achieving an early settlement of the Sino-Japanese War:

1. In my humble view . . . it is not difficult to realize that the American side wants to see Japan alienated from the Axis. In the future we must be on our guard against this. We here have been explaining our attitude on this matter to the Americans in the most explicit way, and I am convinced that there is no misunderstanding on their part. . . .

2. *Whether or not a Japanese-American understanding is reached*, I believe that the central diplomatic issue between Japan and the United States from now on will be whether we succeed in preventing them from entering into the war or they succeed in alienating us from the Axis. . . . *It is a mistake to assume that the Draft Understanding will prevent American participation in the war* and that both the United States and Germany will continue to respect our present position vis-à-vis the Axis. These matters require the utmost effort and concern in terms of Japanese-American diplomacy from now on. (Author's emphasis)

3. From the point of view of the overall situation, and above all from the point of view of settling the China Incident before the conclusion of the European War, it is to Japan's advantage to bring to speedy fruition the proposal [Ambassador Nomura will report to you].[152]

But Iwakuro's telegram arrived well after Matsuoka's revised proposal of May 12 (embodying all the above-mentioned confusions, ignorance, and speculations) had been presented to the American side, and by then it was almost too late to attempt any kind of explanation concerning the actual aims of the Draft Understanding.

Several months later, in mid-November, Foreign Minister Tōgō Shigenori was to comment at a Liaison Conference:

. . . the more closely I examine the documents relating to Japanese-American negotiations to date, the more it seems that things have been bungled. Japan has handed over all its deeds, signed and sealed, to the other side and has gotten none in return.[153]

As this statement indicates, confusions over the Draft Understanding were later to lead to a pattern of negotiations in which only the Japanese side would betray its hand. The U.S. government's June 21 proposal modifying Matsuoka's revised draft made concrete for the first time the basic attitude that Hull had declared to Nomura on April 16. The Japanese side—confused, ignorant, engulfed in speculation—was at first shocked, then overwhelmed by a sense that it had been betrayed by the United States. Contrary to its purpose, the Draft Understanding would in fact compound the difficulties in reaching a Japanese-American understanding thereafter.

6 The Military, Konoe, and the Japanese-American Draft Understanding

Tōjō Does Not Know What to Believe

In his ability to engage in political machinations and to draft statesmanlike policy papers, Iwakuro had few rivals among the key officers of the army at the time, senior or junior. In focusing that ability totally on areas of immediate concern, he was very adept at devising specific measures, but he was also troubled by inconsistencies among them. Although he was an enterprising man who could see what was ahead in the short run, his assertiveness inclined toward braggadocio for want of carefully touching bases beforehand. Tōjō and Mutō, who found Iwakuro somewhat difficult to handle, took advantage of Nomura's request for a special envoy to have Iwakuro transferred to Washington. This was above all a frivolous decision and contrary to the intent of Nomura's request. Nomura, who could not have been expected to know what had transpired in Tokyo, was thus led to the mistaken belief that because Iwakuro had been dispatched at the request of the army, he would be able at least to reflect the intentions of the army and to represent its state of mind.[154] And Iwakuro for his part made the most of this mistaken belief.

By injecting this opportunistic go-getter, prone to braggadocio while he created faits accomplis, into a fluid situation with which Nomura himself had as yet had utterly nothing to do, just at the moment when a draft agreement for peace in the Pacific was being hatched by Ikawa and the two clerics all by themselves, the Japanese government provided Iwakuro with an ideal stage on which to do his own thing. As for Tōjō and Mutō, they were going to have to cope with the consequences of having, through their own frivolity, released a tiger into the wilderness.

When Tōjō received the first report from Iwakuro about the Draft Japanese-American Understanding on April 18, he ordered Mutō—along with Satō Kenryō, chief of the Military Affairs Section; Sanada Jōichirō, chief of the Military Section; and others—to make a routine examination as to what attitude the army should take. Mutō seems to have taken this up with the most enthusiasm,[155] but even he warned: "Is it okay for Iwakuro to be doing this? This telegram is Iwakuro's doing; he schemes too much."[156] After successive meetings on the morning of the 19th—one that included two senior officers, Ishii Akiho of the Military Affairs Section and Nishiura Susumu of the Military Section, and another held within the Military Affairs Section—it was decided "to agree in any case to start negotiations," and Mutō reported this back to Tōjō. In these meetings Ishii got the impression that it had been the Japanese-Soviet Neutrality Pact of April 13 that had made the United States yield to the point of proposing the Draft and that a settlement was bound to be reached between Japan and the United States on this basis.[157] Ninomiya Yoshikiyo, chief of the Army Foreign Relations Office, understood that because the war was going in Germany's favor, the United States had been placed in a predicament and had gradually moderated its position; it would, therefore, propose compromises and make concessions even on the China issue.[158] In general, the Military Affairs Bureau was, like Iwakuro, ready to concede that, if there were absolutely no other alternative, Japan would give tacit consent to American participation in the European war and would not use such participation as a pretext for going to war with the United States, even if that put something of a damper on the Tripartite Alliance.

Tōjō, on his part, was likewise unable to free himself of suspicions about Iwakuro, telling Mutō that the Draft was cock-and-bull. He appears to have been particularly put out by Iwakuro's indulging in intrusive braggadocio without touching base with anyone beforehand. Nevertheless, he and Mutō, not knowing what to believe, were still interested in the Draft. "The foremost and basic concern in the American proposal is to deal with the China Incident," Tōjō wrote to Konoe on April 25. "So we must not miss this opportunity. We must grab it without fail." And Mutō said: "Since this will settle the China Incident it looks great." Satō Kenryō agreed: "Since this really will settle the China Incident, I'd like to make a go of it."[159] As these statements reveal, they may have been so keen on the Draft because the army had by now lost almost any hope of settling the Sino-Japanese War (a war it had itself started) through its own efforts—military, political, or cunning.

Moreover, the army had already become semi-habituated, in Matsuoka's words, to "clutching at" any straw, however weak, that looked as though it might lead to a settlement. Iwakuro's primary objective, to contrive an early settlement of the Sino-Japanese War through this proposal even though it deviated from Matsuoka's policies, was right on the mark in this respect: he was seeking to have this proposal accepted *in toto* by going right to the Army Ministry's sore spot.

The Army and Navy: United in Their Views

The General Staff Office was less encumbered by anxieties concerning Iwakuro. When the unexpected arrival of the first report was announced at the Liaison Conference of April 18, Chief of Staff Sugiyama Gen was cautious:

1. Isn't the United States thinking of this proposal with Germany in mind? Aren't they trying to increase aid to Britain?
2. Aren't there parts that clash with the Tripartite Pact? To what extent do they actually clash? What disadvantages does it give to Germany and what advantages to Britain?
3. Doesn't maneuvering for peace with China diverge from our posture up until now? How about contradictions with the Konoe Declaration?
4. What effect will it have on the establishment of the Greater East Asia Coprosperity Sphere?
5. After examining it fully, should we reject it or start afresh with a revised proposal?
6. What effect will it have on the United States and Britain if we reject it? If we revise it?

. . .

8) We must keep in mind that negotiations with Roosevelt and Hull are already in progress and that international good faith is involved.[160]

The immediate assessment by the War Guidance Office was succinct:

The Japanese-Soviet Neutrality Pact makes it advantageous for Japan to advance to the south. And it will be difficult for the United States to conduct a two-ocean war in both the Pacific and the Atlantic. It appears that the United States does not want war to break out between Japan and the United States.[161]

The next day, when the translated telegrams became available, the War Guidance Office announced its interpretation of the United States' principal objectives in the proposal:

1. To bring about full cooperation between Japan and the United States, based upon two fundamental conditions: that Japan refrain from advancing south by force of arms and that the United States refrain from participating in the war against Germany by force of arms.
2. To have the United States advise Chiang Kai-shek to conclude a general peace through direct negotiations between China and Japan.
3. To bring about world peace through Japanese-American collaboration.

These would amount to a historical change in our foreign policy. However you put it, this is a liquidation of the spirit of the Tripartite Alliance.[162]

On April 20 a conference was held at the behest of the General Staff Intelligence Division. Though noting "that there was need to be on guard lest this should be a grand plot on the part of the United States," those attending endorsed the Draft Understanding with two conditions: 1) that some revisions of the text had to be made so as not to run counter to the spirit of the Tripartite Alliance, and 2) that the China Incident had to be settled once and for all.[163] Their suspicion of an American plot originated in the fact that many members of the Intelligence Division were pro-Axis. Following the conference there was a meeting of the General Staff division chiefs. They were united on "a general course that would undertake the adjustment of diplomatic relations with the United States insofar as that did not run contrary to the spirit of the Tripartite Alliance" and decided "to make revisions in parts of the text so as not to irritate Germany."[164] Further, on the morning of April 21 division chiefs and above from both the Army Ministry and the General Staff were called together and reconfirmed the position taken by the General Staff division chiefs. Following this, bureau and division chiefs from the army and navy ministries and general staffs met and agreement was reached between the army and navy to the same effect (see Appendix 2).[165]

In arriving at this consensus, both the army and the navy presumed the Draft Understanding to be an American government proposal, an illusion widely current within the Japanese government. But apart from this, they came very close to the realities of the situation in their observations regarding the designs of the U. S. government. On the other hand, what they asked that the Draft Understanding take up thereafter—the firm establishment of the Greater East Asia Coprosperity Sphere, the guarantee of demands on

China, strict adherence to the Tripartite Pact, no restrictions on a military advance to the south, and mediation in the European war—were all points that had already been virtually abandoned by Ikawa and Iwakuro in the draft agreement in principle, the April 9 draft, and the Draft Understanding. And it was hardly to be expected that the two clerics, much less the State Department, would reverse their positions and accept these points. Consequently, counterstrategies to "turn" U.S. "designs to our advantage" by inducing the United States to accept these points, however ingenious at first glance, were by their very nature so much willful, and empty, talk from the start. Four days earlier, on April 17, the army and navy had reached agreement on the "Outline of Policy toward the South," and on the 21st they attempted a consensus based on the "Outline" that would reconcile Japan's advance into Thailand and French Indochina with an adjustment of diplomatic relations with the United States, or at least ensure that the two policies were not in contradiction. Had they been more observant of the larger picture, however, they would have found it difficult to turn a deaf ear to the warning Grew's deputy, Eugene Dooman, gave to a Japanese visitor, one Fujii, on April 17: "By joining Germany and Italy in an alliance, Japan had assimilated the Far Eastern problem with the European problem, and it would be idle for Japan to suppose that, so long as she remained an ally of Germany, termination of the China conflict of itself would stabilize her relations with the United States." [166]

A Bolt from the Blue for the Navy

The situation within the navy was even more ambiguous. In the middle of January Toyoda ordered Shiba Katsuo of the Navy Ministry's Naval Affairs Bureau to draft the navy's demands on the occasion of Nomura's proceeding to his new post. Shiba believed that without even the conditions for a four-power accord having been settled upon, there were absolutely no prospects for success if they tried to adjust Japanese-American relations at that point. In his draft, therefore, he said that Nomura "should please be most prudent about entering into concrete negotiations; I would rather you observe and report on the actual situation in the United States." [167] Toyoda approved Shiba's draft, but nothing official was decided because the army insisted on a cabinet decision regarding demands and conditions. The receipt of Nomura's April 18 telegram was therefore even more a bolt from the blue for the navy, which had no connection with Iwakuro. Shiba could not comprehend how it had come about, and although he entertained suspicions about the nature of the proposal, he was simply in a daze. Eventually, after consulting War Guidance Office Chief Ōno Takeji, Shiba concluded that it would be futile to negotiate with the United States by doing things on a small scale, and that Japan had to be prepared to swallow the outcome in silence after diplomacy on a grand scale had been undertaken. From this perspective, on April 19 Shiba drafted a telegram to Attaché Yokoyama in Washington, which was approved by Naval Affairs Bureau Chief Oka Takazumi. It said:

> At first glance the Draft Understanding looks promising, but since the United States maintains an idealism more suited to textbooks, I suspect there are knotty problems lurking here concerning the Tripartite Pact and troop withdrawal from China. The text of the telegram is not clear as to how these are to be dealt with concretely. An imprudent way of doing things is not desirable. If negotiations are not skillfully brought to a conclusion, there is also the danger that we could be dragged into war by the United States. We must avoid being entangled out of ineptitude. We should not enter negotiations. Convey this to the ambassador.[168]

As of November 15, 1940, the navy had already taken the second step in anticipation of war with the United States by activating stage one operations for mobilizing the fleet. Furthermore, the navy's endorsement of the "Outline of Policy toward French Indochina and Thailand" on January 30, 1941, "contained within it the determination not to flinch . . . from the possibility that a worst-case scenario might arise in which events would ultimately lead to war with Britain and the United States," as Fleet Commander-in-Chief Yamamoto Isoroku later pointed out. In taking account of this broad trend within the navy, Shiba's argument for prudence had a measure of reason to it. On the other hand, that trend also gave spontaneous rise to the obverse view, so to speak, among middle-echelon officers of the Navy General Staff: that the Draft Understanding was one big political ploy on the part of the United States, that it really could not stand up from the viewpoint of those who believed in the premise that war between Japan and the United States was inevitable, and consequently that to come out strongly against the Draft was the way to avoid war for the present.[169] But Nagano Osami, who had been appointed chief of the Navy General Staff on April 9 to succeed Prince Fushimi (who had resigned at long last), was simply overjoyed. Shallow, with no inclination to look into such matters as the nature of the draft of broad trends in the United States, he exclaimed: "No-mura's a terrific guy! It couldn't have been done without Nomura. Let's get on with it right away."[170] And on this matter Navy Minister Oikawa Koshirō also took a nonchalant and inattentive stance toward the activities of the middle-echelon officers, telling Inoue Shigeyoshi: "Should we get into a war with the United States? I'd have to say it would be better not to."[171]

Inoue, who had allied himself with Yamamoto some years earlier in stubborn opposition to strengthening the Anti-Comintern Pact with Germany, had been chief of Naval Aviation Headquarters since the autumn of 1940. Toyoda Teijirō had left his post as vice navy minister on April 4, 1941, having accepted the Commerce and Indus-try portfolio in exchange for promotion to admiral. It was precisely in this interim that Inoue happened to be acting vice minister. When he received Shiba's draft telegram destined for Yokoyama, he realized that it would undermine Nomura's policy of no war between Japan and the United States. Inoue called on Oikawa at his private residence to seek his views but found it difficult to extract firm answers. He therefore made revisions on his own responsibility that virtually gut-ted the telegram. Dissatisfied with these revisions, Oka and Shiba wound up canceling its transmission altogether.[172]

The navy minister continued to be noncommittal as usual. The new chief of the Naval General Staff was shallow. Toyoda and Fus-himi, who had endorsed Nomura's appointment perfunctorily and as a matter of convenience, had both left active duty in the navy. From the summer of 1940 middle-echelon officers of the Navy Ministry and General Staff had continued to move steadily forward in their readiness to go to war with the United States. The only naval leader opposed to all this and supporting Nomura was Acting Vice Navy Minister Inoue, who returned to his primary post in late April after the vice ministership had been entrusted to Sawamoto Yorio, a man with a weak sense of self. Such was the state of the navy as repre-sented by Oka, Naval Operations Division Chief Fukudome Shigeru, and Naval Intelligence Division Chief Maeda Minoru when they came to the April 21 consensus of views with their counterparts in the army—Mutō, Tanaka, and Army Intelligence Division Chief Oka-moto Kiyotomi. As a result, that consensus was far from being the backing by "the general will of the navy" (Toyoda) that Nomura had continued to hope for in the United States. Nonetheless, Attaché Yokoyama received a return telegram from the Navy Ministry that sounded quite positive:

The army and navy are united in their view that Japanese-American relations should be adjusted on the basis of Nomura's April 16 telegram. Although some points require modification, the services have completed their investigation in that regard. The Foreign Ministry is also in general agreement. We expect to telegraph instructions once we have decided on our position after the foreign minister returns to Tokyo on April 22.[173]

The Truth Behind Konoe's Endorsement

In December 1940 Konoe had been strongly interested in and somewhat hopeful about the activities of the two clerics while they were in Japan, and with some degree of sympathy he had tacitly promoted those activities.[174] He had also been favorably disposed toward Ikawa's trip to the United States. Konoe received the Drought memorandum of December 14 from Ikawa and the draft agreement in principle from Ikawa via the *Tatsuta Maru* around April 12. But for all that, there is scant reason for believing that Konoe had examined these documents closely, understood their fundamental thinking, or even placed much hope in them. In late February, when Finance Minister Kawada Isao handed him a telegram Ikawa had sent through Nishiyama Tsutomu in New York, Konoe was disposed to say: "I wonder if Ikawa can pull it off; it's not really all that easy, you know."[175]

Speaking at a press conference on the evening of April 11, Konoe seemed in a sanguine frame of mind:

> One of the real purposes of the Tripartite Alliance, to put it bluntly, is preventing American participation in the [European] war. We must make [the United States] understand that purpose. I do not think [relations with the United States] are all that bad. No real problems of consequence have appeared on the diplomatic front. Nothing much has changed from before. . . . There are a lot of problems, but I don't think we have a situation here in which we have come up against such an impasse that none of them can be resolved, that no action can be taken.[176]

Despite having been twice sent basic documents by Ikawa, however, Konoe was surprised when the Draft Understanding arrived. He then proceeded to give it serious consideration. Nomura's two telegrams (text of the Draft and explanation) reached the Foreign Ministry during the night of April 17 and the following morning, and around 11 o'clock on the morning of the 18th Vice Foreign Minister Ōhashi called on Konoe, who was concurrently acting as foreign minister. Ōhashi found Konoe in the midst of a cabinet meeting but managed to give him an interim report. At 5:30 p.m. he visited Konoe again, armed with the complete decoded texts. The following modifications in Konoe's hand (parts by another person?) appended to items 2, 3, 6 and the addenda of the Draft suggest his immediate response:

2. The attitudes of both governments toward the European war.
"Shared attitude of both Japan and the United States (hasten its conclusion)."
The government of the United States is firm in "desiring the earliest settlement of the European war and the restoration of world peace."
"In the event that an actual state of belligerency arises [between America and Germany, the Tripartite] Pact goes into effect."
3. Relationship between the two governments concerning the China Incident.
"Respect" for the Open Door policy, but its interpretation and application "will be adapted to the changing situation," etc.
6. Economic activity of both nations in the southwestern Pacific area.
"Does this include Thailand and French Indochina?"
"The United States will recognize Japan's natural (economic) expansion in the south, particularly" for resources in that region for instance, etc.
Addenda. Announcements.
"Recognition of Manchukuo."
"It has been decided to hold a Japanese-American conference on the maintenance of peace in the Pacific."
"No mention at all that Japan has altered its China policy." [177]

Konoe's intentions as far as the Draft are concerned may be reasonably ascertained if we look at these modifications in conjunction with the following handwritten notes by someone close to Konoe:

Item: American demands on Japan.
1) Restoration of the Open Door.
2) Arms truce in the Pacific. Avoidance of a Pacific war.
3) Japan is to cut itself off spiritually from the Tripartite Alliance.
Is the timing of the American proposal based on their judgment that, with the conclusion of the Japanese-Soviet Neutrality Pact, Japan's southern advance is inevitable?
Item: Prevention of Japan's military advance to the south.
Item: Japanese demands.
1) Suspension of aid to Chiang Kai-shek.
2) Recognition of Manchukuo.

Item: Debatable points.

1) Matsuoka's meetings in Berlin: should we seek Germany's understanding on this?

Problem of unilateral (prior) notification.

2) Reject the Understanding if the United States intends thereby to strengthen aid to Britain and to participate in the war in Europe.

3) Should the United States actually enter the war in Europe, this Understanding will be considered null and void.

4) Proceed with the Understanding on the basis of promises that Japan will refrain from advancing south by force and that the United States will not enter the European war.

5) Should the impression be entertained that Japan will return to the status quo ante that would be absolutely disastrous.[178]

Thus, in his assessment of American designs and his grasp of Iwakuro's objectives Konoe had quite an accurate understanding of the situation. But in line with his January 29 remarks in the lobby of the Privy Council he remained adamant that the terms of the Tripartite Pact were to be strictly applied and that there was to be no restoration of the status quo ante in Sino-Japanese relations. Whereas Tōjō and Sugiyama Gen, representing the army, were cautious at the evening session of the April 18 Liaison Conference because views within the army had not yet been finalized, Konoe expressed sympathy with the policies of Ōhashi and others of the Matsuoka school. On April 19 he had the following telegram of inquiry sent to Nomura for reference in the deliberations in Washington:

1. Will there not be criticisms that the Draft Understanding prevents our advancing to the south by force, secures the British rear, enables the United States to pull out of the Pacific to concentrate on aiding Britain, and thus in actuality runs counter to the spirit of the Tripartite Alliance? . . .

3. From the standpoint of our showing good faith toward Germany, we could, before making a decision on the Draft Understanding, give some thought to attempting a joint Japanese-American mediation of the European war or the like. What are the possibilities of something like this?

4. Although the waves in the Pacific will calm down for the moment as the result of reaching this Understanding, there is no doubt that our position will be damaged should Germany and Italy win. And even should Britain and the United States win, will they not disregard this Understanding, joining together to oppress us as they did after World War I?

5. Where it states that the American attitude toward the European war "will be determined solely and exclusively by considerations of its own national welfare and security," does not that make it clear that the United States intends to disregard this Understanding and join the war, should that be deemed necessary to prevent the collapse of Britain?[179]

Questions (1) and (5) went to the heart of the critical ambiguities accompanying the delicate compromises worked out in Washington; together with the desire to show good faith toward Germany expressed in (3) and the distrust of the United States in (4), they reveal Konoe's and Ōhashi's pro-Axis orientation.

On the morning of April 19 Kido and Ōhashi met for one hour and a half and were "united in concluding that after careful study of ways not to lose good faith with Germany and Italy nor to collide with our firm national policy of establishing the new order of the Greater East Asia Coprosperity Sphere, we must strive for realization of the Draft Understanding."[180] The same day Konoe asked Ōhashi to telegraph Nomura to the effect that we "agree in principle with the Draft Understanding." Ōhashi did not comply.[181]

This, then, is what Konoe's "agreeing in principle" actually came down to. The army, navy, and Konoe agreed to use this Understanding to promote an adjustment in Japanese-American relations. An examination of the actual substance of the agreement, however, leads one to call it an exercise in semantics. And in its illusions about the nature of the Draft Understanding on the one hand, and its being grounded on mistaken military judgments regarding developments in the war between Britain and Germany on the other, Konoe's "agreeing in principle" departed even further from reality.

7 Matsuoka Rejects the Draft Understanding

Matsuoka Makes Up His Mind

From December 1940 onward the Japanese career diplomats in Tokyo and Washington grew increasingly mistrustful of Ikawa and the two clerics. Then, on April 18, Nomura's telegrams suddenly arrived. The Foreign Ministry had received no reports about the discussions leading up to the Draft Understanding, nor had there even been any notification of the fact that private talks with the United States on a matter of such importance were in progress. The immediate reaction in the ministry was one of wild joy.[182] Further consideration, however, led to the conclusion that behind all of this might lie a delicate situation of which the Foreign Ministry was unaware, and these suspicions were heightened by the fact that Ambassador Nomura had requested no instructions whatever from the foreign minister in undertaking a matter of such importance.

Ōhashi and other ministry officials at first thought that the Draft Understanding might have been the result of diplomatic maneuvers on the part of the army to use the United States to settle the Sino-Japanese War. Then they grew more and more suspicious that the Draft Understanding was the result of a deliberate plot to make the gutting of the Tripartite Pact a fait accompli while Matsuoka was out of the country; after all, the Draft had been presented while Konoe was still acting as foreign minister and Matsuoka, en route home, was still two days out of Manchouli.[183] On this latter point their suspicions were not unfounded. On April 7 Ballantine had visited Drought, who told him that

> it was desired to act on this matter prior to Matsuoka's reaching Tokyo, as it was feared that otherwise Matsuoka upon his return would create difficulties. . . . the Japanese Army and Navy were behind the proposals and . . . the only difficulties so far encountered were from the Japanese Foreign Office. If prompt action were taken, Matsuoka [upon his return] would be confronted with an accomplished fact and he would have to either go along with it or resign.[184]

On the point that the army was using the United States to settle the Sino-Japanese War, that was a policy that originated solely with Iwakuro after he arrived in the United States. But Ōhashi and others in the Foreign Ministry could not have known the circumstances surrounding Iwakuro's assignment to Washington. It was only natural that they should conclude that the army had dispatched this highly reputed go-getter to the United States for that purpose, reluctantly relieving him of his important post as chief of the Military Section, and they also suspected that this policy devised by Iwakuro alone had been the hidden intent of the army from the time it had transferred him. In light of Tōjō's and Mutō's consent to the Draft Understanding, moreover, their suspicions were not that far off the mark, but Ōhashi and his colleagues went too far when they concluded that this was the army's diplomatic policy. In fact, this policy should in all respects be seen as Iwakuro's scheme and his alone.

Nomura was firmly convinced that the Draft Understanding would be "okay with the navy," his conviction originating in the pledges he had been given by Toyoda and Prince Fushimi when he accepted his assignment to Washington. Moreover, Konoe had personally given Nomura his strong endorsement of Nomura's policies. On top of that there were the frequent communications from Ikawa. The army could hardly reject the Draft, what with its sore spot having been seized upon. Only Matsuoka was left, and even he could be won over.[185] Or so Iwakuro may have calculated when he sent his telegram, a cunning device to the effect that the Draft Understanding was Hull's proposal. And in line with such calculations, both services and Konoe had clearly confirmed their agreement to the Draft Understanding, however much that assent may have been an exercise in semantics. In fact, the only one yet to make up his mind on the Draft Understanding was Matsuoka.

At the outset of this chapter I discussed in some detail the logic of Matsuoka's policy toward the United States between January and April 1941. To bring that logic to its final destiny by going to Washington himself, even Matsuoka had to pay attention first to strengthening his political position in Japan. Eugen Ott, the German ambassador to Japan, had reported after meeting with Matsuoka on December 19, 1940, that "I have the impression that the Foreign Minister desires to enhance the importance of his policy and person by conversation with the Reich Foreign Minister [Ribbentrop] and possibly through being received by the Führer."[186] During discussions with German leaders in Berlin, he revealed, with singular frankness, his policy toward the United States but could not conceal his anxiety about his political future. He told Hitler on March 27 that:

> Unfortunately he did not control Japan, but had to bring those who were in control around to his point of view. . . .
> Matsuoka then requested urgently that the representations which he had made be treated as strictly confidential, since, if they became known in Japan, those among his Cabinet colleagues who thought differently from him would probably become alarmed and would seek to get him out of office.[187]

On April 4 he told Hitler:

> In Japan, however, many people refused to follow this line of thought. In those circles Matsuoka was considered to be a dangerous man with dangerous ideas.
> . . . he must inform him [Hitler] of the regrettable circumstances

that he (Matsuoka), as Japanese Foreign Minister, in Japan itself did not dare to say a word about the plans which he had set forth to the Führer and the Reich Foreign Minister. . . . in these circumstances he could not state how soon he would be able to hold a conference with the Japanese Prime Minister or with the Emperor about the questions which had been discussed. He would first have to go into developments in Japan closely and carefully, in order to determine a favorable occasion on which to give Prince Konoye and the Emperor the true picture about his real plans. The decision would then have to follow in a few days, for otherwise the problems would be talked to pieces. If he were not able to put through his plans, it would be an indication that he lacked sufficient influence, power of persuasion, and tactical ability. But if he could put them through, it would show that he had attained great influence in Japan. He personally believed that he would be able to put them through.[188]

In the conclusion of this statement Matsuoka showed a measure of self-assurance, but that slightly shaky confidence in Berlin seems to have been transformed into boundless arrogance, even regarding his political future, when, on his journey home aboard the Trans-Siberian Railway following his successful conclusion of the Japanese-Soviet Neutrality Pact with Stalin on April 13, he received the telegram from Ambassador Steinhardt in response to his overture to Roosevelt.

Two days before Matsuoka reached Tokyo, British Ambassador Sir Robert Craigie reported that "Matsuoka's stock is so high that there is now a fairly strong movement . . . in favour of substituting him for Prince Konoye as Prime Minister."[189] Privy Seal Kido learned via Kabayama Aisuke, president of the America-Japan Society, that when Matsuoka visited former Privy Seal Makino Nobuaki, he had said in effect, "I think we must have Konoe take charge of the current situation, but should the emperor order me to form a cabinet in the event of an emergency I would not hesitate to do so."[190] It thus appears that in May 1941 the idea of a Matsuoka cabinet was seriously entertained.[191]

Matsuoka's Three Principles

Ōhashi had deep doubts about the Draft Understanding and did not comply with Konoe's request to telegraph his "agreeing in principle," insisting on waiting until Matsuoka returned a few days later. On April 18 Konoe sent word to Matsuoka at Manchouli Station that he wanted to talk with him by telephone immediately, and the minute

Matsuoka arrived at Dairen on the 20th Konoe got in touch by telephone and pressed him to return to Tokyo at once. When Matsuoka arrived at Tachikawa on the 22nd, Ōhashi informed him that a Draft Japanese-American Understanding had been received which in content and origin was utterly incredible. To Matsuoka it was as if a bucket of cold water had been poured over his head just as he was arriving in Tokyo. A Liaison Conference was convened at 9:20 p.m. the same day. "The Nomura draft," Matsuoka declared, "has it all wrong. All I had done up until now was simply to propose [to the United States] that it should advise Chiang to seek peace. I have had nothing to do with a complete adjustment of diplomatic relations. There is the precedent of the Ishii Lansing Agreement as well, so give me a while to think it over [about two weeks to two months]." [192] At around 11 p.m. Matsuoka excused himself while the conference was still in session. Assuming Matsuoka needed time to think the matter over, the conferees adjourned the meeting. And when Konoe sent for him on the night of the 23rd, Matsuoka replied, "Let me make a judgment after I have had a while to forget what I did in Europe." Konoe acquiesced.

Matsuoka continued to be as disgruntled as before, and Ōhashi and his colleagues were helpless to do anything. There were several reasons why Matsuoka should have been incensed. First of all, despite his having been delegated full powers over foreign policy at the July 1940 Ogikubo conference Konoe had convened with his prospective army, navy and foreign ministers, a grand plan that totally ignored and circumvented him had materialized while he was away. During that time he had laid the groundwork for his policy toward the United States. The result of his tour of Germany and the Soviet Union was that he "had created a neutrality treaty with the Soviet Union and joined forces with Germany though he had not asked Germany for this, leaving only the United States to deal with." [193] Now the egoistic Matsuoka seemed obsessed that Iwakuro, whom he had arbitrarily counted among his supporters, had not only pushed him aside but poured boiling water down his throat, while Konoe, through Ikawa, had joined in, privately consenting to this and betraying his pledge to him.

Talking with Japanese reporters aboard the train from Manchouli to Tsitsihar, Matsuoka made remarks critical of the Konoe cabinet. In a public speech at Hibiya Hall on April 26 reporting on his European trip, Matsuoka reasserted that the cabinet's foreign policy was too weak and too lukewarm to keep up with the fast pace of world events. These remarks stung Konoe and the rest of the cabinet, and with

Konoe's tacit consent, the stenographic pamphlet of the Hibiya speech, which had been broadcast by radio, was banned. Produced by Matsuoka's boundless arrogance, these criticisms of the Konoe cabinet immediately produced an emotionally charged movement censuring the Konoe cabinet and calling for a cabinet organized by Matsuoka; they also intensified political opposition to the Draft Understanding.

Finally, the draft agreement for peace in the Pacific by the two clerics, Nomura's policy of no war between Japan and the United States, and Iwakuro's efforts to neutralize the Tripartite Pact in order to use the United States to settle the Sino-Japanese War would each and severally have fundamentally warped the direction and course of Matsuoka's policies, given the logic of his policy toward the United States, and in one stroke would have reduced all his efforts to naught. Matsuoka could not contain his indignation no matter how much he tried. At the Liaison Conference of May 29, he stated:

> Nomura was up to this before I made my appeal to the United States from Moscow. Before Nomura left I gave him a note I had written which said the opposite of what Nomura has now done. I didn't put the priests up to what they did. It was not I who gave Ikawa the money [for his passage to America]. I know who it was, but don't ask me about that now.[194]

And again at the Liaison Conference of June 27:

> While in Europe I sent a personal message to the United States with the intention of preventing the U.S. from entering the war and of having the U.S. suspend aid to Chiang. After returning to Tokyo I saw the American reply, which was different from what I had expected. It turned out that way because other people got into the act. . . . In the end, ultimately, that undermined my getting a purchase on the United States.[195]

Prompted by personal feelings, by calculations about the domestic political situation, and by his own policy toward the United States, Matsuoka took a stance in fundamental opposition to the Draft Understanding. At the Liaison Conference of May 3 he proposed for the first time three absolute conditions for any adjustment of Japanese-American relations:

1. It must contribute to a settlement of the Sino-Japanese War—in other words, the United States has to wash its hands of China.

2. It must not contravene the Tripartite Pact.
3. It must not breach international good faith [toward Germany]—in other words, it must prevent the United States from entering the European war.

Even the army was surprised by Matsuoka's stubborn adherence to these conditions. Although the army had vacillated somewhat with regard to the third condition, it had been insistent on the first and second from the start; it therefore agreed to all three conditions. Thus the army gave its approval to what might be called "Matsuoka's three principles."

Mutō, together with Chief Cabinet Secretary Tomita Kenji and others, had tried almost every evening since late April to persuade Matsuoka to agree to another Liaison Conference, but Matsuoka resisted until the May 3 conference was finally arranged. Once that conference was over, however, Matsuoka nonchalantly set out on a pilgrimage to the Grand Shrine at Ise, saying he had to report after his return from abroad. Mutō waited for Matsuoka to return to Tokyo, then pleaded over and over again until Matsuoka finally consented to a Liaison Conference on May 8. At this conference Matsuoka presented the following grandiose argument to which no one responded:

It is highly probable that the United States [will enter the European war]. If it does, there is no question but that the war will become a protracted one. If it lasts ten years, Germany will beat the Soviet Union and then advance into Asia. In that event, what position should the Empire take?

The conference giving every appearance of having become a one-man show, Matsuoka disclosed what he had in mind:

1. The Draft Understanding is secondary [in terms of preventing the United States from entering the European war]. Even if the Draft Understanding were put in place, it would not serve to prevent its entering the war.
2. Because we must in any event keep the United States from entering the war, we must come up with something stronger to forestall that eventuality. We must make the Draft Understanding something that will serve to prevent the U.S. from entering the war.[196]

Hitler has been patient up to now, but he just might take on the United States. In the event that Germany does so, I think it proper to argue that according to the Alliance pact Japan is also bound to take on the United States. But that won't do for diplomacy now, and my thought is that what I would do next is try to keep the United States from entering the war and make the United States wash its hands of China.[197]

That Matsuoka's first principle happened to coincide with Iwakuro's objective tells us something of Matsuoka's powers of insight. But to achieve that objective, Iwakuro had deemphasized the point about preventing the United States from entering the war so that the Draft Understanding could primarily be used to bring about an early settlement of the Sino-Japanese War. But precisely because of that deemphasis by Iwakuro, Matsuoka considered the Draft Understanding of little significance and sought to use it to revert to his original policy, which required the firmness of will to intimidate and pressure the United States through the Tripartite Pact. Consequently, at the May 12 Liaison Conference he declared:

> The focus of our diplomacy is on keeping the United States out of the war, and [to that end it is first] directed at making the United States stop its convoying activities [against Germany]. [Should that fail and the United States] come to the point of entering the war [against Germany] as the result of its convoying, there will be nothing we can do.[198]

At the previous Liaison Conference of May 8 Matsuoka had said:

> Even after an understanding [with the United States] has been put in place, war cannot thereby be ruled out. Should [American] patrolling intensify [and lead to a collision with Germany on the high seas], an understanding of this sort will vanish into thin air. And when that happens, Japan will also have to do something.[199]

He had followed this up with a telegram to Nomura on May 9:

> Should things fall apart [and Japan must unavoidably carry out its obligations as an ally under Article 3 of the Tripartite Pact], it is to be feared that any understanding in place between Japan and the United States will go up in smoke. You and I must look that fact squarely in the eye.[200]

Such conclusions were only natural in light of Matsuoka's "three principles."

On the issue of Japan's basically unbreakable obligation to go to war under Article 3 of the Tripartite Pact, Nomura, Iwakuro, and the Army Ministry, however different their respective intentions, had granted the United States a broad interpretation of its right of self-defense and had tried to restrict to as few as possible those instances that would obligate Japan to go to war. Contrary to this, Matsuoka had consistently used that obligation as a means to pressure the United States and by insisting on its strict application had brought the opposition between his view and theirs out into the open. This position compelled Matsuoka to say that Japan would go to war in the event of a collision between Germany and the United States on the high seas, and thus he expressed for the first time his intention to engage in intimidation and pressure. Revision of the Japanese-American Draft Understanding would now be undertaken on the basis of Matsuoka's established policy of intimidating and pressuring the United States, a position diametrically opposed to the respective aims of the two clerics, Iwakuro, Nomura, and key officers in the army.

Strict Adherence to the Tripartite Pact Is Reaffirmed

On May 6 Matsuoka informed Ambassador Ott in concrete terms that he

> would try to proceed with the tactics of making the United States commit herself not to enter the European war. . . . At the moment he was having a study made of the question whether a Japanese protest was not in order against the patrol activities by American armed forces [in the Atlantic], which amounted to proclaiming an American security zone by unilateral action.[201]

Prior to this he had presented a revised draft in keeping with this objective to the Liaison Conference of May 3, the first Liaison Conference to take up the Draft Understanding; his draft was duly adopted. Then, knowing that forwarding this draft to the United States would be held up for the time being because of sentiment favoring consultation with Germany beforehand, Matsuoka insisted on presenting to the United States as trial balloons a draft Japanese-American neutrality pact and an oral statement. Despite the reluctance of others at the conference, he convinced them to leave both matters up to him. That same day he instructed Nomura to deliver the oral statement to Hull immediately as Japan's interim reply; at the same time, Nomura was instructed to sound out U.S. willingness to conclude a Japanese-American neutrality pact by bringing up the question casually with Hull as Nomura's "on-the-spot idea about which he would appreciate a fair measure of promptness." In proposing this neutrality pact Matsuoka "intended to try out a kind of diplomatic blitzkrieg."[202] But Hull, when such a pact was suggested by Nomura on the 7th, showed no inclination whatever to take it up, using as a pretext Nomura's own words: "I am not in receipt of instructions."[203]

The main points of the oral statement frankly expressed various observations Matsuoka had made during his last trip to Europe and the conclusions he had drawn therefrom:

> The German and Italian leaders are determined never to have peace by negotiation; they demand capitulation. They seem satisfied that the war is as good as won even at the present stage. . . . I may also add for what it is worth that these leaders feel that the American entry into the war will not materially affect the final issue, although they are ready to admit that in that event, the war is likely to become protracted. Whatever views Your Excellency or the president may hold, it is, I trust, always worthwhile and interesting to know what other parties are thinking. Of course, I reserve my own opinion on this point but I must confess that my sole and primary concern is, as Your Excellency must know by my utterances on several occasions, that the American intervention is fraught with a grave danger of prolonging the war to the untold misery and suffering of humanity, entailing, who knows, in its wake, an eventual downfall of modern civilization. In that eventuality, there would be no more question of democracy or totalitarianism left on earth. Even at this moment, I shudder at the mere thought of such a dire possibility. The key to prevent or to hasten such a possibility being translated into probability is largely held in the hands of the president of the United States. This has been my view ever since the outbreak of the European war.
>
> I need hardly add that Japan cannot and will not do anything that might in the least degree adversely affect the position of Germany and Italy to whom Japan is in honor bound as an ally under the Tripartite Pact. Such a caution on Japan's part, I trust, will be readily appreciated by Your Excellency.[204]

Matsuoka hereby enlarged upon the logic of his policy toward the United States, ascribing it to the leaders of Germany and Italy, and concluded by reaffirming Japan's position of strictly adhering to the Tripartite Pact. Nomura, however, feared that Matsuoka's frankness would offend Hull and therefore did not hand over the oral statement but simply read through parts of it. He then asked: "There are various things wrong with what is written here, but shall I give it to you anyway?"[205] Hull already knew the gist of the oral statement through the MAGIC intercepts, and therefore replied that that was not necessary. On May 9 Matsuoka followed up with further instructions to Nomura:

> I cannot but earnestly hope ... that the United States will please refrain from making things so unbearable that [Germany and Japan] are driven to the point of having to take hostile action against the United States, given that the United States has come so swiftly to the aid of Britain that it has finally reduced Germany to the unavoidable conclusion that the United States had in fact attacked Germany.[206]

And he repeated his demand that the United States refrain from aiding Britain in view of Japan's strict adherence to the Tripartite Pact.

Matsuoka's revised draft was being delayed out of concern for prior consultation with Germany. Even Matsuoka, however, could not overcome the demands of the army, which was being pressured by Iwakuro, Yokoyama, and Nomura, and instructions were finally sent out at noon on May 12 to present the revised draft to the United States. But on the 13th Matsuoka on his own initiative sent the following provocative memorandum to Hull, making his stance perfectly clear:

> It must have been clear from what I have often stated publicly or otherwise that my decision to follow the *pourparler* between Your Excellency and Ambassador Nomura and open the present negotiation was based on the premises that the United States would not enter the European war and that the United States government would agree to advise Chiang Kai-shek to enter into a direct negotiation with Japan with a view to bringing about peace between Japan and China at the earliest possible date. Of course it must have been plain from the start that on no other premises would or could Japan possibly come to any understanding of the sort held in view in the present negotiation.[207]

The basic premises of Matsuoka's revised draft having been made so clear, there was nothing for the United States to be in the least bit hopeful about. On the contrary, the Matsuoka revised draft served only to arouse indignation and suspicion within American government circles.

As was to be expected, upon receipt of this memorandum Nomura that very day requested instructions that would allow him "to hold off delivering it for the time being, since it is my humble opinion that to present such a memorandum as you have instructed me to at this time would make talks extremely difficult and on the contrary would impede reaching an understanding."[208] Matsuoka overrode him on the 15th, directing that

> The government finds it necessary that our demands with regard to preventing the United States from entering the war and America's advising the Chiang regime to seek peace be proposed to the American side in writing, so as to leave no latitude for misunderstandings later on about our relations with Germany and Italy or about our domestic relations. Although these are incorporated in our revised draft, and although we have great sympathy with your position given the gravity of the matter, kindly do as cabled.[209]

As if he thought that overriding Nomura would not be enough and to make doubly sure, Matsuoka met with Ambassador Grew on May 14 for the first time since returning from Europe. According to Grew, Matsuoka told him that:

> in the face of our supplying Great Britain with war materials . . . Hitler had shown great "patience and generosity" in not declaring war on the United States. He. . . knew that Hitler desired to avoid such a war but it was doubtful whether his patience and restraint could continue indefinitely. . . . if, in spite of previous forbearance, Hitler should. . . sink our ships [convoying] in the Atlantic and if we Americans should then attack the German submarines he would regard this as an act of American aggression which would call for deliberation as to the applicability of Article III of the Triple Alliance Treaty. . . and he thought there was no doubt that such deliberation would lead to war between Japan and the United States.
>
>   This issue he said, therefore, lies exclusively in the hands of President Roosevelt. . . . in view of the present American Government and actions he felt that the "manly, decent, and reasonable" thing for the United States to do was to declare war openly on Germany instead of engaging in acts of war under cover of neutrality.
>
> . . .
>
> He adds that this is only his own opinion and that there would have to be deliberation. . . with Japan's allies, in which deliberation Japan would have but one out of three votes.[210]

The concluding part of Matsuoka's statement to Grew suggested that Japan, Germany, and Italy might reach a decision on the basis of a majority vote in such a deliberation. It is noteworthy that Matsuoka, who had been of the opinion up to this point that this was, from a textual interpretation, properly left to the *independent* deliberations of each contracting party, now allowed room for flexibility on this point. In reporting this shift in Matsuoka's interpretation to Washington on May 27, Grew commented: "I however incline to the opinion that in his talks with me he follows the carefully studied policy of painting the darkest picture of what will happen if the United States gets into war against Germany, probably in the mistaken belief that such tactics may serve to exert a restraining influence on American policy."[211] Walter Duranty later sent home an account of his interview with Matsuoka, in which Matsuoka is reported to have said:

> Japan entered into the Tripartite Pact to keep the United States out of the war. If the United States were now to get involved in a fight with Germany, Japan would feel bound in loyalty and honor automatically to fight against the United States, whether or not war is officially declared.
>
> In answer to my question, "Are you seriously making the statement, meaning that if an American convoy or patrol clashes with a German airplane or submarine, you will regard it as a sufficient cause for a clash between Japan and the United States?" Matsuoka answered "Yes." However, I believe that Matsuoka did not quite mean what he said. My own guess is that Matsuoka was using me to make his last threat to the United States: "If you fight, we fight. You must bear the responsibility for the consequences."[212]

The Draft Understanding Is Completely Rejected

Matsuoka's change in interpretation may have been the final expedient to emerge from his policy of intimidating and pressuring the United States. In any case, on May 12 his revised draft, drawn up with that policy in mind, was presented to the United States.[213] The main revisions were as follows.

1) The Tripartite Pact. Matsuoka's revised draft stated that "the government of Japan maintains that its obligations of military assistance under the Tripartite Pact among Japan, Germany, and Italy will be applied in accordance with the stipulation of Article 3 of the said Pact." This stemmed from the belief that, "If we must have any stipulation at all, in addition, it would be important to have one which would clarify the relationship of this Understanding to the aforementioned Pact." In Nomura's judgment, however, "If we consider the three Axis nations as one and inseparable and remain faithful to the alliance to the extent of committing group suicide, there can be no room whatsoever for an agreement [with the United States]."[214] Thus the revised draft destroyed utterly the plans that Nomura, the two clerics, and Iwakuro each had on this issue.

2) *The Sino-Japanese War.* The revised draft declared: "The government of the United States, acknowledging the three principles enunciated in the Konoe Statement and the principles set forth on the basis of the said three principles in the treaty with the Nanking Government as well as in the Joint Declaration of Japan, Manchukuo and China, and relying upon the policy of the Japanese Government to establish a relationship of neighborly friendship with China, shall forthwith request the Chiang Kai-shek regime to negotiate peace with Japan." Therewith all eight conditions for peace, which, as the preconditions for advising Chiang, were to be guaranteed by the Japanese government and approved by President Roosevelt, were deleted. "The deletions were made because achieving an understanding between Japan and the United States by making each one of these a stipulation would create the impression that Japan had been dictated to by the United States on these issues." Based on a request on the part of the military, it was further added that: "We should obtain an understanding, in a separate and secret document, that the United States would discontinue its assistance to the Chiang Kai-shek regime if Chiang Kai-shek does not accept the advice of the United States that he enter into negotiations for peace. If the United States finds it impossible to do this, a definite pledge by those responsible would suffice."

It may have been that Matsuoka and others were deeply troubled by the ambiguous nature of the difference between "mediation" and "good offices" in the telegrams sent by Nomura and Iwakuro about the Draft Understanding. In any event, the idea of a conditional mediation by Roosevelt, consistently promoted by the two clerics, was completely eliminated, and what the United States was now told to do was simply to swallow *in toto* the existing arrangements between Japan and the Wang Ching-wei regime and merely advise Chiang to enter into peace negotiations without interfering in any way with the terms for peace.

Matsuoka made this point unequivocally in a telegram he sent to Nomura on July 15, the day before his resignation:

The main point of the draft was simply to convey to the American government for its reference the fundamental policy which is to be the basis of peace negotiations and to do no more than request that the United States advise the Chiang regime to enter peace negotiations. That was done with no intention of getting an agreement beforehand between Japan and the United States on the basic terms for peace. The policy that the China Incident must be solved solely between Japan and China and that intervention or interference by a third power must be rejected is firmly maintained by the Imperial Government even today.[215]

In addition, the U.S. government had already deleted from the April 9 draft the pledge to suspend aid to Chiang Kai-shek. Ignorant of this, the Japanese military was merely beating a dead horse.

3) The southern advance. The phrase "without resorting to arms" was deleted on the grounds that: "The present international situation shows signs of unprecedented chaos, and changes of any kind may occur at any time. Things being contingent upon how the international situation develops in the future, the Empire finds it difficult to guarantee that it will not resort to force of arms should by any chance there be provocation by another party. Moreover, it goes without saying that the direction this international situation takes from now on is not something that Japan alone can decide. We therefore believe, on the contrary, that being explicit on this point will avoid deceiving oneself and others."

It had been one of Nomura's basic policies, consistently maintained since the negotiations over his appointment in the summer of 1940, that a southern advance should not be undertaken. In his item-by-item explanatory telegram of April 18 as well, Nomura had stated positively that "the Empire's not resorting to force of arms in moving southward is the basis of the entire Draft Understanding."[216] But this was disregarded by Matsuoka, who harbored the notion of taking Singapore by surprise attack.

4) A conference in Honolulu. This provision was deleted in its entirety on the ground that: "Instead of this it would be desirable to exchange letters in which consideration would be given to a conference between the president and the prime minister, or other representatives of theirs who would act in their stead, should both the United States and Japan deem it necessary after having taken into consideration the effects of the present Understanding." Cool to the idea of a Konoe-Roosevelt conference, Matsuoka hereby tried to make room for himself to come forward in place of Konoe, should circumstances permit, in order to carry out his own policy.

Further deletions were made in the policies of both nations regarding naval forces and shipping in the Pacific, financial cooperation between the two nations, and political stability in the Pacific. All these deletions and the thorough and severe manner of Matsuoka's revisions gave not a bit of leeway to the United States. So much so was this the case that Matsuoka, still fuming with anger, declared in a dictated synopsis sent to Konoe the day after his resignation: "The content of our revised draft of the Japanese-American Understanding, in its basic principles, runs completely counter to the demands of the United States, namely, that Japan should break away from the Tripartite Alliance and return Sino-Japanese relations to the state that existed prior to the Manchurian Incident; in your wisdom Your Excellency, I am certain, is well aware that there is not one chance in ten thousand that the United States will accept our proposal."[217] The aims of those who had drawn up the Draft Japanese-American Understanding had now been fundamentally negated.

Matsuoka and Germany

On April 16, the day the Draft Understanding was completed in Washington, Ambassador Ōshima in Berlin sent an important report to Konoe, who received it just before the Draft Understanding arrived on the 18th. Ōshima said:

> Concerning Telegram No. 413, I submit the following opinion as the result of consultations with Vice Admiral Nomura Naokuni and the army and navy attachés. . . . [In the event of a German counterattack [sic—trans.] against the Soviet Union], even should the Stalin regime survive, its forces will undoubtedly be weakened. A reduction in Soviet pressure on our northern frontier may be expected. Even in the worst eventuality, one in which the war does not progress as Germany expects and German and Soviet forces reach stalemate, pressure from the Soviet Union on our country will abate as a matter of course.
>
> Further, the outbreak of war between Germany and the Soviet Union is exactly what Britain and the United States wish, as they desire to see the war expanded. They would gladly welcome this and would endeavor to aid the Soviet Union. However, it is our judgment that in the final analysis neither Britain nor even the United States will be able to provide the Soviet Union with any great substantial aid; this will have hardly any effect on the outcome of a war between Germany and the Soviet Union. . . .

. . . we deem it in the best interests of our empire not to rush north but to wait for an opportune moment. We should first stride forth on the great road toward the establishment of the Greater East Asia Coprosperity Sphere and concentrate on the conquest of Singapore, the strategic base in the Far East for the Anglo-American forces that are the basic factor standing in our way on this. . . . The defeat of Britain in Europe is now unavoidable and the Empire has doubly insured itself [through the Neutrality Treaty and the Tripartite Pact?] against the Soviet Union. Such a state of affairs greatly influences the pressure the United States can exert in the Far East, and even if war does not break out between Germany and the Soviet Union, it can be said to present the perfect opportunity for the execution of our policies. We believe that the moment has come for Japan to formulate forthwith a counterplan that would be in accordance with the above line of thinking and to decide when that is to be carried out and by what means, once the full understanding of Germany and Italy has been obtained.[218]

Ōshima's telegram contained the relatively superficial observation that a new situation had arisen in which prospects for war between Germany and the Soviet Union were high, and he insisted that the only way to deal with this situation was to embark on the conquest of Singapore with the full understanding of Germany. Ōshima was more buoyantly optimistic than Matsuoka, who thought the chances of avoiding war between Japan and the United States were at best fifty-fifty. Ōshima's telegram might have emboldened Matsuoka, for it backed up his policy toward the United States, that policy having been reinforced by his visit to Europe.

The May 18 Liaison Conference, hurriedly convoked without Matsuoka, failed to reach any decision because opinion was divided as to whether or not Japan should inform Germany of the Draft Understanding. After Matsuoka excused himself from the Liaison Conference of May 22, those remaining were inclined toward proceeding with talks with the United States without obtaining Germany's full understanding. On route from Tachikawa airbase to Tokyo on the day he returned from Europe, however, Matsuoka had told Ōhashi straight away that it was necessary to have Germany's understanding.[219] And on May 3 Matsuoka had obtained the concurrence of the Liaison Conference to his assertion that "we should proceed on the assumption that we confidentially inform Germany and Italy of its general character based on the revised draft and that if Germany and Italy have suggestions we at least listen to them."[220] That night Matsuoka set out for the Grand Shrine at Ise, and in his absence, on

May 4, Europe-Asia Bureau Chief Sakamoto Mizuo spoke confidentially to the German and Italian ambassadors:

> Foreign Minister Matsuoka finds every reason to suspect that in presenting this Draft the United States has as its ulterior motive the attempt to concentrate its entire strength on aiding Britain by temporarily stabilizing the situation in the Pacific region. The proposal must be studied with care. It is an unshakable fact that the keynote of the imperial government's diplomacy is the Tripartite Pact. We are in the midst of studying a counterproposal expressly from the standpoint that, by properly handling the present American proposal, we shall keep the United States out of the war, thereby making it possible to turn that proposal in such a direction as to serve the original purpose of the Tripartite Alliance. . . .
>
> In short, the United States, through this proposal, is undertaking to avoid the danger of a Japanese-American war and, by a palliative that might temporarily stabilize the situation in the Pacific, to turn its attention to the Atlantic. Japan will never under any circumstance allow the United States the liberty of being able to press on with its aid to Britain without anxiety for its future as the result of consummating a Japanese-American understanding. The United States regards this agreement primarily as a political "gesture" and obviously intends to utilize the signing of the agreement for propaganda purposes. We shall prepare careful countermeasures against this beforehand. *Our immediate national policy is to assist Germany and Italy with all our might to ensure them victory in quick order.* (Author's emphasis) [221]

En route back from Ise by train on May 5, Matsuoka telegraphed directly to Ribbentrop: "Since my return home my sole concern both day and night has been somehow to make Roosevelt be more reflective and have him refrain from reckless actions. Although his recent impetuous behavior [Roosevelt's May 4 speech at Stoughton] has driven me virtually to the point of total despair, I have yet to give up my last hope. Nay, I dare not give it up." [222] The following day Ott called on Matsuoka, who urged the ambassador to inform him confidentially of German reactions:

> He said that he had utilized the intervening time [since the arrival of the Draft Understanding] to work on the Admiral [Suetsugu Nobumasa], pointing out especially the feelings in activist circles of younger officers of the Army and Navy who decidedly would reject such a policy. . . .
>
> He would be grateful for receiving as soon as possible the views of the Foreign Minister on the American proposal, in order to face unavoidable argument in the sphere of domestic policy. [223]

On the 10th Matsuoka twice inquired whether Ott had received a reply from Berlin with regard to the "American proposal." At Ott's request and in anticipation of the reply from Berlin, Matsuoka promised to postpone the communication to the American government that had been announced for that day or the next.[224] On the 11th Matsuoka replied to Ott that he was willing to put off sending instructions to Washington until noon, May 12 (Japan time).[225]

It had been Matsuoka's original plan to submit the revised draft approved on May 3 to the United States once he had heard informally from Germany. But as the result of several telegrams that arrived from May 10 into May 11, the view had gained ascendancy in the military that the revised draft must be presented before Roosevelt's May 14 speech:

> the president will deliver an important foreign policy speech this coming 14th, in the evening. Because of reports that he will address the issue of convoying [in the Atlantic] we deem it essential that Japanese-American talks begin immediately. . . . According to a confidential tip from a certain influential cabinet member [Walker?] there are chances of restraining America from convoying if Japanese-American talks get underway. (From Attaché Yokoyama, sent May 10).[226]
>
> [According to a private conversation with a certain influential cabinet member], the argument in favor of convoying has become very powerful within the U.S. government. Although the president has suppressed this up until now, at a cabinet meeting on the 8th last he too came around to acknowledging this general trend as unstoppable given the growing clamor of public opinion. It is anticipated that he will touch on this point in his upcoming foreign policy speech on the 14th, but if negotiations between Japan and the United States start before that there are chances of getting the content of that speech changed. In the event that negotiations do not get started, talks between Japan and the United States will be hopeless. (From Nomura, sent May 11)[227]
>
> On the evening of the 10th a confidential agent arrived with the following message, allegedly from Hull: Should the convoying now being contemplated by the United States go into force, that is bound to create a difficult situation in terms of making progress in our talks on the Japanese-American Draft Understanding; but the United States has absolutely no thought of doing anything that would drive Japan into a corner on this account. (From Iwakuro, sent May 11)[228]

In the end, without waiting to ascertain Germany's reaction, Matsuoka instructed Nomura at noon on the 12th to present the revised draft. As Matsuoka later pointed out in his May 24 telegram to Ōshima, "In order to remain loyal to the Tripartite Pact through thick and thin, I overcame the constant impatience of the military and others (this had absolutely nothing to do with what you called in your telegram the influence of the status quo faction; on the contrary, the army and navy were most ardent on this), and although I encountered any number of difficulties I did postpone sending out a reply for one week."[229]

Just after he sent his directive to Nomura, Matsuoka received Germany's reaction from Ott, the essence of which was:

It goes without saying that the Japanese government is itself in the position to judge best to what extent the American president's proposal restricts future Japanese action within the Greater East Asia Coprosperity Sphere. The German government has no other choice but to recognize this proposal as emanating from the American president's carefully laid plan to make it appear that there has been a reduction of tension in the Pacific region, thereby eradicating fears among antiwar elements within the United States, in order to press forward in the predetermined direction of entering the war. The only way to block the American government leaders' resolution to enter the war is to make unquestionably clear the fact that American entry into the war will of necessity bring about Japanese intervention. Thus there is no doubt that the American president is attempting first of all to neutralize this fact so that it will be easier to take aggressive action in Europe.

Clearly it is the policy of the American government step by step to intensify actions (patrolling and convoying) without declaring war but in de facto violation of neutrality, wait for counterattacks by Germany and Italy, and then shift the responsibility for the outbreak of war to the Axis powers. The German government deems it appropriate that the Japanese government keep the following points in mind in responding to the American proposal:

1. It must be stressed that the actions now being taken by the American government, namely, actions in violation of international law such as patrolling and convoying, are deemed to be actions on the part of the American government deliberately designed to provoke war, the continuation of which will of necessity compel Japan to enter the war.
2. It must be clearly indicated that the Japanese government is prepared to study the American proposal if the American government refrains from these actions.

In view of the grave impact this matter has on the contracting parties to the Tripartite Pact, the German government entreats the Japanese government to notify the German and Italian governments unofficially of the contents of its final reply, and to solicit their opinions, prior to dispatching it.[230]

Although it was only to be expected, this reaction on the part of Germany was consistent with Matsuoka's strategy in making his revisions.

Matsuoka Becomes Isolated

Because of his insistence on obtaining the understanding of Germany and Italy, and also because there were hints that he desired to form his own cabinet, Matsuoka was rapidly pushed aside and isolated from the mainstream of politics as May progressed. However, there was little in the way of an influential grouping squarely opposing his policy toward the United States.

On May 8 Tōjō ordered the Army Ministry's Military Affairs Bureau to investigate and draft a policy concerning "the attitude Japan should take if the United States enters the war against Germany." Mutō entrusted the task to Ishii Akiho. The Ishii plan, which was submitted to Tōjō after deliberations on May 10 and 11, was unanimously approved by the Army Ministry. In essence, it proposed the opportunistic argument that Japan was not bound in an official way by Article 3 of the Tripartite Pact and should sit tight and watch world developments for the time being.[231] But even an argument of this extent could not be brought up for discussion in the Army General Staff, where the pro-Axis position was ascendant among some members. The army, navy, and Konoe had agreed at the April 18 Liaison Conference, before Matsuoka's return from Europe, that an adjustment of diplomatic relations with the United States should proceed on the basis of the Draft Understanding, but by May 3, barely a fortnight later, they readily consented to Matsuoka's revised draft that would essentially kill the Draft Understanding.

On February 7, just before Nomura arrived in Washington, Matsuoka had instructed him:

> I have endeavored on such occasions as the recent Imperial Diet interpellations to make it perfectly clear that the capacity of our national strength has neither dissipated nor wasted away. . . . Although it is a fact that our national strength has dissipated to a certain extent, its capacity is not as exhausted as American officials incessantly propagate. . . . Please make every effort to explain this fully [to influential persons both in and out of the American government].[232]

On May 31, after the revised draft had been approved, he sent Nomura instructions in which he emphasized the improvement in Japan's international position:

> The difference in the international position of the empire today as compared with the days [of the first Sino-Japanese and the Russo-Japanese wars] is greater even than that between heaven and earth. . . . In view of the international position of our imperial nation and the situation in East Asia today, I have no intention whatsoever of requesting the United States to mediate or the like. My intention is solely to advise the American authorities simply to tell Chiang Kai-shek, "You had better negotiate directly with Japan or the United States will terminate aid.." . . In the future, please pay particular attention to this point and make it absolutely clear to the American authorities that the attitude and determination of our imperial nation are completely different from what they were in the past.[233]

Was it really proper for Matsuoka, in the dark as he was about all the assessments that had been made of the nation's material strength, to hold forth with such utter assurance? The army and navy had given their consent to the Draft Understanding on April 21 in an attempt to turn U.S. designs to Japan's advantage, partly from the standpoint of restoring and sustaining national power. Surely they could have brought Matsuoka into line simply by showing him their separate assessments of the nation's material strength and then asking him to ponder the matter.

Why might the army, the navy, and Konoe have followed Matsuoka's lead in handling the Draft Understanding? In the first place, the more his political isolation in Japan grew and the more he came to realize just how unlikely it was that he would become prime minister (the prerequisite for the coherent implementation of his policies toward the United States), the more Matsuoka brandished his diplomatic prerogatives with reckless abandon: far from being able to engage him in discussion, Konoe and the army and navy alike found Matsuoka more and more difficult to handle. Second, the prime minister and the military both appear to have thought initially that the Draft Japanese-American Understanding might have been the product of a Matsuoka peace offensive in collaboration with Germany and Italy, and they could hardly go back and look into this on their own without involving Matsuoka. For example, notes by someone close to Konoe record that the Draft resulted from Matsuoka's conversations in Berlin. The Army General Staff also noted, "In short, the 'point' is whether or not Matsuoka had reached an understanding with Germany; [but as became apparent later] no understanding with Germany and Italy had been reached at all."[234] Third, the respective interpretations of the Draft Understanding given by the two clerics, Iwakuro, Nomura, and the Army Ministry with regard to the Tripartite Pact were all somewhat labored from a textual standpoint; by contrast, Matsuoka's interpretation was less forced. Finally, having themselves insisted on concluding the Tripartite Pact, Konoe and the army and navy now hesitated to oppose Matsuoka's interpretation head on, and therefore their objections could not help but be of limited force.

In the end, Konoe and both services turned around and accepted Matsuoka's revised draft, thereby defeating the intent of the Draft Japanese-American Understanding. Consent had been given with relative ease to two basic policies that were completely incompatible. Was such a state of affairs a symptom that the turning of state policy-making into exercises in semantics, so characteristic of the Konoe era, would become even more acute?

Behind this ceaseless movement toward semantic agreements over state policy, however, substantive actions had nonetheless been taken. Matsuoka, for example, spoke of war between Japan and the United States—implicitly with Grew, explicitly with Duranty. And the navy was making steady progress in its readiness for war with the United States. Detecting such fissures in the substance of state policy, the emperor did not hold back his misgivings. When Matsuoka reported to the Throne on May 8, the emperor asked him about the relationship between adjusting Japanese-American relations and the Tripartite Pact. Matsuoka replied: "That is not to run counter to the Tripartite Pact; a Draft Understanding that would do so will not be put in place."[235] On May 12, however, Matsuoka told the navy's Captain Ishikawa Shingo that as the result of this reply to the Throne "things might go the way the emperor wishes."[236] The War Guidance Office of the Army General Staff had trouble interpreting what Matsuoka was saying: "It is not clear whether he meant by this that only a Draft Understanding that accords with his thinking will be put forward, or whether he was implying that he would resign if forced [by Konoe and the military] to do something against his liking."[237] Konoe wrote in his memoirs that Matsuoka had replied to the Throne that "if, out of excessive preoccupation with the problem of the United States, Japan were to betray Germany and Italy, he would have no choice but to tender his resignation."[238] And Konoe also recorded that on the 23rd Matsuoka had told him, "As a loyal subject I have no choice but to obey His Majesty's wishes."[239] Taking all this into consideration, it is difficult to understand how Matsuoka could ever have been so confident about his political future, let alone the idea of his becoming prime minister.

8 Hull Rejects the Japanese-American Draft Understanding

Grew's Proposals Are Ignored

During May and June, starting from the time Nomura had requested instructions on the Japanese-American Draft Understanding, the communications he received from Matsuoka all ran counter, and in the extreme, to the policy of no war between Japan and the United States that he had put into the Draft Understanding. Caught between the objectives he was pursuing in the Draft and Matsuoka's directives (in particular, Matsuoka's oral statement of May 3, his revised draft of May 12, and his memorandum of May 13), Nomura found it difficult to adopt a clear and concrete position on each item of the Draft.

Deeply dedicated to improving Japanese-American relations ever since his appointment, Nomura had constantly appealed to both governments to change their psychologies and the atmosphere between them. He first appealed to Konoe and Matsuoka:

> Should the United States begin convoying and eventually declare that a state of war exists, that will pose an enormous problem for our country. We must somehow bring about an understanding at this time and change today's psychology of war to a psychology of peace. (Dispatch of April 15)[240]
>
> Our first axiom should be to handle properly the actual problems that exist between Japan and the United States, limiting to the absolute minimum debate over matters of principle. Although it is nearly impossible to eradicate in one stroke the serious and complex issues that have accumulated over many years between the two countries, once both sides begin to move toward an understanding, grudges will be gradually dispelled, to be followed by the growth of friendly feelings. If such a situation were to materialize right now, it should gradually become possible to check the attitude of the United States toward the larger war and then change it. Consequently, I have taken up matters of substance in the belief that it would be to our advantage to put first priority on achieving practical results. . . . (Dispatch of May 8)[241]

I have repeated the same thing [to Hull] every time we have met, but what with one step forward and one step backward [no] progress has been made. I told him that the Draft Understanding was originally aimed at transforming the psychologies of both our peoples from war to peace, not at composing a diplomatically clever document; while we are dillydallying around, something unexpected will happen and all our efforts will come to naught. (Dispatch of May 29)[242]

On May 20 he told Hull that he "hoped that we would not be disposed to dwell upon technicalities" and that "it would be a pity if we failed to reach an understanding through disagreement on words."[243] And in his memoirs Nomura recorded that on May 21 he told Hull virtually the same thing he reported to his government in his telegram of May 29: "The original goal of the Draft Understanding is to switch the war psychology of both our peoples toward peace; concocting up a clever diplomatic document ought to be put off to another day."[244] On the 28th he told Hull that "there would be no war between Japan and the United States, as . . . once the proposed agreement was concluded it would have a profound effect upon Japanese psychology which would cause a weakening in the influence of the jingoes."[245]

Nomura did not want to get mired down in debates over either principles or technicalities. Consequently, there was in fact not one instance of Nomura's having given a reply that would satisfy the United States, even on the matter of the Tripartite Pact, while on several occasions he made vague statements to the effect that "if an agreement were reached with the United States, the psychological effect in Japan would be such that there would be no possibility of Japan interpreting its obligations under the Tripartite Pact adversely to friendly relations with the United States."[246]

In the meanwhile, Grew had sent several important reports, such as those of May 26 and 27, in which he repeatedly suggested to Hull that in his judgment the situation in Japan was still fluid and divided, and there would be no substantial loss even if the United States were to trust Japan for the time being; therefore, the United States should make its position unequivocally clear beforehand as well as leave Japan room to maneuver.[247] But the Far Eastern division of the State Department, led by Hornbeck, paid little attention to these reports, or rather it simply ignored them. The division's policies, which were contrary to Grew's, can be extracted from Hornbeck's memoranda at the time.

1) Self-righteous moralism:

" . . . it would be unwise, inexpedient and of doubtful morality for the Government of the United States . . . to associate itself with any movement or any effort on the part of any other government or nation to eliminate or to disregard or to weaken or to undermine the principle of nonrecognition." (May 15)[248]

2) Prosecution-like judgments:

"For forty-five years [since the Sino-Japanese War of 1894–95] Japan (the Japanese) has been the great disturber of the peace of the Pacific. . . .

. . . [Japan] might in the course of the next three or four or five years undergo a change first of mind and then of heart. That, however, would have to come not of success in making treaties—with Germany, with the Soviet Union, *with the United States*—but by quite another process, a process not of encouragement but of discouragement.

Japan (some Japanese) has fooled the United States in and with diplomatic exchanges no less than five times during the past thirty-three years." (May 23)[249]

"The first essential toward renunciation of an objective of conquest by force is the development within the nation which cherishes that objective of a real conviction of the futility of the effort which it is making. This can be brought about only on the basis of evidence of failure or of comparative incapacity to succeed. Development of such a conviction takes time. . . . until Japan's militant leadership has shown to its own people to be *not possessed* of the capacity to take *and to hold.*" (April 18)[250]

3) Distrust of Japan:

"*These* Japanese are engaging us in conversations . . . *in order* to enable Japan to straddle—with one foot resting on a German platform and the other foot resting on an American platform; *in order* to make it possible for Japan to hold on to some of the loot which she gained in China, to collect additional loot as opportunity develops, and to be in position to collocate herself, as the world conflict progresses and when it ends, with whichever side seems to be . . . victorious." (May 23)[251]

"I feel it my duty in fairness to you [Hull] . . . to let you know that to the best of my knowledge every officer of the Department . . . shares in the misgivings to which I have been and am giving expression. . . . " (June 10)[252]

Hornbeck's simplistic formalism reprovingly asserted that nothing could be done until after the military collapse of Japan; he had virtually no sensitivity to or perception of the ever-changing power balance in the Far East among Japan, the Chinese Nationalist government, Chinese Communist political power, and the Soviet Union. Accordingly, the day after the Draft Understanding was completed, the Far Eastern Division submitted a memorandum with the objectives of aiding China to the fullest extent possible and of exerting ever greater economic pressure on Japan, short only of embargoes on commodities such as oil, which Japan regarded as vital to its existence.[253]

Hull Flatly Rejects the Nomura Formula

Hull entered the talks with Nomura in essential agreement with such a policy. His view, however, was broader than Hornbeck's and his statements always reflected shifts in the actual state of American-German relations. In the first place, Hull "dwelt on the need of drawing up the proposed agreement in clear-cut and unequivocal terms so that the agreement would speak for itself. . . . he was not interested in an agreement of a temporizing character. . . . "[254] He considered that specific matters naturally revolved around three points: 1) a guarantee by Japan that it would not advance southward for the sake of military conquest; 2) a guarantee by Japan that it would not go to war for the sake of Germany if and when the United States were drawn into the war; and 3) a satisfactory settlement between Japan and China. In his talks with Nomura, Hull always had these points in mind. Nomura's formula, with its emphasis on psychological conversion, was flatly rejected by Hull, and the focus of their conversations inevitably reverted back to debates over principle or to technicalities involving specific matters. Below are Hull's main utterances on these three points and on Matsuoka's stance.

1) Prevention of a military advance southward by Japan:
May 11: "I asked the Ambassador whether his Government had in mind any method of giving absolute assurances that it would not use either force or threat of force for purposes of conquest in the southwestern area of the Pacific or other countries."[255]
May 12: "As for the provision about a southern advance there is still nothing much by way of guarantees."[256]

2) Military intervention in the Atlantic and preventing the Tripartite Pact from going into force:
May 7: . . . "I would not be candid if I did not say to him that I could not give any assurances of further patience in the event of further

delay [in Japan's reply] for the reason . . . that this country . . . is determined that Hitler shall not get control of the high seas. . . . "[257]

May 11: ". . . with things moving as rapidly, no one could tell . . . what any day might bring forth. . . .[United States] resistance [against Hitler] would be to the maximum extent within the minimum of time, and that this in its very nature would constitute necessary self-defense against an avowed world-wide aggressor, and in no sense could be construed as an act of offense . . . in the light of the world nature of the movement of aggression on Hitler's part."[258]

May 28: ". . . if we went into an agreement with Japan [per Matsuoka's revised draft], critics would assert, unless the Japanese Government could clarify its attitude toward its obligations under the Tripartite Alliance in the event that the United States should be drawn into the European war through action in the line of self-defense, that there was no assurance as to Japan's position."[259]

3) Withdrawal of Japanese troops from China:

May 11: "I . . . inquired as to whether there were any definite plans in the mind of his Government in regard to when the Japanese troops would come out of China, and what assurances, if any, there were that they would actually come out under a mutually satisfactory arrangement."[260]

May 20: "One [point that he would like to bring up] was in regard to the joint defense against communism and the other was in regard to the stationing of Japanese troops in certain parts of Chinese territory."[261]

June 2: . . . "the policy of keeping Japanese troops stationed in China indefinitely . . . was an extremely important point in the situation. . . . "[262]

4) Taking exception to Matsuoka:

May 7: . . . "such conduct and action [by Matsuoka and others] were in the opposite direction of the entire spirit and policy of the [Draft Understanding] . . . and instructions [by the Japanese government] authorizing him to make it a basis for the beginning of negotiations."[263]

June 2: . . . "one was forced back to the inquiry of whether Japan really is seeking this sort of settlement, or whether she is only seeking a way to get out of China, and otherwise to go forward with methods and practices entirely contrary to the principles. . . . "[264]

June 7: "According to information we have obtained, the Japanese government seems not necessarily enthusiastic about this problem, and we have learned that it differs fundamentally from us on various important points. If this is true, there is no point in continuing our talks. However much Japanese-American relations deteriorate, we shall guarantee the safety of your person, and friendship between us as individuals will remain unchanged."[265]

Surely Nomura was hesitant to report to Tokyo this last comment, in which Hull probed into policy differences between Matsuoka and Nomura. And there is scant evidence that Nomura actually transmitted the remark Hull made on June 3: "Because of Matsuoka's declarations, many in America doubt if Japan is in fact sincere in desiring to maintain peace in the Pacific. This puts me in a very difficult position."[266] Nor that of June 15: "Hull commented on a declaration Matsuoka made to Italy and then said that he had obtained from Tokyo information that Matsuoka and company are attempting to destroy the Draft Understanding."[267]

On this score, Iwakuro was in a less constrained position than Nomura. In a frank report to Tōjō on May 2, Iwakuro had stated:

> As I see it, Mr. Matsuoka is postponing sending instructions in response to my earlier report in order to use the intervening time to send up "trial balloons" in the newspapers. Given the situation in the United States today, this will have no effect except to antagonize American leaders. I am convinced that if Mr. Matsuoka continues on with his "gesture diplomacy," all our efforts up till now will be for naught. I believe that what we should do now is put a quick stop to this gesture diplomacy and, by sending return instructions as soon as possible, have the ambassador endeavor to set up preliminary negotiations between Japan and the United States; once that is done we should take a suitably grand course of action—a conference between Japan and the United States or a visit by Mr. Matsuoka to the United States (although representatives of the army, navy, and foreign ministries here in Washington all agree that his trip would not be effective).[268]

The Factors Behind Hull's Insistence on a Reply

Around May 10 Hull suddenly began to urge that Japan give assurances with regard to its position on the Tripartite Pact. This originated primarily from the following factors. On April 15 Roosevelt had decided to patrol against and pursue German submarines in the western Atlantic and to notify Britain that he would do so. On April 18 Admiral Ernest J. King, commander-in-chief of the Atlantic Fleet, secretly ordered these measures carried out and on the 21st ordered the formation of patrol squadrons. Now all that remained was the military intervention of convoying, but that would be possible only if the United States were determined not to flinch from actual clashes with the German navy in the Atlantic. Behind King's orders lay the fact that Germany had on March 25 issued a declaration extending its naval war zone to a portion of the Greenland coast in a manner that would encircle Iceland. In response, the United States on April 28 greatly advanced the boundary of the western hemisphere to the east, to longitude 26° west, thus incorporating within that hemisphere a portion of the new German naval war zone. By doing so, the United States navy was poised to intervene militarily in that zone in the name of defending the western hemisphere.

Such being the case, it is hard to say that Nomura's May 8 report on his conversation with Hull the previous day was particularly accurate, given that it went no further than to convey Hull's utterances just as he gave them:

> [Hull] said that the United States has now reached the point where speedy action is required, that negotiations must be undertaken before it is "too late," and that the United States cannot tolerate Hitlerism spreading over the seven seas and is therefore resolved in the name of defense to resist for ten or even twenty years in order to protect the rights and interests of the United States (Hull enlarged upon this by saying that such is the right of every nation). Hull repeatedly said this was of course defensive. He told me that partly because all his colleagues had urged him to undertake negotiations quickly, negotiations must be undertaken promptly, without vacillation or hesitation, before it is "too late." Hull urged that Japanese-American negotiations get started in the most emphatic tones I have ever heard him use.[269]

And in interpreting Hull's chief concern as being to get started on negotiations rather than to probe into whether or not Japan would give assurances, Nomura's report can hardly be called accurate either:

> Consequently, the United States will soon embark on convoy operations, stepping up the patrols in which it has been engaged. Since convoying would be carried out only with the willingness to risk war, the danger is great that the United States will enter the war once it goes into effect. Facing such a delicate situation, the United States would find it disadvantageous if both Japan and Germany were to become hostile nations at the same time. It is therefore understandable that the United States should attempt to readjust its relations with Japan, which poses less danger to it. We can be confident that the American desire to open negotiations on the basis of the so-called Draft Understanding

is underwritten by such developments. . . . It would appear that the president and a minority of his close associates have come to recognize that Japanese national character differs from that of Germany or Italy and that Japan is not necessarily as aggressive as Germany and Italy. They seem to have come to believe that rapprochement between Japan and the United States would also be advantageous to their country (please note that this is not absolutely necessary to them).[270]

Hull Waits for War to Break out Between Germany and the Soviet Union

Unlike the Japanese government, Hull was largely familiar with the background to the Draft Understanding. Whereas the Japanese government erroneously thought that the Matsuoka draft was a modification of an American proposal, Hull was able to make the correct interpretation that what the Japanese government intended in terms of an adjustment of diplomatic relations had, in the Matsuoka revised draft, been authoritatively expressed for the first time.[271] On the other hand, when the British ambassador, Lord Halifax, called on Undersecretary of State Sumner Welles on May 23 and conveyed to him that "the British Government is in possession of information which convinces it that the German and Italian Governments have received full reports [from Matsuoka] concerning existing conversations between the Japanese Ambassador in Washington and the Secretary of State," Welles noted that this information was already in the possession of the State Department.[272] As this reveals, from at least the beginning of 1941 the United States had been successfully deciphering the Foreign Ministry's incoming and outgoing telegrams. The German embassy in Washington had already reported on April 28 that according to "an absolutely reliable source, the State Department is in possession of the key to the Japanese coding system and is therefore also able to decipher information telegrams from Tokyo to Ambassador Nomura here regarding Ambassador Ōshima's reports from Berlin."[273]

Hull was thus in direct or indirect possession of Ambassador Matsuoka's oral statement, his revised draft, his May 13 memorandum—everything. And when he became aware of the important telegrams exchanged between Matsuoka and Ōshima, which are discussed below, Hull found it all but impossible to overcome his mistrust of Matsuoka. On the other hand, he told Halifax on May 16 and Chinese Ambassador Hu Shih on the 23rd that thus far he "had not taken any of these things seriously."[274] To Halifax he further expressed the view that the chances of reaching an understanding with Japan probably did not exceed one in ten.[275] Despite this pessimism about reaching an understanding, however, Hull continued his frequent and courteous conversations with Nomura, largely playing for time until the right moment. During this time Hull was also walking a tightrope between a hard and a soft posture toward Japan: while stepping up economic pressure on Japan, he did not want on that account to provoke Japan into an armed advance to the south. That was also the import of representations to the United States by Britain, Australia, and Holland, which were threatened directly by a Japanese armed advance to the south.

That "right moment," needless to say, was the commencement of war between Germany and the Soviet Union. Since late January the U.S. government had been of the firm conviction that Hitler would decide to attack the Soviet Union. They had calculated that if the talks with Japan could be dragged out until that moment, the revolutionary changes in the international situation that would follow in its wake would be sufficient to smash to smithereens the illusory Axis policy of Matsuoka and the military.

On June 21, certain that war between Germany and the Soviet Union would break out the following day, Hull for the first time presented Nomura with what the U.S. government had in mind in the form of a counterproposal accompanied by an oral statement. The U.S. counterproposal was a document that developed explicitly the principles that Hull had repeatedly stated to Nomura throughout May and June with regard to the three critical matters: an armed advance to the south, the Tripartite Pact, and the stationing of troops in China. The counterproposal was so severe that had Japan accepted it *in toto,* the Japanese, in the words of Herbert Feis, would have been given "only a chance to live at peace, and by hard and patient work earn the means of living on their crowded islands. . . . no premium, no consolation prize, for returning to the company of peaceful and orderly states and accepting a place below the salt."[276] The first Draft Understanding, originating in the vision of the two clerics of an agreement for peace in the Pacific, had now been totally rejected by the American government as well.

The oral statement that accompanied the counterproposal contained the following passage:

Unfortunately, accumulating evidence reaches this Government from sources all over the world, including reports from sources which over many years have demonstrated sincere good will toward Japan, that some Japanese leaders in influential official positions are definitely committed to a course which calls for support of Nazi Germany and its policies of conquest and that the only kind of understanding with the United States which they would endorse is one that would envisage Japan's fighting on the side of Hitler should the United States become involved in the European hostilities through carrying out its present policy of self-defense. . . . So long as such leaders maintain this attitude in their official positions and apparently seek to influence public opinion in Japan in the direction indicated, is it not illusory to expect that adoption of a proposal such as the one under consideration offers a basis for achieving substantial results along the desired lines? . . .

The Secretary of State has therefore reluctantly come to the conclusion that this Government must await some clearer indication than has yet been given that the Japanese Government as a whole desires to pursue courses of peace such as constitute the objectives of the proposed understanding. . . .[277]

Hull further elaborated on this point when he handed a transcript of the oral statement to Nomura, saying, "It seems to us that the Japanese Government would decide either to assume control of those elements in the Japanese body politic which supported Nazi Germany and its policies of aggression or to allow those elements to take over entire charge of Japan's policies."[278] And on June 22, the day of the awaited outbreak of war between Germany and the Soviet Union, Hull asked Nomura whether that war "might not affect the situation in such a way as to render it more easy for the Japanese Government to find some way along the lines indicated" by the United States.[279] In making such remarks, Hull was not merely sounding out Japan's reaction to the German-Soviet conflict; he was further suggesting that Japan, by relieving Matsuoka of his post, might alter its pro-Axis policy. However, to expect that this suggestion, when presented together with the accusatory severity of Hull's counterproposal, would win over the Japanese was perhaps excessively self-indulgent.

Matsuoka Throws in the Towel

On June 10 Hornbeck felt compelled to write Hull:

As I envisaged this matter, Father Drought has taken upon himself and is playing the role of a promoter and salesman. My conjecture is that he first "sold" the idea of a negotiation and if possible an agreement to certain Japanese and that he has been since and is doing his utmost to "sell" the idea to you (and through you to the President): Drought is the pushing and the pulling agent in the matter. He has enlisted as his aides the Postmaster General and the three Japanese [Ikawa, Iwakuro, Nomura?]. . . . As a go-between, he has brought those gentlemen and you (with your aides) into what amounts—no matter how it may otherwise be technically described—to a negotiation.[280]

In other words, however frequently Hull repeated by way of covering himself that these were no more than preliminary and informal investigations, by the very fact that he met frequently with Nomura and discussed problems between their countries there was no gainsaying that negotiations were indeed in progress. On the other hand, when he met with Nomura for the first time, Hull had reserved the right of the American government to present its official views at a later time. The June 21 counterproposal was nothing more than the first exercise of that right.

From the outset the Japanese government had been under the illusion that the Draft Understanding was an official proposal to which the U.S. government had no serious objections. It had therefore regarded the continuation of the Nomura-Hull talks as a natural development in Japanese-American negotiations, and this American counterproposal inevitably came as a severe shock. Military Affairs Section Chief Satō, who had responded favorably to the Draft Understanding, was so stunned that he felt like rubbing his eyes or pinching himself. Thereafter, indignation and suspicion began to take hold throughout the army, which felt that the negotiations had to be a plot on the part of the United States acting out of bad faith. Despite this trend in the army, Tōjō and Oikawa conferred with Konoe and on July 4 sent Matsuoka the following note with Konoe's thoughts:

1. The consequences of adjusting our diplomatic relations with the United States cannot but be unsatisfactory as far as Germany's needs are concerned. That is bound to give rise to unpleasant emotional undercurrents among the alliance signatories for a while. But this is unavoidable.
2. An adjustment in diplomatic relations with the United States is necessary for three reasons: (a) to increase our national strength through the acquisition of commodities from abroad, (b) to exclude the possibility of an American rapprochement with the Soviet Union, and (c) to speed up peace maneuvers with Chungking.
3. From this point of view, it is not only necessary to continue the negotiations with the United States that are now being conducted; we also think that from the larger perspective of carrying out national policy we must strive to bring them to a prompt conclusion. From Your Excellency's farsighted point of view an understanding be-

tween Japan and the United States might be impossible, but . . . at
this time we cannot but hope that we will succeed in this by putting
forth our best efforts, even though we make some concessions.[281]

We have already seen not only that the original Draft Understanding
had been rejected by both Matsuoka and Hull, but also that Matsuoka's revised draft and Hull's counterproposal were fundamentally
incompatible and could not be reconciled. That being the case, the
foundations for adjusting Japanese-American relations had been utterly destroyed for the present. Apart from Konoe and Tōjō, who
were unable to face this situation squarely, it was only natural that
Matsuoka would be reluctant to come up with a new solution to
the deadlock.

Deeply displeased over the whole matter and having become
greatly concerned for the future of the Tripartite Pact, Germany
reiterated its concerns once again on May 17:

The German government is of the view that the best way to restrain
the United States from entering the war would be the complete refusal
to take up negotiations on the [Draft Japanese-American Under-
standing]. . . .

If, however, the Japanese government considers that it cannot avoid
negotiations with the American government about Japanese-American
relations, at least the appearance of those detrimental effects [men-
tioned above] must be made impossible beforehand, since the United
States is in actuality (if not strictly by international law) an enemy of the
Axis powers. It is therefore necessary that the fundamental point of a
Japanese-American agreement shall be to establish firmly, clearly, and
succinctly, the duty of the American government not to intervene in
the war between Britain and the Axis powers (in a form much clearer
than has been stipulated up to now) and the duty of Japan arising from
the Tripartite Pact. Moreover, the remainder of its provisions must all
be made dependent on that fundamental point. Under these circumstances, the question of the formula adopted becomes of greatest importance. . . . Deviating from or weakening the absolute minimum [of
Matsuoka's revised draft] would lead toward a deterioration of the
situation and by its consequences would result in contradiction of the
spirit and intent of the Tripartite Pact and could make the pact illusory.[282]

Ōshima pursued this logic even further in his report of May 20,
which rested on the skewed judgment that "the war in Europe is now
developing more and more to the advantage of Germany and Italy; a
major development is to be expected in a few months":

1. There is not the least doubt that the American proposal [the Draft Understanding] is anything more than a makeshift American scheme to detach Japan from the Tripartite Pact.
2. To attempt to solve the China Incident through the good offices of the United States would give rise to serious trouble in the future.
3. Japan would have to abandon, at the moment of greatest opportunity, an invasion to the south and, even more, miss out on the prospect of conquering Singapore at any time it pleased. I believe that it is absolutely necessary [therefore, that a Japanese-American agreement at least] be firmly based on the principle of facilitating German and Italian operations against Britain, demands that the United States observe [strict] neutrality toward the European war [by suspending patrol and convoy operations], and clarifies our obligation under the Tripartite Pact to enter the war. No agreement should be concluded unless the United States accepts these conditions.[283]

Matsuoka had earlier sent Ōshima a telegram, dated May 10, which expressed his convictions regarding what Ōshima had reported here. "Whatever understanding may be reached between Japan and the United States," it stated, "we are resolved to avoid absolutely anything which might adversely affect the Tripartite Pact to even the slightest degree."[284] At the June 22 Liaison Conference, the foreign minister presented his own assessment of the situation: "America's intentions are a plot to maintain peace in the Pacific by deceiving Japan, to alienate Japan from its obligations under Article 3 of the Tripartite Pact by resolving to enter the war in Europe."[285] In a prior telegram to Ōshima on June 9 Matsuoka had expressed a judgment of Roosevelt's intentions that was right on the mark (see Appendix 3).[286] And in a conversation with Konoe on May 23 he had made his choice abundantly clear:

Leaders of the army and navy seem more or less to want to have an understanding even if that would be unfaithful to Germany and Italy. With such a timid attitude, what then? . . . In any case, [in the event of a clash between the United States and Germany on the high seas] Japan would necessarily be pressed to clarify its position for or against the Anglo-American side and the German-Italian side. In that eventuality, I, as foreign minister, shall insist that we join the latter.[287]

Moreover, Matsuoka was pessimistic about the future of his own revised draft. As Ott reported:

... He was not very hopeful about [the negotiations with the United States], as he was of the personal opinion that developments in the United States would continue to move rapidly in the direction of entrance into the war. (May 6) [288]

As responsible Foreign Minister it was incumbent upon him under the Tripartite Pact to do everything calculated to keep the United States from entering into the European war. He was willing to admit that his effort had only little chance of leading to success. In his audience with the Emperor he had estimated that chance at 30 percent. (May 14) [289]

... he regarded the prospects of Japanese-American negotiations with extreme skepticism, and counted as before on America entering the war soon. His motive in negotiating with the U.S.A. was purely to delay or prevent the United States from entering the war, if possible. ... (May 18) [290]

At the May 22 Liaison Conference Matsuoka stated, "I judge prospects for success in the negotiations to be three out of ten." [291] And after receiving Hull's counterproposal Matsuoka seems to have thrown in the towel, for he declared to the Liaison Conference on June 22, "Even if I am told to carry on with diplomacy, I think that diplomatic maneuvering with the United States is over and done with at this point." [292]

TWO

Leaning Toward War

1 The Navy Induces the Resolve to Go to War with the United States

The Shake-up in Navy Leadership

In September 1940 a shake-up in the Navy Ministry began with the appointments of Oikawa Koshirō and Toyoda Teijirō as navy minister and vice minister. It was completed, for the time being, in November with the arrival of Oka Takazumi, Takada Toshitane, and Ishikawa Shingo at their posts as chiefs of the restructured Naval Affairs Bureau and of the Bureau's First and Second Sections, respectively. The shake-up at the Navy General Staff was finally completed with the appointments of Nagano Osami as chief of staff and Fukudome Shigeru as chief of the Operations Division in April 1941, having begun inconspicuously with the posting of Tomioka Sadatoshi as chief of the Operations Section in October of 1940.

Back in the fall of 1939, following Yonai Mitsumasa's resignation as navy minister, Admiral Yamamoto Isoroku had confided to Harada Kumao that "it is absolutely essential for the sake of the nation that Admiral Yonai serve as chief of the Navy General Staff . . . into the foreseeable future. From this standpoint I want to stop as best I can any movement to have him shoulder the prime ministership. . . . The navy has produced a goodly number of admirals, but should Prince Fushimi resign, there really is only Admiral Yonai to succeed him as a chief-of-staff whom . . . one can truly rely on in terms of both character and judgment. There are people like Nagano . . . but that is out of the question."[1] About the same time, Hirata Noboru, a naval aide-de-camp to the emperor, proposed to Privy Seal Yuasa Kurahei:

> In any case it seems that a cabinet change is not far off, and I would like to leave you with one and only one request. I would like you to make anyone prime minister but Admiral Yonai. . . . He would be a

hard person for the navy to replace. He is a man we must keep as a military man [on active duty], and have him be either commander-in-chief of the Combined Fleet or chief of the Navy General Staff. It is common practice for a military man to leave active duty when he becomes prime minister. Once he leaves active duty it is extremely difficult for him to return. For the sake of the imperial navy, I must request that you please keep this firmly in mind.[2]

When he was ordered by the emperor in January 1940 to take the premiership, Yonai voluntarily resigned from active duty and, as Hirata had feared, it was difficult for him subsequently to regain that status.

Nevertheless, Yamamoto and others like him did not change their views thereafter. In late October or early November 1940 Yamamoto put it strongly to Oikawa:

Unlike pre-Tripartite Pact days, great determination is required today to make certain that we avoid the danger of going to war [with the United States]. I think that it will not be enough to change one division chief [i.e., the Operations Division chief of the Navy General Staff] or to switch the vice minister of the navy. First, the Navy General Staff. Either we make Yonai chief-of-staff or put up Yoshida [Zengo—trans.] or Koga [Mineichi] as vice chief (although neither appointment might be possible) and have Fukudome assist them. We should make Inoue [Shigeyoshi] vice minister of the navy. Without strengthening naval leadership to the point where all work together from top to bottom, we will not be effective.[3]

But Oikawa, showing his inherent disposition to avoid knotty problems, was not willing in the least to take on the kind of "grand restorative turnabout" that Yamamoto urged and took "no position one way or the other."[4] As Yamamoto added in a postscript, his entire proposal was made with the objective of making Yonai central in rebuilding the navy to the point where an attitude of no war with the United States would prevail:

Whom should we seek at the top echelons after Yoshida's setbacks? Things are apt to be very difficult unless men such as Yonai, Koga, and Inoue rise to the occasion. Even then, should it still come to war, we will have no choice but to resign ourselves to it as having been truly inevitable and to fight resolutely.[5]

In response to these assertions by Yamamoto, Prince Fushimi went so far as to say, in December 1940, that "I concur in having Yonai return to active duty and succeed me in the future."[6] Nonetheless, Oikawa moved closer to the position of preparing for rather than averting war with the United States. He turned a deaf ear to Yamamoto's ardent appeal and appointed Nagano to succeed Prince Fushimi, then temporized by selecting only one of those Yamamoto recommended, Fukudome Shigeru, to be chief of the Operations Division.

Since the conclusion of the Tripartite Pact in September 1940, and certainly once the "Outline of Policy toward French Indochina and Thailand" had been agreed upon in January 1941, Nagano saw the situation as leading to inevitable war between Japan and the United States.[7] But he lacked the intellect to make proper judgments about that situation, or even, as chief of staff, to understand his responsibility for the stands he took. Just after Fukudome was appointed to his new post in April, Nagano told him that the situation "was like a person on the verge of death: to save him, it is necessary to resort to surgery whether he lives or dies. There is no other way."[8] Nagano resigned himself to the conclusion that war with the United States was unavoidable and its outcome uncertain: "by around the end of the spring of 1941, Japanese-American relations will have become so tense that there will no longer be any prospect that anyone can put a stop to things; we are resigned to the fact that nothing more can be done."[9]

On July 31 Nagano expressed his views on the critical state of Japanese-American relations to the Throne, giving the emperor the impression of "appearing to be strongly opposed to the Tripartite Pact and to be of the opinion that so long as it existed, an adjustment in relations between Japan and the United States was impossible."[10] And in a memoir written after the war, Nagano recorded that "quite unexpectedly the Tripartite Pact was concluded," making Japanese-American relations worse.[11] But the fact of the matter is that at a conference of naval leaders held at the time the pact was concluded, Oikawa had told Yamamoto that "the Supreme War Councillors are expected [to announce] their approval of the pact via our senior colleague, Nagano."

In assisting this Nagano, moreover, Vice Chief of Staff Kondō Nobutake was content to be manipulated by his subordinates, so much so that he consistently parroted the logic of middle-echelon officers: in his March 4 talk with Ambassador Ott, for example, Kondō said, "We've got to recognize that if Japan lays its hands on Singapore or the Dutch East Indies, there is a great possibility that America will come out fighting."[12] In addition, the newly appointed Fukudome was also inclined to play the role of liaison-mediator and, as far as his subordinates were concerned, was much more pliable than his predecessor, Ugaki Matome.[13] As a result, the Navy General Staff came increasingly under the sway of middle-echelon officers, the core group at section chief meetings. Nagano himself was reduced to volunteering that "because the section chiefs are the ones most in the know, I accept their views."[14]

As for the Navy Ministry, Oikawa rejected Inoue, who had been suggested by Yamamoto, and selected, as vice minister to succeed the outgoing Toyoda, Sawamoto Yorio, who had a weak sense of self-identity. Subordinate to him was Oka Takazumi, likewise a liaison-mediator type, and with this, actual power in the Navy Ministry fell even more into the hands of the section chiefs of the Naval Affairs Bureau and, secondarily, of the Armaments Bureau.

Selling the Navy's Top Leaders on "Resolving to Go to War with the United States"

The stage was now set for the First Committee (on policy) to go into action.[15] From November 15, 1940, when the order on preparatory fleet mobilization operations stage one was issued, until May 1, 1941, the navy's preparations for war proceeded rapidly; and the more irreversible the momentum of a steady build-up became, the greater was the weight given in the Navy General Staff to the pronouncements of the First Committee, which rode that momentum. A report to the Throne on the preparatory fleet mobilization had been made on October 28, 1940, and on January 7, 1941, the emperor had authorized the navy to issue orders. Thereupon, on the basis of the fleet reorganization order of January 15, the 11th Air Task Force was formed, combining the 2nd, 3rd, and 4th Air Corps. On January 7 another report to the Throne on preparatory fleet mobilization was made. On March 31 the emperor approved the issuing of orders, and in accordance with the fleet reorganization order of April 10, the 1st Air Task Force, composed exclusively of aircraft carriers, and the 3rd Fleet were formed; both were to engage in operations to occupy the south in close cooperation with the army. On March 31 the chief of the Navy General Staff reported to the Throne that with these measures "expeditionary forces have essentially been built up to the level of mobilization for wartime called for in this fiscal year [1941], keeping aside the 5th Fleet and some other ships and air forces [for anti-Soviet operations]; we are now ready to meet any exigency [with the United States]." And this "mobilization for wartime" was so great that it would be sufficient "to maintain for the present the military forces as reorganized this time, without augmentation beyond the completion of the new construction envisaged in the revised plan for military preparations—unless the situation hereafter becomes greatly strained."

The remaining problem, he stated, was that "although it was necessary to requisition a further one million tons or so of specially outfitted warships and other vessels, that would have a severe effect on the procurement and transport of critical domestic goods; because it is possible to outfit most of the ships within three months after their requisition, as things stand now we should hold off on requisitions." [16] Augmenting preparations for war in this way, the navy had indeed come one step away from the total wartime mobilization that would occur with the huge requisition of one million tons.

At this point the First Committee urged that the "Outline of Policy toward the South," forged on April 17 as the first official agreement between the navy and the army, be put into effect. No matter what the army thought it to mean, the Outline was based on the First Committee's logic that the exercise of military force in Indochina and Thailand would lead to an embargo against Japan by the United States, which in turn would lead to Japan's conquest of the Dutch East Indies, finally resulting in Japan's resolving on war with the United States. Together with the Second Committee (on war preparations), the First Committee studied ways to put the Outline into effect for more than a month. [17] On June 5 it drafted "The Position to Be Taken by the Imperial Navy under the Present Circumstances," prepared under the signature of First Committee member Ishikawa Shingo (see Appendix 4). [18] As the chief of the Naval Affairs Bureau's Second Section, Ishikawa then obtained the approval of Naval Affairs Bureau Chief Oka, Navy Vice Minister Sawamoto, and Navy Minister Oikawa. In that document the First Committee took the basic position that as far as Japan was concerned the navy alone held the ultimate key to war or peace between Japan and the United States. And on that premise the First Committee made one study after another covering all manner of things, such as the availability of commodities, international conditions, trends within the army, general domestic trends, and cargo capacity and fuel supply should war break out. As a result, it concluded firmly, and received the approval of the top naval leadership, that the navy must immediately make clear its resolve to go to war with the United States and must guide the government—and above all the army, which had misinterpreted the "Outline of Policy toward the South" as a sign of the navy's unwillingness to go to war with the United States—in the direction of resolving on war. At the same time, it decided that Japan must embark without delay on a military advance into Thailand and French Indochina.

Attached to this draft was the notation, "separately circulated to the Navy General Staff." It is assumed that either the chief of the War Guidance Office or the chief of the Operations Section submitted a document to the same effect, along with operational studies, to Operations Division Chief Fukudome, Vice Chief of Staff Kondō, and Chief of Staff Nagano for their approval, which was obtained from all three. The leaders of the Navy General Staff could never have approved this conclusion by the First Committee unless they were confident of success in a war with the United States, that being the key factor in any such decision. However, it is impossible to know what was specifically said or written on the matter, because neither the Navy General Staff position papers nor its "Assessment of the Operational Situation," which suggested that Japan could wage war against the United States, are available for study.[19] But by April 1941, when Fukudome became chief of the Operations Division, the Navy General Staff section chiefs conference had already swung over to war, and Tomioka had impressed upon Fukudome that "the prospects of winning are good enough; let's make up our minds to join battle now."[20] This general trend was also confirmed by "A Study of War," the product of a study group set up by the section chiefs conference at the time of Tomioka's arrival at his post in October 1940, which had concluded its work in March 1941. That study had determined that if Japan quickly occupied the south, it could somehow carry on a war with the United States for about two or three years.[21] The study group itself had served as a sort of operations subcommittee of the First Committee.

Ishikawa praised "A Study of War" as a document that would contribute to "unifying the thinking of concerned staff and at the same time set the standard for handling the current situation." Since the navy had already set out on the road to full-scale mobilization for war with the United States, a sort of "charter" to unify the thinking among the navy's middle-echelon officers and above was considered indispensable before anything could be done. But this was not the sole objective of the study. The study group also desired that officers make up their minds quickly about whether or not to go to war with the United States, lest they blunder when an emergency arose, because if the logistics of fleet mobilization were out of phase and did not move forward as expected on the budgetary and matériel fronts, plans simply could not be carried out. In short, no action could be taken unless the top leaders were resolved to go to war with the United States. Of even greater import, middle-echelon officers had goaded the top leaders for a decision and had obtained their written agreement that the navy at least was resolved on going to war with the United States. From the standpoint of the middle-echelon officers, they had in any case succeeded in obtaining a decision from the navy's leaders that would allow them to proceed with logistical mobilization, regardless of whether the leadership's agreement to resolving on war was literally acted upon thereafter.[22] With this major accomplishment the work of the First Committee was virtually over.

The administrative results of this were first seen in July, when October 15 was set as the date for completing phase one preparations in preparatory fleet mobilization operations stage two, which had been scheduled for activation after war started. As previously noted, preparatory fleet mobilization operations stage one had begun on November 15, 1940, but they had not progressed as anticipated because of problems related to matériel production facilities, labor power, and transport capabilities. The July decision actually eliminated the distinction between the first and second stages, and preparations were to be undertaken as necessity and time demanded. This meant accelerating preparations for war, such as preparing for battle, immediately completing that construction not yet finished but necessary before the first units went into action, beginning the construction of warships and other vessels designated for rush wartime construction, and requisitioning a massive 784,000 tons of specially outfitted warships and other vessels needed for use by the expeditionary forces.

On July 18 Oikawa submitted the following conditions that would have to be met if he were to continue on in the third Konoe cabinet: 1) firm adherence to the "Outline of National Policies in View of the Changing Situation" adopted by the Imperial Conference of July 2; 2) completion of the basic preparations for war against Britain and the United States required to achieve those national policies; and 3) a promise that the new cabinet would put even greater emphasis on completing those preparations, above all on the completion of naval war preparations.[23] All these conditions were for the purpose of guaranteeing the completion of preparatory fleet mobilization operations stage two.

Yamamoto Is Enraged

In putting together "A Study of War," Ishikawa argued from the large perspective that the only way out of the dire situation in which Japan found itself was to make clear its resolve to go to war with the United States and to advance by force of arms into Thailand and

Indochina without delay.[24] In contrast, Ōno was of the opinion that prompt action was necessary only with respect to measures needed to place Japan in an impregnable position, without regard for international developments; if this created a risk of war with the United States, so be it.[25] Tomioka knew that the United States was unlikely to acquiesce in a Japanese military advance into Thailand and French Indochina, and that it might come to war if things went badly; but he was convinced that Japan had to muster up its courage and take the risk.[26] Thus two members of the Navy General Staff went beyond making clear Japan's resolve to go to war and supported an immediate advance by military force into Thailand and French Indochina, fully affirming the preordained logic that this would result in an American embargo, which in turn would lead to Japan's readiness to go to war with the United States.

Nagano, as always taking in everything proposed by the section chiefs, fell in line and immediately declared that even if a military advance into French Indochina did by chance lead to war with the United States, that couldn't be helped—what was bound to happen was bound to happen.[27] Breaking with his usual practice since taking office of giving approval without comment, Nagano asked a member of the War Guidance Office who came seeking his approval to send troops into southern Indochina, "Who participated in this study? This means war [with the United States]"—and then approved it.[28] A year or so after the war had begun, Nagano reminisced to Reserve Admiral Kobayashi Seizō: "We sent troops into French Indochina with the resolve to fight [the United States]; of course, that was done in light of the attitude of the United States [referring to embargoes against Japan and other measures]."[29]

When the advance into southern Indochina was brought up at the Liaison Conferences of June 11 and 12, Matsuoka was opposed: "If you go ahead with this, it will lead to a clash with Britain and the United States—is that all right with the high command?" And when Army Chief of Staff Sugiyama remained silent, Nagano spoke up: "Then we will fight; we will strike [Britain and the United States] decisively."[30] Nagano spoke so forcefully that Sugiyama was baffled about what he really had in mind. Quite possibly, the mood of the entire Navy General Staff, from Nagano on down, had already been reflected in a broadcast made on May 27 by Hiraide Hideo, chief of the First Section, Navy General Staff Intelligence:

Should economic pressure by a group of hostile nations violate our right to exist, the Empire will naturally have to rise up in self-defense.

> . . . Our navy's preparedness has reached a level unprecedented in our
> nation's history. . . . Should any nation be so heedless as to provoke us,
> our navy is ready to smash it with one blow. We have more than 500
> warships and nearly 4000 airplanes.

In fact, Hiraide had made the broadcast without consulting his superiors; he had discussed it with his friend Tomioka and both thought
it would be all right to make such a speech.

In November 1940 Admiral Yamamoto, seeing that the Navy General Staff was reluctant to do so, went ahead on his own authority and
conducted a wargame on operations against the Dutch East Indies.
Part of his objective was "to suggest through this exercise how truly
insufficient matériel mobilization and military strength were for this
(i.e., how possible it was to bring it off), and to give key officers . . . at
the center a true understanding on this."[31] Yamamoto's views were
shared by Naval Aviation Chief Inoue, who judged that troops certainly could not be sent into southern Indochina unless Japan were
prepared for war with the United States. When Vice Minister Sawamoto reported at an information session for bureau and division
chiefs on July 4, 1941, that the southern advance had already been
finalized as national policy, Inoue was indignant that a decision of
such magnitude as war or peace with the United States had been
decided so off-handedly. He argued vehemently that "the air force is
simply not prepared for war; I cannot take the responsibility [for air
force readiness] if war breaks out between Japan and the United
States."[32] In place of the silent Oikawa, Sawamoto merely reiterated
that "the decision has been made, so there's nothing we can do about
it; we will take care from now on."

Several days later, at a briefing session for fleet commanders on
Oikawa's decision to send troops into southern Indochina, 2nd Fleet
Commander Koga Mineichi responded sharply: "How could he make
a decision on such a grave matter so lightly and arbitrarily, without
even hearing out the fleet commanders? If it does come to war we
can't win simply because we're told to do so. What the hell does the
Navy General Staff think about this decision?" Yamamoto was en-
raged when Nagano took refuge from Koga's criticism in a lie: "Since
this was the government's decision, we really have no choice, do
we?"[33] Like Yamamoto and Inoue, Nagano and Oikawa had been
well aware of the logical sequence that sending troops into southern
French Indochina would provoke the United States into declaring a
total embargo against Japan, which would thereupon resolve to go to
war with the United States. But whereas Yamamoto and Inoue de-

cided to do all they could to prevent that logical sequence from happening, to exhaust every means to turn what was already a bad situation around, Nagano and Oikawa took the position that such a sequence was inevitable and watched from the sidelines as events unfolded, ambiguous as always about Japan's chances of success.

The analysis of the British-German war situation in "A Study of War" was likely the product of mutual discussion among members of the Navy General Staff. Their assessment might have been influenced in part by Ambassador Ōshima's telegram of April 16, which began with the statement that "I respectfully submit the following opinion as the result of consultations with Vice Admiral Nomura [Naokuni] and the army and navy attachés":

> As I have reported in successive telegrams, it is evident that Germany has completed all preparations for submarine and air warfare, as well as for landing operations, in the assault on Britain. This has been confirmed by a navy observation team led by Vice Admiral Nomura, which has personally inspected these German facilities on the western front. Seen impartially, it is reasonable to conclude that a German attack on Britain, even taking into consideration American aid to Britain, will end in success for Germany.[34]

On this point the senior Nomura had reported from Washington the day before a more straightforward observation that took in the larger picture:

> Should Japan participate in the war, the Japanese navy would bear the great responsibility of having to take on the combined naval forces of the United States and Britain almost singlehandedly. And this fact will not be altered in the slightest by German-Italian ascendancy over the continent or by how things progress in the battle of the Atlantic.[35]

Let us now pause for a moment and take an overview of developments in the battle of the Atlantic. In preparation for German landing operations, Britain had diverted to anti-invasion patrols large numbers of naval vessels that hitherto had been used for patrolling against German submarines. Considerably greater effort was also put into patrolling waters where German submarines lay in wait than into convoying. Slow escort vessels not yet equipped with sonar and radar, moreover, were of no use against "wolf pack" operations by German submarines that at night attacked convoys on the surface in the manner of torpedo boats. As a result, German submarine operations up until the end of 1940 had been very successful. In October Britain lost 103 ships totaling 443,000 tons, two-thirds of which was attributable to German submarine operations. If sinkings continued at this rate, it was clear that Britain's supply lines on the high seas would be severed. But at the start of 1941 Britain's convoy capabilities increased greatly as the result of the 50 destroyers and newly completed escort vessels of various kinds acquired in the destroyers-for-bases deal with the United States. At the same time, Germany had neglected submarine construction and could not replace the 31 submarines it had lost since war broke out; by the end of 1940 the number of submarines in actual operation had been reduced to a low of 22 boats. With the steady improvement in Britain's convoy organization and training, and the solid cooperation between its navy and air forces, the war to destroy Britain's commerce in the Atlantic began to ease up somewhat from the beginning of 1941.[36]

It has already been noted that on September 14, 1940, Hitler had ordered the cancellation of the planned invasion of Britain. When that decision is taken into consideration, the absence of strategic judgment on the part of the Navy General Staff becomes even more pronounced. Yet the First Committee's "A Study of War" still took as its "premise" that "the invasion of Britain will be entirely successful" and that German ascendancy in the war to destroy commerce in the Atlantic would continue. From the standpoint of strategic judgment, therefore, "A Study of War," in basing its position on such mistaken judgments, built a castle of sand.

The Army Too Will Not Flinch from War with the United States

The Military Affairs Bureau of the Army Ministry came to virtually the same judgment as the navy's First Committee on the issue of advancing into French Indochina, then into Thailand, and finally into the Dutch East Indies. The bureau became concerned about the need to include the south in Japan's resource sphere, by military conquest if necessary, when, in addition to the difficulties encountered in Japan's economic agreement with Indochina and the deadlock in Japan's negotiations with the Dutch East Indies, it added into the equation movements toward the encirclement of Japan. These included the military conference held among Britain, the United States, and the Netherlands at Singapore on April 21–27, as well as the further intensification of economic pressure against Japan by the United States. However, on the basis of the navy's assessment of the

British-German war situation, the bureau calculated that Britain might surrender to Germany at any moment and was acutely aware that that moment would be precisely the golden opportunity, spelled out in the previous year's "Main Principles for Coping with the Changing World Situation," for Japan to rush out and seize Singapore. Finally, the bureau became strongly convinced of the need to transfer the necessary army bases from northern to southern Indochina. On May 1, therefore, Military Affairs Section Chief Satō Kenryō indicated to his section: "This won't do. We'll really be bottled up. Draft a plan with the idea of putting our troops into southern French Indochina."[37] Satō had not given up all hope on the Draft Understanding, but it was his judgment that it would be dangerous to hold off from creating a self-sufficiency zone in commodities merely out of fear of offending the United States.[38] In contradiction to Ambassador Nomura's cabled report that "the Empire's not resorting to force of arms in moving southward is the basis of the entire Draft Understanding," Satō believed that the negotiations with the United States could be made compatible with a southern advance by force of arms, and he resolved to push both lines simultaneously.

Once its draft plan was completed, the Military Affairs Section began negotiations with the War Guidance Office of the Army General Staff on May 6. Although the Operations Section had of course concurred, the War Guidance Office was, however, opposed. Vice Chief of Staff Tsukada Osamu also opposed the draft plan on the grounds that its objectives in employing troops were not precise. On May 15 the War Guidance Office put forward its own revised draft on setting up military bases in the south and began talks with the Second Section of the Naval Affairs Bureau and with the Navy General Staff's War Guidance Office. On June 2 the two service ministries and both general staffs came to the tentative agreement that military bases should be set up in southern French Indochina and Thailand, that the army and navy should present the matter directly to a Liaison Conference, and that a confidential understanding should be sought with Foreign Minister Matsuoka beforehand.

Immediately upon his return from Europe, Konoe told Tōjō on April 25, Matsuoka had "insisted on the conquest of Singapore at all costs."[39] The foreign minister, however, indicated his strong disapproval, as he had done before, of the idea of military agreements with Thailand and French Indochina for the establishment of bases. On June 5, in the face of efforts by Mutō and Oka to win him over, Matsuoka rejected the idea out of hand: "I won't budge on the issue of these military agreements unless there is a plan to conquer Singapore" based on the resolve to go to war with Britain and the United States. Instead he countered with the argument that:

> Thailand and French Indochina will immediately report to Britain and the United States. Britain and the United States will then take the initiative from us. Once we determine to go ahead, I will strike a bargain in three days. Twice up to now I have asked whether the high command was resolved to do this, whether this was all right with the military, but there has been no reply.[40]

Cornered, Mutō returned to his office. He abandoned the agreed upon plan for setting up bases and went back to the original Satō plan, directing that "a thorough-going plan be drawn up that will have troops being stationed in southern Indochina; with that we'll get [Matsuoka] out of the way."[41] And he also ordered that a rationale for the proposal be drafted for the Liaison Conference. The task was undertaken by the Military Affairs Section in collaboration with the War Guidance Office. Primarily as a measure to win Matsuoka over, a draft was produced that took into account Matsuoka's counterargument by including the sentence: "If, as a result of the military agreements, Britain and the United States should by any chance rise up, Japan shall resolutely launch an assault on Singapore."[42] Although the army would sound out the navy about all this on June 10, it had hereby taken the first step toward coming out with the rhetoric of "will not flinch from war with the United States." In using the term "war against the United States" in policy statements, even as a figure of speech, it appears that the process of turning state policy-making into literary exercises had hit rock bottom. Unwittingly, Mutō and his colleagues were playing around with war against the United States. And viewing the navy in the same light as they viewed themselves, they may well have thought that the navy too was taking a rhetorical stance on war with the United States.

However, the army's War Guidance Office still interpreted the "Outline of Policy toward the South," which had just been generally agreed to by the two services on April 17, simply as the product of the navy's concern for itself vis-à-vis the United States and of its wariness about an advance to the south by military force. It was skeptical about the navy's reactions, telling Satō, Army General Staff Operations Section Chief Doi Akira, and others that if that Outline "can be changed, and if it is possible to get the navy to change its position, let's try to get the navy to do so."[43] So, unexpectedly for the

army, but only naturally in light of the First Committee's position
paper of June 5, the naval officers in charge readily agreed on June
10 to the army's rhetoric with regard to sending troops into southern
French Indochina: "We will not flinch from war with Britain and the
United States if they counterattack." Furthermore, the navy's key
leaders seconded this on the afternoon of the 11th by merely polishing it to read: "We will not flinch from taking the risk."[44] But this
agreement on the part of the navy was not mere rhetoric. At the
Liaison Conference held immediately after this Nagano spoke so
forcefully against Matsuoka's opposition that Sugiyama was baffled,
as noted above. Because of Sugiyama's hesitation on the matter,
the Liaison Conference adjourned, deferring its decision until the
following day. At the Liaison Conference on the 12th Nagano spoke
as forcefully as before, so that an actual decision was reached on the
policy of moving south, to which were attached three stipulations
based on Matsuoka's objections.

The army's War Guidance Office stood by its observation that
"the navy's use of military force against southern French Indochina
depends on whether it is resolved on war with Britain and the United
States. After hesitating and hesitating up until now, the navy has
finally gotten off its backside. But it is still not clear whether or not it
has resolved to go to war with Britain and the United States. The
same goes for the army."[45] Ever since the conference of army and
navy bureau and division chiefs on June 10, the first held since
receipt of the telegram reporting the certainty of war breaking out
between Germany and the Soviet Union, counterplans for that war
actually began to impinge upon the argument for sending troops into
southern French Indochina, and the argument in favor of advancing
north continued to gain strength within the Army General Staff. To
fend off concrete preparations for a northern advance, the navy
became even more insistent that Japan go in the direction indicated
by its First Committee's position paper. And in fact Mutō's argument
for sending troops into southern French Indochina was, so to speak,
just the right bandwagon to jump on.

The Fragility of the Army's Southern
Advance Argument

On the basis of the June 12 Liaison Conference decision, the cabinet
and officials concerned from the navy, army, and Foreign Ministry
agreed on the 14th to draft a memorial to the emperor. When the
draft was shown to Matsuoka, he would not endorse it, claiming that

it differed from what had been agreed to. From the 16th to the 22nd Oka on behalf of the navy, now working closely with the army's Mutō, shuffled the rhetoric of the draft around in continuous parleys with Matsuoka, finally getting Matsuoka to agree to the deletion of the June 12 "stipulations."

From the 11th on Nagano had assumed de facto leadership at liaison conferences. Consequently, in bringing about a formal decision at the June 25 Liaison Conference it was the navy, rather than the army, that played the chief role. That decision was precisely what the conclusion of the First Committee's study had asked for. It was the army that had proposed that article 3 in the original army-navy draft be included in the "Measures for Advancing the Southern Policy" that were formally approved on the 25th: "Should Britain, the United States, and the Netherlands interfere with the execution of this policy and, there being no way to overcome this, make it unbearable for Japan in terms of its self-preservation and self-defense, Japan shall not flinch from risking war with Britain and the United States." For the army this was nothing but rhetoric to win Matsuoka over. However, Oikawa, Nagano, Oka, Fukudome, and their colleagues, who had all approved the First Committee's position paper, had added the phrase "shall not flinch from risking" out of their fundamental strategy that it was "necessary to induce" the army "in the direction of resolving on war against the United States." But in doing so they were expressing their genuine and vigorous approval. The army's resolve to go to war with the United States, which it had toyed with rhetorically to win Matsuoka over, was thereby thrown back in its face by the navy as a genuine decision. On the 11th the army and navy had reached formal agreement on this modification. Although article 3 was subsequently deleted from the formally approved text because of Matsuoka's persistent opposition, by bringing it up the army, as far as the navy was concerned, had nonetheless put itself in the position of being formally bound to resolve on war with the United States. Right after the June 11 meeting, for example, Operations Division Chief Tanaka Shin'ichi pointed out that "the proposition that we are resolved on war with the United States" had become "widespread," and Operations Section Chief Doi Akio confided on the 15th that "if the situation compels us, we are prepared even to take on Britain and the United States." And it appears that Sugiyama responded to a query at the meeting of the Supreme War Councillors on June 30 that "if Britain and the United States challenge us, [war] will be unavoidable."[46]

Ever since it had embraced the draft of the "Main Principles for Coping with the Changing World Situation" in June of 1940, the army had exerted its utmost efforts to limit its antagonists to Britain and the Netherlands, or to Britain alone, should war result from the exercise of military force in the south. It later arrived at the judgment that Britain and the Netherlands were inseparable, but even then it still could not break free from the idea that military force could be exercised in the south on the principle that a war would at all times be limited to Britain and the Netherlands and that at least the United States would keep out. It was thus that the army arrived at the 1941 "Outline of Policy toward the South."

In the process, however, the army never came up with a clear and thorough-going grasp of its own position regarding the relationship between Britain and the United States when it came to military operations in the south. It did not adhere to the principle of separating the two countries so firmly and consistently that it would absolutely refuse to agree to military operations on any other terms, so that if the navy asserted that military operations in the south could not be separated from war with the United States, then the army would simply call off those operations altogether. This is indicated in various phrases that appear in the army's original draft, such as that Japan "will endeavor *to the utmost* to limit hostilities to Britain and Britain alone," or that Japan "will carry out this policy, *striving to* avoid war with the United States" (author's emphasis). In short, the army's position was ambiguous: it *wanted in so far as possible* to limit hostilities to Britain, *to pull it off somehow* without getting involved in a war with the United States. The army did not reject the use of military force in the south, but it did not want war with the United States either. Thus, it was the army's view that Japan should move steadily ahead with the exercise of military force in the south, while from time to time patching up relations with the United States through such devices as the Japanese-American Draft Understanding. It was a point of view that looked at the Anglo-American relationship with unfounded optimism—self-indulgently, one-sidedly, focused all but exclusively on what was convenient for the army. Another reason for the army's adherence to this point of view from the spring of 1940 into the spring of 1941 may very well have been that, having failed to come to a balanced assessment of the war situation in Europe, it was still dreaming about profiting from Germany's military achievements. With regard to U.S. policy directions too there was a pronounced tendency toward over-optimism, deriving from speculation that German threats and pressure would ultimately *somehow* control this for them, much like pinning all their hopes on the power of almighty Buddha.

To summarize, a fundamental ambiguity and fragility lay hidden behind the army's opportunistic policy, consistently maintained since the summer of 1940, that military force should be exercised in the south. Since that same summer the middle echelons of the navy had been equally consistent in strictly adhering to the proposition that Britain and the United States were inseparable and that the exercise of military force in the south would mean war with the United States. On that basis they had pressed for formal alignment with the army on June 11, borrowing the phrase "will not flinch from risking war with Britain and the United States." Rather than calling off the exercise of military force in the south, however, the army simply switched suddenly to the point of view that if the navy thought that way, then it would be perfectly all right to go to war with the United States. Unable to maintain a consistent position on the inseparability of Britain and the United States, the army did not have the backbone to oppose stoutly the navy's position and caved in without offering any perceptible resistance.

As the result of weakness and opportunism, therefore, the army now moved toward resolving on war with the United States. But the prime mover in this was surely the navy, above all its First Committee. When the emperor's chief aide-de-camp, Hasunuma Shigeru, contacted the Army General Staff on June 13, he expressed unease and misgiving about why the navy had suddenly become so obdurate. On October 20 this same Hasunuma told the new navy minister, Shimada Shigetarō, that back in June, although both the army and navy had agreed on a policy of no war with the United States, the navy had changed its position overnight because of the opposition of a certain section chief in the Navy Ministry, and that the palace thought the present situation had been brought about by the navy. These comments are indicative of just how astute the palace's observations were.[47]

2 Preparing for War with the United States and the Soviet Union

The Army Is Flustered by Reports That War Will Break out Between Germany and the Soviet Union

Soon after his arrival in Germany at the start of February 1941, Ambassador Ōshima became aware of the serious deterioration in relations between Germany and the Soviet Union, which he reported to Matsuoka when the foreign minister arrived in Berlin on March

26. Because Matsuoka paid no heed, Ōshima sent word to army headquarters via Colonel Nagai Yatsuji, who had accompanied Matsuoka, that "Germany's attitude toward the Soviet Union has worsened and Germany now appears to be resolved on war with the Soviet Union, but please keep the fact that German-Soviet relations are not good strictly confidential." Nagai's message was received with a mixture of credence and doubt and left at that. Then, on April 16, about ten days after Matsuoka had started home, Ōshima reported on the results of his talks with Hitler (March 18), Ribbentrop (April 10), and Stahmer (April 14):

> ... when I met with Foreign Minister Ribbentrop. ... he said that, depending on what moves the Soviet Union makes, Germany might well go to war against the Soviet Union—this year even. ... It is common knowledge in Europe that Churchill has recently been extremely active in trying to enlist the Soviet Union into his camp. The same goes for the United States. ... He replied that consequently there is the thought that, depending on the circumstances, it would be to Germany's advantage to crush the Soviet Union beforehand while it is unprepared. ... [In light of what Hitler, Foreign Minister Ribbentrop, and Stahmer have said] it is considered quite probable that Germany will [attack the Soviet Union] in parallel with an attack on Britain. ... I ask that this telegram go no further than the prime minister, the army and navy ministers, and the chiefs of the general staffs. I ask in particular that you convey to these people my hope that they make every effort to keep this telegram confidential.[48]

Toward the end of April several telegrams were also received from Sakanishi Kazuyoshi, a military attaché stationed in Germany, reporting signs of imminent war between Germany and the Soviet Union, but this only made Mutō angry that Sakanishi was being carried away by German bluster.[49] On May 13th, however, Sakanishi reported, on the basis of information obtained from German Army Intelligence Division Chief Gerhard Matzky: "Relations between Germany and Soviet Union critical. Advisable Yamashita army investigation team return Japan immediately."[50] Even the army was finally compelled to think that the outbreak of war between Germany and the Soviet Union was quite conceivable. Both the Army Ministry's Military Affairs Section and the Army General Staff's War Guidance Office set to work that same day on drafting proposals on the position the army should take in such an eventuality. Even so, the string of telegrams received from Ōshima on the 5th and 6th of June came as something of a bolt from the blue for the army:

> Both Hitler and Ribbentrop reported that war between Germany and
> the Soviet Union was probably unavoidable. (Dispatch of June 4)

> The gist of what Foreign Minister Ribbentrop told me is as follows:
> Relations between Germany and the Soviet Union have become partic-
> ularly bad as of late and the possibility of war has increased im-
> mensely. . . . (Dispatch of June 5)

> The impressions I got as the result of talks with Hitler and Ribbentrop
> on the 3rd and 4th of June are as follows: (1) . . . war between Germany
> and the Soviet Union should now be seen as inevitable; (2) as for the
> timing on going to war . . . it is to be inferred that Germany will act
> decisively on this within a short time. (Dispatch of June 5)[51]

On June 5 and June 6 the leading officers of the Army Ministry and
General Staff met repeatedly to debate countermeasures drafted by
the War Guidance Office, but the debates were so agitated that virtually nothing could be settled. On the 7th a meeting of Army General
Staff division chiefs was held, with Sugiyama and Operations Division
Chief Tanaka absent. A general consensus was reached on three
points of principle: (1) the Axis alliance is to be the keynote of policy;
(2) strategic deployments to the north and south are to be promptly
completed to enable Japan to respond to any kind of situation that
might arise; and (3) preparations are to be made even though we are
unable to decide which direction to attack, north or south. As before,
however, they found it hard to come up with concrete plans. What
then after this? Do nothing? Do something? If something, the north
first or the south?[52]

No further progress was made at the conference of division chiefs,
convened at noon on the 8th, that greeted Sugiyama on his return to
Tokyo. An all-day discussion among Mutō, Satō, Sanada, and their
colleagues at the Military Affairs Bureau on the 8th also concluded
that, should war come about between Germany and the Soviet Union,
it would most likely become protracted like the Sino-Japanese War.
They informally decided to:

1. Watch how the situation develops for the time being. *If an extremely
   advantageous situation emerges* as the war progresses between Germany and the Soviet Union, dispose of the Soviet Far Eastern
   Army in one blow by the exercise of military force and solve the
   long-standing northern problem.
2. *If German victory becomes certain* once it has turned its sword on Britain after having cut down the Soviet Union, carry out an armed ad-

vance into such areas of the south as are necessary beyond southern French Indochina and bring them within our sphere of influence.[53] (Author's emphasis)

On the 9th Mutō reported their decision to Tōjō and, having obtained Tōjō's overall approval, began discussions with Tanaka.

In its opportunistic posture, Mutō's proposal was a direct extension of the ideas contained in the previous summer's "Main Principles for Coping with the Changing World Situation." Its wait-and-see directionlessness, leaving the decision to go north or south completely up to future developments in the European situation, was proof of its opportunism. How could Japan hold fast to a policy predicated on the emergence of "extremely advantageous" conditions for itself? What on earth would Japan do if extremely advantageous conditions did not come about? What if, as was very likely, conditions unfavorable to Japan should come about? That Mutō put aside any serious investigation into these questions was indicative of the self-indulgent optimism to which the army had clung ever since the "Main Principles" were adopted. Nor, as members of the War Guidance Office pointed out on June 9, did the Mutō proposal take into the slightest account the fact that the "Outline of Policy toward the South," agreed upon between the army and the navy on April 17, had limited the contemplated southern advance to Thailand and French Indochina. Sugiyama, however, was of no mind to be clear and precise at the conference of Army General Staff division chiefs convened on the 9th. Influenced by the forceful views of Tanaka, who had returned to Tokyo that day, the conference decided to exercise military force to the north. And when Tanaka insisted further that Japan "should exercise military force by seizing an opportune time of its own making," not waiting to take advantage of an opportune time to present itself,[54] he carried the argument on this as well.

The Army Ministry, however, stuck to the Mutō plan, by which Japan would essentially wait for the persimmon to ripen until the right moment to pick it and go no further in the interim than to keep a watchful eye on the north. On June 13 the ministry agreed that the words "of its own making" should be deleted from the phrase "seizing an opportune time of its own making," and based on such semantics a compromise was reached between the Army Ministry and General Staff the following day. But this did not eliminate the actual disunity between them regarding the attitude Japan should adopt in the event of German victory.

On the 18th an urgent telegram was received from Ōshima:

Ribbentrop replied that "although I am not in fact authorized to speak to your very sensitive question [about when Germany would go to war], if it is necessary for Japan to prepare itself then it would be desirable that preparations be made within two weeks at the latest." (Dispatch of June 17).[55]

Now no one could doubt that there would be war between Germany and the Soviet Union.

The Substance of "Resolving on War Against the United States"

By contrast, the Navy Ministry quickly decided on its policy (June 7) when Ōshima's telegrams were received on June 5 and 6:

Measures for Dealing with the New German-Soviet Situation

1. The Empire will not intervene in the new German-Soviet situation but will keep close watch for the time being while making ready to respond to changing circumstances.
2. Our military strength both on land and at sea vis-à-vis the Soviet Union shall be maintained largely at the current level, with the exception of reinforcing certain units.

. . .

4. Military preparations both on land and at sea shall be completed in readiness for a challenge by Britain and the United States.

. . .

8. Japan will move immediately to implement the following measures vis-à-vis Thailand and French Indochina:

    1. Accelerate carrying out the "Outline of Policy toward French Indochina and Thailand";
    2. Augment forces in French Indochina as conditions permit, particularly in order to bolster operations against China.
9. Measures to be taken once military moves vis-à-vis Thailand and French Indochina have been implemented shall be determined as the situation develops.[56]

This decision was made two days after the First Committee had presented its study. Five days later, the Navy Ministry and General

Staff reached a tentative compromise with the army on the matter of setting up military bases in southern French Indochina and Thailand.

Immediately after war broke out between Germany and the Soviet Union, a Naval Affairs Bureau officer pleaded with Nagano not to let the navy be drawn into the war by the army. Nagano retorted: "You're telling me. We're on the verge of war with the United States!"[57] Standing on its basic policy of "inducing" the army "in the direction of resolving on war with the United States," the navy's consistent position throughout the remainder of June was to exert every effort to curb schemes for war against the Soviet Union that would compete with accelerating a military advance into Thailand and French Indochina and war with the United States.

At the conference of army and navy bureau and division chiefs on June 10 the navy's intentions were still not clear to the Army General Staff. Its counterproposal of June 20 to the army's draft proposal of June 14, however, made clear the navy's insistence that military preparations be focused on the United States:

1. When to exercise military force depends on conditions at the time [such as the state of American embargoes against Japan]; taking advantage of an opportune time is to be rejected.
2. Military preparations for advancing south shall be completed, but military preparations for advancing north [against the Soviet Union] shall be kept at the present level.[58]

The second proposition was clearly an expression of the navy's resolve to go to war with the United States. On June 11 the navy had already given its genuine approval to the army's rhetorical pledge that it would not "flinch from war with the United States," and it now demanded that the army honor that pledge.

The conference of army and navy bureau and division chiefs on the afternoon of June 23 finally wore to a conclusion after four hours. The main points in the bargain struck between the two services were:

1. Although the navy tried to impose limits on a military solution in the north by attaching various conditions, the army draft was finally accepted.
2. The navy, however, was greatly worried that the army would pull out of the south if a military solution in the north were undertaken. It therefore attached one condition, that "no obstacles shall be placed in the way of maintaining basic readiness for war with

Britain and the United States in the south." The army concurred completely on this; there was no need to stipulate this one particular condition but for the navy's distrust of the army.[59]

Each service secured the agreement of its leaders to this compromise, leaving unresolved the latent discrepancy that in effect the navy emphasized preparations against Britain and the United States while the army emphasized preparations against the north. Thereafter it was merely a matter of moving ahead with administrative routines. A few revisions were made at the conference of army and navy bureau and division chiefs on the 27th. Then Mutō and Oka talked with Matsuoka on the 28th and made further revisions. The resulting draft was approved by the Liaison Conference held that same day. Finally it was swallowed whole, with no changes, at the July 2 Imperial Conference, producing the following "Outline of National Policies in View of the Changing Situation":[60]

PART I. POLICY

1. Regardless of what changes may occur in the world situation, the Empire shall firmly adhere to the policy of building a Greater East Asia Coprosperity Sphere, thereby contributing to the firm establishment of world peace.

2. In order to press forward on resolving the China Incident and in order to establish a firm foundation for self-preservation and self-defense, the Empire shall take steps to advance southward and shall solve the northern problem as changing circumstances permit.

3. The Empire shall remove all obstacles in the way of achieving these objectives.

PART II. PROSPECTUS

1. We shall increase pressure from the southern region in order to accelerate the submission of the Chiang regime.

   As changing circumstances permit, and at an appropriate time, we shall exercise our right of belligerency against the Chungking regime and also seize hostile foreign settlements.

2. The Empire shall continue diplomatic negotiations and promote various other necessary measures with regard to those regions in the south important for self-preservation and self-defense.

   For this purpose we shall make ready for war with Britain and the United States. We shall first carry to a successful conclusion our policies toward French Indochina and Thailand as set forth in the "Outline of Policy toward French Indochina and Thailand" and "Measures for Advancing the Southern Policy," thereby strengthening arrangements for a southern advance.

The Empire shall not flinch from war with Britain and the United States in order to achieve these objectives.

3. Though the attitude we take is to be founded on the spirit of the Tripartite Axis, we shall not intervene for the present in the war between Germany and the Soviet Union. We shall make military preparations in secret against the Soviet Union and deal with the situation on an independent basis. In the meantime, we shall carry on diplomatic negotiations, always in careful readiness for that eventuality.

Should the war between Germany and the Soviet Union develop in a direction advantageous to the Empire, we shall solve the northern problem and ensure stability in the north by exercising military force.

4. In carrying out 3 above, no great obstacles shall be placed in the way of maintaining basic readiness for war with Britain and the United States when it comes to deciding what measures are to be taken, particularly in deciding to exercise military force.

5. In keeping with national policy, we shall strive to the utmost through diplomatic measures and other means to prevent the United States from entering the war, but in the event that the United States should enter the war, the Empire shall act on the basis of the Tripartite Pact. The Empire shall, however, decide independently as to when and how military force is to be exercised.

6. We shall proceed immediately to a thorough strengthening of our domestic wartime organization, endeavoring in particular to strengthen the defenses of the homeland.

7. Concrete measures shall be drawn up separately.

Item (2) in Part II of the "Outline" expressly confirmed the "Measures for Advancing the Southern Policy" adopted at the June 25 Liaison Conference, doing no more than to dress them up as comprehensive state policy. The focus throughout the "Outline" was on balancing a solution to the northern problem with the promotion of a southern advance. Out of opportunism, Mutō and his colleagues strove to prevent Japan from going to war with the Soviet Union in a premature response to the war between Germany and the Soviet Union, while limiting the southern advance to Thailand and French Indochina until that future time when it would be expedient to go farther. The Army General Staff's War Guidance Office thought it prudent to leave the question of a northern or southern advance undecided for the time being and to continue to make preparations without resolving on war. Thus, the Army Ministry and General Staff were unable to arrive at an agreement to go south or north, or go to war against the Soviet Union immediately or wait for an opportune moment to arrive. The navy was, of course, single-minded in its resolve to go to war with the United States. And Matsuoka, as we shall discuss presently, was bent solely on immediate war with the Soviet Union. Under such circumstances the "Outline" did nothing more than establish a compromise among these views that was based on pure semantics. Consequently, although it was a momentous state policy to the effect that Japan would "not flinch from war with the United States," this decision had been inherently ambiguous from the start and was subject to whatever interpretation the parties to it wished to make.

Although the controversial phrase "will not flinch" had once been deleted from the "Measures for Advancing the Southern Policy" because of Matsuoka's objections, it was reintroduced into the "Outline" with the positive approval of the navy, but as an expression of rhetorical resolve on the part of the army, which was still trying to throttle Matsuoka's opposition. This phrase, to which both the army and the navy had agreed on June 11, now became national policy; therewith, Japan as a nation—not just the navy, not just the army—unquestionably set forth on a course toward war with the United States. But the decision had by no means been reached on the basis of a definite and conclusive unity of purpose or a scrupulous and painstaking investigation.

At the Imperial Conference of July 2 Privy Council President Hara Yoshimichi asserted openly:

> I consider war with Britain and the United States, mentioned in item 2 of the Prospectus, a very serious issue. . . . The Empire does not desire to start a war with Britain and the United States while at war with the Soviet Union. . . . If we take action against French Indochina, I think there will be war with Britain and the United States; what do you think? . . . The question to which I would like a clear answer is whether or not the United States will enter the war if Japan goes into French Indochina. . . . I would like to avoid a collision with Britain and the United States insofar as possible. . . . I believe that in this instance at least Japan on its part should avoid belligerent action toward the United States.

Yet when he heard the responses of those who proposed the "Outline" he stated: "Good. Then that is exactly what I think. . . . I completely support the plan proposed today for the above reasons."[61] That he was so easily reassured might well be proof that neither the government nor the high command took the phrase "will not flinch from war with Britain and the United States" in anything more than a quasi-rhetorical sense.

The Army and the Navy Go in Opposite Directions

The navy was suspicious of this newly adopted state policy. For example, on July 5, just three days later, Nagano advised the Throne: "Under the present circumstances we should move promptly to solve the southern problem."[62] Then on the 12th Navy Vice Chief of Staff Kondō presented Army Vice Chief of Staff Tsukada with a document whose main points were:

1. There will be no change in the distribution of factories for matériel mobilization [administered] by the army and the navy.
2. No workers in navy [administered] factories are to be recruited for army mobilization.
3. Navy preparations for action against the north will not be completed until the end of August.
4. The navy desires that army preparations for war in the area of Manchuria be discreetly carried out.[63]

The Army General Staff's War Guidance Office surmised that the navy's "true intent" in this document "was clearly to restrain the army [its Special Exercises for the Kwantung Army]" and that the navy "may have been dismayed by the army's preparations against the Soviet Union."[64] On the other hand, the way the army went about its preparations could hardly be called faithful to the Outline's decision that "we shall not intervene for the present in the war between Germany and the Soviet Union. . . . We shall make military preparations in secret against the Soviet Union."

In view of the severity of Siberian winters, northern operations would have to get under way no later than the beginning of September. On June 27 the War Guidance Office noted that should a golden opportunity arrive for going to war with the Soviet Union after early September, "we shall miss the opportunity for war even if we make preparations after resolving on war at that time. If we do not resolve on war now, full-scale preparations cannot be carried out in time. In saying this, however, we are not that confident about resolving on war immediately."[65] Thus the War Guidance Office writhed between the uncertain arrival of a god-sent opportunity and the seasonal limitations on commencing military operations. On the 30th it argued impatiently: "We are going to miss out on a golden opportunity. That opportunity depends first and foremost on developments in the war between Germany and the Soviet Union during the next few days. That will solve everything." But at the same time it consoled itself, saying: "When all is said and done the war guidance of the Empire, which continues to follow in the wake of Germany's war guidance, is weak. As a result we just may have to miss the opportunity to go to war." But saying that "rhetoric is rhetoric—that's inevitable when the reins of government belong equally to the army and navy,"[66] it still aimed above all else to solve the northern problem through a unilateral interpretation of a semantically contrived state policy.

Immediately before he was summoned back to Tokyo by telegram, Tanaka had been persuaded by Kwantung Army commander Umezu Yoshijirō that Japan would not be able to solve the northern problem alone and that the outbreak of war between Germany and the Soviet Union would be the opportunity of a lifetime.[67] After returning to Tokyo on June 9, Tanaka was adamant that the north should come first. Even after the draft proposal for the Imperial Conference had been formally approved by the Liaison Conference on June 28, he continued to insist that the phrase "to make ready military preparations with the resolution to exercise force" against the Soviet Union be added to the explanation that Sugiyama was to make to the emperor.[68] Echoing Tanaka, Tōjō told a gathering of army reserve generals he had invited over on the very evening after the Imperial Conference that "the general situation truly presents the opportunity of a lifetime."[69] Around the same time, Tōjō also revealed to Satō Kenryō that: "In cooperation Japan and Germany will achieve complete victory [over the Soviet Union]. Alone Germany might get bogged down, but with Japan's cooperation Germany will win. [Even if the United States were to intervene in a war between Japan and the Soviet Union] that will take time, and in the meantime we will take care of the Soviet Union."[70] Both statements indicate that Tōjō was disposed toward a "north first" policy.

Tanaka wasted no time in taking advantage of this trend in Tōjō's thinking and succeeded in getting his approval to activate massive preparations against the Soviet Union. Finally, in early July the so-called "Special Exercises for the Kwantung Army" were activated, which was to lead to the concentration of sixteen divisions against the Soviet Union through reinforcements by two divisions from Japan to the Kwantung Army (twelve divisions and two air groups) and from the Korean Army (two divisions). In addition, all of the 200 rear-support companies that belonged directly to the Kwantung Army, as well as supplies for military operations, were gathered in Manchuria in accordance with plans for full-scale operations against the Soviet Union (based on 20 to 25 divisions). The resulting mobilization, which took about three months, reached a scale unprecedented since the founding of the Japanese army.

This concentration of rear-support troops and supplies had been carried out prior to resolving on war with the Soviet Union and in full knowledge of the conspicuous imbalance between that support and the forces in the field. Behind this undertaking the Army General Staff's original intentions could be detected: Once forces were mobilized and concentrated in Manchuria they could be used either in the south or in the north; the important thing was to get them mobilized even if the army was unilaterally interpreting state policy thereby. On July 16 the Army General Staff discussed operations against the Soviet Union, concluding that "the main body of the army's forces is in the north, and the solution to fundamental problems lies in the north," while at the same time acknowledging that "these plans are of course founded on how [the war between Germany and the Soviet Union] goes."[71]

Although the "Outline of National Policies in View of the Changing Situation" had been adopted at the highest level, that of an Imperial Conference, the document was nothing more than one great exercise in semantics. This can be inferred from the fact that after it was approved the army and navy viewed it differently and went in quite opposite directions in carrying it out.

Matsuoka Turns a Deaf Ear to Reports that War Between Germany and the Soviet Union Is Imminent

In March Matsuoka was in Berlin, and Ribbentrop had "told him that relationships between Germany and the Soviet Union had so deteriorated that a war might break out at any time (this is confirmed by the minutes of their meeting). Ribbentrop also believed that having been told this much the foreign minister of any nation [including Matsuoka] should have inferred that war would break out."[72] While he was in Berlin, Matsuoka nonetheless maintained his belief that the German posture toward the Soviet Union was bluster and concluded that there would be no war between them.[73] In Moscow on his way home Matsuoka told Nishi Haruhiko, Japan's minister to the Soviet Union, that he considered it questionable whether Hitler would really attack the Soviet Union.[74] On April 8 he remarked to U.S. Ambassador Steinhardt that:

The Germans were fully prepared to invade the Soviet Union but had no intention of doing so unless the Soviets substantially reduced deliveries to Germany. He expressed the opinion that the rumors of a German attack on the Soviet Union had been given out by the Germans in order to frighten the Soviets into maintaining deliveries.[75]

Having returned to Tokyo on April 24, Matsuoka further stated at a plenary session of the Privy Council that "if Germany can intimidate the Soviet Union by taking an attack posture, there will be no need for Germany to take up arms. Whether or not Germany and the Soviet Union are on the verge of war is a fifty-fifty proposition."[76]

Consequently, Matsuoka did not heed the advice given him by Ōshima in Berlin against concluding a pact with the Soviet Union. As far as such a treaty was concerned, he replied on April 4 just before his departure for Japan via Moscow, "I know exactly what to do."[77] Two days later, escorting Matsuoka by train as far as the Soviet border, Ōshima again pointed out the possibility of war between Germany and the Soviet Union and strongly counselled Matsuoka to give up the idea of a neutrality pact with the Soviet Union. Matsuoka parried this by saying, "I'll think about it."[78] While stopping briefly at Malkinia on the Soviet border, Matsuoka was surprised to receive word of the German army's advance that morning on Beograd, and turning to his personal secretary, Kase Toshikazu, as the train was about to pull out, he declared, "That does it; we've got our pact with the Soviet Union."[79]

Thus Matsuoka concluded the neutrality pact with the Soviet Union, fully aware of the objections of Ribbentrop, Ōshima, and others. In doing so he may have felt compelled first of all as a matter of face, given the way in which the Tripartite Pact had been concluded, to set up at least the appearance of collaboration among Japan, Germany, Italy, and the Soviet Union whatever the realities of Germany's relations with the Soviet Union might have been. Second, having secured Japan's rear to the north he may have wanted to go to the United States and grapple with Roosevelt, bracing himself between the twin pillars of the Tripartite Pact and the Soviet-Japanese pact.[80] In addition, he may have hoped thereby to forestall a rapprochement between the United States and the Soviet Union. On April 13 he told the German ambassador to the Soviet Union, Count von der Schulenburg, that "the Neutrality Pact. . . . would result in an appreciable strengthening of the position of Japan as over and against America and England."[81]

Not surprisingly, former Foreign Minister Shidehara Kijūrō criticized the Soviet-Japanese Neutrality Pact as "erratic diplomacy akin to mere child's play" (March 22), pointing out that "diplomacy is not supposed to be acrobatics" (April 16). Employing the legal discourse of the able official, Shidehara went on to argue that "one wonders how Article 3 of the Pact of Alliance among Japan, Germany and Italy can be reconciled in practice with Article 2 of the Soviet-Japanese Neutrality Pact."[82] The truth of the matter is that the neutrality pact was the product of a compromise between Matsuoka's aims and those of Stalin, which were to avoid war on the Soviet Union's eastern and western fronts simultaneously, to encourage Japan to advance southward, and to hasten a clash between Japan and the United States. Neither Matsuoka nor Stalin was unaware of the kind of legal difficulties pointed out by Shidehara and doubtless neither meant to bring them up. On the day the pact was signed, Matsuoka paid a courtesy call on Ambassador Schulenburg and assured him, in reply to the ambassador's query, that "the forthcoming conclusion of the Pact, of course, in no way affects the Tripartite Pact. [Although] the Pact [did not have] any provision to this effect in it . . . the Russians had not brought up this question, and accordingly he had not gone into it either."[83]

After his return to Japan, Matsuoka repeated this point to his vice minister, Ōhashi Chūichi. He then clarified his one-sided interpretation: the axis of Japanese foreign policy was the Tripartite Pact and all other treaties were valid only insofar as they did not conflict with it; consequently, if Germany and the Soviet Union were to go to war, Japan would not be bound by the Soviet-Japanese Neutrality Pact.[84] In fact, Matsuoka had made this point at a press conference early on the morning of April 20 just after he left Soviet territory, and he reiterated it on April 23, just after he arrived at Tachikawa:

I should like to say in a word that the recent Soviet-Japanese Neutrality Pact, along with its proclamation, has not the slightest effect whatever on the Tripartite Pact, which constitutes the axis of our foreign policy. Nay, not only does it have no effect. . . . it can be said to have reinforced the Tripartite Pact.[85]

When he reported to the Throne on June 6, Matsuoka referred to Ōshima's telegrams: "Ambassador Ōshima's observations notwithstanding, my view of German-Soviet relations is that there is a 60 percent possibility of their reaching an agreement and a 40 percent possibility of their going to war."[86] Until June 18, when Ōshima's June 17 telegram was received, Matsuoka had maintained that it would not come to war between Germany and the Soviet Union, that the Soviet-Japanese Neutrality Pact was a temporary expedient, and that Japan would not be pressed to choose between the Tripartite Pact and the Neutrality Pact.

The sudden outbreak of war between Germany and the Soviet Union on June 22 decisively upset this posture, and at the June 25 and June 27 Liaison Conferences Matsuoka was contrite: "To tell the truth, I concluded the Neutrality Pact because I believed that Germany and the Soviet Union would not go to war. Were the situation such that there would be war between the two, I would have acted more cordially toward Germany and not concluded the Neutrality Pact."[87] "We cannot abandon the Tripartite Pact. I should have abandoned the idea of a Neutrality Pact from the start."[88] Forced to make a choice, however, on the evening of the 22nd Matsuoka reported to the emperor that "now that war has broken out between Germany and the Soviet Union, Japan should cooperate with Germany and attack the Soviet Union."[89] Well before this, on May 6, soon after his return from Europe, Matsuoka had told Ott:

> If war should break out between Germany and the Soviet Union, no Japanese Prime Minister or Foreign Minister would be able to keep Japan neutral. In such a case Japan would be impelled by natural consideration to join Germany in attacking Russia. No neutrality pact could change anything in this respect.[90]

And on June 22 he told Ott, "I, for one, still believe that Japan, in the end, would not be able to remain neutral toward the clash [between Germany and the Soviet Union]."[91]

On June 25 Matsuoka avoided a candid reply to Soviet Ambassador Constantin Smetanin on the issue of observing the Soviet-Japanese Neutrality Pact:

> Our position vis-à-vis this question, I have enunciated sometime ago in my statement after my return from Europe. The Tripartite Pact is the foundation of Japan's foreign policy. Should this war [between Germany and the Soviet Union] and the neutrality pact contradict this foundation and the Tripartite Pact, the neutrality pact would cease to be effective.[92]

Then, on July 4, Matsuoka commented to British Ambassador Craigie:

The Tripartite Pact imposed on Japan no obligation to enter this war on Germany's side. Similarly, Japan would not be prevented by the Neutrality Pact from taking any action arising out of this war which the preservation of Japanese interests might demand. Thus Japan's liberty of action in respect of the situation created by the German-Soviet war remained unaffected, whether by the Tripartite Pact or the Neutrality Pact.[93]

Matsuoka Switches from Going South to Going North

On April 24, right after his return to Tokyo, Matsuoka gave the Privy Council his estimate of the war situation in Europe: "Although [German] preparations for the invasion of the British homeland are complete and its execution is attendant only on Hitler's orders, Hitler has made no definite statement whatever. . . . It seems he is confident of reducing Britain in mid-year by intensifying air and submarine attacks on Britain."[94] On this basis Matsuoka began reasserting in blunt terms his long-standing argument for a decisive surprise invasion of Singapore. On May 8 he reported to the emperor that "should the United States enter the [European] war, Japan, as a matter of course, must side with Germany and Italy and attack Singapore."[95] Similarly, at the May 22 Liaison Conference, Matsuoka insisted that "we should conquer Singapore."[96] On June 5 Matsuoka countered Mutō's and Oka's arguments by saying, "I won't budge on the issue of military agreements [with Thailand and French Indochina] unless there is a plan to conquer Singapore."[97]

Sometime in May, Matsuoka invited the Operations Division chiefs of both services, Tanaka and Fukudome, to come and see him. Being sticklers about protocol, they sent their two section chiefs, Doi and Tomioka, in their stead. Matsuoka plied them with an agitated jumble of questions about operations to conquer Singapore. Could they undertake this or not? Would they succeed or not? What prior preparations were necessary? Had both services in fact made up their minds to do this or not?[98] Given the tenor of his debates with military representatives at Liaison Conferences since the beginning of 1941, it seems that by mid-June Matsuoka had arrived at the conclusion that neither the army nor the navy had operational plans or intentions to launch a decisive surprise invasion of Singapore, that, in his words, both services were "farting around." Just at this time he received Ōshima's report that war between Germany and the Soviet Union was imminent. So at the June 30 Liaison Conference Matsuoka declared: "A great man changes his mind. Previously I advocated advancing south, but now I advocate advancing north."[99] However much this soliloquy by Matsuoka might have struck the other participants as being empty posturing on a grand scale, Matsuoka had indeed made a great south-to-north turnaround in mid-June, shifting from his longstanding argument for a surprise invasion of Singapore to insisting on an attack against the Soviet Union, for at least the two reasons mentioned above. Moreover, this was not the first time Matsuoka had made a 180° turnaround when he ran into a blind alley; such behavior was part and parcel of Matsuoka's nature.[100]

Yet Matsuoka had never given the army and navy a full and careful explanation of why he had favored a surprise invasion of Singapore up to mid-June, or of why he insisted after this time that, regardless of the Soviet-Japanese Neutrality Pact, acting in concert with Germany was the axis of Japanese diplomacy. Instead of aggressive arguments for both courses of action, all that surfaced in the debates throughout May and June was Matsuoka's passive resistance primarily to exercising military force in the south. That merely made the army and navy even more bewildered about his true intentions.

Before going on, let us look at some of the statements Matsuoka made at Liaison Conferences during this period.

1) Opposition to exercising military force to the south: "We might get into a war with Britain and the United States that we did not plan on." (June 3) "There is a good chance that this would cause war with Britain and the United States." (June 11) "If we carry this out we will collide with Britain and the United States." (June 12) "If we go south we join battle with Britain and the United States. Even by advancing into French Indochina we might join battle with Britain and the United States." (June 27) "Striking south is playing with fire." (June 28) "We must stop playing around with fire in dealing with the south. My predictions have never been off the mark. If we go after the south a fire will start and we will be hard pressed by Britain and the United States. Can the chiefs of the high command guarantee that this will not happen?" (June 30)[101]

2) Japan's response to war between Germany and the Soviet Union: "According to Ōshima's telegram, Germany and the Soviet Union will go to war next week. Such an eventuality will lead to world war. Britain and the Soviet Union will become allies. The United States will enter the war on the side of Britain. I think we must carefully consider such developments. . . . There will be war between Germany and the Soviet Union. Don't we have to look into this?" (June 16)[102] "If we judge that the German-Soviet war will end

quickly, we cannot say that Japan will go neither south nor north. . . .
Go after the north first. . . . We should go after the north first then
the south. . . . If we wait and see how things shape up, as the draft
proposal of the high command suggests, we will be encircled by
Britain, the United States, and the Soviet Union." (June 27)[103]

It may very well be that behind these superficial remarks there lay
hidden Matsuoka's policy toward the United States. While he was in
Berlin during March, Matsuoka had estimated that if within six
months Singapore could be captured by a decisive surprise attack,
any threat to Japan from the United States could be warded off
within that time frame. His opposition to negotiations over setting up
military bases in French Indochina and Thailand was almost certainly
based on a judgment that by wasting time in Thailand and French
Indochina, it would require more than six months for Japan to capture Singapore, which would cause a crisis in Japanese-American
relations. In fact, on March 29 Matsuoka frankly told Ribbentrop that
"if the capture of Singapore should take longer and were perhaps
protracted for as long as a year, an extremely critical situation with
America would develop, which he did not yet know how to meet."[104]
Plainly, Matsuoka would have opposed any proposal for stationing
troops in southern French Indochina as a prelude to the conquest of
Singapore if only on the basis of the six-month limit on holding out
against the United States.

With regard to attacking the Soviet Union, his argument on June
27 was also tied to the time limit for holding out against the United
States:

> If we go after the Soviet Union quickly, the United States will not join
> in. In fact, the United States can't help the Soviet Union. The United
> States has always disliked the Soviet Union. On the whole, the United
> States will not enter a war [between Japan and the Soviet Union]. . . . If
> we go to war with the Soviet Union, I am confident that I can control
> the United States by diplomacy for three or four months.[105]

In its essential outline, Matsuoka's policy was to make a sudden conquest of either Singapore or Siberia but without bringing on war
with the United States; it was based on using the Tripartite Pact for
intimidation and pressure and premised on quick German victories
over both Britain and the Soviet Union. That policy was bound to
lead him into head-on collisions both with the navy, which was trying
to induce the army to resolve on war with the United States, and with
the army, which wavered between war against the United States and

war against the Soviet Union without daring to venture forth on either. But Matsuoka never put forward the positive side of his assertions, nor did he explain fully the logic of his position. This only served to deepen the widespread distrust toward him and to increase his political isolation.

At the Liaison Conference of June 30 Matsuoka made his final proposal: "Postpone stationing troops in southern French Indochina for about six months." But when Konoe, in a rare move for him, supported both services by stating that "if the high command is prepared to go ahead, we will go ahead,"[106] Matsuoka's opposition since January to stationing troops in southern French Indochina ran completely out of steam, and his policies toward both the south and the north were buried forever.

Revolutionary Changes Take Place in Japan's International Environment

The fundamental problem for Japan with regard to the Tripartite Pact was whether Germany could really be an effective ally in terms of Japan's relations with the United States. Given its geographical position between Japan and Germany and its vastness, the Soviet Union could isolate those two nations from each other any time it wished. Thus, the Soviet Union's attitude toward both countries was vital to their effective cooperation as allies, and the outbreak of war between Germany and the Soviet Union isolated Japan and Germany from each other, making cooperation between them virtually impossible and robbing the Tripartite Pact of its efficacy.

To make matters worse, Britain then entered into an alliance with the Soviet Union and thereby indirectly made the United States a quasi-ally of the Soviet Union. Both Japan and Germany had now made enemies of the three great powers of the world: Britain, the United States, and the Soviet Union. Isolated from Germany, with the United States a quasi-ally of the Soviet Union, Japan faced a revolutionary change in its international environment, a grave situation that could not be easily disposed of by a god-sent "golden opportunity" without assuming as self-evident a swift and sweeping German victory. This meant "of course that Japan is again at the crossroads" (Grew dispatch of June 27).[107] Consequently, debates on state policies at Imperial Conferences now presented Japan with a "golden opportunity" to look into more consistent and coherent foreign policies consonant with this revolutionary change, to get rid of preconceptions, and to make a thoroughgoing investigation of the course it had taken since the Tripartite Pact was concluded, without lapsing into discussions about a directionless preparedness or incoherent rhetoric about how the situation would develop.

Early on the morning of June 25, Konoe presented his objections to the army-navy draft proposal informally adopted two days earlier. It was quite normal for a prime minister to take such a step, but when Mutō explained somewhat deceptively to Chief Cabinet Secretary Tomita Kenji that the proposal was intended "to restrain the Army General Staff, which was inclined to attack the Soviet Union no matter what,"[108] Konoe readily accepted this and immediately withdrew the objections he had taken the trouble to make. Possibly as a result of Tomita's report, Konoe wrote on a document distributed at the Imperial Conference of July 2 that the advance into southern French Indochina "was to restrain the die-hards."[109] The matter of stationing troops in southern French Indochina had been discussed from June 5 on, apart from and prior to the June 23 draft proposal; it just so happened that the decision on this was made at the Liaison Conference which took place on the afternoon of the day Konoe presented his objections, and Konoe's concurrence was apparently influenced by Mutō's deceptive explanation that morning.

Some years later Konoe stated that "as soon as the war between Germany and the Soviet Union started, Suzuki Teiichi and Itō Nobufumi advised me to abrogate the Tripartite Pact, and I presented the matter to the Five Ministers Conference."[110] While the first part of his statement is true, he did not refer the matter to the Five Ministers Conference. The truth is that Suzuki, who had proposed that the pact be abrogated, consulted Tōjō at Konoe's suggestion, and Tōjō replied that this was essentially for the foreign minister to decide. Konoe then talked with Matsuoka, but in the face of the foreign minister's objections made no effort to insist on abrogation.[111] In any case, it is not true that Konoe grasped the "golden opportunity" presented by the outbreak of war between Germany and the Soviet Union to demand that the army (once again enthusiastic about help from almighty Buddha) and the navy (which persisted in its policy of "inducing" the government "in the direction of resolving on war with the United States") both go back to their drawing boards. It might have been too much to expect such strength of will from Konoe, who had as recently as June 20 revealed to Kido his desire to resign because of Matsuoka.[112]

In contrast to Konoe's passivity, the only person in the cabinet who dared to criticize the ambiguous and semantic compromises between the army and navy was Matsuoka, even though his position rested throughout on a mistaken judgment about the war between Britain and Germany. Outside the cabinet, criticism came from Ambassador Nomura, who argued repeatedly for an independent reexamination that was above all else discriminating about the limits of national strength. Nomura also perceived the logical sequence that a southern advance by military force would provoke a total embargo against Japan by the United States which would in turn lead to war with the United States. Even before his departure for Washington he had prepared a memorandum, based on his policy of no war between Japan and the United States, in which he wrote that "it seems that all that remains [to be embargoed by the United States] now is oil, and the United States will not hesitate to place oil under embargo either."[113] Shortly before the outbreak of war between Germany and the Soviet Union, Nomura warned against advancing south by military force: "Despite the fact that a majority of influential people has advocated an oil embargo, Hull and the State Department are holding back out of diplomatic considerations."[114] Once war broke out, he issued a warning against advancing either north or south to take advantage of the situation:

> If, in connection with the war between Germany and the Soviet Union, we are resolved to exercise armed force to the south, we can be sure that there will be absolutely no room left for adjusting Japanese-American relations. . . . If, moreover, we rush to join with Germany and enter the German-Soviet war, that will bring about a swift deterioration in Japanese-American relations and will likely bring us one step away from war between Japan and the United States. (Dispatch of July 3)[115]

Nomura appealed to Oikawa as well:

> As things now stand, it is to be feared that in the last analysis Japan will make enemies of Britain, the United States, the Soviet Union, China, the Netherlands—all of them. There will be enemies everywhere—east and west, north and south. Japan will have no choice but to deal with this critical situation all by itself. . . . Today we truly stand at a crossroads. At this juncture . . . I am painfully aware of the necessity to conceive of ways to overcome this critical situation, resolutely and on our own. (Dispatch of July 10)[116]

But saying this to Oikawa was like shooting an arrow into a sponge.

On the day the German-Soviet war broke out, the emperor summoned Kido and pointed out that "Matsuoka's policies will have us marching aggressively both to the north and to the south. . . . I am greatly concerned whether this is appropriate in light of our national strength, among other things."[117] In their concern for national strength the emperor and Nomura echoed one another across the seas.

3 Toyoda Diplomacy Gets Under Way

Hull's Oral Statement

Hull's counterproposal arrived in Tokyo on June 24—the day before the formal decision to station troops in southern French Indochina, and the day after the informal decision by a conference of army and navy bureau and division chiefs on countermeasures to cope with the outbreak of war between Germany and the Soviet Union. That is, it arrived in the midst of the quarrels between the army and navy and Matsuoka over whether to advance north or south or both immediately after war between Germany and the Soviet Union had broken out. Under the circumstances an examination of Hull's counterproposal was shelved until after the July 2 Imperial Conference decision.

Matsuoka's July 2 telegram to Japanese envoys abroad, somewhat toning down in expression the substance of that day's Imperial Conference decision, was immediately put to decoding by the United States. Roosevelt, who feared first and foremost that Japan would mount a sudden attack on the Soviet Union, forwarded a veiled warning[118] to Konoe on the 6th (Japan time). On the 7th Matsuoka, still fuming over Hull's oral statement, counter-attacked, saying that he would like to avail himself of this opportunity to ascertain definitely whether the United States really intended to intervene in the European war.[119] The United States responded to this on the 16th by reiterating, following the format of Hull's oral statement, that:

> Any intimations or suggestions that the United States should desist from its policy of self-defense and protection [in opposing Nazi movements] would in actual fact range those making such suggestions or intimations on the side of those favoring or facilitating the aims of the aggressor nations to conquer the world by force.[120]

To which Matsuoka shot back on the 17th:

> The Japanese Government . . . cannot . . . pass unnoticed any intimation or suggestion on the part of the American Government, or, for that matter, any governments, to invoke unlimitedly the so-called right of self-defence, claiming the right to extend it wherever they like.[121]

This was tantamount to a nasty parting of the ways between Matsu-oka and Hull.

With the United States widely disregarding its own neutrality laws, Matsuoka's rebuttal was more valid, logically speaking, than were Hull's assertions. Japan, however, faced a far more complicated domestic political situation in terms of coping with so nasty a parting of the ways. The Liaison Conference of the 10th, more than two weeks after Hull's counterproposal and oral statement had been received, set about examining these two documents for the first time. Matsuoka called attention to the following points, among others:

1. This demands a reorganization of our nation's cabinet, or at least "hints" rather blatantly at that. Such acts are historically rare. Only among nations that differ markedly in their comparative strengths are there a few examples of this (and even these are extremely rare). Most are limited to cases involving dependencies or protectorates.
2. If we were to accept even half of the American proposal, this would ultimately lead to Japan's withdrawal from the Tripartite Pact.
3. We shall have to abandon the Empire's fundamental policy of establishing a new order in Greater East Asia and other established state policies of great import—recognition of the Nationalist government [of Wang Ching-wei—trans.] in Nanking, its further nurturing and strengthening, and the thorough chastisement of the Chungking regime [of Chiang Kai-shek—trans.].
4. We shall have to modify our great objective of making secure our leadership in East Asia. Over the years the foundations for this have finally been built, at the cost of overcoming numerous obstacles, of thrice risking the nation's destiny, and at the sacrifice of more than two hundred thousand lives and enormous state revenues. We would have to allow British-American meddling in Sino-Japanese affairs, which in turn would make it impossible to resolve local Sino-Japanese problems—that is, to stabilize the East Asian situation at large.
7. We shall be doing no less than approving United States utterances and actions toward Germany to date, and in that respect we shall naturally be forced to decide to withdraw from the Japan-Italy-Germany pact.
8. By the single fact of having achieved an understanding with Japan in regard to the Sino-Japanese Incident and the entire area of the southwest Pacific (excluding of course the Pacific Ocean in the western hemisphere), the United States will relieve the anxieties of American citizens and in addition intimate to Germany and Italy

that Japan will withdraw from the Axis Pact. This would expedite American entry into the European war, and Japan would be concurring in just that.

9. Turning to the future, the United States will try to set in place an effective foundation for meddling in Sino-Japanese negotiations, for keeping an eye on Japan's behavior in these negotiations and other matters, while at the same time casting barbs of criticism and denunciation.

10. In essence, the aims of the United States are to weaken Tripartite Pact ties among Japan, Italy and Germany and to obliterate the Nanking government at one stroke, forcing Japan to recognize the Chungking regime as the legitimate government of China. Although the United States will urge Chiang Kai-shek to make peace through direct negotiations with Japan, the quid pro quo will be for the Japanese government to propose its basic conditions for those negotiations to the United States government; taking the stance that it had approved these conditions, the United States government (and Britain) will then boast to the Chinese and to its own citizens that it had in fact acted as a mediator. Finally, the United States seeks to eradicate any claim on Japan's part to establish a Greater East Asia Sphere and by every means possible to facilitate the maintenance of the status quo—that is, preservation of the old order.

On this basis Matsuoka concluded, and the Liaison Conference voiced no outward opinions to the contrary, that:

I need not point out that the oral statement, given even the slightest appreciation for the dignity of the Empire and Japan's independence as a nation, must be rejected out of hand. If, however, we still feel that we must continue negotiations on the Draft Understanding itself (of course, if the United States were Japan, these negotiations would have been indignantly broken off long ago), this minister believes that the only recourse is to continue to adhere to our counterproposal decided upon in May this year, and to accept only those few phrases in the American proposal that have no effect on the points enumerated above. I therefore conclude with regret that there are no prospects for agreement in the present negotiations; but if we are to break them off, prudence and care are required over timing and method.[122]

The following day Matsuoka sent Nomura his conclusion that this oral statement "was equivalent to calling for the reorganization of our cabinet, suggesting as it does that even if an understanding between Japan and the United States is reached, its implementation is well-nigh impossible so long as questionable ministers remain in the present Konoe Cabinet."[123] At the Liaison Conference of the 12th he added the contention that, "so long as I am foreign minister I cannot accept it; I submit here and now that we reject the statement and that we cannot continue negotiations with America any further."[124]

The navy brought up its demands at this same Liaison Conference:

1. We think that negotiations should be conducted on the basis of established policy; if in the case at hand there is fear that negotiations will be broken off, we should resort to an interim measure, whereby negotiations will be prolonged at least until we have finished stationing forces in French Indochina.

2. We have no objections to the Foreign Ministry's revised draft in response to the United States proposal of June 22. If taking a strong stand on this immediately increases the probability of a rupture, however, it would be appropriate to moderate that draft somewhat in accordance with the policy in 1) above. However, the following three points are set down to make the claims of the Empire perfectly clear, so as not to bequeath troubles to a later date; other than that, we ultimately have no difficulty with the purport of the United States proposal:

   a) Attitude toward the European war: Should the European war expand, Japan will take an autonomous position in support of its treaty obligations and its own security and defense.

   b) The question of peace between Japan and China: The overall provisos are to be based on Konoe's three principles. The United States is to do no more than recommend a truce and peace negotiations; it is not to intervene or interfere in the peace terms (we shall draw up articles of understanding in the event that Chiang Kai-shek does not respond to the recommendation).

   c) In regard to "political stability in the Pacific region," we revise this so as not to circumscribe the exercise of such military force by the Empire as may be required under the circumstances.[125]

Supporting the navy, Army Chief of Staff Sugiyama voiced his opposition to Matsuoka, saying that "it is appropriate to leave room for negotiations" with the United States. All three of the navy's points were consequential provisions that had been deleted from Matsuoka's revised draft by Hull's counterproposal. In reviving them, the navy was merely pressing for an agreement based on a reversion to Matsuoka's revised draft—that is, Hull's voluntary restoration of these three provisions in his counterproposal. The phrase "other than that, we ultimately have no difficulty with the purport of the United States proposal" had no significance whatever in terms of reaching a compromise. Except for the hard-core Axis faction in the Army General Staff, army and navy views on the Tripartite Pact mostly inclined toward a policy of expediency, to the effect that it was imperative to preserve the alliance with Germany in order to take advantage of German victories rather than to threaten and intimidate the United States by brandishing Japan's obligations under Article 3. They by no means concurred with Matsuoka, who held solely to the latter position.

In insisting on still "leaving room for negotiations," the army and navy did possess some sense of realism regarding the Tripartite Pact. However, Sugiyama's insistence on flexibility, even in resolving the war between Japan and China and exercising military force in the south, was so unrealistic that it provoked a retort from Matsuoka at the July 12 conference:

Room for what? . . . What [other concessions] would you put in? . . . If we say we won't use armed force in the south, that might work. Anything else?[126]

Matsuoka had already criticized the military for opportunism at the Liaison Conference two days earlier:

I am unhappy that there are so many so overburdened by the China Incident that they lose sight of their own ideals and take to thinking that dumplings are more important than flowers, to put it colloquially.[127]

Nonetheless, the Conference decided *inter alia* (1) to quash Matsuoka's appraisal that "if we continue to negotiate by firmly holding to" my revised draft "and are kicked around [by America] until we are finally kicked out, we might then be able for the first time to give up on negotiations" (July 12), and (2) to reject the oral statement but continue the negotiations with the object of bringing them back to the Matsuoka revised draft. When Tōgō Shigenori examined the particulars of Hull's counterproposal for the first time immediately after becoming foreign minister in Tōjō's cabinet, he told Kase Toshikazu:

Now I understand why Matsuoka foresaw the failure of the negotiations and insisted on dropping them. What is incomprehensible is why the cabinet was so optimistic about succeeding in the negotiations without softening the terms of our demands.[128]

Be that as it may, as a result of this decision Matsuoka first sent instructions to Nomura on the 14th to press Hull to withdraw the oral statement, explaining that:

> If it were the other way round and the United States government had had this kind of an "oral statement" thrust upon it from the Imperial government, what its response would have been hardly overtaxes the mind. Given that the United States government concludes that so long as there is no change in the composition of our present cabinet the implementation of a Japanese-American understanding would be "illusory" even if it were reached, the present cabinet is of absolutely no mind to discuss that proposal seriously. The oral statement ought even to be taken as a document of severance insofar as the current negotiations involving the present Japanese government are concerned. Regrettably, we are led to the conclusion that there is no other recourse but to reject this oral statement out of hand.[129]

On the 15th Matsuoka issued a revised proposal that brought the Hull counterproposal closer to his earlier revised draft.

The fact that from the outset the Matsuoka revised draft and the Hull counterproposal were totally incompatible and irreconcilable had been discerned by Matsuoka, who had made this clear at the Liaison Conference of July 10. Although he had been forced to issue this revised proposal, Matsuoka's objective at this point was to buy time, in keeping with the demands of the military that the rupture of negotiations be put off until the stationing of forces in French Indochina had been completed. "While I regard coming to an agreement on the Draft Understanding to be well-nigh impossible, I have taken sufficient care to prolong negotiations as long as possible in view of state policy."[130]

Matsuoka Exits

On the 17th Matsuoka grumbled to Konoe that "in spite of my view that notification of our rejection of the oral statement should precede the submission of [my revised proposal] by several days, there were those in government circles who adhered to the opinion that both should be submitted at the same time; they brought this up with Your Excellency and attempted to undermine the foreign minister's policy, [but] the foreign minister dealt with the situation strictly from his own point of view."[131] It was in fact Konoe himself, as well as the army and navy, who adhered to the opinion that both should be submitted at the same time. Tomita, Mutō, Naval Affairs Bureau Chief Oka, and the chief of the Foreign Ministry's America Bureau, Terasaki Tarō, shared that view and spent all day on the 14th mustering support for simultaneous submission. Konoe also asked Foreign Affairs Counselor Saitō Yoshie, who had paid a call that same day, to convey this to Matsuoka. But complications arose when Saitō, under orders from Matsuoka, telegrammed at 11:30 that night instructions to serve only notice of the rejection of the oral statement, whereas the following morning Terasaki, who had taken Konoe's wishes to heart, telegrammed the revised proposal as well, on the cognizance only of Ōhashi Chūichi and without a word to Matsuoka. With that, Matsuoka was to plunge once again into a frontal collision with Konoe. Following the Liaison Conference on the 10th, Konoe had consulted in secret with Army Minister Tōjō, Navy Minister Oikawa, and Home Minister Hiranuma Kiichirō concerning Matsuoka's assertions against the Hull counterproposal and oral statement. At a further conference of the four on the 15th on how to cope with this collision, Tōjō stated that "at this point we have no choice but to take decisive action, either by replacing the foreign minister or by having the entire cabinet resign—one or the other."[132] Oikawa and Hiranuma agreed.

Nearly a month earlier Konoe had complained to Kido that he "was at a loss to understand Matsuoka's attitude,"[133] revealing on June 20 that he was so vexed over this that he might resign. On July 5 Konoe had again stated that he "could not grasp what Matsuoka really had in mind." There was no concealing the sudden deterioration in Konoe's relations with Matsuoka, and even back on the 20th Kido had advised Konoe "to have Matsuoka resign, and only if Matsuoka refuses to resign should you assume responsibility for disunity in the cabinet."[134] And again, on July 15, Kido had "encouraged him to seek the dismissal of the foreign minister to avoid in so far as possible a change of government at this time."[135]

It was hardly possible for Konoe to have only Matsuoka resign, given that back when he had proposed his roster of cabinet ministers to the emperor in July 1940, the emperor had twice cautioned him: "I wonder about Matsuoka as your foreign minister." Konoe, however, had insisted on having his own way on this. Therefore, a year later, on July 16, he felt compelled to have the entire cabinet resign.[136] Wishing to avoid a change of government if at all possible, Kido then petitioned the Throne that Konoe be ordered to form a new government. The Imperial Command was issued to Konoe on the afternoon of the 17th and the formation of his new cabinet was completed on the afternoon of the 18th. The real purpose in revamping the cabinet, of course, was to dismiss Matsuoka. In his place as foreign minister appeared Retired Admiral Toyoda Teijirō, who was transferred from his previous post as minister of commerce and industry.

Toyoda's Policy Concerns

Hull's suggestion in his oral statement, that Japan's Axis policy be reconsidered upon the removal of Matsuoka, had thus been accepted by Konoe, the army, and the navy. It therefore followed as a matter of course that a reconsideration of Axis policy would subsequently be taken up by the third Konoe cabinet in its dealings with the United States. But if Matsuoka's dismissal had been largely a foregone conclusion when toward the end of June he had plunged into head-on collisions with the army and navy and then with Konoe, why did Konoe, the army, and the navy, insist on making him carry out a negotiating policy that would attempt to bring the Hull counterproposal around to Matsuoka's revised Draft Understanding? They probably thought they would still be able to "leave room for negotiation" in dealing with the United States, even by reverting back to Matsuoka's revised draft, if they took Hull's suggestion to mean only the ejection of Matsuoka the individual and then simply got rid of Matsuoka the individual. However, Hull's suggestion also included a request that Japan reconsider its Axis policy, and if they evaded this request and merely rehashed Matsuoka's revised draft, they would find themselves in a position just as irreconcilable with Hull's as before, no matter who was foreign minister. From the very outset, therefore, Foreign Minister Toyoda found himself between a rock and a hard place in terms of relations with the United States.

Immediately after being appointed foreign minister, Toyoda invited over for a chat members of the Naval Affairs Bureau, former subordinates when Toyoda had been vice navy minister. It would not do, he told them, to change Matsuoka's policies suddenly.[137] At the first Liaison Conference of the new cabinet on July 21 he spoke out in place of the silent Konoe:

> Because I thought it would be troublesome if our ambassadors and ministers to various countries were given to think that there might be changes in state policies, I sent telegrams stating that there would be

no change in established policies. I was particularly careful to send word to Ōshima . . . saying carry on as before. At the same time, I summoned the German and Italian ambassadors in Tokyo and told them that even though there has been a change in foreign ministers there is no change whatever in the attitude of the Empire. Besides, having been vice navy minister when the Tripartite pact was concluded, I am strongly obligated to it. I played a part when that pact came into being; make changes I will not.[138]

It was from this stance that he sent the following telegram to Ōshima on the 31st:

The act of occupying southern French Indochina has struck a great blow in the Pacific that will prove a set-back to the United States and Britain, to say nothing of the Soviet Union; this is something that will surely help Germany. Relations between Japan and the United States will now continue on the path of deterioration even more swiftly than before, and this will show how great a blow to the United States this act has been. Even though I am cognizant that Germany on its part is somewhat disgruntled over our negotiations with the United States, I continue to hope that Japan will block United States' participation in the war, no matter what the sacrifice.[139]

Even ten days before he resigned as foreign minister on October 18, Toyoda told both Ambassador Ōshima and Ambassador to Italy Horikiri Zembei:

I believe that the action [of stationing forces in southern French Indochina] has had the effect of strongly diverting Britain and the United States, above all the United States, to the Pacific, and that this has been in line with Germany's true aims. In fact, I must say that the sudden turn for the worse in Japanese-American relations of late corroborates that effect.[140]

However, the measures that Toyoda actually took based on such a stance amounted to nothing more than an opportunistic policy of getting by on a case-by-case basis, just as when he had agreed to the Tripartite Pact as vice navy minister. Concretely, they amounted to a technique for substantially revising, by installments at Liaison Conferences, a state policy that had just been approved at the July 2 Imperial Conference, and for giving pledges one after another to both the United States and the Soviet Union that were contrary to state policy. The distinctive feature of Toyoda's foreign policy is to be discerned in its step by step gutting of the substance of Matsuoka's policies, while continuing them in form. His foreign policy was also in line with Konoe's covert attempt to abandon the Tripartite Pact when he changed foreign ministers.

Toyoda was able, with Konoe's understanding and support, to gut the substance of state policy only because that policy had been from its inception nothing more than a grand exercise in semantics, as the way it came about proves. In their attempts to interpret and put into effect this semantic state policy in a self-serving way, therefore, Toyoda's foreign policy and the Army's Special Exercises for the Kwantung Army were much the same. However, the army, which had taken the self-centered, indulgent, and contradictory attitude of carrying on with Matsuoka-like policies without Matsuoka, became apprehensive over Toyoda's gutting techniques and soon set about counteracting them. Moreover, the United States was able to decode Toyoda's telegrams to Ōshima in Berlin and interpreted Toyoda's double-dealing as a scheme to placate both the United States and Germany until Japan could assess the course of the war between Germany and the Soviet Union after it had gained control over French Indochina. When counteracted by the army and hedged in logically by the United States, how could Toyoda's opportunistic approach to foreign policy, based as it was on getting by as the occasion demanded, possibly avoid self-destruction?

Abandoning War Against the Soviet Union

When the Army General Staff's War Guidance Office heard of Toyoda's appointment as foreign minister, it took the view that "if it is in the nature of the new cabinet to destroy the Axis [Alliance—trans.] in substance and to rely on the United States and Britain, the army's voice vis-à-vis the recent change of government has been extinguished"; "the actual destruction of the Tripartite Alliance is to be feared."[141] On the 19th Operations Division Chief Tanaka drafted a strongly worded statement of opinion to be presented to the new government's first Liaison Conference on the 21st, the gist of which was that "the high command questions the true intentions of the government and will take a defiant attitude if compelled to do so; should the government abrogate the Tripartite Axis, there will be grave repercussions in the high command."[142] He obtained Army Vice Chief Tsukada's approval, and it turned out that the Navy General Staff, from Vice Chief Kondō on down, had no objection either. On the 20th, however, Sugiyama expressed his opposition and gutted the strongly worded portions. The following desiderata were subsequently presented to the Liaison Conference of the 21st:

> We recognize that a change of cabinets in the midst of growing domestic and international tensions, and while various policies of the Empire are in progress, has profound repercussions, and it is truly gratifying that the new cabinet has been formed so swiftly. The army and navy staffs of Imperial Headquarters will be unsparing in giving strong and loyal backing to the new cabinet.
>
> Although the government's aspirations have already been clarified in its declarations and other pronouncements, the high command would like on this occasion to set forth a number of desiderata:
>
> 1. The basis for state policies to be pursued by the Empire at present is clear from the "Outline of National Policies in View of the Changing Situation" adopted at the Imperial Conference of July 2, and various domestic and international policies based on the "Outline" must be carried swiftly to completion. In particular, the high command requires that those military measures toward French Indochina now in progress be executed precisely as previously decided (in both content and timing) and enjoins on the government that its policies conform strictly thereto.
> 2. With regard to war preparations to the south and the north already set in motion to deal with the present critical situation, these brook no delay or postponement.
>   Although firmly convinced that the government will naturally adhere to established policy in this regard, we wish on this occasion to call once again for their vigorous and faithful execution.
> 3. With regard to adjustments in diplomatic relations between Japan and the United States, we ask that the established policy be firmly adhered to at all times, and especially that care be taken in carrying them out so as not to run contrary to the spirit of the Tripartite Axis.
>   Note: By established policy . . . is meant the spirit of the instructions given to Ambassador Nomura on May 3 and July 14. . . .[143]

Item 3 was insurance against a Konoe-Toyoda turnabout in foreign policy that the high command sensed was coming. But note that Item 3 did not say Tripartite *Pact* but explicitly and deliberately stipulated "Axis spirit." Here we see the army as usual putting stress on taking advantage of the victories of the German army rather than on fulfilling treaty obligations against the United States.

Moreover, Ambassador Ōshima in Berlin had come up with a

forecast of war between Germany and the Soviet Union and changed his position in a flash from that in his telegram of April 16 in which he had advised his superiors to attack Singapore. Now he was deluging his superiors with opportunistic arguments for going to war with the Soviet Union, taking the victory of the German army over the Soviet Union as self-evident:

> Today a key nation in the Tripartite Alliance, the Empire took the lead in the world of the future by concluding the Anti-Comintern Pact; for it not now to make its attitude clear would be regrettable in the extreme for the honor and prestige of the Empire. Although this envoy too acknowledges that there will be domestic difficulties and realizes the difficult predicament of Your Excellencies, now is no time for debates. What is needed is manly resolve, and I would urge you to determine our attitude with dispatch. Please transmit this telegram to the army and navy. (Sent June 28)[144]
>
> The deepest impression that this envoy got from conversations with both Hitler and Ribbentrop [on July 14] was that Führer Hitler (and of course Ribbentrop) is greatly displeased with Japan's attitude since the war between Germany and the Soviet Union broke out, although given their personalities they did not say so directly. Consequently it is my judgment that if Japan continues hereafter to take the attitude it does today even Hitler will take to despairing over Japan, and the danger of the Tripartite Alliance becoming utterly void in spirit will be very great indeed. Although it goes without saying that there is no need for the Empire to be dragged about at the inclination of Germany and Italy, if the Empire is to keynote its diplomacy on the Tripartite Alliance as it has to date we need, and with dispatch, to make our attitude absolutely clear. (Sent July 19)[145]

While clamoring about "the Axis spirit," however, the Army General Staff remained hesitant to do anything concrete about attacking the Soviet Union. As late as the Liaison Conference of August 1 Sugiyama and Tōjō both expressed the view that it "was not necessarily so" that the war between Germany and the Soviet Union would become protracted:

> The fact that the fighting in the West [Russia] is not progressing rapidly at present means, on the contrary, that the Soviet Union is playing into Germany's hands, and it is probable that this will lead to blitzkrieg warfare by Germany. The Soviet Union will find it increasingly impossible to carry out a protracted war. One cannot jump to the conclusion that the war between Germany and the Soviet Union will be protracted.[146]

On July 30, however, the Operations Section had forecast that the German army "might take one to two weeks to reach Moscow, and one week for the attack on Moscow—altogether three weeks at the least; at that juncture we will take a reading of the situation, possibly in late August." Even earlier, on July 25, the Operations Division itself had noted that "the argument that we should strike north is slipping gradually into the shadows."[147] That was the state of play in the Army General Staff.

In view of the severity of the Siberian winter, Japan would have to initiate war against the Soviet Union by the beginning of September at the latest.Thus it was necessary for the nation to reach a decision between early and mid-August. But there were prerequisites for reaching that decision, all dependent on help from almighty Buddha: the transfer of half the Soviet Far Eastern Army to the European front, a two-thirds decrease in Soviet air power and tanks in the Far East, as well as confirmation that there would be a German blitzkrieg against the Soviet Union. On the other hand, at the beginning of August the Army General Staff's Soviet Intelligence Section reported to Sugiyama its judgment of the war situation, forecasting that it would be impossible for German forces to make the Soviet Union surrender during the current year and that subsequent developments would produce a war of endurance not necessarily to the advantage of Germany.[148] Thus, the judgment should have been reached that an opportune moment for going to war with the Soviet Union, one that depended on help from almighty Buddha, was hardly in the offing. Even the German army's Heinz Guderian, the genius of ar-mored vehicle operations, judged on August 2 that the war had reached a critical turning point, reporting this to Hitler on the 4th.[149]

The Soviet Intelligence Section's forecast was on the mark. With that in mind, Sugiyama notified Army Minister Tōjō on the 9th of the army's decision "not to exercise military force against the Soviet Union during the current year, regardless of developments in the war between Germany and the Soviet Union."[150] On the same day Tanaka advised Mutō "not to take action to the north during Septem-ber."[151] This explicit rejection of an attack "during September" may have been meant to leave open the possibility of attacking the Soviet Union in the latter half of October, even in the face of winter, should an opportune moment arise. It may also have stemmed from a desire not to give the Military Affairs Bureau a pretext for slowing down the "Special Exercises for the Kwantung Army," which had gotten under way in July and about which the emperor had expressed reservations to Sugiyama on July 31:

> The Special Exercises for the Kwantung Army are giving other coun-
> tries a bad impression, and Japan's position steadily worsens. How
> about putting a stop to mobilizing the Kwantung Army from here
> on? [152]

Brushing aside the emperor's wishes, the army massed the great bulk
of its uncommitted troops and supplies in Manchuria following the
August 9 notification to Tōjō. Furthermore, the decision to do so was
confined to the army; not even the navy, to say nothing of the
government, was to be informed. Thus it would appear that the army
was still keeping the navy in check without interrupting its northern
advance posture.

Prior to this, however, Toyoda himself had in fact given up on
going to war with the Soviet Union. The "Guidelines for Diplomatic
Negotiations with the Soviet Union," which Toyoda presented to the
Liaison Conference of August 1, were adopted on the 4th. Despite
stating in its opening paragraph that "the Empire will be careful not
to place restrictions on its future course of action," the "Negotiation
Policy" section of the "Guidelines" contained the sentence: "the Empire declares that it will fulfill its obligations under the Soviet-Japanese Neutrality Pact." [153] When Toyoda made this clear-cut statement
to Ambassador Smetanin on the 5th and added by way of elucidation
that so long as the Soviet Union abided by the Treaty of Neutrality
Japan would have no cause to attack the Soviet Union without provocation, [154] Smetanin was ecstatic:

> Up until now I had had misgivings about what was in store, but your
> gracious words have clarified matters. I shall notify my government
> explicitly of what you have said. The foreign minister has been kind
> enough to give me his gracious thoughts on a matter that touches upon
> the keynote of diplomatic policies. . . . Allow me to express my deepest
> gratitude for your having spoken so openly and with such complete
> clarity. [155]

And yet this clear-cut statement and supplementary elucidation actually gutted one of the July 2 Imperial Conference decisions: "Should
the war between Germany and the Soviet Union develop in a direction advantageous to the Empire, we shall resolve the northern problem . . . by exercising military force."

Thus, in early August both Tōjō and Toyoda gave up on going to
war with the Soviet Union, while keeping one another mutually in the
dark. Whereas the army's position was to postpone implementation of

the decision because the prerequisite stipulated in approved state policy—that the war between Germany and the Soviet Union develop in a direction advantageous to the Empire—had not yet been fulfilled, it was distinctive of Toyoda's foreign policy to give those he was dealing with, in this case the Soviet Union, pledges in point-blank disregard of state policy.

Repercussions of the Rupture in Economic Relations with the United States

Meanwhile, Toyoda was faced with the freezing of Japan's assets in the United States on July 26 and with the announcement of a total embargo on oil on August 1. Putting off until later the main business of an overall adjustment in diplomatic relations with the United States, he therefore immersed himself in the single matter of reviving commercial treaties. The day after the August 4 Liaison Conference Toyoda presented the United States with a plan for a regional settlement:

1. Japan has no intention of stationing troops in the southwest Pacific beyond French Indochina; troops will be withdrawn from French Indochina as soon as the war between Japan and China is settled.
2. Japan will guarantee the neutrality of the Philippines.
3. The United States will cease military measures against Japan in the southwest Pacific; once this is agreed, the United States will urge both Britain and the Netherlands to do the same.
4. The United States will cooperate in Japan's acquisition of natural resources in the Dutch East Indies.
5. The United States will promptly take such measures as are necessary to restore normal commercial relations.
6. The United States will act as a mediator to bring about direct negotiations between Japan and China and will also acknowledge Japan's special position in French Indochina even after troops are withdrawn.[156]

Given that the four concessions asked of the American side were far greater in scope than the two concessions offered by the Japanese, this plan was surely an overly sanguine plea by a Japan fallen onto hard times as the result of ruptured economic relations. Furthermore, items such as (3) wistfully hoped to get something for nothing, and the latter half of item (6) would only serve to make the Americans wary once again. Setting aside all these problems, the very proposing of item (1) with an eye to reaching an agreement was to give the

United States a pledge that would have virtually gutted one of the items approved by the July 2 Imperial Conference: "We shall first carry to a successful conclusion our policies toward French Indochina and Thailand . . . , thereby strengthening arrangements for a [further] southern advance." Here again is that distinctive feature of Toyoda's diplomacy.

However, this kind of diplomatic response by Toyoda was not the only reaction to the shock of America's decisive rupture of economic relations with Japan. An entirely different reaction emerged within the army and navy, where pressure began to mount for decisiveness as opposed to the "getting-by-first" measures taken by Toyoda.

4 Converting to a War Footing

The American Rupture of Economic Relations Strikes Home

The July 2 Imperial Conference reconfirmed the state policy to station troops in southern French Indochina. As a result, the army on July 5 announced the formation of the 25th Army based on the 2nd Imperial Guard Division and the 21st Independent Mixed Brigade.[157] Preparations for dispatching occupation forces commenced when July 24 was set as the date for the 25th army to sail from Sanya, Hainan island. On July 21 the two chiefs of staff presented to the new government the above desiderata, which stressed in no uncertain terms that "in particular, the high command requires that those military measures toward French Indochina now in progress be executed precisely as previously decided (in both content and timing). . . ." Whether or not the two chiefs of staff had done so, this was already a state policy that had been approved at the highest procedural level, an Imperial Conference. The new cabinet was naturally bound by it unless it convened another Imperial Conference and changed it. On July 12, a few days before resigning as foreign minister, Matsuoka had sent instructions concerning Japanese forces for the occupation of southern French Indochina to Katō Sotomatsu, ambassador to the Vichy government:

> I sense that our demands are once again running into difficulties, despite our repeated concessions over French Indochina. Although these are demands that the Empire does not in fact want to make. . . . it is a truly unavoidable procedure at this point. In this regard please

start negotiations with the French immediately and get a definite answer from them by the 20th (Japan time).[158]

On the 15th, Konoe sent Pétain a personal letter along the same lines.
Toyoda followed this up on the 19th, the day after he became foreign
minister, by sending Katō the further instruction that he demand a
reply from the Vichy government by noon on the 23rd. By the 21st,
a Franco-Japanese understanding for the joint defense of French
Indochina had been reached. A detailed accord based on the understanding was drafted on the 23rd and signed on the following day.
On the 24th, therefore, the Army General Staff ordered the 25th
Army to sail from Sanya as planned, thence to commence the peaceful occupation of southern French Indochina. Landings in southern
French Indochina began on the 28th.

The U.S. government's reaction was immediate and severe. On the
evening of the 25th it announced that Japanese assets in the United
States would be frozen on the 26th. Britain and Canada followed suit
on the same day, as did the Dutch East Indies on the 28th. On the
28th the Dutch East Indies also suspended its oil agreement with
Japan. Then, on August 1, the United States finally announced an
embargo against Japan on everything except cotton and foodstuffs.
Oil was included. The rupture of economic relations was a severe
blow, far more damaging to Japan in its immediate and tangible
effects than the U.S. notification of the 23rd that talks with Japan
were to be discontinued, with the impending Japanese occupation of
southern French Indochina being given as the excuse. For Japan, the
embargo was tantamount to a world-wide embargo. Its trade with
Europe had already been cut off. Except for incidental shipments,
imports of war matériel from Central and South America had also
been all but suspended by a thoroughgoing British-American corner-
ing of the market.

Since April the Cabinet Planning Board had been at work on a
fundamental plan for mobilizing matériel from the second quarter of
fiscal 1941 on, but it had been compelled to make basic changes in
that plan as the result of the outbreak of war between Germany and
the Soviet Union. On July 29 the Board finally presented to the
government and high command its "Desiderata Bearing on the Empire's Prosecution of War from the Standpoint of the Mobilization
of Matériel" to confront the new situation (see Appendix 5). The
conclusion, part 3 of the "Desiderata," came directly to the point.
From the standpoint of a plan for mobilizing matériel, Japan had
now arrived at the crossroads of deciding on war or peace. It was

essential to put war guidance on a firm footing so that a plan for mobilizing matériel could be activated in the event of resorting to war:

> Up to the present we have tried to enhance the nation's strength by relying on Britain, the United States, and others to acquire resources, but that is now becoming very difficult. Should present conditions continue, the Empire will shortly become impoverished and unable to hold its own. In other words, the Empire stands at the point of no return and must make a final decision, immediately and without hesitation.
>
> For guidance in military operations . . . it is desirable to set forth an optimal plan at the high command level that will make it possible to convert the fruits of war into productive practical uses in as short a time as possible.[159]

On August 22 the cabinet adopted the matériel mobilization plan for fiscal 1941 brought forward by the Cabinet Planning Board. In that plan the Cabinet Planning Board had come up with an even more negative forecast on matériel mobilization for fiscal 1942:

> Based on present conditions our forecast of production capability anticipates significant decreases because of shipping, oil, raw material and other shortages. Our forecast of supply capability projects that there will be a very significant decrease in matériel even if anticipated quantities from special stockpiles in Manchuria and China and imports from French Indochina and Thailand are included; particularly in regard to the kinds of oil for civilian use, such as fuel oil, gasoline, etc., and essential resources such as bauxite, there will be close to nothing from the beginning of the fiscal year.
>
> When looked at from the standpoint of mobilizing matériel, and taking all the above conditions into account, it is apparent that it is necessary now, today, to take immediate and resolute action on measures necessary for self-preservation.[160]

Nagano Advocates War

The June 5 document produced by the navy's First Committee concluded that, "although N-maneuvers [Japanese-American negotiations] are to continue, we must promote hard-line diplomacy [toward Thailand and French Indochina] . . . without regard for those maneuvers"; "it is our intention to break off N-maneuvers as the occasion calls for, depending on the progress of this hard-line diplomacy." On June 7, the day after Ōshima's telegram about the inevitability of

war between Germany and the Soviet Union, the Navy Ministry decided that "we should adhere to established policy as far as N-maneuvers are concerned, but under the circumstances these negotiations
must be concluded promptly, successful or not."[161]

At the last Liaison Conference of the second Konoe cabinet on
July 12, Nagano drew on these arguments and was the only one to
make a statement in support of Matsuoka: "If Matsuoka says that [the
United States] will not change its attitude no matter what Japan
says, what's wrong with doing what he says [and breaking off the
negotiations]?"[162] And at the new cabinet's first Liaison Conference
on July 21 he went so far as to assert:

> There's a chance now for victory against the United States, but things
> will get tougher as time goes on; by the second half of next year we
> won't be a match for them anymore. . . . We can occupy the Philippines
> if we strike now, and if we take the Philippines it will be a push-over
> after that.[163]

From the time he became navy chief of staff in April 1941, Nagano
had taken to the logic that a military advance to the south would
provoke a total embargo against Japan, which in turn would force
Japan into a war against the United States. As we have just seen, he
did not waver from this. Now, in late July, he openly advocated war
against the United States *even before the United States froze Japanese
assets* (the 26th Japan time). On the 25th, *the day before that event,*
Kobayashi Seizō called on Nagano and was told:

> The situation has turned around suddenly over the last six months.
> Things have come to such a pass that there is nothing else to do but
> stand resolute and break the iron chain that [the United States] has not
> yet finished [strangling us with]. There is absolutely no hope for a
> compromise through diplomatic negotiations or the like. I too recog-
> nize that the people are exhausted. But the only way out is to fight.
> Having said "go this way, go this way" up to now, I can't very well
> suddenly go in the opposite direction, can I?[164]

Not surprisingly, Nagano grew even more bellicose after Japanese
assets were frozen. On July 31, for example, he told the emperor that
"at this juncture, on the contrary, we have no choice but to come out
fighting." The emperor followed up: "The document you submitted
shows that we will win, therefore I too believe we will win. But a great
victory like the Battle of the Japan Sea will be difficult." Nagano was
constrained to reply that "a great victory like the Battle of the Japan

Sea is out of the question, and I am even uncertain whether we can win or not." This made the emperor most anxious, and he told Kido that "this means embarking on a war of desperation, which is truly dangerous."[165]

On the 22nd Grew had cautioned Hull that:

> I do not doubt that the Department has given careful consideration to the thought that more may be gained by letting the Japanese Government know of our intentions, privately and without publicity, preferably through Admiral Nomura if this has not already been done, before rather than after a Japanese occupation of bases in Indochina. . . . A clear unambiguous statement of such intentions might conceivably exert a deterrent effect, but, once an occupation were effected, Japanese prestige would render subsequent withdrawal out of the question. It would seem to be a grave error to allow American-Japanese relations to advance one step further on the road to potential war through any possible misconception on the part of the Japanese Government as to the determination of the United States to take positive action in the event of certain contingencies.[166]

Grew's advice was not followed, but even if it had been, it would have had no impact on the navy, which had taken into account the possibility that a total embargo would be invoked while troops were occupying southern Indochina and had gone ahead with this anyway.

Just as it had in the series of discussions leading up to the Imperial Conference of July 2, however, the army continued until the very end to cling to its self-serving judgment that there would be no total embargo. Had an unofficial warning from the United States government along the lines advised by Grew been received before the Imperial Conference on July 2, the army might have reconsidered its position. In any event, Grew's advisory was not made around the time of the Imperial Conference. When Sugiyama reported to the Throne that the June 25 Liaison Conference had decided to station troops in southern French Indochina, he stated that this action "would have no effect on foreign countries whatever."[167] At the Imperial Conference he insisted that "stationing forces in French Indochina will most certainly provoke Britain and America. . . . But stationing to the extent we have in mind at this time might put a force-out on their maneuverings in Southeast Asia."[168] Nomura's telegram of the 23rd had reported:

> As to the effect our southern advance is having on Japanese-American relations, there have been quite precipitous developments today. . . .

The southern advance is seen here as going one step this side of severing diplomatic relations. In my judgment the reason for this sudden change in atmosphere toward Japan is that the United States considers our southern advance to be the first step toward our advancing into Singapore and the Dutch East Indies.[169]

When Toyoda brought this up and repeated observations to the same effect at the July 24 Liaison Conference, the army's War Guidance Office belittled the telegram: "One can't help being amazed at how hysterical the telegram from Nomura is. This office dissents."[170] And it kept on with this line of thinking:

We firmly believe there will be no embargo so long as we go no further than stationing troops in French Indochina (the 25th).
   This office does not consider [the freezing of assets] a total embargo, and it is our judgement that the United States will not invoke one. It might come sometime, but it is our judgment that this will not happen this year or early next (the 26th).[171]

Consequently, the army was totally nonplussed by the resolute measures taken by the United States.[172]

Ever since the Hull counterproposal arrived, the army had been infatuated with the idea that once Matsuoka was out of the way there would be room for accommodation: the United States would act as mediator in the Sino-Japanese War, tacitly acquiesce in Japan's military advance southward, and even reach an overall adjustment in diplomatic relations with Japan. Rudely awakened by America's decisive actions, the army not surprisingly gave up on this. In its place, the anger and mistrust that had been growing against the United States since the end of June was to become decisive.

The Determination of the Army General Staff: No More Than Skin Deep

Informed that the United States had frozen Japanese assets, middle-echelon officers in the Operations Division of the Army General Staff stiffened their backs and insisted on a military solution. By the 28th opinion was rife that war with Britain and the United States was inevitable.[173] On August 2 Operations Division Chief Tanaka informed the Operations Section that "it looks to me like war both to the south and to the north is inevitable."[174] The Army Ministry's Military Affairs Section had also firmly resolved to go to war with Britain and the United States, proposing that an Imperial Conference be held to obtain formal approval for commencing operations in the south. On the 9th the "Outline of Imperial Army Operations" was adopted, calling for a halt to the Special Exercises for the Kwantung Army during the current year and ending with the statement that Japan should now "accelerate preparations for war with Britain and America in the south, with the goal of completing them by the end of November." [175]

The army's War Guidance Office, however, was unable to rid itself of gnawing doubts about the future, despite being at the center of these trends. For example:

1) On the chances of victory.

"Should we resolve to go to war with Britain and the United States? A long drawn-out war with the United States must be avoided. Even if there is no chance for victory in a war with Britain and the United States, is there no chance of not losing?" (August 8)

2) On Axis policy.

"Should we capitulate to Britain and America? We oppose withdrawing from the Axis. Can we capitulate to the United States at this late date? Does the honor of the Empire allow apparent withdrawal, not to speak of actual withdrawal?" (August 8)

3) On banking on Germany.

"Is there is no way out besides going to war or capitulating? Do we not have the option of delaying as long as possible the outbreak of war between Japan and the United States by making temporary compromises that will not tarnish the honor of the Empire? Or at least the option of restraining the United States and getting oil until such time as Germany again intensifies its attacks on Britain?" (August 8)

4) On the intentions of the United States.

"On what diplomatic terms shall we proceed with the United States? Diplomatic success is highly doubtful if we make only a partial retreat or capitulation; if we capitulate totally the United States will deliver oil. If we only agree not to advance south, will the United States deliver oil or not?" (August 8) [176] "Even if we can pull through by acquiring oil on a temporary basis by means of diplomacy, what if the United States perfects its naval and air armaments in the interim? Should that occur, will we not be immobilized when our oil supply is stopped?" (August 12)[177]

"Does the United States truly desire a long-term peace in the Pacific or not? Is it not that they want only a temporary peace in the Pacific in order to get out of their present predicament? If the former, there just might be room for diplomatic measures made possible through trust between the Japanese and American authorities concerned. At present, however, mutual trust is problematic." (August 13)[178]

On the other hand, Navy War Guidance Office Chief Ōno Takeji told a gathering of middle-echelon officers from both services on July 29 that:

The army cannot come to a resolution on this without the navy's doing so. The navy will most certainly come to a resolution within a few days and, once this has been cleared at the top, it will make its intentions perfectly clear to the army.[179]

That same day it was reported that Navy Chief of Staff Nagano had stated flatly, "This means war."[180] Of course, this was only natural in light of what Nagano was to report to the Throne on the 31st, as noted above. The army also found out that the navy's administrative authorities had also resolved to go to war with the United States.

Sure enough, the navy formally presented its "Plan for Carrying Out the Empire's Policies" at the August 16 army-navy conference of bureau and division chiefs. The gist of the Plan was that Japan should push forward simultaneously with preparations for war, to be completed by late October, as well as with diplomacy. If a diplomatic agreement could not be reached by the middle of October, Japan would exercise force. Just before the conference a member of the navy's War Guidance Office had informed the Army General Staff that "the 'Plan' was drafted by our superiors."[181] That the leaders of the Navy General Staff had resolved on going to war with the United States can also be amply inferred from the fact that the navy had informed the army on the 15th of the concrete measures it would like taken in preparation for such a war: "1) war preparations are to be concluded by October 15; 2) the army-navy operations agreement is to be carried out on September 20; 3) 300,000 tons are to be requisitioned in August, the same again in September, and a further 500,000 tons after the middle of September (only this last measure is pending)."

On August 18 the army's War Guidance Office presented a revised draft of the navy's Plan to Tanaka, whose uncompromising view that "a resolution" had to be made at once led to further revisions. Sugiyama and his subordinates gave this second revised draft their general approval and it was transmitted to the Army Ministry on the 19th. The ministry produced a counter-draft on the 20th, "a thoughtful draft, to put it in a good light," that endeavored to incorporate "the import of the navy's proposal to complete preparations for war without resolving on going to war" for the present.[182] This accorded with what a member of the navy's War Guidance Office emphasized on the 20th: "It should be put into the kind of prose that will pass muster at the top; even a rotten draft will do for now if we can get it by at the top and put on more pressure."[183]

On the 22nd and 23rd the Army General Staff deliberated additions to its second revised draft proposed by the Army Ministry and then arrived at its final version, which was sent back to the Army Ministry. Sugiyama was "unclear about where the true intention" of the document lay but nonetheless "seemed the very picture of composure," while Vice Chief Tsukada was "very firm-willed, as if he had arrived at a resolution for war after having suffered one gnawing doubt after another for about a month."[184] But what had the Army General Staff solved by this? They had not even resolved the one question that had given its War Guidance Office such gnawing doubts on the 8th: "Even though there is no chance of victory in a war with Britain and the United States, is there no chance of not losing?"

Those most involved in terms of their army responsibilities were Chief of Staff Sugiyama, Vice Chief Tsukada, and Operations Division Chief Tanaka. Yet all three had limited careers as far as actual operations were concerned, and none had wrestled with questions of national strength and war-making capability. They had resolved on war without having first thought through the issues of how that war would be actually conducted, the conditions under which it would be fought, or what it would take to win. Their capacity to give mature, thorough, and judicious attention to such basics of war leadership was attenuated indeed. Tanaka, however, was both clever and a man of action. Sugiyama and Tsukada seem to have been overpowered by his forceful and positive arguments, going along with him without making any substantial investigation of their own.

What might account for such a positive attitude on Tanaka's part? It was the Army Ministry's responsibility to assess the nation's physical capacity to sustain a war, while the actual prosecution of a war with the United States would fall to the navy. Ever since July 1940, when the "Main Principles for Coping with the Changing World Situation" was adopted, the navy had consistently assured the army that there were chances for success,[185] and therefore Tanaka must have assumed that the navy really did stand a chance. Although he had lost hope that the German army would bring the war with the Soviet Union to a conclusion during the current year, he still expected Germany to win in 1942. In essence, he went along with the navy on the chances for success against the United States, while banking on the god-sent golden opportunity to be afforded by German victory in the coming year. In any case, there is no evidence that in arriving at its resolution for war the Army General Staff had joined with the Army Ministry in a rigorous assessment of the nation's strength, or with the Navy General Staff in an exhaustive examination of Japan's chances for success against the United States. There is no better proof of how subjective and no more than skin deep this resolution was than the statement made by a pale and haggard Tsukada at daybreak on November 2, when the upshot of the Tōjō cabinet's reexamination of state policy was to arrive at the same "resolution" as that reached in August:

> No one was willing to say, "that's okay, I'll take blanket responsibility for the war, even a protracted war." We have simply reconciled ourselves to the conclusion that war is inevitable. . . . If Britain falls, the United States ought to have second thoughts. Five years from now you ask? How should I know what military operations, politics, or diplomacy will look like?[186]

Replace Nagano and Oikawa?

Toward the end of August Secretary to the Navy Ministry Enomoto Shigeharu called on Kobayashi Seizō and expressed his anxieties: "Nagano was moderate until the other day but just recently he has become altogether bull-headed; it looks like he is being dragged along by the jingoists."[187] Kobayashi understood this to mean that Nagano was being pressured by middle-echelon officers and had lost his composure, becoming rashly assertive. Kobayashi visited Konoe on August 22 and cautioned him:

> I think that Nagano has recently become a hard-liner because he has lost his equanimity as the result of ill health and of pressure from middle-echelon officers in the navy who are close to middle-echelon

officers in the army. Nagano's show of toughness makes no sense, given that the navy's matériel preparations, for instance, are inadequate for a long war.[188]

Konoe then expressed his hope that Nagano would be replaced:

Nagano has taken moderate positions for some time now, but lately he has rashly come out with a hard line, just like Sugiyama. That troubles me. (It is clear), in fact, that His Majesty has very little confidence in Nagano. It seems that Nagano cannot even answer His Majesty's questions readily, even correcting himself at times, and His Majesty tells me that he has had just about enough. I too hope that Nagano will be relieved. He does belong to the high command, however, and it would not do for me to propose this to the navy minister even though I am the prime minister. I have, in fact, mentioned my personal opinion to Toyoda Teijirō [former navy vice minister], but in any case, I want you people to use your influence to ease Nagano out somehow.[189]

Having broached the subject, Kobayashi took it upon himself to consult each of the navy elders—Yonai Mitsumasa, Okada Keisuke, and Takarabe Takeshi—on the 24th or 25th. They were all of the same opinion. Kobayashi reported this to Toyoda at the end of the month and pressed him to use his good offices in the matter. But Toyoda declined, skirting the main issue by saying:

Replacing Nagano is fine, but what is more imperative is to replace the navy minister first. Even when a matter concerns the navy, Oikawa doesn't say a word [at cabinet meetings]. Even if you pump him he won't give an opinion. If the navy minister would only pull himself together and stand up for what he believes, there would hardly be any occasion for Nagano to take such a hard line at Liaison Conferences.[190]

Takarabe had pointed out to Kobayashi that "if Konoe spoke plainly to Oikawa, wouldn't that be quickest and simplest?" But Konoe would neither engage in a heart-to-heart talk with Oikawa nor would he replace him. And because of the friction between Konoe and Toyoda the original matter of replacing Nagano was also dropped.

During this episode Yonai told Kobayashi:

Yamamoto would be good as Oikawa's successor. If that poses problems, Yamamoto and Oikawa could switch places. In any event, I think it essential that Yamamoto be in Tokyo [as navy minister].[191]

In light of the fatal results of Oikawa's equivocation over the next month and a half, Yonai's observation went right to the navy's weak spot.

The "Essentials for Carrying Out the Empire's Policies"

On August 25 Tōjō, Mutō, Satō, Sugiyama, and Tsukada met to discuss the Army General Staff's final version of the "Plan for Carrying Out the Empire's Policies." Following further discussions between Mutō and Tanaka that same day, agreement was largely reached. In doing so, the Army Ministry's Mutō would have nothing to do with pursuing a rigorous assessment of Japan's matériel strength and merely immersed himself in the arts of semantic compromise, largely to rein in the navy. The maneuvering to reach a semantic compromise continued when the army-navy conference of bureau and division chiefs resumed on the 27th and 28th. In the meantime, reasoning that it would further the resolve to go to war, the army revised the phrase "resolves to go to war" in the navy's original draft to read "based on the resolve to go to war." The navy then altered this to read "based on the resolve not to flinch from war." In this fashion, on the 30th both sides reached a consensus decision on the draft "Essentials for Carrying Out the Empire's Policies" (see Appendix 6).[192]

A supplement to the draft included "limits on what the Empire can agree to" in negotiations with the United States. An "addendum" to the supplement expressly stated with respect to those "limits" that interpretations of the Tripartite Pact and actions thereunder were to be made with complete autonomy. A "note to the addendum" contained the proviso that "the above in no way alters the Empire's obligations under the Tripartite Pact." Things like this were stylistic perfections in the art of semantic compromise among the respective opinions of the Army General Staff, the Army Ministry, and the navy. The Army General Staff adhered firmly to its "Axis spirit," which was to bank on Germany. On September 2 Sugiyama went so far as to write Konoe that there must be no wavering on three provisos: adherence to the Axis alliance, realization of the Greater East Asia Coprosperity Sphere, and no withdrawal of troops from China. In contrast, Mutō grew stronger in his self-serving enthusiasm for a possible negotiated agreement with the United States, and just before the Liaison Conference on September 3rd he became embroiled in a fierce argument with Tanaka over whether it was actually necessary for Japan to fulfill its obligations under the Tripartite Pact.

At the Liaison Conference itself Oikawa strongly objected to the phraseology of the concluding sentence in Article 3 of the proposed "Essentials," which stated: "In the event that we cannot obtain our demands by early October, we shall resolve to go to war with the United States." An agreement was finally reached when this was revised to read, "In the event that by early October *there is still no prospect of obtaining* our demands through diplomatic negotiations. . . ." (author's emphasis.) The War Guidance Office pointed out that Oikawa's revision "actually guts the draft, going to the very core, the pivot on which everything turns; [whether there is no prospect] will come up for extensive debate once again in early October." Consequently, when that office heard that Oikawa's revision had carried verbatim at the September 6 Imperial Conference, it "was not overcome by the feeling that anything in particular had been decided." With the exception of the debate on Oikawa's revision, the Liaison Conference of September 3 went forward with astonishing smoothness when compared to the June 25 Liaison Conference (which decided to station troops in southern French Indochina) or that of June 28 (which decided on state policy in response to the German-Soviet war). In only one discussion of just seven hours they lightheartedly approved the draft "Essentials." Surely this is evidence of the flatness of debate after Matsuoka departed.

The Army General Staff immediately began preparing for the September 6 Imperial Conference, compiling materials to answer questions from the participants. Among the questions and answers it prepared, the following are worth noting:

1) QUESTION: Is war with Britain and the United States unavoidable?
ANSWER: The construction of a New Order in East Asia, centering on the Empire's disposition of the China Incident, is unshakeable national policy. However, United States policy toward Japan rests on a status quo world view that would obstruct the Empire's rise and expansion in East Asia in order to dominate the world and defend democracy. The policy of Japan is in fundamental contradiction to this. Collisions between the two will finally develop into war after periods of tension and relaxation. This may be said to have the nature of historical inevitability. So long as the United States does not alter its policies toward Japan, the realities of the situation will reduce the Empire to the point of no

return where it cannot help but resort to war as the final means of self-preservation and self-defense. If for the sake of a temporary peace we were now to yield one step to the United States by a partial retreat from state policy, the strengthening of America's military position will lead to its demanding further retreats of ten steps then a hundred. Ultimately, the Empire will wind up having to do whatever the United States wants it to do.

2) QUESTION: If the terms [demands] enumerated in the "Supplement Part One" are not accepted in their entirety, will this cause a breakdown in diplomacy [with the United States]?

ANSWER: Once we promise [as per the Supplement Part Two] not to exercise force in the south, China must without fail do exactly as our Empire wishes. Without question the absolute requisite to this end is the stationing of necessary troops. If we withdraw all our forces, for instance, China will not heed what we say, and Japan will not be able to survive. And of course, once we do promise not to exercise force in the south, we must have the Americans refrain from engaging in such actions as would threaten the national defense of the Empire. If they do not accede to the conditions we have presented, we must take the view that they harbor designs to bring Japan to its knees; thus, it is clear that if we make concessions we will soon be put to their poisoned swords.

3) QUESTION: With the kind of demands and limits on what we can agree to as those in the Supplement, what is the outlook for negotiations with the United States?

ANSWER: They will be successful only if there is a spirit of mutual concession between Japan and the United States. If the United States only demands concessions from Japan, which is its present attitude—and in particular tries to make us abandon our disposition of the China Incident and the construction of a Greater East Asia Coprosperity Sphere, as well as insists that we withdraw from the Tripartite Alliance—there is little probability of success.

4) QUESTION: What is the outlook in the war between Germany and the Soviet Union, and what operations by the German army are anticipated after this?

ANSWER: The probability is great that the German army will annihilate the main Soviet field armies by the end of October or the beginning of November; that, occupying the main part of Soviet Europe, it will take on a beaten

Soviet army with part of its powerful forces and then commence operations in the Caucasus, Near East, and North Africa. Because of this we judge as follows:

1. The line of advance this fall will be a line connecting the White Sea, the eastern side of Moscow, and the Donbas.
2. From around the time the above operations in Soviet Europe are concluded, operations in the Caucasus will next be launched, soon to be followed by operations in the Near East and North Africa.
3. As far as operations against Britain are concerned, air raids will gradually intensify with the redeployment of air power now assigned to operations against the Soviet Union. The war to destroy commerce will also be stepped up. But landing operations will probably be postponed until next spring or summer, after operations in the Near East and North Africa are concluded.

It is virtually certain that Germany will sweep through the greater part of Soviet Europe within the year and that the Stalin regime will flee east of the Urals. . . . It is clear that the Stalin regime, having lost Soviet Europe, will weaken with the passage of time and lose its capacity to prosecute the war.[193]

The answers to questions 2) and 3) reveal the following scenario: adherence to Matsuoka's revised proposal, which would lead to failure in negotiations with the United States, which in turn would lead to resolving on war with the United States. A carbon copy of Matsuoka's arguments, the answer to question 1) speaks to the fact that there was still no reconsideration based on strategic outcomes, even when it came to resolving on war with the United States. Moreover, the answer to 4) leads us to infer that Japan's chances largely depended on the German army.

In any event, the army came up with a way of unilaterally foreclosing the government's options. Once the consensus among army-navy bureau and division chiefs was reached on August 30, it had Colonel Mabuchi Itsuo, chief of the Information Division, make a pro-war radio speech on September 1—prior to bringing up the issue of going to war at the September 3 Liaison Conference. And on the same day the navy also activated the fiscal 1941 plan for full wartime mobilization and put the final touches on mobilizing the fleet for war—without waiting for a state policy decision and without consulting the army or the government.

The Emperor Reproaches Sugiyama

The navy's first formal reference to its chances for success against the United States, chances that the army had already deduced, was Nagano's statement at the Imperial Conference of September 6 (see below). His main line of argument was that a war against the United States would be a protracted one, but that successful operations during its first stages could make for the preservation of an invincible position, establishing the first and fundamental requirement for prolonged operations. Thereafter those operations would depend on the nation's total strength and developments in the international situation.[194] This was to constitute the basic thread through all of Nagano's pronouncements on the chances for success until war broke out in December. That the Army General Staff also went along with this line of reasoning may be deduced from the forlorn answer it prepared to another question in its brief for the September 6 Imperial Conference:

> QUESTION: What is the outlook in a war with Britain and the United States—in particular, how shall we bring the war to a conclusion?
>
> ANSWER: In any case, by occupying the necessary areas to the south. . . . we should be able to consolidate an invincible position; by taking advantage of conditions in the interim, we can entertain hopes of being able to bring the war to an end.[195]

The emperor was clearly aware of the desperation that lay behind Nagano's abstract arguments on the chances for success, as in his report to the Throne on July 31, and expressed "extreme apprehension"[196] over Japan's prospects in a war with the United States as set forth by Nagano and Sugiyama.

When on the afternoon of the 5th Konoe secretly informed the emperor beforehand of the contents of the Liaison Conference's final draft, the emperor asked him: "The order in which the particulars of the plan are set down is a bit strange. Why aren't diplomatic negotiations put first?" Konoe replied lamely that the draft "did attach primary importance to diplomatic negotiations, just as if diplomatic negotiations were put first in the plan." When the emperor went on to voice doubts regarding operational matters as well, Konoe asked him to summon the chiefs of the high command and withdrew.[197] At six that evening Konoe attended as the two chiefs responded to the emperor's questions. According to the Konoe Memorandum and Kido's deposition, the following exchange took place:

EMPEROR: If something happens between Japan and the United States, how long does the army really believe it will take to clear things up?

SUGIYAMA: If limited to the South Seas, I would expect to clear things up in three months.

EMPEROR: You were army minister at the time the China Incident broke out, and I remember you saying: "The Incident will be cleared up in about a month." But it still hasn't been cleared up after four long years, has it?"

SUGIYAMA: China opens onto a [vast—trans.] hinterland and military operations could not be conducted as planned.

EMPEROR   (raising his voice in reproach): If the hinterland of China is vast, isn't the Pacific Ocean even more vast? What convinces you to say three months?

(Sugiyama lowers his head, unable to reply; Nagano comes to the rescue with an explanation.)

EMPEROR: The high command understands that as of today the objective is to emphasize diplomacy, correct?

SUGIYAMA,
NAGANO: That is correct.

Although the emperor had questioned him about land warfare in a general war between Japan and the United States, Sugiyama had deliberately limited his replies to initial operations in the south, so it was only natural for the emperor to keep after him. But more important, this exchange suggests that the emperor lacked confidence in Sugiyama, who merely followed Nagano's line with haphazard indirection. In fact, that evening Military Section Chief Sanada Jōichirō argued that "at this critical juncture it is a sorry matter for the chief of the Army General Staff not to have His Majesty's confidence; we've got to get him replaced."[198] But Sugiyama got by without resigning.

Moreover, the emperor had twice made sure that diplomacy would come first. Neither Konoe nor the two chiefs of staff could be in any doubt about his wishes on this. And Konoe had been made aware of his wishes both times, once directly and once while in attendance. Of course, the Meiji Constitution did not give the emperor a veto power; nor was it necessary for the emperor's officials to accede to his wishes in the first place. The point is that if they did accede to his recommendations, the emperor's officials would be liable for them as their own voluntary acts of advice and assistance, in this instance as those of the prime minister and both chiefs of staff. Thus, once they had agreed when the emperor made sure that "the objective is to emphasize diplomacy," it was only right that Sugiyama and Nagano work with Konoe to rewrite the draft "Essentials" accordingly. This was especially so considering that it was perfectly clear to anyone who gave the document an unbiased reading that a deadline on diplomatic negotiations was a device to trigger the resolve to go to war, and that Konoe's replies to the Throne were so lame as to be unsupportable in this context. But all three dared not do a rewrite, and they went before the Imperial Conference on the following day with the draft "Essentials" unchanged.

A Stormy Imperial Conference

The Imperial Conference began at 10 a.m. and followed the usual format. First, statements were made by Prime Minister Konoe, Chiefs of Staff Nagano and Sugiyama, and Cabinet Planning Board Director Suzuki Teiichi. Then Privy Council President Hara Yoshimichi, as prearranged with Privy Seal Kido, stressed the need for the utmost in diplomatic efforts to break the deadlock:

> In perusing the draft it would appear that war is primary and diplomacy secondary. However, I take it that we are to make out-and-out efforts now to achieve a diplomatic breakthrough; only when those fail will we have to go to war.

Sugiyama was about to rise in response to this when Oikawa stood up and repeated the same lame interpretation that Konoe had given to the Throne the previous day:

> The import of the draft is just as Hara interprets it. War preparations in Article 1 and diplomacy in Article 2 carry the same weight. A resolution on Article 3 will be made at a cabinet meeting and then given imperial sanction.

Hara made doubly sure about what Oikawa had committed himself to:

> The import of this proposal has been clarified by your comments. Because this draft was approved at a Liaison Conference, I am persuaded that the high command also agrees with the navy minister, and that puts my mind at ease. When Prime Minister Konoe goes to the United States, it is essential for him to feel that his main objective is to

adjust relations somehow or other through diplomacy, bearing in mind that we shall be preparing for war while doing everything possible in terms of diplomacy. If this proposal receives the Imperial Assent, I ask your cooperation in supporting the prime minister's mission to the United States, and in avoiding the worst possible situation between Japan and the United States.[199]

Then suddenly the emperor raised his voice: "The question Hara has just asked makes sense; why doesn't the high command answer?" He then took a piece of paper from his pocket and read out a *waka* composed by the Emperor Meiji:

> Across the four seas
> All are brothers.
> In such a world
> Why do the waves rage,
> The winds roar?

"I always read this composition with humility," he added, "endeavoring to be instructed in the late emperor's peace-loving spirit." Taken aback, Nagano and Sugiyama replied to the effect that "we are in complete agreement with the import of what Hara said."[200] Thereupon this singularly stormy Imperial Conference came to a close.

Immediately after the conference Kido recorded that the emperor had told the high command that it "must cooperate fully in diplomatic maneuvers."[201] It was rare for the emperor to make remarks at any of the conferences around this time, much less remarks in anger. On the other hand, the emperor himself had previously made it clear that he wished to make Imperial Conferences, which had lapsed into ceremonies for rubber-stamping prepared documents, opportunities for the kind of thorough examination of state policies that would satisfy him. On August 11 he told Kido:

Imperial Conferences up to now have been really perfunctory, so this time I thought I might try asking questions until I am sufficiently satisfied. In this connection, how about leaving out of these conferences staff people, such as the chief of the Military Affairs Bureau, and having them composed of the following: prime minister, foreign minister, finance minister, army minister, navy minister, director of the Cabinet Planning Board, the chief of the Army General Staff, the chief of the Navy General Staff. To these it might be good to add the three field marshals and admirals of the fleet. I would like you to consult thoroughly with the prime minister about these participants.[202]

And twenty minutes before the Imperial Conference of the 6th convened, he again made clear to Kido that he wanted to ask questions himself at the Imperial Conference that day. Kido had done nothing about the emperor's suggestions on the composition of Imperial Conferences, which basically went in one ear and out the other, and now he opposed the emperor's wish to ask questions directly:

> Since Privy Council President Hara is expected to ask questions concerning the points about which Your Majesty has serious doubts, it would be most appropriate for Your Majesty, at the very end, to issue an admonition to the effect that because the decision this time is a grave one that might lead to a war in which the nation's destiny will be at stake, the high command must cooperate fully in bringing success to our diplomatic maneuvers.[203]

It might well be that the deaf ears and obstruction of Kido, the extremely lame interpretations put forward by Konoe and Oikawa, and the lack of concern shown by Sugiyama and Nagano in presenting an utterly unrevised "Essentials" to the September 6 Imperial Conference despite having the previous day accepted, as his responsible advisers, the emperor's "objective" "to emphasize diplomacy," all led the emperor to a rare expression of anger. Only the emperor, in abandoning semantics, truly agonized at this crossroads between peace and war. Lacking a veto power in the first place, and having his plan to ask questions thwarted by Kido, this was probably all the emperor could constitutionally have done. In any event, his remarks suddenly changed the atmosphere of the Imperial Conference, making it diametrically opposed to one of textual concerns with the semantics of state policies.

The Sole Opportunity to Wipe the Slate Clean

The army was the most keenly impressed by this sudden change of atmosphere. Upon returning to his office from the conference, Tōjō exclaimed: "His Majesty's wish is for peace, I tell you!"[204] And Mutō blurted out excitedly to a member of the Military Affairs Bureau: "War is absolutely out of the question! Listen up now. His Majesty told us to reach a diplomatic settlement on this, no matter what it takes. We've got to go with diplomacy."[205]

On the face of it, the state policy approved at this Imperial Conference would no doubt convert the nation's strength overwhelmingly to a war footing. Once put in motion on a national scale, it would be very difficult to call it off, much less restore the status quo ante, because of the massive faits accomplis that would have subsequently accumulated. At the very instant that this policy of changing the nation's orientation from negotiating peace to going to war was about to be approved, the emperor's remarks transformed the atmosphere of the conference and the army instantly submitted to him. This was the one and only golden opportunity that would allow Japan to change its mind about preparing for war and to "wipe the slate clean."

Years later Konoe himself wrote that "Sugiyama was apprehensive and Tōjō had been deeply moved by the emperor's remarks."[206] *If* at this conference Konoe had accepted the emperor's remarks and had said that he would that very day withdraw the proposal to rework it along the lines the emperor called for and on the responsibility of the government, and *if* he had immediately set about reworking the proposal to accord with "the objective . . . is to emphasize diplomacy" as the emperor wished, there is no small possibility that Konoe might have succeeded on the domestic front, apart from the question of relations with the United States, given the sentiments expressed by Tōjō and Mutō and the pledges given to the emperor by both chiefs of staff. Konoe and Toyoda, however, had grown used to viewing state policy as semantics since the summer of 1940, and on October 12, just before resigning, Konoe told Suzuki that "that [Imperial] Conference was an informal matter to begin with,"[207] and Toyoda described the Imperial Conference decision as "rash."[208] Kido also stated at the Conference of Senior Statesmen on October 17, "The fact is that a very serious decision was hastily reached at this Imperial Conference."[209] Such statements reveal how little attention they had paid to the gravity of the decision; as usual, they simply rubber-stamped the text without pursuing a thorough examination as the emperor had wished. And they blithely let go by the one and only opportunity they had at the time to "wipe the slate clean."

When the Army General Staff proposal was finalized on August 23, the army's War Guidance Office went so far as to predict that, "The chief of the Army General Staff and his subordinates have serious doubts about whether the Army General Staff proposal does in fact coincide with the views of the government; the downfall of the cabinet is inevitable [should the two conflict—trans.]."[210] But feeling that words were merely words, even when it came to a state policy that determined on war or peace, Konoe had gone ahead with plans for direct talks with Roosevelt—not so much in parallel with that state policy decision as unrelated to it. And it was Konoe's hope for the fuluie that whatever this semantic state policy might have approved, it could be aborted if adjustments in diplomatic relations between Japan and the United States could be worked out in direct talks. Konoe also hoped that even though there was a deadline of early October on diplomatic negotiations, a scant month away, that too could somehow be extended by manipulating the phrase "no prospect." Such hopes naturally meant that he was trying to gut the text of an approved state policy through negotiations with the United States, which in turn would provoke the military to oppose him.

5 Toyoda's Diplomacy Fails

Konoe Argues for Direct Talks

The United States froze Japan's assets in the United States on July 26, but Konoe remained optimistic. On the 30th his private secretary, Ushiba Tomohiko, informed James Espy, third secretary at the American embassy, that although "Admiral Toyoda had been very pessimistic over the events that had occurred since his assumption of office, Prince Konoye on the other hand appeared to view the situation quite optimistically."[211]

When Konoe chatted with Tōjō and Oikawa on the evening of August 4, he expressed confidence that he could maintain peace in the Pacific through direct talks with Roosevelt, and he asked for their support. Konoe then ventured to elaborate:

1. The issue is not to bridge the differences with the United States at whatever cost, nor of course should we play the coquette and then submit in our haste to bridge the differences. . . . From the very outset we must be ready to walk out and come home if Roosevelt doesn't come across.

2. If it comes to war after we have done all that can be done, that can't be helped. In that case we will have come to a resolution and the people will also be fully prepared. Moreover, it will be clearly understood by the world in general that we have shown good faith in going to such lengths, and this may be of some use in alleviating a deterioration in world opinion. I think it necessary both domestically and internationally to do all we can do.

3. Consequently, what is involved here is our being fully prepared for war with the United States.[212]

The reverse side of Konoe's optimistic self-confidence may have been a calculation on his part that underestimated the military: if only a summit materialized and an agreement were reached on adjusting diplomatic relations, the military would not be a problem. But the straightforward Tōjō took what Konoe had said at face value, using the opportunity to advance parts of what Konoe had elaborated as the army's preconditions for a summit conference. Aware that by July 28 talk was rife in the Army General Staff that war with the United States and Britain was inevitable, on August 5 Tōjō and Mutō approached Sugiyama and Tanaka, respectively, to seek their approval:

> We can't say that Konoe can't go to the United States. We figure it's 80 percent certain that his trip will end up a failure, but even if he does fail we'll have pinned the prime minister down about not resigning.[213]

But they still had their doubts, because trying to pin Konoe down "might be like trying to nail jelly to a wall."[214]

Nonetheless, Sugiyama and Tanaka gave their conditional approval in writing that same day:

> Holding firmly to the fundamental objectives for N-Maneuvers set out in the revised proposal, we shall make one last effort. If Roosevelt misinterprets our Empire's true intentions and persists in pursuing the same old policies, no objections can possibly be raised to prevent our confronting this with resolute determination to join battle with the United States.[215]

Here was expressed the faint hope that Hull still might reverse his position and agree to one of Matsuoka's revised proposals, even at a time when indignation and suspicion toward the United States were becoming more and more decisive in the army. And it preserved a shred of the self-serving assessment that continued even after assets were frozen, one evident ever since the army and navy had forced a reluctant Matsuoka to send out his re-revised proposal in mid July.

As for the navy, Nagano based his position on the First Committee's position paper and took the lead at liaison conferences from July 12 on in advocating that negotiations between Japan and the United States should be broken off and that Japan should go to war. Ishikawa, who had authored the First Committee paper, also got angry with the army, calling the plan for a summit meeting "an odd artifice."[216] On the other hand, Oikawa gave his complete approval to that plan the very day Konoe proposed it, even though preparations for dispatching expeditionary forces would be virtually complete by

September 1. He even added that he hoped the summit would succeed. Oikawa's equivocal attitude when it came to managing departmental affairs stood in stark contrast to that of the straightforward Tōjō, and it is worth noting that that attitude grew more and more pronounced as the day of his resignation in mid-October approached.

After Japanese assets in the United States were frozen, Konoe reported almost daily to the emperor on each new development as it suddenly occurred: July 28, 29, 30, 31, August 2, 4, and 6. On August 7 the emperor urged him to proceed at once with direct talks as proposed. Konoe had instructions cabled to Nomura immediately, initiating his plan for a summit conference:

> The present state of affairs between Japan and the United States is fraught with extraordinary tensions as the result of misunderstandings between the two nations and the scheming of third parties, whatever we will on our part. Aware that we cannot let things drift as they are now, we are convinced that at this juncture the only way to overcome this dangerous state of affairs is to explore the possibility of rescuing the situation by means of direct meetings and a frank exchange of views between Japanese and American leaders.
>
> In our opinion there are also pertinent matters for discussion in the first American proposal. If the United States agrees, Prime Minister Konoe himself desires to make an official trip to Honolulu and talk intimately with President Roosevelt. In this regard we would like Your Excellency to sound out the American side immediately, emphasizing that his proposal is based on our earnest wish to maintain peace in the Pacific.[217]

In subsequent telegrams Toyoda also importuned Nomura:

> In his heart-to-heart talks with the president, the prime minister will not limit himself to the August 5 proposal [a plan for a local solution] but will try to come up with a breakthrough in the situation from the larger perspective of preserving world peace. Please leave no misunderstandings on this point in your representations to the United States government. (Dispatch of August 12)[218]
>
> Public opinion in Japan being just and fair, it will endorse a proper adjustment of relations with any country whatever. (Dispatch of August 15)[219]

Hull, on the other hand, had decided that by this time there was no leeway whatever for him to reconsider his position. The third Konoe cabinet had done no more than oust Matsuoka, and had continued his policies virtually unchanged; now it had gone ahead and stationed troops in southern Indochina. On August 6 Nomura presented Hull with the plan for a local solution, Hull having appeared at his office for the first time in around two months. Hull all but refused to consider it, saying that "he was frankly pessimistic over the prospect of getting anywhere with a proposal such as that. . . . he . . . felt doubtful that there was any prospect of being able to deal at this time with any proposal of the Japanese Government. . . ."[220] "He cannot but be deeply discouraged when it comes to contemplating the succession of actions Japan will take thereafter. There is no room for conversations if Japan does not give up its policy of conquest by brute force. Nothing is to be expected from Japan as long as its government leaders call what the United States is doing a policy of encirclement" (Nomura dispatch of August 6).[221]

During the August 9–12 Atlantic Conference, moreover, Sumner Welles had reported to Sir Alexander Cadogan, Britain's permanent undersecretary for foreign affairs, that when these proposals were delivered Hull had indicated to Nomura that "he was in no hurry whatever to consider the messages. . . or even to read them."[222] Secretary of War Henry L. Stimson wrote in his diary for the period August 7 to August 9 that Hull had "made up his mind that we have reached the end of any possible appeasement with Japan and that there is nothing further that can be done with that country except by a firm policy and, he expected, force itself." Hull and Stimson concluded that "the invitation [to a summit conference] is merely a blind to try to keep us from taking definite action."[223] "Not budging an inch," Hull gave Nomura his reply to the plan for a regional settlement on the 8th:

> The use of force by the Japanese government contradicts what Your Excellency and I are consulting over. So long as there is no change in that policy there is no basis for consultations. . . . We can begin consultations only when Japan stops using force. (Nomura dispatch of August 8)[224]

He made it clear that the cabinet change in Japan had produced no grounds for changing the July 23 notification that talks would be broken off. Nomura then brought forward the plan for a summit conference. Hull showed little interest, saying he was not confident about conveying it to Roosevelt as long as there was no change in Japanese policies.

Roosevelt's "Ultimatum."

On the 8th Roosevelt was on the high seas en route to Placentia Bay, Newfoundland, for the Atlantic Conference with Churchill. Three months after the conference Churchill wrote his old friend General Jan Smuts that Roosevelt had gone "so far as to say to me, 'I may never declare war; I may make war. If I were to ask Congress to declare war they might argue about it for three months.' "[225] British Secretary of State for Dominion Affairs Viscount Cranborne also wrote to Robert Menzies, prime minister of Australia, that

> the general impression derived by our representative at the Atlantic meeting was that, although the United States could not make any satisfactory declaration on the point, there was no doubt that in practice we could count on United States support if, as a result of Japanese aggression, we became involved in a war with Japan. . . . [Roosevelt] assured [Halifax] on 31st July that this would still be the United States attitude in the event of such a Japanese attack.[226]

Roosevelt had thus resolved that he would no longer flinch from war with Japan, and his statement, announced at the Atlantic Conference and ultimately destined for Nomura, was in the nature of a warning. Both Stimson[227] and Hull[228] referred to Roosevelt's statement as an "ultimatum." Upon his return to Washington on August 17, however, Roosevelt called for Nomura and spoke in terms that would lead Japan not to place particular importance on the "ultimatum" aspect of his warning. The president then handed Nomura two written statements, the first containing a warning regarding any further military advances. The second was quite conciliatory:

> the thought of Prince Konoe and of the Japanese Government in offering this suggestion [for a summit conference] is appreciated. . . .
> In case the Japanese Government feels that Japan desires and is in position to suspend its expansionist activities, to readjust its position, and to embark upon a peaceful program for the Pacific along the lines of the program and principles to which the United States is committed, the Government of the United States . . . would be glad to endeavor to arrange a suitable time and place to exchange views. The Government of the United States, however, feels that, in view of the circumstances attending the interruption of the informal conversations between the two Governments, it would be helpful to both Governments, before undertaking a resumption of such conversations or proceeding with plans for a meeting, if the Japanese Government would be so good as

to furnish a clearer statement than has yet been furnished as to its present attitude and plans.[229]

As to the first statement, Nomura reported:

> Having said that neither he, the Secretary of State, nor I, the Ambassador, were professional diplomats, and having indicated that he had no intention of following diplomatic usages, he took particular pains to point out that this was neither a diplomatic instrument nor an *aide memoire* but only a note setting down what he was trying to say. . . . While saying that even after he read the note he really did not want to say these things, he intimated that it might be appropriate to make things clear.

As to the second, he merely went on to say that

> going to Honolulu would be difficult geographically. He has been forbidden from taking airplanes. It might be difficult for the Japanese prime minister to come to San Francisco or Seattle, so how about Juneau? How many days does it take from Japan? . . . What do they say the weather will be in mid-October? . . . Having read this to me he did not at all relish the closed door that now exists, but that was done as an unavoidable response to Japanese actions and therefore it is up to Japan to open the door first. This time it is Japan's turn. (Nomura dispatch of August 18)[230]

The prior expression of Japan's attitude requested in the reply was not particularly made as a prerequisite for holding a summit meeting, nor on the whole was Roosevelt averse to such a meeting despite having issued the warning. This made Nomura feel that "it seems he intends to go ahead if conditions are right." Roosevelt's response was genuinely affable, courteous, and cordial to the last.[231] Nomura's cabled report about the tone of the meeting did indeed give a more accurate account of their entire conversation than did the American record.[232] And Konoe, who was obsessed with holding the summit itself rather than with its content, was naturally disposed to place higher value on Roosevelt's affability than on the contents of the written warning and the reply.

Expediting the Meeting with Roosevelt

Having obtained the approval of the Liaison Conference on August 26, Konoe issued the so-called "Konoe Message" that same day, explaining that:

The preliminary informal conversations, disrupted July last, were quite appropriate in both spirit and content. But the plan heretofore under consideration, which was to continue the conversations until such time as they could be validated by both heads of government, is not suited to the present situation in which developments are proceeding swiftly and which threatens to produce unforeseen contingencies. I consider it of the utmost necessity that the two heads of government first meet directly and discuss from a broad standpoint all important problems between Japan and the United States, covering the entire Pacific area and without being bound to previous conversations through ordinary channels, and explore whether it is possible to save the situation. Details may be left to negotiations between competent officials as need be after the summit meeting. Such is my aim in making the present proposal. I sincerely hope that you, Mr. President, will extend me your full appreciation on this and reciprocate. Given the above circumstances I hope that the meeting will take place as soon as possible. From various considerations I think that Hawaii would be appropriate for the meeting.[233]

Toyoda was worried that the military might just hold a conference of army-navy bureau and division chiefs in hopes of converting to a war footing, and thus upset the timetable of the plan to hold the summit meeting. He therefore cabled Nomura that same day: "Right now the situation both internationally and domestically is extremely tense and we have come to the point of pinning our last hopes on a meeting between the prime minister and the president." And he suggested gutting state policy by arguing that, "you should bear in mind our view that the summit meeting is by no means bound strictly [to Japan's response of August 26 to the American reply of August 17]."[234] He reiterated to Nomura on the 28th that: "On my part I deem it essential that, once our respective views have been made clear, points of compromise be discovered through a spirit of mutual conciliation; I think that for this purpose the meeting between the two heads of government will be most effective."[235]

On the 27th Nomura had called on Hull, delivered the Konoe Message, and requested a meeting with Roosevelt, who received the ambassador the following day. According to Hull,

the President said to the Ambassador that he could say to his Government that he considered this note a step forward and that he was very hopeful. He then added that he would be keenly interested in having three or four days with Prince Konoye, and again he mentioned Juneau.[236]

Nomura reported that Roosevelt had complimented the tone of the message and "praised it highly as being a truly fine idea; he seemed to have no objections to setting an early time [for the meeting], but he could not give an immediate reply as to a date."[237] However, when Nomura met privately with Hull that same night, Hull told him:

> When both heads of government meet, consequences of the gravest nature will ensue should certain issues fail to be resolved because of one side's obstinacy. Therefore, if and when a meeting between the two does take place, it should be a formality for reaching a final decision (Hull used the word "ratification") of those issues, their having been largely resolved beforehand.

In short, he gave Nomura reason to think that "there will be little chance for a summit meeting unless it is apparent that basic issues are being handled with the utmost care and attention, that careful thought is being invested from every possible angle, and that both sides are virtually agreed on fundamental principles."[238]

Despite Hull's reservations, Konoe continued to count on Roosevelt's affability, and he refined his scheme when he conferred with Ikawa, Ushiba, and others at Hakone for three days starting on the 29th. Toyoda too was greatly disposed toward optimism at the Liaison Conference on August 30.

Grew and Hornbeck Cross Swords

When Ambassador Grew in Tokyo wrote his diary summary for the month of July, he predicted:

> The vicious circle of reprisals and counter-reprisals is on. . . . Unless radical surprises occur in the world, it is difficult to see how the momentum of this downgrade movement in our relations can be arrested, nor how far it will go. The obvious conclusion is eventual war.[239]

For Grew, Konoe's proposal for a summit meeting might have caused something of such a radical surprise. On August 18 Toyoda personally requested him to exert his efforts on behalf of the summit, and Grew proceeded to turn his talents to persuading the State Department toward its realization. In subsequent communications, Grew developed the following arguments:[240]

1) The summit offers a golden opportunity.

"The opportunity is here presented. . . . of avoiding the obviously growing possibility of an utterly futile war between Japan and the United States. . . . " (Dispatch of August 18)

". . . it offers a definite opportunity to prevent the situation in the Far East from getting rapidly worse. . . . " (Dispatch of August 19)

2) The consequences of rejection.

". . . we must accept almost as a mathematical certainty the thought that if this outstanding and probably final gesture on the part of the Japanese Government should fail, either by rejection of this proposal in any form or by the meeting, if held, proving abortive, the alternative would be an eventual reconstruction or replacement of the present Cabinet with a view to placing the future destiny of the nation in the hands of the army and navy for an all-out-do-or-die effort to extend Japan's hegemony over all of 'Greater East Asia' entailing the inevitability of war with the United States." (Dispatch of August 19)

3) Japan will make concessions.

"[The Japanese government is] . . . in full knowledge that the proposed meeting. . . would be utterly futile unless the Japanese Government were prepared to make concessions of a far-reaching character." (Dispatch of August 19)

4) A concrete plan.

"Since it is presumed that a detailed formulation of a general plan of reconstruction of the Far East could not probably be worked out in advance, it would be eminently desirable that the military and economic measures of the United States which are now inexorably pressing on Japan be relaxed point by point *pari passu* with the actions of the Japanese Government in the direction of implementing its proposed commitments. If our Government followed this suggested course it would always retain in its hands the leverage which would contribute to Japanese implementation of its commitments. If an adjustment of relations is to be achieved some risk must be run. . . . " (Dispatch of September 5)

The State Department's Division of Far Eastern Affairs, and Hornbeck in particular, was utterly opposed to Grew's views. That Division sent up the following reports.[241]

1) The United States government should sit tight.

"Japan is in a weakened and a perilous position; Japanese leaders are contending among themselves and are uncertain and fearful; . . .
    It is the Japanese who are eager for and who are asking for this conference;
    This approach, by one element in Japan's leadership, is a confession of internal weakness and external weakness;
    The real 'crisis' is in Japan.
    . . . we have everything to gain and little or nothing to lose by standing firm on our principles and our policies." (September 2)
    "The facts of the situation that now exists are working real hardship to Japan (as a nation at war) but are not working any real hardship to the United States. This condition of 'tension' can continue for an indefinite period without our suffering much." (September 5)

2) Japan is powerless.

"The Japanese Government has no intention of making war on the United States." (August 30)
    "We are not in great danger vis-à-vis Japan and Japan is not capable of doing us any great injury. . . . Were Japan to attack us, we could. . . maintain a sound defensive position while we prepared for an ultimate offensive." (September 5)

3) Surgery is necessary.

". . . the kindest and the soundest course for foreign countries, especially the United States, to pursue would . . . be that of bending every effort toward ensuring a thorough defeat and a complete discrediting of the armed efforts of the military militaristic leadership. . . . For Japan to enjoy political health, may it not be, is it not, essential that the cancer of militant militarism which is deeply imbedded in the Japanese body politic be destroyed and eliminated?" (August 27)

That Hull was more influenced by Hornbeck's opinions than by Grew's frequent reports from Tokyo may be judged from the fact that, in contrast to Grew, he looked on indifferently as the Konoe cabinet reached the end of its tether. On September 3 Hull told Australian Minister Richard G. Casey that "the situation was rather critical on account of explosive domestic politics in Japan, and that things seemed to be coming to a head or to a showdown between the Konoye Government and the extremists, with the latter apparently gaining ground."[242]

On the same day Roosevelt summoned Nomura and read to him an oral statement as well as a written reply to the Konoe Message. He then consoled Nomura:

> I, Prince Konoe, Your Excellency, and the Secretary of State are all working for peace in the Pacific. But both Japan and the United States have vocal publics, and I have received a stream of telegrams demanding that there be no changes in our policy in order to accommodate Japan. I am therefore very sincerely sympathetic toward Prince Konoe.[243]

Roosevelt's written reply was an indirect rejection of the Konoe Message, pointing out that it would be difficult to agree to a summit conference without preliminary talks. The oral statement, on the other hand, brought to the fore the four principles Hull had drafted and delivered to Nomura on April 16 as well as Hull's counterproposal of June 21, asserting that the United States government

> seeks an indication of the present attitude of the Japanese Government with regard to the fundamental issues under reference. . . . The Government of Japan will surely recognize that the Government of the United States could not enter into any agreement which would not be in harmony with the principles in which the Government of the United States and the American people . . . believe.[244]

In essence, even with regard to the preliminary conversations that would be prerequisite to a summit meeting, the United States reaffirmed its stance that no agreement between Japan and the United States could be entered into unless Japan retracted all its previous proposals—the Matsuoka drafts of May 12 and July 15 and the plan for a local settlement—and agreed to Hull's counterproposal. It administered the coup de grace to Konoe's and Toyoda's plans for gutting the substance of state policies, to say nothing of the ray of self-serving hope that the army and navy had entertained in Matsuoka's final draft.

The Willingness to Make Concessions at a Summit Conference

Nomura, however, had repeatedly and accurately reported this unyielding attitude on the part of the United States prior to the warning he cabled on August 18. Although he relayed word for word Roosevelt's affable statements at their meeting on the 17th, Nomura had been continuously reporting observations prior to this that left no doubt about the fundamental attitude of the United States:

> July 8: "It is impossible for me to believe that if we continue now with a resolute attitude they will finally give in."[245]
>
> August 6: "From what I gathered [from Hull] today, it is now all but impossible for the Empire to get its intentions across to responsible officials in the United States whatever explanations we make; there is no mistaking that the United States government has made up its mind to take in stride any contingency whatever."[246]
>
> August 7: "In short, I believe they will counter each move we make, step for step, and never back down."[247]
>
> August 8: "In short, they insist that negotiations can only begin when Japan stops using armed force. They will never back down on this point. There is no longer any room for talks unless there are changes in our policy."[248]
>
> August 9: "So long as Japan proceeds with its present policies, the policies of the United States will move forward accordingly. Moreover, the attitude of the United States government is that the stationing of troops by Japan in southern Indochina has decisively influenced the direction of Japan's policies (the president and the secretary of state are absolutely of one mind on this point and it would be a mistake to make a distinction between the two). In light of this, it is with true regret that I observe that they will not be moved merely by the prime minister's personal intervention. Consequently, I believe it will be difficult to overcome the deadlock unless on this occasion the government explores some means or other for making the United States change its policies."[249]

Nomura therefore ceased to pin any hopes on a summit meeting, and on August 18 he recommended that Japan change its policy so as to bring about modifications in the policy of the United States: at this time when, "if I may express myself frankly, we are standing at the crossroad between war and peace," Japan "should in general take the path of strengthening itself based on a position of independence and self-reliance, without going too far to one side [Germany] and without running such risks as would endanger the nation, . . . working cooperatively" even on the Hull counterproposal.[250] Behind this recommendation, of course, lay Nomura's accurate observations on the attitude of the United States and his broad perspective on Japan's international environment and national strength. That assessment had been expressed to Toyoda over and over again ever since Toyoda's appointment as foreign minister:

July 19: "Looking at our current national predicament, it seems that there will be no way to engage in direct mutual assistance with our allies Germany and Italy if communications with them are ruptured; with British, American, and Soviet suspicions toward us growing and the China Incident expanding, we are gradually being surrounded by foes on all sides. . . . I am painfully aware that, given our exposed, isolated and vulnerable position in the Far East, our foreign policy must issue forth from the principle of 'Japan first' to preserve the autonomy of the Empire. But it is safest to act prudently, within the limits of our national power, without relying idly on countries whose support is problematic. It would not be wise, in our haste to achieve success, to rush into a collision with the Anglo-American powers and take the initiative in engaging their crack troops."[251]

July 28: "I would hope that we shall operate from a position of autonomy, without counting solely on the complete victory of Germany and Italy."[252]

July 29: "Developments in East Asia are today taking a turn for the worst, as we move toward taking on singlehandedly the United States, Britain, Holland, China, and the Soviet Union. It appears to me that while we endeavor to restrain the United States for Germany's sake, we are unwittingly courting the danger of going to the point of war with Britain and the United States all by ourselves."[253]

August 18: "Even if Germany achieves a brilliant victory, our national strength is now being consumed and it is inconceivable that we shall be able to achieve the results we desire if we fight Britain, the United States, the Soviet Union, and Holland in the Far East by ourselves. If things go badly for Germany such results are beyond imagining."[254]

Nomura's recommendation for a change in Japanese policy posed difficulties for Konoe. He had obtained the emperor's approval of the July 2 Imperial Conference decision which declared that Japan would "promote various . . . measures with regard to those regions in the south important for self-preservation and self-defense," and that it would "not flinch from war with Britain and the United States in order to achieve these objectives." Then, on September 3, Konoe and Toyoda had agreed to an Imperial Conference proposal that would convert Japan to a war footing vis-à-vis the United States. When this proposal was formally approved on September 6, the entire nation had embarked even more conclusively on a course toward war with the United States. Although neither Konoe nor Toyoda felt much compunction about gutting semantic state policies, they would certainly have found it difficult to change drastically a decision that had just been adopted at an Imperial Conference. Therefore, they may have resorted instinctively to the strategy of gutting that decision at a summit meeting that would be held overseas, away from Japan.

On the evening after the September 6 Imperial Conference Konoe pursued that strategy when, with the understanding of Tōjō and Oikawa, he met secretly with Grew at a friend's home, in the company of Ushiba and Dooman.

> Prince Konoye recognizes. . . that only he can cause the desired rehabilitation to come about. . . .
> . . . he is confident that the divergencies in view can be reconciled to our mutual satisfaction, . . . both the Ministers of War and of the Navy have given their full agreement to his proposals to the United States. . . .
> . . . Prince Konoye told me that from the inception of the informal talks in Washington he had received the strongest concurrence from the responsible chiefs of both the Army and the Navy. . . . he voiced the conviction that since he had the full support of the responsible chiefs of the Army and Navy it would be possible for him to put down and control any opposition which might develop within those elements.
> . . . Prince Konoye feels confident that all problems and questions at issue can be disposed of to our mutual satisfaction during the meeting with the President. . . .
> . . . as soon as he had reached agreement with President Roosevelt and had so reported to the Emperor, the Emperor would immediately issue a rescript ordering the suspension forthwith of all hostile operations.[255]

Three weeks later, on September 29, Grew followed this up with a long report that contained his considered judgment. He urged that the debate over principles be suspended:

> If we expect and wait for the Japanese Government to agree in the preliminary conversations to clear-cut commitments of a nature satisfactory to our Government in point both of principle and of concrete detail, the conversations will almost certainly drag on indefinitely and unproductively to a point where the Cabinet and those supporting elements who desire *rapprochement* to the United States will reach the conclusion that the American Government is merely playing for time and that the outlook for an agreement is hopeless. In such a contingency, . . . [t]he downfall of the Cabinet and its replacement by a military dictatorship with neither the temperament nor the disposition to avoid a head-on collision with the United States would be the logical outcome.[256]

He also noted that Japan had actually made concessions:

I would point out, however, that with regard to the specific case of Japan's relations with the Axis the Japanese Government, while consistently refusing to give an undertaking overtly to renounce membership in the alliance, has in actual fact shown itself ready to reduce to a dead letter Japan's adherence to the alliance by indicating readiness to enter into formal negotiations with the United States. It is therefore not unlikely that the Prime Minister might be in a position to give directly to the President an engagement more explicit and satisfactory than already vouchsafed during the preliminary conversations.[257]

Grew's views were supported by British Ambassador Craigie, who reported to his superiors on September 30:

the main difficulty appears to be that, while the Japanese want speed and cannot yet afford to go beyond generalizations, the Americans seem to be playing for time and to demand the utmost precision in definition before agreeing to any contract for a step of rapprochement. . . . It seems apparent that the United States does not comprehend the fact that by the nature of the Japanese and also on account of the domestic conditions in Japan no delays can be countenanced. . . . But the risks must be faced in any case, and (Grew) and I are firmly of the opinion that on balance this is a chance which it would be inexcusable folly to let slip.[258]

Grew's recommendations from August onward depended critically on whether Konoe and Toyoda could gut state policies. Toyoda, who had expected to accompany Konoe to the summit, said years later that, "fully intending to follow through if we went, we were ready to settle everything on the spot, even the withdrawal of troops [from China], and then seek the emperor's sanction."[259] In the opinion of the army's War Guidance Office at that time (August 19), "if the summit talks did take place, they would probably not break down and a negotiated settlement would be reached based on a temporary compromise adjustment."[260] Ishii Akiho, a senior member of the Army Ministry's Military Affairs Section, predicted that Konoe would try to do his best, but Roosevelt would probably not go along with him; then Konoe would cable Tokyo that nothing further could be accomplished and the army would stand firm; finally, Konoe would seek the emperor's sanction, the emperor would issue a message to the army, and that would be the end of that. At that point, according to Ishii, there would be a 70 percent chance of a negotiated agreement.[261] Similarly, in the Navy Ministry, Naval Affairs Bureau Chief Oka opined that "once Konoe meets with Roosevelt, things might get settled on the spot, so something may come of it if he goes."[262] Oka's subordinate, Shiba Katsuo, also noted that if they did meet, Konoe could be easily coaxed along.[263]

The State Department Fails to Respond

Grew's appraisals elicited no response from the State Department; they were rarely referred to. Grew must have felt his efforts were akin to throwing stones into a lake in the middle of the night, when not even a ripple could be seen. He later learned that his arguments had been given no credence whatever and it was clear to him that his reports were not appreciated. When he met with Hull following his return to the United States, he wondered whether all of his dispatches had actually been forwarded to the secretary of state for him to read.[264] In any event, in the days after Grew's September 9 report on his meeting with Konoe, the State Department's policy remained "almost completely inflexible."[265]

The "Essentials" put before the Imperial Conference on September 6 had been approved by the Liaison Conference three days earlier, when Toyoda had introduced alongside the "Essentials" a new proposal to be sent to the United States.[266] As soon as it was approved, he transmitted it to both Grew and Nomura (September 4): "Judging it utterly impossible to get a meeting under way by late September if we reiterate such bureaucratic and legalistic arguments as have been advanced in the past, and given that we have already made every effort to say what had to be said, having expressed our views and also sent a message from the prime minister, we will now express our views frankly and discover points on which we are agreed regarding this proposal, both preliminary and substantial."[267] Toyoda was thus trying to guide the proposal toward confirmation at a late September summit conference. Two pledges of great importance were included in the proposal that would have virtually gutted the Supplement of the "Essentials" about to be approved by the Imperial Conference of September 6:

1. Upon the achievement of full normal relations between Japan and China, Japan is prepared to withdraw troops from China as swiftly as possible in accordance with agreements between Japan and China.
2. Japan's attitude toward the war in Europe will be governed by concepts of protection and self-defense; Japan's interpretation of the Tripartite Pact, and its actions thereunder, in the event that the

United States enters the war in Europe, will be made with complete autonomy.[268]

The latter assurance in particular was given at a time when the United States navy was intervening militarily against Germany in the Atlantic, the shoot-on-sight policy against German submarines having been in operation since August 26. Precisely on September 4, when this policy provoked the German submarine attack on the U.S. destroyer *Greer*, we find Konoe and Toyoda in the midst of tacitly eviscerating the Tripartite Pact by disregarding Japan's obligations thereunder. Both thought that such a pledge "would win over the American side, it being a pledge of great importance that anyone could easily assent to and indicating generally just how far the Empire was willing to go to 'meet' American wishes" (Toyoda dispatch of September 5).[269]

Toyoda's proposal, however, crossed paths with Roosevelt's oral statement and reply of September 2 rejecting the proposed summit meeting. Neither these two great pledges, made with such effort, nor the hopes that Konoe had expressed to Grew on the night of September 6 were of any avail in eliciting the desired response from the United States, which remained as inflexible as ever.

The Japanese Proposals Intensify Distrust of Konoe.

Having perceived that the propositions in the plan for a local settlement would produce a deadlock, the Foreign Ministry worked with Mutō on September 17 to produce a comprehensive plan for a readjustment with the United States. Army Vice Chief of Staff Tsukada suggested the following day that its submission to the Liaison Conference that day be postponed because the Army General Staff needed to do preliminary work on it. Sugiyama was adamant on an investigation of this Foreign Ministry-navy plan, which was in fact laid before the Liaison Conference that day, and Nagano backed him on this. The only decision reached was "to decide swiftly on the Empire's final attitude concerning N-maneuvers and to make it known to the United States."[270] After a meeting of division chiefs that night, the Army General Staff explained its views about the plan to Mutō prior to the meeting of bureau chiefs from the army, navy, and foreign ministries on the 19th. Mutō conveyed these views fully to the Foreign Ministry, which drew up a revised plan following deliberations presided over by Shigemitsu Mamoru.[271] But the Army General Staff was still not satisfied. On the evening of the 19th the top leaders of the Army

Ministry and General Staff met and decided on the army's opinion of the plan. Sugiyama explained the army's position to the Liaison Conference of the 20th, and it was adopted almost in full. Herewith Japan's final attitude to be made known to the United States was at long last settled upon.

Indignant over Toyoda's gutting, the army, so to speak, put the guts back into Toyoda's revised plan for a local settlement of September 4. Toyoda's revision had contradicted the Supplement of the September 6 Imperial Conference decision, and it gave rise to unfounded misgivings that "The Basic Terms for Peace Between Japan and China" adopted by the September 13 Liaison Conference had been inaccurately transmitted to Nomura. So the army purposely had the text of "The Basic Terms" attached word for word as a supplement to the plan approved by the September 20 Liaison Conference. The third condition, relating to joint Sino-Japanese defense, stated:

> In consequence of [agreements between Japan and China] and based on existing arrangements and precedents, Japanese troops and ships will be stationed in specified areas for such periods as may be necessary.

Article 3 of the main body of the text declared:

> For the sake of promoting and realizing. . . a settlement of the China Incident, the government of the United States will use its good offices with the Chungking government to have it enter into negotiations with the Japanese government in order to terminate military actions and restore peaceful relations, and it will engage in no measures or actions such as will hinder the measures and efforts of the Japanese government to settle the China Incident.[272]

The army's action in effect aimed to retract unilaterally the momentous pledges sent to the United States by Toyoda on September 4. For a fortnight Japanese policy had oscillated wildly, and it is not surprising that Toyoda hesitated to present this latest plan to the United States. Finally, under pressure from both chiefs of staff he sent it out to Nomura on the 25th as simply a summary of the various opinions to date [and not as a policy decision—trans.].

Throughout this period the attitude of the United States remained as inflexible as ever. When he met with Nomura on August 28, Roosevelt was concerned "whether an invasion of Thailand could be expected during the conversations with Prince Konoe just as the invasion of Indochina occurred during Secretary Hull's conversations with Your Excellency."[273] Soon after, for example, Navy War Plans

Director Captain Richmond Kelly Turner called on Nomura particularly to tell him that, "Should a conference of the leaders of the two governments be held without a definite preliminary agreement, and should, in the meantime, an advance be made into Siberia, the President will be placed in a terrible predicament."[274] In short, as Turner told Terasaki Hidenari, first secretary of the Japanese embassy in Washington:

> it is doubtful that. . . the present Japanese cabinet. . . has the support of the Army, and if the Military finds itself at variance with the opinions of the cabinet, the cabinet might be overthrown at any time. Therefore, the United States cannot help feeling a little trepidation in broaching any negotiations with the Japanese Government under these circumstances. (Nomura dispatch of October 16)[275]

Adding to these fears over the ability of the Konoe cabinet to control the military, the marked discrepancy between what intelligence reports and decoded intercepts revealed as Japan's actual policies and the Konoe-Toyoda proposals further deepened the misgivings of the United States. The situation in Tokyo was one almost incomprehensible to a student of politics: to write compositions was to make state policy, and state policy became an exercise in writing compositions; so when Konoe set his hand to the actual gutting of such semantic state policies, he succeeded only in intensifying the distrust of the United States, which deemed his efforts to be a strategy of deception. On September 20 Nomura warned him bluntly that "the United States is fully cognizant that Japan is appeasing the United States while engaging in policies of military force."[276]

Negotiations Are Virtually Broken Off

The "Comprehensive Plan for a Readjustment with the United States" was received by Hull on the 27th. He suggested the outlines of a reply to Roosevelt, at Hyde Park, who replied on the 28th:

> I wholly agree with your pencilled note—to recite the more liberal original attitude of the Japanese when they first sought the meeting, point out their much narrowed position now, earnestly ask if they cannot go back to their original attitude, start discussions again on agreement in principle, and reemphasize my hopes for a meeting.[277]

Having obtained Roosevelt's complete agreement, Hull ordered a reply drafted along the lines he advocated. This he delivered to

Nomura on October 2, prefacing it with the comment: "In order to maintain peace in the Pacific a temporary patchwork understanding will not do; the United States desires an explicit agreement."[278] The reply, having first reiterated once again Hull's four principles, then generalized that:

> From what the Japanese Government has so far indicated in regard to its purposes this Government derives the impression that the Japanese Government has in mind a program that would be circumscribed by the imposition of qualifications and exceptions to the actual application of those principles.

Concretely, it stated:

1. The inclusion in the conditions for peace between Japan and China of such a provision as the stationing of troops in specified areas for an indeterminate period is open to objections.
2. The step the Japanese Government has taken with regard to the Tripartite Pact is appreciated. It would be helpful if the Japanese Government could give further study to the question of additional clarification of its position.[279]

To put it in plain terms, these two stipulations demanded, first, that in the Sino-Japanese War Japan accept its own defeat and China's victory, totally abandoning any and all standing it had gained thus far in Manchuria, China, and Indochina as well as all future prospects. Second, with respect to the Tripartite Pact, it was not enough merely for Konoe and Toyoda to put their under-the-table gutting of state policies into practice nor for Japan to look on silently as the United States intervened militarily in the Atlantic; Japan was to liquidate forthwith its alliance with Germany.

Nomura knew Tokyo would "no doubt be disappointed with this, but I will send it on."[280] On October 7 Toyoda had complained to Grew "that it was his impression that the Government of the United States wished the Japanese Government to revert at once and unqualifiedly to the *status quo* which prevailed four years ago."[281] On September 29 Hull had already met with Admiral Stark and told him in extreme confidence that "conversations with the Japs have practically reached an impasse."[282] "As stern as a righteous schoolmaster,"[283] Hull all but broke off the talks with Japan. Meanwhile, Konoe, having lost hope that a summit meeting would take place, announced to Kido on September 26, prior to receiving Hull's reply and the day after Toyoda had dispatched the "Comprehensive Plan," that he intended to resign.[284] His vacillating behavior exasperated Tōjō: "He decides great matters rashly, without deliberating carefully beforehand; he gives every indication that he thinks he can chuck a thing out like a worn-out pair of shoes whenever it becomes slightly inconvenient to him."[285]

6 Konoe Reaches the End of His Tether

Completing Preparations for War

The September 6 Imperial Conference decision stated at the outset that "the Empire shall complete preparations for war by the approximate deadline of late October, based on the resolve not to flinch from war with the United States (Britain and Holland)." It thus became state policy to concentrate the nation's energies on completing preparations for war within a two-month period. For the army this was precisely the right moment to shift from preparing for war against the Soviet Union to preparing for war against the United States, Britain, and Holland—and from a semi-wartime setup to a definite war footing. That meant implementing, by early October (that decision's designated date "to resolve to go to war") the deployment of operating forces, the requisitioning and outfitting of ships, the establishment of air and naval bases as well as supply bases, and the stockpiling of supplies and munitions for military operations. All these measures and others were to be carried out in one month. On September 18 the order to prepare for military operations was issued, and the army began by deploying its forces for South Seas operations to south China, Taiwan, and northern Indochina.

On the other hand, leaders from the Navy Ministry and General Staff had decided in August 1940 to step up preparations for war immediately, aiming to commence preparatory fleet mobilization stage one operations on November 15, 1940. Since then the navy had made steady progress in implementing those preparations—that is, its plans for mobilization, as tables 2.1 and 2.2 reveal.

With the implementation of the total war organization for 1941 (dated September 1, 1940), Nagano was able to report to the Throne on August 26 that "over 90 percent of all vessels and units planned for the fiscal year's war footing have been organized into the Combined Fleet, and we are in a position to cope with any emergency."[286] Vessels totalling 230,000 tons were requisitioned at the start of stage one in November 1940, as were 784,000 tons during stage two from July to September of 1941; with their renovations completed, the

Table 2.1*

AN OVERVIEW OF THE AUGMENTATION OF NAVAL PREPARATIONS IN THE PERIOD PRIOR TO THE OPENING OF HOSTILITIES

| Date | War Preparations Made | New Naval Formations and Construction (Completed) | | | | Tonnage of Warships & Other Vessels Requisitioned (Minus that Discharged from Service) | Notes |
		Fleets	Squadrons and Navel Base Squadrons	Warships & Other Vessels	(Units)		
May 1, 1940			Torpedo Squadron (3rd) 5th Squadron 18th Squadron Submarine Squadron (5th)	Cruisers Seaplane Tenders	3 1	@320,000 (already requisitioned)	
Nov. 15, 1940	Implementation of the operational organization for 1941. Start of Stage one operations for deploying forces.	6th Fleet (3 submarine squadrons) formed.	Air Squadrons (2nd, 7th, 6th) Torpedo Squadrons (6th) Combined Air Squadrons (3rd, 4th) Naval Base Squadrons (1st, 3rd, 5th)	Cruisers Submarine Tenders	12 3	@230,000	Extensive revision of the wartime program; first mass requisitioning of shipping.
Dec. 27, 1940				The "Zuihō" (formerly the "Takasaki") is put in service after reoutfitting had been completed.			

Date	Fleet/Force	Unit	No.	Tonnage	Notes
Jan. 15, 1941	11th Air Force (21st, 22nd, & 24th Air Squadrons) formed.	2nd Naval Base Squadron; 6th Naval Base Squadron	Gunboat Units — 3; Special Minesweeper Units — 4; Subchaser Units — 5; Defense Units — 2; Air Wings — 1	@86,000	85% of regular warships and other vessels to be mobilized for wartime now outfitted.
Jan. 31, 1941			2nd Submarine Unit		
Mar. 31, 1941			The "Hachijo" completed. 4th Destroyer Unit		
Apr. 10, 1941	3rd Fleet (16th, 17th, 5th Torpedo Squadrons; 12th Air Squadron; 6th Submarine Squadron) formed. 1st Air Force (1st, 2nd & 4th Air Squadrons) formed. Hainan Garrison Authority established.	16th Squadron; 4th Air Squadron; 23rd Air Squadron	Battleships ("Fuso," "Kongō," "Haruna") — 3; Cruisers ("Myōkō," "Kuma") — 2; Aircraft Carriers ("Akagi," "Zuihō") — 2; Special Submarine Tenders — 2; Special Air Wings — 2	@91,000	

Table 2.1 (*Continued*)
An Overview of the Augmentation of Naval Preparations in the Period Prior to the Opening of Hostilities

Date	War Preparations Made	New Naval Formations and Construction (Completed)			Tonnage of Warships & Other Vessels Requisitioned (Minus that Discharged from Service) (Units)	Notes
		Fleets	Squadrons and Navel Base Squadrons	Warships & Other Vessels		
May 1, 1941	6th Fleet Hdqrs. becomes independent.		6th Submarine Squadron ("Chō-gei;" 9th & 13th Submarine Units) 1st Submarine Squadron Hdqs.	"Uji" completed.		
May 15, 1941				30th Minesweeping Unit		
Jul. 15, 1941	Start of stage two deployment operations.		3rd Submarine Squadron			
Jul. 25, 1941		Formation of 5th Fleet.			@122,000	Start of 2nd mass requisitioning.
Jul. 31, 1941		Formation of Southern Fleet.				
Aug. 11, 1941		Combined Fleet Hdqrs. becomes independent. 1st Fleet Hdqrs. est.	11th Squadron dissolved. 4th Naval Base Squadron.	Reoutfitting of the "Ōtaka" (formerly the "Kasuga Maru") completed.	@387,000	

Date						
Sep. 1, 1941	Implementation of total war footing for 1941.	11th Air Force Hdqrs. becomes independent.	21st Air Squadron Hdqs. 5th Air Squadron ("Shōkaku," "Ōtaka")	Special Garrison Force	@275,000	Mobilization of regular warships and other vessels for wartime close to completion; expeditionary forces virtually readied.
Sep. 25, 1941				"Zuikaku" completed.		
Oct. 1, 1941			7th Naval Base Squadron Maizuru Defense Squadron Shizuumi (Chinkai) Defense Squadron Ōshima Naval Base Squadron Razu Naval Base Squadron	Cruisers ("Ashigaru") 1 Tainan Air Wing Komatsushima Air Wing	@101,000	Priority is shifted to domestic front forces, supply corps.
Oct. 15, 1941			22nd Squadron 24th Squadron Yokohama Patrol Squadron Kure Patrol Squadron Sasebo Patrol Squadron	Special Marine Brigades 3 Special Cruisers 9 Subchaser Units 6 Minesweeper Units 9 Special Minelayer Units 2 Special Seaplane Tenders 2 B-Class Aircraft Cruisers 2 Special Gunboats 19		The bulk of newly requisitioned and special construction warships and other vessels are on a wartime footing.

Table 2.1 (*Continued*)
An Overview of the Augmentation of Naval Preparations in the Period Prior to the Opening of Hostilities

Date	War Preparations Made	New Naval Formations and Construction (Completed)			Tonnage of Warships & Other Vessels Requisitioned (Minus that Discharged from Service)	Notes
		Fleets	Squadrons and Naval Base Squadrons	Warships & Other Vessels (Units)		
Oct. 21, 1941		Southern fleet incorporated into the Combined Fleet.				
Oct. 31, 1941			9th Naval Base Squadron	4th Submarine Unit "Tsugaru" completed. Battleships ("Yamashiro") 1 Special Seaplane Tenders 1		
Nov. 20, 1941	Ōsaka Garrison Authority established.		9th Squadron (2 light cruisers) Sasebo Naval Yard Special Combined Marine Corps Kure Coast Guard Squadron Sasebo Coast Guard Squadron Maizuru Coast Guard Squadron 11th Special Naval Base Squadron 32nd Special Naval Base Squadron	"Shōhō (formerly the "Kengi") reoutfitted. Marine Units 3 Special Minesweeper Units 2	@428,000	3rd mass requisitioning.

Date					Notes
Dec. 1, 1941	4th Fleet Hdqrs. becomes independent.	18th Squadron Hdqrs.			
Dec. 10, 1941	11th Combined Air Squadron 12th Combined Air Squadron.	Special Cruisers Special Gunboats Special Seaplane Tenders Subchaser Units Minesweepers	1 4 1 1 4	@119,000 Grand Total: @1,979,000	Vessels second to be outfitted for stage two operations are largely in service.
Dec. 16, 1941		Completion of the "Yamato."			
Dec. 31, 1941		Special Cruisers Minesweeper Units	1 3		

* Compiled from JDA Archives.

Table 2.2*
AN OVERVIEW OF VESSELS REQUISITIONED
AND VESSELS ASSIGNED
TO THE FLEET

	Vessels Requisitioned**		Of These, Vessels under Special Construction		Vessels Assigned to the Fleet	
	NO.	TOTAL TONNAGE	NO.	TOTAL TONNAGE	NO.	TOTAL TONNAGE
Nov. 15 1940	265	312,000	86	190,000	86	185,000
End of Dec. 1940	342	488,000	157	355,000		
End of Jan. 1941	354	521,000			156	357,000
End of Feb. 1941	366	529,000				
End of Mar. 1941	378	575,000	170	386,000		
End of Apr. 1941	399	616,000	168	381,000	163	381,000
End of May 1941	398	603,000	169	392,000		
End of Jun. 1941	409	617,000				
End of Jul. 1941	467	737,000	194	407,000		
End of Aug. 1941	670	1,114,000	205	434,000	201	407,000
End of Sep. 1941	783	1,377,000	473	943,000		
End of Oct. 1941	798	1,442,000	571	1,138,000	557	1,126,000
End of Nov. 1941	1011	1,867,000	613	1,351,000		
End of Dec. 1941	1153	1,979,000	816	1,649,000	747	1,484,000

*Compiled from JDA Archives.
** According to the register of requisitioned vessels, June 1, 1943.

outfitting of specially equipped vessels for use by the expeditionary forces was also nearly done.[287] The navy's preparatory fleet mobilization involving expeditionary force vessels for front line action had already been completed by September 1, irrespective of formal state policy decisions, and it can be assumed that preparations for war with the United States were also nearly completed as far as the navy was concerned. Consequently, the job of pressing the government to resolve on war or peace naturally fell on the shoulders of the army, which had just begun genuine preparations for war. And for the army, which had barely started to get moving, there were just too many reasons why it could not perform this task adequately without a clear signal from the government.

The Difficulty That Would Cause the Negotiations to Go up in Smoke

The hard-line views of Operations Division Chief Tanaka against Toyoda's diplomacy when it got under way, though toned down by

Sugiyama, were apparent in the desidcrata Sugiyama presented to
the Liaison Conference on July 21 on behalf of both chiefs of staff
(see p. 153). From mid-August on, the army's War Guidance Office
had fumed over the directions in which Toyoda's diplomacy was
going, hinting that a change of cabinet would be desirable:

August 15: "Indications are rife that he will calmly pull out of the
Axis."
August 25: "The clouds of estrangement from the Axis are thick-
ening."
August 30: "An attitude is called for that will prod the government forward so that it will not be reduced to a state of virtual submission to
the United States; there might be a cabinet change as the result."[288]

Toyoda's revised "Plan for a Regional Settlement" of September 4
had offered pledges of great importance that would gut the "Essentials for Carrying Out the Empire's Policies" the Liaison Conference
had just the day before decided to submit to an Imperial Conference.
Doubts and suspicions arose over his "new arrangements between
Japan and China," and deepened when he sent "deceptive" dispatches[289] to the United States about the terms set by the Imperial
Conference of September 6.

On September 15 Tanaka pointed out that the attitude of the
government toward a summit meeting "is not necessarily what the
high command thinks it is; I would like us to explain in no uncertain
terms that after a compromise is reached between Japan and the
United States, the situation could become utterly intolerable for Japan from the standpoint of national defense, and to urge that the
government reflect on this."[290] Around the same time, Operations
Section Chief Hattori Takushirō pressed the Military Affairs Section
to prevail upon the army minister "to go to the palace, every day and
alone if need be, and urge upon the emperor the need to go to war
[with the United States]."[291] By now, Tanaka and Hattori had become the nucleus of the pro-war group in the Army General Staff.
Sugiyama allowed himself to be influenced by such subordinates,
instead of doing the opposite by impressing upon them the official
pledges he had made to the emperor, which he limited to the confines
of the Imperial Conference chambers. Thereafter, the army's war
advocates took as their sole "imperial mandate," their sole "imperial
standard," the provision for "stationing of troops under new arrangements between Japan and China" in the Supplement to the "Essentials" approved by the September 6 Imperial Conference. This provision would be the difficulty that would cause the negotiations to go

up in smoke, given that Japan knew the United States had no intention of accepting such arrangements.

Although there is little doubt that Konoe and Toyoda transcended the limits of textual interpretation in their gutting of state policies, the Army General Staff's categorical insistence on the right to station troops was justified neither by the main text nor by the Supplement of the "Essentials." That was a frantic effort to uphold what was no more than a footnote to the Supplement by taking it out of context, and hardly a balanced interpretation of state policy either. However, even though it was only a footnote, it allowed the Army General Staff to put forward far more effective formal arguments, inasmuch as these rested on the text of a state policy approved by an Imperial Conference. Moreover, after the order to prepare for South Seas operations was given on the 18th, the Army General Staff could no longer dismiss that state policy as a mere writing exercise, and what they now faced was not the give-and-take of conceptual debates but inescapable decisions on what to do about tactical objectives and deployment limits regarding the men and matériel they had in reality begun to deploy over the ocean to the south. That is, the Army General Staff had in fact begun to implement the Imperial Conference decision to "complete preparations for war by the approximate deadline of late October"; and although the phrase "in the event that by early October there is still no prospect of obtaining our demands" allowed for some postponement of the deadline, they had come to the point where they could not actually complete preparations for war by late October if a decision on war or peace were not made by around October 15 at the latest.

On September 23 the Operations Section of the Army General Staff drafted a position paper for the September 25 Liaison Conference in which it discussed when to resolve on war with the United States—that is, "the turning point for choosing between political and military strategies." The draft was distributed to the relevant units of the Army Ministry and General Staff, and the army's War Guidance Office began discussions with the Navy General Staff on the 24th so as to be able to convey to the government the demand from both general staffs that this turning point must be no later than October 15.

Nagano had been advocating war since before the United States ruptured economic relations, and after the discussions of the 24th he drafted the following proposal, jointly signed by Sugiyama and to be presented to the government at the Liaison Conference of the 25th, "On the turning point between politics and war and the moment for deciding on whether there are prospects for success in diplomatic negotiations" (see Appendix 7):[292]

As for the moment to resolve on war with the United States (Britain and Holland) in accordance with the "Essentials for Carrying Out the Empire's Policies," great importance is to be attached to operational requirements, and whether it will be politics or war shall be decided by October 15 at the latest

Tōjō Confronts Konoe, Toyoda and Oikawa

The government responded to the Army General Staff on this with the statement, "acknowledged without major comment."[293] In fact, Konoe did go to the extent of replying to Sugiyama at the Liaison Conference that "I fully understand this proposal; then again, I do have to get ready to leave in early October to meet with Roosevelt."[294] In actuality the proposal seems to have come as quite a shock to Konoe. Following the conference he went on to query Tōjō and Oikawa, who had accompanied him to his official residence, if that proposal was really meant to be a strong demand. "It is a strong demand," Tōjō replied appropriately, "but it is not so much a demand as merely a faithful statement of what was decided at the Imperial Conference and therefore cannot be changed."[295] Konoe appeared nonplussed. Having heard this exchange, Oikawa may have sympathized with Konoe's predicament, because after returning to his office he called for Ishikawa Shingo and directed him make a determination, unconstrained by previous policy decisions, as to whether a decision for war or peace should be made at this time. Oikawa further directed Ishikawa to investigate how Konoe's previous resignation had been dealt with, possibly because he felt that this shock would start Konoe thinking about suddenly resigning again.[296]

In fact, Konoe told Kido explicitly on the 26th that he intended to resign, saying that he had no choice if the army intended to resolve on going to war on October 15 no matter what. That same day the Army General Staff revised its position: "the prime minister seems to have had a great change of heart [after acknowledging the proposal]."[297] But Konoe confined himself to his private villa at Kamakura from September 27 to October 1, avoiding any discussion with the army about the merits of the proposal. All Konoe did before going to Kamakura was to have Toyoda cable Nomura on the 26th what he had urged upon Grew:

> We have confidentially decided not only on the ship [*Nitta Maru*] that will transport the prime minister and his entourage but also on the members of that entourage, which will include General Doihara [Kenji] for the army and Admiral Yoshida [Zengo] for the navy. We are in a position to depart any day. . . . The Imperial government hopes for an answer from the government of the United States [about when the meeting is to take place] as soon as possible. . . . At this point, time is of the essence in every respect, whether it be from the standpoint of the international situation or from that of the domestic situation. . . . This is the reason we are troubling the United States again for its prompt and sincere consideration, and we would be much obliged if you were promptly to obtain a definite answer one way or the other; it would be most convenient for us if in due course the date of the meeting were to be set between October 10 and October 15.[298]

With rumors spreading rapidly about a new cabinet because of Konoe's absence from Tokyo, and with political instability mounting, the examination of the high command's proposal turned into a debate primarily between the high command and Tōjō, who endorsed it, and Oikawa, who seemed to sympathize with Konoe's plan to gut the Imperial Conference decision. On the 27th Tōjō met with Oikawa and confronted him directly with the question: "You seem to be intent on changing the Imperial Conference decision, is that right?" Unable to admit to such an intention, Oikawa explained himself in Konoe-like fashion: "The world situation is changing from one moment to the next, and I fear that Japan will plunge rashly into the vortex of a world war all by itself."[299]

Invited to Kamakura on October 1, Oikawa told Konoe frankly that "we must be prepared to do nothing less than swallow whole the United States proposal; if the prime minister is prepared to move forward on this basis, the navy will of course lend its full support, and I am convinced that the army will also follow suit." To this Konoe replied: "That's a relief; that's where my thinking also lies."[300] Thus they came to a mutual agreement to try and change the Imperial Conference decision.

On October 2 Oikawa reported this agreement to Toyoda and expressed the hope that Toyoda would devote himself to reaching an agreement and would exercise prudence in dealing with the reply to the United States. When he met with Tōjō that same day, however, Oikawa did not inform him of the agreement and reported only that "he had been asked by the prime minister about how things stood with the navy." Confidential collaboration among Konoe, Toyoda, and Oikawa had now begun to distance them from Tōjō, who was like the political representative of the two high commands.

The United States reply of October 2 was a declaration that conversations were at an end concerning all proposals made by Japan after troops had been stationed in southern Indochina, including the September 20 "Comprehensive Plan for a Readjustment with the United States." Once he received this reply, Nomura accurately reported to Tokyo (October 3) on how things stood:

It is my sense that Japanese-United States negotiations have finally reached a "deadlock." . . . I think there will be no change in [U.S.] policy toward Japan unless there is a great change in the world political situation and unless Japan does an about-face in its policies.[301]

In light of the United States reply and this telegram from Nomura, it was plain for everyone to see that there was "no prospect of obtaining our demands through diplomatic negotiations" by early October, as stipulated in the Imperial Conference decision. At the morning briefing for the Liaison Conference of the 4th, the atmosphere was that "the conference this afternoon should decide that there is no prospect." Opinion was divided over Toyoda's draft reply presented that afternoon:

TOYODA: It could well be that with this memorandum as a foundation, the United States intends to seek a gradual turn for the better in Japanese-American relations.

TŌJŌ: This is not a reply that rejects or accepts Japan's proposal, but the true intentions of the United States are clear enough. Japan must carefully look into the future to see whether or not it should adhere to its past policies. Because the matter is of such great importance, it is necessary to set the draft reply to the United States aside for the time being and study it carefully. The Four Principles are very problematical as well.[302]

The conference adjourned with statements by both chiefs of staff, without going into Toyoda's proposal. Nagano reiterated his pet argument that "this is no time for discussion; I want a decision fast."[303] And the Naval Affairs Bureau also concluded that Hull's reply meant that war could no longer be avoided.[304]

The emperor had underscored his own position when Tōjō reported to the Throne on September 11 by telling him that "my desire to avoid war was made clear to the army minister by my statement at the Imperial Conference, was it not?" Tōjō replied, "I have fully taken to heart Your Majesty's wishes and am bending every effort to reach a negotiated agreement."[305] In truth, until he looked into the U.S. reply at the October 4 Liaison Conference, Tōjō had adhered faithfully to this reply to the Throne. However, the American reply was based on Japan's acceptance of Hull's Four Principles, which Tōjō took to mean a reaffirmation of the Nine Power Treaty.* Because Tōjō was concerned about preserving what Japan had won in the Sino-Japanese War, this roused his animus against the United States to a fever pitch. Moreover, in order to reach agreement, the army minister had no recourse but to compromise with the Army General Staff by accepting more or less what it asserted, because the General Staff was structurally beyond the jurisdiction of the army minister and because the army lacked a mechanism for collective leadership like the navy's First Committee.

Finally, Tōjō had an inflexible and hidebound sense of responsibility. Once an Imperial Conference had approved a proposal submitted to it, that proposal was, in his view, almost as sacred as an imperial proclamation; those responsible for advising and assisting the emperor on such a decision were duty bound to carry it out to the letter. Once the U.S. reply was received, therefore, Tōjō no doubt saw it as the self-evident duty of the emperor's ministers to conclude that there was "no prospect" of Japan's obtaining its demands and to "immediately resolve to go to war with the United States." In any case, from October 4 on Tōjō put his heart and soul into persuading Konoe, Toyoda and Oikawa to decide promptly on going to war.

Fukudome Makes a Statement of Great Importance

On October 5 the Army Ministry and General Staff held a meeting of division and bureau chiefs that lasted for eight hours. Having determined that there was "no prospect" for diplomacy, they urged that an Imperial Conference "be promptly requested of the emperor to resolve to go to war."[306] On the other hand, leaders from the Navy Ministry and General Staff (minus Nagano) met and decided that "given the firm resolve of the prime minister we will talk to the army minister tomorrow, consulting with him about postponing the date

* Hull's four principles were almost identical to the four principles presented at the Washington Conference by Elihu Root. Root's four principles in turn became the womb from which the Nine Power Treaty was born, thus Tōjō's interpretation was accurate.

[to resolve on going to war] and moderating the terms [decided at the Imperial Conference], provided that there is still room for diplomacy."[307] Toyoda or Tomita was to report this to Konoe. When Konoe met with Tōjō that evening he revealed his anxiety by asking:

> Can't we separate the United States and Britain? Is there no way not to take on the United States in a war? Is there no room for giving thought to improving the expression "stationing troops"?[308]

To all of which Tōjō apparently answered no. At a meeting of army-navy bureau and division chiefs on the afternoon of the 6th, Naval Affairs Bureau Chief Oka Takazumi declared that "there are prospects" of obtaining our demands through diplomacy if we change the Imperial Conference decision and "reconsider the matter of stationing troops." Moreover, because Britain and the United States were not inseparable, he asked: "Can't we think of ways to proceed without taking the Philippines" and without going to war with the United States?[309] Navy Operations Division Chief Fukudome Shigeru also made a statement of great importance:

> I have no confidence in South Seas operations. As far as losses of ships are concerned, 1.4 million tons will be sunk in the first year of the war. The results of the new war games conducted by the Combined Fleet are that there will be no ships for civilian requirements in the third year of the war. I have no confidence.[310]

Navy Ministry and General Staff leaders met again that evening (Nagano joined while the meeting was in progress) and reconfirmed the policy decided the previous day. Following up on Oka's earlier statement, Oikawa asked: "I'll try as hard as I can to prevent a clash between the army and navy, but would it be all right to go ahead and negotiate [with the army about changing the Imperial Conference decision] without being concerned over starting a quarrel?" Pro-war Nagano objected: "I wonder about that." Vice Minister Sawamoto, Vice Chief of Staff Itō Seiichi, and Oka were present, but none voiced support for Oikawa, who found himself left in the lurch both in the Navy Ministry and the General Staff when the meeting adjourned.[311] When Tōjō and Sugiyama met that night, they decided to convey the following army policy to Konoe:

1. The army judges that "there is no prospect" in negotiations between Japan and the United States; consequently, we will have to re-

solve to go to war. In any case, the army affirms that the Four Principles are unacceptable.

2. No changes whatever (including phraseology) are to be made with regard to stationing troops.

3. If the government says "there are prospects," there is no objection to carrying on with diplomacy until October 15.

And referring to the statement Fukudome had just made to the bureau and section chiefs, Sugiyama asked Tōjō:

> If the navy's claim is correct, that there will be zero vessels for civilian requirements in the third year as the result of shipping losses, then existing state policy has been built on a dangerous foundation. Is this acceptable to the government?

In the end, they agreed that if Fukudome's statement were in fact true, the army and navy ministers and both chiefs of staff would have to accept responsibility and resign for having petitioned the Throne to sanction an Imperial Conference decision to start a war they had no chance of winning. To make sure about this, they then decided that the Army General Staff should put two questions to the Navy General Staff: 1) "Do you lack confidence about going to war in the South Seas?" 2) If so, "will you try to change the Imperial Conference decision?"[312]

Tōjō Demands Clarification

As the result of such activity by both the army and navy, the next day, October 7, was a busy one. Meeting followed meeting: Sugiyama and Nagano met, Tōjō and Oikawa met twice, there was a meeting of senior army and navy section chiefs, Konoe and Tōjō met. At his meeting with Sugiyama, Nagano did not take the Imperial Conference decision "based on the resolve not to flinch from war" to be rhetoric or elegant prose,[313] and he simply rejected the army's two-point inquiry and Fukudome's warning on which it was based. He then related:

> Overly extending the deadline for the negotiations will upset the timing for going to war and make it difficult to carry out operations; therefore, we will be in a real bind if the deadline is extended, negotiations are continued, and then we are told to go to war because the negotiations didn't go well. Thus, extending the deadline to carry on negotiations is to be made conditional on the certainty that a negotiated adjustment

will result; it is hardly possible to agree to go rambling on with pointless negotiations. Although certainty of success also depends on the attitude of the United States, Japan must first determine its own attitude and then proceed with the conviction that success will be certain; to test the waters without such a conviction is not appropriate in this instance. If we hold to the attitude that we have already said what needs to be said, if we concentrate on theoretical debates or minor revisions, no adjustment is remotely possible. The problem is first and foremost to examine whether a more fundamental change of course is possible and, if so, to have the confidence that an adjustment will most certainly result. And once the deadline is postponed and negotiations have begun, we must by all means see to it that these negotiations succeed.[314]

They reached a meeting of minds at this point and Oikawa was notified.

Almost parallel discussions were taking place between Tōjō and Oikawa, their first talk beginning at 9 a.m. Tōjō began by reporting on his talk with Konoe on the evening of the 5th:

Tōjō: The United States' attitude is that Japan must withdraw
           from the alliance, put the Four Principles into practice un-
           conditionally, and stop stationing troops. Japan cannot yield
           on these points.
Konoe: The focus is on the stationing of troops. What if in principle
           we aim at withdrawing troops, while stationing some troops
           in the name of protecting resources?
Tōjō: That's just a ploy.
Konoe: I want to do things prudently. We've got the atmosphere of
           the Imperial Conference [brought about by the emperor's
           statements]. The United States need not be seen as pursu-
           ing a policy of delay. Then there is the Craigie cable [men-
           tioned in the previous section].
Tōjō: It is improper to treat the Imperial Conference as a for-
           mality.
Konoe: Of course. I want to study the matter. Can the United States
           and Britain be separated?
Tōjō: The outcome of staff studies is that [they cannot be sepa-
           rated]. For the navy that cannot be done strategically. Our
           position now is based on their inseparability.[315]

Tōjō and Oikawa then began an inconclusive exchange of views, after which they parted for the time being:

Tōjō: Differences of opinion seem to have emerged between the
           army and the navy over whether to determine on peace or

war, but these differences can surely be adjusted by impartial examination. It goes without saying that state policy centers on the army and navy. I would like to state the army's view on the U.S. memorandum. The United States does not concede an inch. Its position is to compel Japan to submit, both nominally and actually. There are three essential points in the memorandum.

1. Attitude toward Europe. The United States has clearly expressed its wish that Japan withdraw from the Tripartite Pact.

2. Hull's Four Principles. The United States forcefully insists that they be put into practice, but these are a reconfirmation of the Nine Power Treaty. Japan's efforts since the Manchurian Incident and up until the China Incident have been based on the conviction that the Nine Power Treaty can no longer be valid as the result of the changed situation in East Asia. The conception of a Greater East Asia Coprosperity Sphere surely rests on this conviction as well.

3. The problem of stationing troops. Withdrawing Japanese influence from northern China and Mongolia will affect the existence of Manchukuo. This being the absolute minimum demand, we cannot depart from it in principle or in practice.

I think there are no prospects on the diplomatic front, but this is a difference of views. We cannot give in on two points: stationing troops and rejecting the Four Principles.

OIKAWA: The attitude of the United States should not necessarily be deemed one of enmity. I deem it essential to continue the negotiations because there is hope on the diplomatic front. I am of no mind to change the Imperial Conference decision nor do I intend to raise objections over resolving on war. But I am not confident. What the high command means by "confidence" is victories at the start of hostilities; what the situation will be in two or three years is still under investigation. Another Imperial Conference is needed.

TŌJŌ: If the navy has no confidence about a war, we must reconsider our position. Bearing weighty responsibility [for advising the Throne] we must of course change what has to be changed.[316]

Because Oikawa did not make himself perfectly clear, his true intentions remained obscure to Tōjō, who surmised only that he was inclined to avoid going to war.

Meanwhile, a conference of senior army and navy section chiefs had begun at 10 a.m. The army chiefs inquired closely into what Fukudome and Oka had really meant by their statements the previous day, focusing particularly on the chances of success in relation to ship losses. The navy chiefs "scurried" out of the meeting, but in the afternoon Ishikawa and Ōno of the First Committee visited the Army General Staff office and explained:

> We told the government about ship losses of 1.4 million tons to prompt the government to be prepared for that eventuality. The separability of Britain and the United States was meant to be no more than a suggestion: Might we not at least study the question? The navy does not consider the separability of Britain and the United States to be an issue any longer.[317]

And Shiba Katsuo of the Naval Affairs Bureau contacted Ishii Akiho of the Military Affairs Section to say that "the navy stands pat; don't be led astray by casual pronouncements from the Navy General Staff."[318]

That evening Oikawa returned Tōjō's visit and in the course of their second meeting Tōjō confided:

> We have lost 200,000 souls in the China Incident, and I cannot bear to give it all up just like that. But when I think of all the lives that will be further lost if there is a war between Japan and the United States, we must even think about withdrawing troops. That will be hard to decide.[319]

By suggesting that he would even abandon his rigid adherence to stationing troops if Oikawa would declare openly that he "had no confidence," Tōjō was tacitly encouraging Oikawa to clarify his position.

Finally, Tōjō was summoned by Konoe and they wrangled again from 9:00 p.m. on:

KONOE: As far as the Four Principles are concerned, I think we must recognize equality of opportunity in China; if we can get the United States simply to recognize our special geographical relationship to China, that should do the trick. As far as the Tripartite Pact is concerned, the problem is to let it stand as a document, and I think I can somehow come to terms on this when I meet with Roosevelt. The one remaining problem is the stationing of troops. But if everything else is resolved and only the stationing of troops remains, what then? Can't we take the position of withdrawing troops in principle while stationing troops in practice?

Tōjō: Doesn't the American memorandum deny a special and vital
           relationship between Japan and China? It is dangerous to
           rely on Nomura's conjectures and take an optimistic view of
           this problem. With regard to the problem of stationing
           troops, I find it absolutely impossible to make concessions. I
           have trouble with your assumption that all other pending is-
           sues will be resolved. [When that is no longer an assump-
           tion] we can then think about what to do. But I would like it
           understood that even in that event there will be consider-
           able difficulties.

Konoe: "Immediately" in article 3 of the Imperial Conference deci-
           sion is troublesome; this ought to be examined further.

Tōjō: What's the purpose of examining it? If you intend to over-
           turn the decision of the Imperial Conference, that is a truly
           grave matter. Do you have some misgivings, some doubts?
           Is there some suspicion in your mind that this ought to be
           overturned? Should you let your doubts out into the open,
           that will be a big problem. By now we have had our fill of ex-
           amining both war and operations. And we are all discharg-
           ing our responsibility for advising and assisting the Throne.
           Should you make it known that you have doubts, you will
           bear a grave responsibility in terms of the September 6 Im-
           perial Conference.[320]

Despite Tōjō's opposition, Konoe apparently summoned Oikawa
again at 11 p.m. and announced that "I have persuaded Tōjō."[321]

Two points ran consistently through Tōjō's arguments that day.
First, he was accurate in his judgment that, in light of the American
response, "there is no prospect of obtaining our demands" through
diplomacy. Second, if at this point the navy truly had no confidence
about a war with the United States, and if Konoe truly had doubts
about the Imperial Conference decision, that meant they had obtained the emperor's consent at an Imperial Conference to a proposal
that was premature and insufficiently examined, and that in both the
government and the high command those responsible for advising
the emperor bore a grave responsibility for having done so. Despite
there being no prospect of success in diplomacy, therefore, Tōjō
argued that once they were all clear about their responsibility, what
had to be changed would have to be changed. A change in the
situation now depended on what directions Konoe and Oikawa would
take—their attitudes having been ambiguous up to that point—and
on how explicit they would be in the face of such articulate assertions
by Tōjō.

The Army and Navy Sound Each Other Out

Further meetings between Tōjō and Oikawa on the evenings of the 8th and 9th failed to resolve anything. But on the 9th Oikawa did say that the October 15 deadline was "immovable" as "the turning point for choosing between political and military strategies," to that extent moving a step closer to Tōjō's position.[322] But when Nagano started to repeat his statement of the 7th at the Liaison Conference on the 9th, Oikawa cut him off.

Around this time Ishikawa and a member of the Naval Affairs Bureau visited Oikawa at his private residence in the dead of night and urged: "We think it inevitable that things turned out this way, and we would like you to make a decision between peace or war on your responsibility as the minister of state in charge of naval affairs." Because Oikawa gave no indication of having made up his mind, Ishikawa presented him with a pointed written opinion the next day.[323] Meanwhile, former Navy Chief of Staff Prince Fushimi made a very radical report to the Throne: "You should resolve promptly on going to war."[324] This provoked both pointed questions and disappointment on the part of the emperor. Although Oikawa was thus isolated in both the Navy General Staff and the Navy Ministry, his attitude remained as ambiguous as ever. On the 10th a report was sent in by the army's eavesdropping machinery: "There are indications that the palace, Konoe, Toyoda, and Oikawa are closing ranks and will clamp down on Tōjō, [gut the Imperial Conference decision], and swallow whole the American reply."[325] Konoe had previously gotten rid of Matsuoka, and now Tōjō, speculating that "this time it's my turn," came out spoiling for a fight with Konoe, Toyoda, and Oikawa.

Tōjō's argument with Konoe and Toyoda was over the issue of holding to the stationing of troops; with Oikawa, it involved the chances of success in a war with the United States. Konoe's assertion to Tōjō on the evening of October 7 that "the only problem remaining is the stationing of troops" was probably based on Ambassador Nomura's reports. At his September 3 meeting with Roosevelt, the ambassador had turned to Hull and explained: "Of the three problems that are pending, two (the Tripartite Pact and the close relationship between Japan and China) have been agreed upon in principle"; only the problem of withdrawing troops remained.[326] Reporting to Tokyo on October 3, Nomura had repeated the judgment that "among the three pending issues, two have already been solved for the most part; what remains is the problem of stationing troops."[327]

The United States, however, had actually declared that conversations were at an end and did not consider that any solution had been reached on either the question of the Tripartite Pact or that of nondiscrimination in China. Tōjō's counterargument on the evening of October 7, that "it is dangerous to rely on Nomura's conjectures and take an optimistic view," was far more perceptive as to the actual state of affairs in the United States. To Tōgō, who was soon to take over from Toyoda with the assurance that the only issue pending was that of stationing troops, it was "becoming clearer and clearer that understanding is lacking in Washington on the other two problems as well."[328]

The principle of a joint Sino-Japanese defense against communism had been consistently asserted by Japan ever since Foreign Minister Hirota Kōki had enunciated his Three Principles to the Diet in January 1936. It was Konoe's first cabinet that had made the Arita Declaration (December 1938), which repudiated the Nine Power Treaty that Hull's Four Principles sought to enforce by calling for a New Order in East Asia. And on the basis of Konoe's explanatory statements to the Imperial Conference of July 2, 1941, the following state policy had been adopted: "Regardless of what changes may occur in the world situation, the Empire shall firmly adhere to the policy of establishing a Greater East Asia Coprosperity Sphere, . . . The Empire shall remove all obstacles in the way of achieving these objectives." In other words, the first and second Konoe cabinets had consistently repudiated the Nine Power Treaty and vowed to establish a New Order in East Asia and a Greater East Asia Coprosperity Sphere. Thus it was only natural from a logical standpoint for Tōjō to insist that the third Konoe cabinet could not contemplate abandoning the special and vital relationship between Japan and China either.

Even Tōjō, however, was a layman when it came to assessing the navy's chances of success in a war with the United States. Instead of sticking to a judgment he had made on his own, all he could do was rack his brains over where the navy really stood. Moreover, with Tsukada's approval the Army General Staff had in fact resolved on war back on August 23 by relying primarily on the navy's predictions about a war with the United States, as well as by banking on Germany. Were the navy now to become uneasy about its predictions, as was suggested not only by Oikawa but also by Fukudome, this might so disturb both the army's resolve for war and its war preparations already in progress that they would collapse immediately. Thus Tōjō had to be deadly serious about looking into this. As Kido Kōichi explained at the October 17 meeting of the senior Statesmen: "I went over that point in some detail with Tōjō; even the army fully understands that it is impossible for Japan to plunge into a war with the United States without genuine resolve on the part of the navy."[329] Around October 9 Ishikawa pointedly asked Oikawa to make up his mind on resolving to go to war. But on the 10th Ishikawa did not give a firm answer when the Army Ministry's Ishii pressured him by saying:

> If it comes to war between Japan and the United States, the navy will have the leading role. What about that? Isn't the navy confident about standing up to this? If not, we will have to reconsider, so at least tell me what is really on your mind.[330]

On the contrary, he went around telling top naval leaders that "the army is trying to get the navy to say openly 'no can do'; don't let the army pass the buck to the navy."[331]

Konoe did in fact tend to deal with difficult problems by trying to set the army and navy against each other, a tactic the navy warily called "getting the buck passed by Konoe."[332] Ishikawa may well have considered the queries for clarification from Ishii and others to be activity of this nature, emanating chiefly from Konoe. Be that as it may, now that the situation had reached its denouement, Ishikawa appeared to be scheming to put the responsibility for deciding on peace or war back onto Konoe or the army, even though he had written the First Committee position paper himself. After his meeting with Tōjō and Oikawa on the 7th Konoe had remained silent, having only one further meeting with Oikawa on the 8th. Finally, on the 11th he sent word through Chief Cabinet Secretary Tomita that a very important meeting of only the Five Government Ministers would be held at his private residence at Ogikubo the next day to discuss the issue of peace or war. When Tomita, accompanied by Oka, visited Oikawa soon after midnight, Oikawa clearly went along with Ishikawa's warnings when he said:

> I want to avoid a war between Japan and the United States at this time. I persist in hoping that negotiations will continue. Unlike the army, moreover, there is absolutely no fear that the lower echelons of the navy will get out of hand if we don't go to war. There is entirely no need for worry on that score.
>
> However, it is not possible for the navy to state clearly and openly

222 LEANING TOWARD WAR

that we are opposed to this war from a navy standpoint. Because deciding on whether or not to go to war is a political issue, it is proper that the prime minister should decide.[333]

Tomita was unable to obtain a commitment from Oikawa to support Konoe and left after repeating his hope that at least "you will please endeavor to give strong support to Konoe at tomorrow's meeting and restrain the army so that the negotiations between Japan and the United States can continue."

On the morning of the 12th Oikawa summoned Sawamoto, Oka, Itō and Fukudome to a conference of top leaders, at which it was decided to insist on three points at the Ogikubo meeting: (1) a change of government must be avoided at this time; (2) in any event, present conditions do not justify going to war, and the actual situation must be clarified by pursuing diplomatic negotiations further; (3) these responses are to be kept *entre nous*.[334] Oka then telephoned Tomita:

> At the meeting to be held today the navy minister intends to state that the decision on peace or war is entirely up to the prime minister. He can go no further than that. The navy minister cannot make a statement for or against going to war. That is an issue for the prime minister to decide. At the meeting it would be good if we could get the prime minister to say clearly that war must be avoided.[335]

Tomita immediately telephoned this information to Mutō, who replied that he would promptly relay his reaction to Oka, which would be that: "If the navy is loath to go to war, then I want them to say that clearly, straight from their own mouths. If they do that, we will put a stop to the pro-war arguments in the army."[336]

Tomita then called on Oka and put it bluntly: "If the navy says 'no can do,' we will get the army under control one way or the other, so tell me what the situation really is."[337] But Oka refused to change his position. Throwing in the towel, Tomita reported to Mutō: "I didn't get through to Oka; have the army and navy talk together directly." This time Mutō went to see Oka, but just as before, Oka would not budge an inch,[338] and the meeting broke up. Mutō reported this to Tōjō.

Oikawa Misses His Last Chance

Preceded by such wrangling, pitting Tomita and Mutō against Oikawa and Oka, the Ogikubo meeting began at 2 p.m. and lasted for four hours. There was, of course, only one item on the agenda: to decide whether or not there was any "prospect of obtaining our demands through diplomatic negotiations." Two almost identical memoranda drafted by Sugiyama[339] (based on Tōjō's oral statement immediately after the meeting) and Tomita[340] (dictated by Konoe, also immediately after the meeting) present the main points raised at the meeting:

Tōjō:	I think that negotiations between Japan and the United States hold no promise whatever. The obstacles with regard to the stationing of troops are particularly great. But then if you say we will yield on this, that is another problem.
Oikawa:	I think we are now at a very important crossroad: Do we resolve on war? How far do we go with negotiations? If we decide to keep on negotiating to the very end, we will set aside war preparations and proceed solely with diplomacy, but only on the condition that negotiations promise to be successful. We cannot allow this policy to be changed in midstream. In other words, it is essential to make up our minds not to resort to war for perhaps several years. Which road we take I leave to the decision of the prime minister.
Konoe:	What does the foreign minister think about the prospects for negotiations?
Toyoda:	I cannot say with absolute confidence; that depends on what the other side has to say.
Tōjō and Oikawa:	We will be in trouble if we are strung along and then wind up in a war anyway.
Konoe:	There are risks in taking either road. The basic problem is which one involves the greater risks, which one we have greater confidence in. I myself have greater confidence in negotiations and therefore want to take that road.
Tōjō:	Hasn't the foreign minister just said he is not fully confident? Such a wobbly position will put me in a bind. I won't be able to persuade the high command to go along. There must be much greater grounds for confidence.
Konoe:	Having compared both options, I for one choose diplomatic negotiations.
Tōjō:	That's the prime minister's subjective view; I can't convince the high command on such a basis as that.
Oikawa:	I agree.
Tōjō:	We will get into trouble if the prime minister makes such a quick decision. What we want to hear from the foreign minister is whether he is sufficiently confident or not.

At this point Tōjō proposed the items of understanding contained in the "Supplement" below, which were agreed to by all present:

KONOE: As for which road we should take, I for one want to go with diplomacy because I have greater confidence in that course. If, in spite of this, you say go to war, I for one cannot take the responsibility.

TŌJŌ: At the Imperial Conference it was decided to resolve on going to war in the event that diplomacy did not work. The prime minister was present, was he not? And did he not agree with this? It is hard for me to understand how, in spite of this, he can now say he cannot take responsibility for going to war.

KONOE: I am saying that I cannot take responsibility if, in spite of my having greater confidence in one route, you tell me to take the other in which I have none. The Imperial Conference made a decision about what to do in case one route became completely hopeless. Today the situation is that such a decision is yet to be made; what's more, the situation allows much greater confidence in one route over the other.

SUPPLEMENT

Neither changing our policy on the issue of stationing troops or those policies of central concern to that question, nor jeopardizing the fruits of the China Incident, we are confident that we can achieve diplomatic success in negotiations between Japan and the United States virtually by the deadline desired by the high command.

On the basis of such confidence, we shall proceed to seek a diplomatic settlement.

In proceeding with the determination to do so, we shall discontinue preparations for military operations.

We shall study what the foreign minister will and will not be able to do in this regard.

(The army minister gave assurances when asked by the president of the Cabinet Planning Board if the army would be content with this.)

In the above exchanges, Konoe and Toyoda argued that there were prospects for diplomatic success, since two of the pending problems had been largely resolved and the remaining problem of stationing troops could also be resolved if some alterations were embroidered into the Imperial Conference decision. On the contrary, Tōjō argued that there were no prospects for success: not only was there no room for compromise on the matter of stationing troops but also the other two problems had in no way been resolved either. The meeting finally had to be adjourned with both sides remaining opposed in their judgments. Even if both sides had agreed that diplomacy would not succeed, the complexion of the meeting would have changed completely if Oikawa had stated positively that the navy had no chance of success in a war with the United States. Had that happened, it stands to reason that they would have had to rethink what the prospects for resolving the three pending issues would be if they scrapped the Imperial Conference decision and reverted to the basic premise that there must be no war between Japan and the United States. In other words, behind the question of the prospects for negotiations—the issue ostensibly under discussion at Ogikubo—lay the issue of whether or not the navy had any chance of success in a war against the United States. The meeting was limited to representatives of the government without anyone from the Navy General Staff, and Oikawa, representing the entire navy, was perfectly free to state frankly what the navy's chances were. Attended by members of neither high command, both of which were close to being uniformly pro-war, this meeting was precisely the golden opportunity for Oikawa to state "I am not confident," as he had to Tōjō on the 7th. And in their entreaties to Oikawa, Oka, and Ishikawa from the 10th on, Ishii, Mutō and Tomita had encouraged and banked on such a statement.

On October 15 Kobayashi Seizō called on Yonai Mitsumasa, who told him that, "Ten days ago I had a certain third party make a representation to Oikawa that the situation is very grave, and you must make clear the navy's thinking."[341] And after the war had started, Admiral Yamamoto lamented: "If I had been in charge I would have said honestly that there can be no final victory against the United States, I really would have."[342]

Toyoda Soemu, who was recommended several days later as a possible successor to Oikawa, also had his doubts:

> A war between Japan and the United States will largely be the navy's war. It is inconceivable that the navy minister, the very person responsible, could possibly have said "it's okay if we go to war, it's okay if we don't." That would simply be unthinkable behavior for a person conscious of the importance of his responsibility.[343]

In light of Oikawa's ambiguous attitude at such a decisive moment, Konoe, Tōjō, and even Kido could not but have had doubts about the navy's chances for success after the Ogikubo conference. In fact, their attitudes from then on were based on the judgment that there were no chances for success. To that extent, Oikawa had cleverly succeeded in conveying tacitly that the navy's chances were dubious, without having the buck passed to him by Konoe. To do so, however, Oikawa had to pay the exorbitant price of letting the golden opportunity to avoid war go by.

The Navy General Staff's Resolve to Go to War Is Unchanged

The Ogikubo conference adjourned with Konoe and Toyoda as opposed to Tōjō in their judgments as before. Thereafter, neither side revised its judgment. When Konoe presented his letter of resignation on October 16 he wrote:

> Upon careful consideration, I believe we must not conclude that with more time there would still be no hope for success in negotiations with the United States. I also believe there is hope for compromise even now, if on the issue of withdrawing troops, which is considered the most difficult obstacle, we take the attitude of yielding to them as a formality, in effect keeping in substance what we abandon in name.[344]

In a message sent to the Conference of Senior Statesmen on the 17th, Konoe reiterated, as "the difference in views between the government and the army," that:

> The government on its part . . . thinks there are prospects for success even today if the army on its part would relax its terms (which boil down to the issue of withdrawing troops). . . .
> While it is not to be thought that [the United States] has as yet made its true intentions completely clear, the difficult points that remain today largely come down to three: withdrawing troops from China, Japan's attitude toward the Tripartite Pact, and nondiscrimination in trade in the Pacific region. Moreover, these three issues ultimately revolve around the problem of withdrawing troops. Thus it can be said that the sole obstacle in the way of negotiations with the United States is the issue of withdrawing troops.[345]

Tōjō had countered this position at the cabinet meeting on the 14th:

> Problems other than the stationing of troops remain. To say that stationing troops is the key is merely speculation on our part. Even if we yield on this it won't do any good; things won't get settled unless we swallow the whole package. I doubt whether we will be successful even if we yield on this.

And with that he held out on the stationing of troops as well:

Next, the army regards the issue of withdrawing troops to be of great moment. To submit to the contentions of the United States in their entirety will annihilate the gains from the China Incident and by extension threaten the existence of Manchukuo, even affecting Japanese rule over Korea and Taiwan.

Since the Incident started, Japan has had hundreds of thousands of war casualties—dead, wounded, and sick—and has cared for bereaved families several times that number. Several million troops and one hundred million civilians have fought against hardships on and off the battlefield, and billions have already been expended from the national treasury. Yet Japan has adopted a policy of nonannexation and no compensation, an attitude of generosity unexampled among the Great Powers. Japan is merely securing the gains of the Incident by stationing troops. There is no need whatever to defer to the world. There is no need to submit to ingenious pressures from the United States.

If we are reluctant to take an immovable position on north China and Mongolia, the foundation on which Manchuria has been built will be endangered, bequeathing to the future a great source of trouble that will take another war to recoup. Of course, if we want to go back to the little Japan of pre-Manchurian Incident days there's nothing else to be said, is there?

You say we will make good the stationing of troops under the rubric of withdrawing troops, but withdrawal is retreat and armed forces that have lost their morale are the same as no armed forces at all. It is necessary to stipulate clearly that we will station troops. However, we ought to station troops only in essential areas, and military forces other than these ought to be withdrawn in good time.

Stationing troops is the heart of our demands. We must insist on what we ought to insist on. Is it necessary to make one concession after another and then beyond that yield further, to the point of endangering our very life? What is a foreign policy that yields this far? It is submission. Because it will embolden the United States more and more, I don't know where it will end. If you are saying that you are confident of success only by yielding, that I cannot accept.[346]

Yet even Tōjō, while he held firm on the stationing of troops and did not waver in his judgment that "there is no prospect," became increasingly uneasy over Oikawa's attitude regarding the navy's chances in a war against the United States. After the cabinet meeting on the 14th he told Sugiyama:

Oikawa doesn't say he isn't confident, but he seems to talk that way. The matter can't be decided because he won't speak plainly. If the navy

can't come out in favor of war, then we must think of a different way
of proceeding based on that.

Sugiyama then told Tōjō that when "Tomita had asked the navy
[Oikawa?] if it wouldn't please say 'no can do,' Nagano had in effect
responded 'no way.' "[347] When Mutō visited Tomita that afternoon,
he again proposed that:

> It looks like the navy really hasn't made up its mind. If the navy really
> doesn't want war, then the army will have to reconsider. But the navy
> does not outwardly oppose war and tells the army that it's up to the
> prime minister. I can't get things under control in the army merely by
> saying that it's for the prime minister to decide, but if the navy came
> out and told the army formally that it doesn't want war, then I can get
> the army under control. Can't you get the navy to come out and say
> this for me?[348]

Tomita conveyed this on to Oka, whose reply at 3 p.m. was the same
as that in his telephone call on the morning of the 12th.

On the 15th Kobayashi Seizō received a plea from Uchida Nobuya,
in which Okada Keisuke had also concurred: "To prevent the Konoe
cabinet from resigning, we have no choice but to get the navy, which
will play the leading role in a war between Japan and the United
States, to make its attitude clear and to have the navy minister propose that waging war would be against our interest."[349] That same
afternoon Kobayashi visited Oikawa and urged this upon him. As
usual, Oikawa stuck to his position:

> Now is not the time for an immediate rupture in negotiations, and I
> also think we will lose everything if we wage war now. Because I have
> had occasion thus far to express my thoughts to the prime minister I
> think he must certainly be aware of them. . . . It is not possible for me
> [to emphasize my own opinion as a minister of state on a matter of
> such vital importance to the nation].[350]

His response only angered Kobayashi.

The day before, on the other hand, Mutō had ordered Military
Affairs Section Chief Satō Kenryō to ask the Army General Staff:

> Given that the navy minister has said that it's up to the prime minister,
> the navy must be looking to change the decision of the Imperial Con-
> ference and avoid proceeding to a decision on going to war. Is there a
> change, or vacillation, in the attitude of the Navy General Staff? If so,

won't the army too have to change its attitude, because the navy will be the principal in a war with the United States? [351]

A reply came from Army Operations Division Chief Tanaka Shin'ichi: "Because the Navy General Staff has never thought of changing the Imperial Conference decision, the Army General Staff should not change its position; both high commands are in complete unity on this." While this response avoided stating officially what the navy's chances were, it did speak to the fact that the Navy General Staff's resolve to go to war with the United States was unchanged.

THREE

The Decision for War

1 Kido's No War Policy Is Scrapped

Tōjō Presses for a Cabinet Headed by Prince Higashikuni

After his conversation with Oikawa on October 7 Tōjō had gradually come to the conclusion that the navy did not stand a chance in a war against the United States and that further exchanges with the navy would be pointless. In a conversation with Kido one morning around October 14 he shifted his concern from specific steps to be taken to a reexamination of the Imperial Conference decision itself, on the responsibility of those charged with advising the Throne: "We have no choice but to drop issues of responsibility for what has happened up until now," such as having petitioned the emperor for an Imperial Conference decision; "we must consider whether the state policy previously decided upon should be carried out as is or not."[1] In a conversation with Kido on the 16th Tōjō also agreed with Kido's view that "so long as the navy is not confident and determined, the utmost caution must be taken before plunging into a great war that will put the nation's destiny on the line," saying:

> The prime minister cannot make up his mind at this point . . . because the navy does not express self-confidence. If the navy would simply say that it cannot take on a war, then we might be compelled to reexamine the decision of the Imperial Conference. If at this point they say they have no confidence, there will be no choice but to call everything off and start all over again. The decision of the Imperial Conference is a scourge; in fact, this war is not possible without confident resolve on the part of the navy."[2]

Setting out to achieve a breakthrough, he would try to "call everything off and start all over again" by bringing into the government and high command new personnel responsible for advising the Throne at Imperial Conferences.

Meanwhile, at the prompting of Suzuki Teiichi, Konoe had also gone to work on ending the impasse immediately after the Ogikubo conference of October 12. Suzuki had counseled Konoe that "given the way policy deliberations now stand, why not appeal to His Majesty to scrap the decision of the Imperial Conference and continue negotiations with the United States?" Konoe replied that "because that conference was confidential and informal, such an appeal is not out of the question; have a talk with the army minister."[3] When Suzuki brought this up with Tōjō on the 13th, Tōjō pointed out that bringing new personnel into both the government and the high command was the *sine qua non* for starting all over again:

> I cannot agree to this, because both the government and the high command must shoulder the grave responsibility for overturning, for scrapping within scarcely a month, the decision of the Imperial Conference. I can do so only when the top leaders have been replaced.[4]

Informed of Tōjō's reply, Konoe had Suzuki check further with Kido. That evening Suzuki called on Kido, telling him that "for diplomatic negotiations to continue it is necessary to request of His Majesty that the decision of the Imperial Conference be scrapped." Kido answered that Konoe would have to discuss the matter thoroughly with the army and navy ministers.[5] Following a cabinet meeting on the 14th, Konoe made up his mind to have the cabinet resign because of disunity over "the prospects." He then summoned Suzuki, telling him that:

> Given the army's attitude today [at the cabinet meeting], negotiations with the United States are not possible. Since they are not possible, the cabinet has no choice but to resign. Because this resignation is due to the attitude of the army minister, I want you to ask him what thoughts he has about bringing the political situation under control after the cabinet resigns. It is necessary to inform His Majesty about what to expect once the cabinet resigns.[6]

When Suzuki called on Tōjō that same evening, Tōjō replied that he preferred not to offer personal opinions about matters of imperial prerogative, but "were I to venture to speak to your question, I think Prince Higashikuni is the only person capable of managing the present situation; I made this suggestion the other day when I had a talk with Kido."[7] Suzuki conveyed this to Konoe at midnight. Konoe was delighted:

That is really splendid. The prince is bent on opposing the war and has urged me again and again to make a success of the negotiations with the United States. I would therefore like to assist him, by becoming deputy prime minister for that matter. I will inform His Majesty of this myself. I want you to convey Tōjō's and my thinking to Kido immediately.[8]

On the 15th Suzuki called on Kido to apprise him of the views of Tōjō and Konoe. Kido replied:

Before requesting [Prince Higashikuni] to make himself available, it is imperative that a policy on which the army and navy are united, and a prudent policy at that, first be settled upon. We must thoroughly investigate whether the prospects for this are certain.[9]

That afternoon Kido followed up by telephoning Suzuki to make sure "whether Tōjō had agreed to a turnabout in policy for the sake of interservice harmony, or was it his thought to request an imperial prince to resolve this difficult problem?"[10] Suzuki took this question to mean that he should "call on the army minister and ask him whether he would be able to bring the pro-war advocates in the army under control should the prince make himself available and then decide against going to war."[11] When Suzuki called on Tōjō and put Kido's question to him, Tōjō replied candidly about how things stood:

If the army will not be brought under control were a no-war decision reached as the result of the prince making himself available, it cannot be brought under control no matter who steps forward. However, I cannot guarantee at this point whether it can or cannot be brought under control.[12]

Kido received a return call to this effect from Suzuki that evening and noted:

From what he said, it can be inferred for all intents and purposes that Tōjō's thinking is not to plan on interservice harmony beforehand but to try and bring that about entirely through the influence of an imperial prince. On that I cannot give my immediate approval.[13]

Yet when Konoe reported on the proposal for a Higashikuni cabinet to the Throne that afternoon and sought His Majesty's personal opinion, the emperor's pleasure was that:

I would like to proceed with peace to the very end. Were an imperial prince to come forward, he would be like my deputy; for him to do so, therefore, we must have a decision in favor of peace. And because it is without precedent for an imperial prince to come forward, should that occur you must exercise special care in selecting cabinet ministers, etc.[14]

With Kido's approval, therefore, Konoe talked with Prince Higashikuni that evening. Konoe began by saying:

It is without precedent to call on Your Highness's influence, thinking that we must somehow prevent war from occurring. But there is no other way to scrap the existing [Imperial Conference] decision. I spoke with Kido about Your Highness heading the next cabinet, and when this was brought up with His Majesty by Kido, His Majesty also concurred.[15]

Prince Higashikuni's reply showed little knowledge of how things stood:

The navy is said to oppose war and perhaps there are people in the army who do not favor war either. We should organize a fourth Konoe cabinet by dismissing Tōjō, who insists on war, and appointing an army minister who favors continuing negotiations between Japan and the United States; we should press forward to the very end with the conviction that war between Japan and the United States will be avoided. As for a successor to the army minister, I shall do my humble best to help. If in the last instance you cannot bring the army under control even after having resolutely reorganized the cabinet, I shall accept.[16]

Konoe then telephoned Kido and reported that Prince Higashikuni "wants two or three days to consider the matter; it is also his desire to have an interview with the army minister and the privy seal."[17] On the 16th Vice Army Minister Kimura Heitarō called on Prince Higashikuni as Tōjō's emissary. The prince, Kimura informed Tōjō, had said that he would "wait until after he met with the army minister." He then observed that Higashikuni would probably accept if he were to receive the imperial mandate to form a cabinet.[18]

Early on the morning of the 16th Suzuki also visited Prince Higashikuni, claiming to be under Konoe's instructions. "Given the present state of the nation," Suzuki said, "it is especially necessary that Your Highness be gracious enough to make yourself available. This is a sincere request not only from Konoe but from me as well."[19] In

response, Prince Higashikuni suggested an extraordinary, ultracon-
stitutional measure:

> The international situation at present has changed from that which
> existed at the time of the Imperial Conference. With such drastic
> changes in the international situation, of what use is it to be obsessed
> with the particulars of that Imperial Conference decision? Shouldn't
> Prime Minister Konoe have requested another Imperial Conference
> and, after making the army and navy discuss their differences of opin-
> ion thoroughly in the emperor's presence, asked the emperor to make
> the final decision?[20]

Kido Opposes

Suzuki then called on Kido at 8:30 a.m., but Kido made it "clear
that upon mature consideration since yesterday I am opposed for
essentially the following reasons:"

> 1. A request that an imperial prince make himself available is made
>   only as a last resort. Even if, for example, the army and navy were
>   united in their views, force of circumstance might still make it desir-
>   able to have recourse to the influence of an imperial prince. In
>   such a case it would not be impossible to turn to an imperial prince.
> 2. As our conversations since last night have shown, serious problems
>   remain unresolved; it is absolutely improper to ask an imperial
>   prince to remedy such a situation.
> 3. On the other hand, it could be that there is no other person among
>   the subjects of the realm.[21]

Kido then conveyed this statement to Konoe, who was upset when
Suzuki visited him at 3:30 that afternoon:

> Word has arrived from Kido to the effect that he had decided to put a
> stop to His Highness's candidacy, and therefore I consider this line of
> talk to be over and done with. Since Kido might have something in
> mind, the cabinet will resign immediately.[22]

Kido also emphasized the same points to Tōjō when Tōjō paid him a
call. Tōjō was silent for a moment, then asked: "In that case, what on
earth is to become of Japan?"[23]

At 5:00 p.m. Konoe went to the palace and presented his resignation. Herewith the third Konoe cabinet came to an end, having
brought disunity upon itself over "the prospects" and arrived at the

point of being unable to implement the Imperial Conference decision.

From October 7 on, Tōjō had become more and more firmly determined to rescind the Imperial Conference decision and turn the situation around by bringing new personnel into the government and high command; for this purpose he was convinced that no one but Prince Higashikuni could be the new prime minister. Tōjō had singled out Prince Higashikuni because he was invested with the authority of the imperial family and was also clearly against war between Japan and the United States. Once it was inferred that the navy stood no chance of success, it would also be utterly meaningless to continue debating the "prospects" based on the premise that there was some chance of success. Even if the conclusion were reached that there could be no way out in relations with the United States other than to make more decisive and wide-ranging concessions premised on no war between the two nations, to swallow the American reply of October 2 and accept the principle of a full-scale withdrawal of troops from China would be nothing less than to acknowledge utter defeat in the Sino-Japanese War. Official acknowledgement of such a defeat would inevitably involve pursuing the responsibility of those in positions of leadership since the war broke out. Not only would the prestige of the army and navy plummet and morale collapse; but also there would almost certainly be an emotional explosion among the Japanese people, who had been asked to make enormous sacrifices in the name of a holy war. To control these eventualities it would be mandatory to take decisive action by way of a revolutionary diversion. Tōjō told Suzuki on the 14th:

No one else in the realm today has the strength to control the army and navy and redo the [Imperial Conference] draft. At this point there really is no other recourse but to have His Highness come forward.[24]

Then on the 15th Prince Higashikuni asserted: "If I can't control them, who [else] could step forward and do so?" They seemed to have reached the conclusion that the nation could not be rescued from the profound shocks that these across-the-board concessions to the United States and the abandonment of the war in China would cause, unless Japan were under the command of an imperial prince invested with the authority of the emperor—an imperial prince, moreover, who was explicitly against war with the United States.

This was no ordinary cabinet change. Konoe had brought the nation to the brink of war and then balked, resigning abruptly in the midst of the maneuvering around Prince Higashikuni—out of anger at Kido and without ensuring that the basic course to be taken by the succeeding cabinet had been set. His resignation was to bear out the emperor's concern expressed in September the previous year: "Won't Konoe run off the minute he makes a mess of things?"[25] In Tōgō's words, Konoe had left Kido a "bomb with a lighted fuse"—the Imperial Conference decision. And Kido had already rejected Prince Higashikuni when it came to forming a new cabinet that could defuse the bomb.

Paying no heed either to Oikawa's avoidance of an open declaration about the chances for success or to the respective activities of Tōjō, Konoe, and Kido to achieve a breakthrough in the situation, the middle-echelon officers of the navy were the only ones to show any spunk at this point. On the 15th, in Kyoto, First Section Chief Hiraide Hideo of Navy General Staff Intelligence fanned the flames of war by saying:

> Under circumstances such as these, our navy is ready for the worst. Preparations are now complete, up to the hilt, and we are champing at the bit. We have now come to the final fork in the road. This is surely the moment for our navy to set out on its fundamental mission.[26]

Kido's Guarantee: The Key to Deciding on Tōjō

Even after his appointment as lord keeper of the privy seal in June of 1940, Kido had been an opportunistic advocate of a military advance to the south, as on May 15, 1941, when he told Prince Higashikuni:

> We want the Dutch East Indies [because] oil and rubber are a must. [Although] the policy of advancing south is a necessity, in the present circumstances our national strength does not allow an immediate occupation of the Dutch East Indies. They should be put under the joint control of Japan, Germany, and Italy at a peace conference. At present we are advancing our foothold in French Indochina and making it a base for a southward advance; once our national strength has been perfected, we should occupy the Dutch East Indies, peaceably or by taking advantage of the right moment.[27]

On July 31 he also presented the emperor with the formalistic argument that "because the United States is a nation that greatly respects international treaties, it is exceedingly doubtful whether Japan's abrogating [the Tripartite Alliance] now is indeed the way to deepen America's trust; on the contrary, that might just earn its contempt."[28]

Such statements resonated with the attitudes of the second and third Konoe cabinets. But on August 2, when Konoe expressed his usual faintheartedness over taking charge of the political situation, Kido had also suggested that if, after discussing the situation thoroughly with the army and navy ministers, "you do not come to agreement, you will have to resign. After that happens there will be no other recourse but to have the army and navy step in to save the situation."[29] Just before Konoe went to the palace to tender his resignation on the afternoon of October 16, Kido had told Matsudaira Yasumasa, his chief secretary, that "Tōjō seems to have changed his mind over the past several days; if the navy is opposed to going to war, Tōjō will certainly not advocate going to war."[30] Evidently, Kido was leaning toward choosing Tōjō from within the armed forces. It should also be noted that on the previous afternoon Kobayashi Seizō had visited Yonai Mitsumasa, who had mused: "won't it come down to Tōjō with conditions attached?"[31] Konoe, whose cabinet had just collapsed because of Tōjō, also concurred with Kido on Tōjō when they met after Konoe tendered his resignation to the Throne. On the morning of the 17th, therefore, Konoe telephoned Kido that Kido should propose Tōjō, saying that he[32]

> ... concurred completely. Prince Konoe also said that at this time control over the army was the issue to be settled first. If control over the army fell apart, then the negotiations between Japan and the United States would also become a complete mess. Therefore we should have Tōjō take charge. From the way Tōjō has talked over the past two or three days he was not necessarily to be regarded as an advocate of immediate war between Japan and the United States; Konoe was sure that when the emperor spoke with him, he would heed the emperor's words.[33]

Having firmly made up his mind as the result of Konoe's concurrence, Kido convoked a conference of Senior Statesmen at one o'clock that afternoon. Once he had asked each person his opinion, he took the unprecedented action of insisting strongly on Tōjō, at his own discretion. He concluded by saying, "I understand your general inclination on this," and declared the meeting adjourned.

Because this was a complicated cabinet change, Kido had planned to have Konoe attend the conference to explain what had happened and had obtained both the emperor's permission and Konoe's consent on this. But when the appointed day arrived, Konoe was reluctant to attend and ordered Chief Cabinet Secretary Tomita Kenji to write up the particulars of his resignation. Tomita immediately drafted "An Account of the Progress of Japan-U.S. Negotiations and of the Cabinet Resignation." Revised by Konoe and then forwarded, it was read out loud by Kido at the start of the conference.

Wakatsuki Reijirō advanced the most coherent argument at the meeting:

1. I often hear "gradual pauperization" put forward as an argument for war between Japan and the United States, but nothing could be more dangerous; much further study must be given to what will happen if we do go to war.

2. The decision of the Imperial Conference must of course be respected. But to deal with it only as a lawyer would and advocate going to war immediately on the ground that there are no longer any prospects for diplomatic negotiations—what kind of talk is that? Shouldn't a bit more thought be given to political considerations, inasmuch as this is an issue on which we are staking the nation's destiny?

3. If it comes down to Tōjō, I think the reaction abroad will be bad; we must bear in mind that the effect on foreign countries will be very bad.[34]

Wakatsuki proposed Ugaki Kazushige instead. Then Hayashi Senjūrō made a counterproposal. Late on the 16th Tōjō had received a report from Vice Army Minister Kimura about his meeting with Prince Higashikuni and had immediately sent Military Affairs Section Chief Satō Kenryō to inform Hayashi and Abe Nobuyuki that: "For what it's worth at tomorrow's conference of Senior Statesmen, Tōjō hopes for a Higashikuni cabinet."[35] When they heard this, Abe appeared displeased but Hayashi seemed to agree in principle. It was thus that Hayashi made his counterproposal at the conference: "This time how about asking an imperial prince to make himself available to form a cabinet?" He then added that "in view of the state of affairs today, I think we should ask that an imperial prince from the navy come forward," a superfluous remark that self-destructed when Yonai pointed out that "that might be a fine idea in theory, but as a practical matter it doesn't go anywhere, does it [there being no one suitable among imperial princes in the navy]?"[36]

In any case, the first two points made by Wakatsuki were the most telling: reformulate the basic policy on peace or war on the basis of a reexamination of the nation's material strength and, accordingly, adjust the Imperial Conference decision in political terms. But because Konoe, the person responsible for the situation confronting them up to the 16th, had declined to attend, "there was no one who could make a satisfactory explanation with regard to the above."[37] Under these circumstances the much-hoped-for basic proposal aborted, and the conference deteriorated into a discussion largely of such issues as the caliber of individual candidates, putting completely aside any political assessments involving a reexamination of the nation's material strength or a reformulation of the basic policy on peace or war. Perhaps Konoe, having already made up his mind to recommend Tōjō as his successor, took the view that it was no longer necessary for him to go to the conference and press for such a reexamination or reformulation.

At this conference, moreover, Kido violated the convention that a privy seal hardly ever states his own opinions aggressively. "I am unable to agree with you on a cabinet headed by an imperial prince," he told Hayashi, and then asserted:

> If I may start by giving you my conclusion, I think Tōjō should be mandated to form a cabinet. . . . I think the most realistic way to save the situation is for His Majesty to command that the army and navy work in genuine harmony and that the Imperial Conference be reexamined.[38]

When Hara pointed out that "if we do as the privy seal says, I think it will be necessary for His Majesty to give clear directions on policy when he issues his mandate," Kido responded: "I intend to give that point full consideration."[39] Abe, who was related to Kido by marriage, ignored the communication from Tōjō and merely seconded Kido's statements, so that according to Okada Keisuke the conference at times gave the appearance of being a "comic dialogue" between the two. As the conference raced ahead, focusing solely on the selection of a prime minister and with Kido keeping political assessments on the shelf, there was no sign of support for Tōjō among the Senior Statesmen except for Abe until Kido reassured them with his guarantee that:

> If Tōjō is chosen, I will come to an agreement with him. Tōjō is someone who can handle negotiations with the United States. If the emperor speaks to him, he will not start a war with the United States, will he?[40]

Somewhat relieved by this guarantee, the Senior Statesmen reluctantly came to an agreement in favor of Tōjō.

After the war had broken out, and with Japan confronting an adverse war situation, it was this guarantee that led the Senior Statesmen to declare bitterly that Kido bore grave responsibility for such an outcome.[41]

Tōjō Is Stunned

After September 25, when the chiefs of staff had proposed October 15 as the deadline "for choosing between political and military strategies," the army had been determined to hold to this deadline even if it led to a change in government. The army's only fear was that the emperor might make his wishes clear. On the 30th the General Staff's War Guidance Office recorded that "a truly insurmountable difficulty would be for the army to be compelled by extraordinary measures to retreat; the chief of staff and army minister must be prepared to go to the wall over this."[42] On October 10 Colonel Ishii Akiho was told by General Mutō that an alliance seemed to be forming among the palace, Konoe, the Foreign Ministry, and the Navy Ministry to make the army swallow the entire American reply. The Military Affairs Section therefore decided to insist on stationing troops regardless of the emperor's instructions.[43] When the meeting of the Senior Statesmen was announced, the War Guidance Office held its breath, wary of the outcome:

> There are reports that His Highness Prince [Higashikuni] might be installed as prime minister. That would be fine were His Highness determined [to go to war], but if that is not the case the army's position will suffer.
>
> Sometime this evening the emperor may summon both chiefs of staff. Should His Majesty say "desist from war," will the determination of the chiefs of staff hold up? It would be capital if [on that occasion] Navy Chief of Staff Nagano were to submit to the Throne that "war must be resolutely undertaken" and say that he resigns, or even if he were to say that "we must do what we firmly believe in without consulting the Navy Ministry in any way whatsoever." What about our own chief of staff [Sugiyama]?[44]

Meanwhile, Kido had brought the conference of Senior Statesmen to a close and then petitioned the Throne to have Tōjō appointed to head a new cabinet. Toward evening a telephone call summoned an unsuspecting Tōjō to the palace.

On the 16th Tōjō had received word about a tentative decision to make him the next prime minister and had ignored it, being in the midst of moving to his private residence. One hour before the Senior Statesmen met, the Military Affairs Section's Ishii had also heard that the Throne would be petitioned to summon Tōjō, but he put no stock in it either. On the contrary, he anticipated that the mandate would fall on someone else and that imperial instructions would be issued to Tōjō saying, in effect, "Do not persist in stationing troops; cooperate with the new cabinet." For that eventuality Ishii had already drawn up at Mutō's suggestion a long report arguing the necessity for stationing troops that could be presented to the Throne on the spot when Tōjō went to the palace.[45] Consequently, Tōjō himself, as well as Military Affairs Section Chief Satō, could only assume that the emperor was summoning him to reprimand him over the army's obstinacy on stationing troops.[46] Just before he set out for the palace, Tōjō met with Sugiyama and told him that he did not know why he was being summoned but that he would no doubt be questioned about the army's views concerning the Konoe cabinet's resignation.[47] Tōjō also spurned the report to the Throne that Ishii had drafted. "If His Majesty says this is the way it will be, that is that as far as I am concerned; I will say 'yes sir' and withdraw," and he affected a most respectful bow. He then added: "I will not argue with His Majesty. Your fine report is duly acknowledged."[48] Frowning, he turned and left for the palace. At the palace Tōjō received the entirely unexpected command from the emperor to form a cabinet. Waiting for him when he retired from the emperor's presence was Kido, who, on orders from the emperor, conveyed to him, and to Oikawa, the emperor's wishes:

> I gather that His Majesty has just spoken with you about army-navy cooperation and so forth. It is His Majesty's pleasure that when it comes to deciding the cardinal principles of state policy, you examine more extensively and deeply, and give more prudent consideration to, conditions at home and abroad, without being obsessed with the Imperial Conference decision of September 6.[49]

Why Kido Recommended Tōjō to the Throne

That was how Kido carried through on his guarantee to the Senior Statesmen. In November Kido wrote an "Account of the Third Konoe Cabinet Change," in which he recorded that "the Imperial Conference decision of September 6 has been scrapped." As a result, Kido's instructions to Tōjō and Oikawa came to be known as "the emperor's message to wipe the slate clean." In dealing with this cabinet change, Kido had focused on petitioning the emperor to appoint Tōjō and then on having the emperor transmit instructions to him; he clearly noted in his "Account" that in doing so, "I was determined for better or worse to take it upon myself to make the best of the situation."[50]

Tōjō's reasons for turning to Prince Higashikuni have already been discussed. By nature a man of strong likes and dislikes, Tōjō would by no means have been inclined to propose Higashikuni under ordinary circumstances. But because the prince, whom Ogata Taketora described as "a person who never dreamed that people smelled like people," was against war with the United States as well as directly endowed with the authority of the emperor, Tōjō judged that Japan might barely weather the anticipated revolutionary changes only if the mandate fell to Prince Higashikuni. Furthermore, the emperor had already made it sufficiently clear by his unprecedented statement at the September 6 Imperial Conference that he wished to risk revolutionary changes rather than go to war with the United States.

Kido was merely a palace official; the Meiji Constitution gave him no responsibility for advising and assisting the emperor. It would have sufficed for him simply to have used his good offices to have the ministers of state, who had that responsibility, take the emperor's wishes under advisement.[51] Thus, had Kido been truly devoted to implementing the emperor's wishes, he would surely have capitalized on Tōjō's argument for a cabinet under Prince Higashikuni in dealing with this change of government. But in his reply to Suzuki on the morning of the 16th noted above, Kido opposed Tōjō's proposal. Tōjō had realized that Japan had come to the turning point between peace and war with "serious problems unresolved" and without "the army and navy being united in their views"; he therefore advocated that an imperial prince be asked "to remedy the situation" because there was "no other person among the subjects of the realm." For precisely the same reasons, however, Kido was opposed to doing so, and the opposition between the two came down to a fundamental argument over the proper political role for an imperial prince. Kido saw this as grounds for rejecting Prince Higashikuni and argued for Tōjō instead.

After the war, Matsudaira Yasumasa, Kido's chief secretary and the person closest to him at the time, observed that,

> although this is conjecture on my part. . . . Kido probably had it in mind to have Tōjō bring the army under control. As to whether Kido was confident that Tōjō could in fact control the army and avoid an

extremely dangerous démarche, it did not seem that he was fully confident about this. But *if indeed* the army could be brought under control the only person who could do this was Tōjō. And this might have been *wishful thinking* on Kido's part: *if Tōjō were able* to control the army, he would somehow be able to prevent the most dangerous démarche. (Author's emphasis)[52]

Kido's willingness to forge ahead with Tōjō despite such doubts may have been due to what Takagi Sōkichi referred to as his "bow and stern oarlock set-up." With Tōjō, Kido could go one way or the other. If war could be avoided, Tōjō would have the military under control; on the other hand, if war could not be avoided, Tōjō would be preferable to the civilian, antiwar Prince Higashikuni.[53] Suzuki Teiichi, the person most frequently in touch with Kido from the 13th to the 16th, later recalled that Kido opposed Tōjō's plan first because of his habitual concern to constrain the emperor from speaking out, and second out of concern for his own personal safety[54] in the event of the domestic disturbances he feared. Kido himself recorded in his "Sugamo Notes" that he told Konoe after the latter had presented his resignation: "because the driving force is the middle-echelon officers of the army and navy who are committed to the decision of the Imperial Conference, one could say that at this time of extraordinary tensions it is all but impossible to form a cabinet *that would straight away indicate that it would change policy*" (author's emphasis).[55]

The Problem: Kido's "Wiping the Slate Clean"

Tōjō showed his lack of confidence about maintaining control over the army when he said, "I cannot guarantee at this point whether it can or cannot be brought under control." With his bow and stern oarlock set-up, Kido offered Tōjō something to propel him forward: "Wipe the slate clean." This move had probably been thought up by Kido at Suzuki's suggestion when they met on the 13th.

"Wiping the slate clean" meant that Japan's situation should be examined without being bound by the September 6 Imperial Conference decision. But Kido, ignoring Tōjō's pleas, communicated this policy *to the government only*—to Prime Minister Tōjō and to Navy Minister Oikawa, who was about to resign. As a result, the Supreme Command, which was independent of the government, was not notified officially of that policy and thus not bound by it, which prompted a rather emotional disposition against it. And because Kido transmitted nothing of the emperor's wish to annul the Imperial Conference and not go to war with the United States, even when the Tōjō cabinet was in the midst of wiping the slate clean, the Imperial Conference decision never got shelved: war preparations based on the resolve not to flinch from war with the United States moved steadily toward completion by the deadline of late October, and inevitably led the United States to conclude that Japan was on the verge of going to war. Within Japan, it served only to embolden the jingoists, given that the accumulated effects of one *fait accompli* after another simply could not be reversed by a mere reexamination of the situation.

Kido was hesitant to take decisive, revolutionary action. His "wiping the slate clean," deriving as it did from a one-way-or-the-other set-up, was thus fated to wind up a formalistic process. Years later Hirota stated:

> At a juncture when Japanese-American relations were becoming more and more tense, I told Yoshida Shigeru when he called on me, "This is going to be terrible; it's Kido's fault." Yoshida communicated this to Kido, who responded: "I have fulfilled my responsibility because Tōjō has scrapped the September Imperial Conference decision and taken on negotiations with the United States." That is what Yoshida told me.
>
> When Arita, Tōgō and I were invited to Konoe's Mejiro home, Konoe told us that "Kido said he was blameless, because the decision of the September Imperial Conference has been changed."[56]

This, too, would lead us to believe that Kido considered the issue of "wiping the slate clean" as largely a formalistic process.

The heart of the issue, however, lay not in formalistic processes but in dealing with the grim reality of the war preparations that had been readied since September 6 and that continued apace. The new prime minister was responsible for advising and assisting the Throne. Kido's role as a palace official was to render loyal service in the emperor's behalf. Kido would not be able to get at the heart of the real issue without conveying the emperor's wishes on that issue directly and literally to the new prime minister, to the effect that:

> I want all war preparations to cease and the status quo ante restored. I want you to abstain from war with the United States and look for another way for the nation to survive no matter what the sacrifice. I want state policy reconstructed from the very foundation so as not to have a war with the United States under any circumstances.[57]

Even after Tōjō's argument in favor of Prince Higashikuni had been rejected, Tōjō had turned down Army Ministry and General Staff demands throughout October that the emperor's message be sent back and that an uncompromising report to the Throne be made on stationing troops, and on October 17 Tōjō had gone to the palace ready to submit instantly and unconditionally to the emperor. This might have afforded Kido yet another chance to get at the heart of the issue, but he allowed this second opportunity afforded by the cabinet change to go by the boards.

Two opportunities to put revolutionary changes into effect had now been wasted and there was nothing forthcoming to guide Japan at the turning point between peace and war. The sole product of this cabinet change was nothing more than a mere formalistic process: Kido's "wiping the slate clean." The only new faces in the Liaison Conference where it would be discussed were Tōjō's cabinet appointees: Navy Minister Shimada Shigetarō, Foreign Minister Tōgō Shigenori, and Finance Minister Kaya Okinori. The middle echelons of the military—the vice chiefs of staff and the chiefs of the operations divisions, the vice ministers and chiefs of the military and naval affairs bureaus, and those below them, were to a man the same as those during the tenure of the previous cabinet, and governed by the same psychological inertia. Given such substantial continuity, formalistic processes were bound to amount to nothing, however often attempted; no new development in the situation could be expected by resorting to them. So this "wiping the slate clean" was also an exercise in rhetoric on Kido's part, and it is hard to see how Kido had solved in any material way the question that Tōjō had posed the day before: "In that case, what on earth is to become of Japan?"

2. Tōjō Reexamines State Policy

The Stance of the Tōjō Cabinet

The collapse of Konoe's third cabinet was caused by cabinet disunity resulting from a fundamental confrontation between Tōjō on the one hand and Konoe, Toyoda, and Oikawa on the other over the "prospects" as set forth in the September 6 Imperial Conference. Toyoda and Oikawa could hardly expect to remain in office once Tōjō replaced Konoe as prime minister. Tōjō, who now doubled as both prime minister and army minister, selected Tōgō Shigenori and Shimada Shigetarō as foreign minister and navy minister, respectively. With Kaya Okinori as finance minister, these three, plus Tōjō now as prime minister, added a certain freshness to liaison conferences with the high command. But how would they deal with the wide latitude offered by a Kido-style "wiping the slate clean"? That was the problem that the Tōjō cabinet first tackled.

Back in July 1940, when Konoe came stage center again, Tōjō had, for better or worse, so typified in political terms the army's capacity for effective action at the time that he was virtually the unanimous choice of the Army Ministry and General Staff for army minister. His disposition toward efficiency in all work of whatever kind correlated with his insistence that office work be dispatched with lightning speed, earning him the sobriquet "The Razor." He was truly dedicated in performing his duties, and his comprehension seemed to grow spontaneously as his work experience accumulated. And after entering the third Konoe cabinet in July 1941, he was able to free himself from Mutō's influence and exert control over the Army Ministry as its central figure, both in name and in reality.

But was such a person, disposed to administrative precision and razor sharpness, appropriate for the prime ministership as the nation drew nearer and nearer to deciding on war or peace with the United States? In proposing Tōjō to head the new government, Kido gave little or no thought to this crucial question of judgment. It is virtually certain that Kido had carelessly assigned Tōjō responsibilities beyond his ability, given that Tōjō was unlikely to give long and careful consideration to the one grave matter that would determine the fate of the Japanese people; nor was Tōjō likely to give deep and mature thought to creating a far-sighted plan or to put forward strategic initiatives based on insight into future trends. His one prominent characteristic was a vigorous but narrowly focused combative spirit, which would soon manifest itself as an intense desire for personal power and become decisive in establishing his notoriety. At this time it manifested itself primarily as a fierce emotional hostility toward the United States. For a prime minister at the turning point between war and peace this aspect of his character was also certain to produce a seriously defective balance of judgment.

To succeed him as navy minister Oikawa first proposed Toyoda Soemu, commander-in-chief of the Kure Naval Station. Just after he was ordered to form a cabinet, however, Tōjō told Oikawa that he was reluctant to accept his recommendation because Toyoda was well known for his antipathy toward the army: "I have problems with Toyoda. The atmosphere in the army is bad and they are of no mind to cooperate. If you persist in this I will have no choice but to firmly decline [the mandate to form a cabinet]." Informed of this by Oikawa when he returned to the office, Vice Minister Sawamoto, Vice Chief of Staff Itō, and Naval Affairs Bureau Chief Oka argued strongly against Tōjō in support of Toyoda. Anxious as always not to have the buck passed to him, however, Oikawa did not agree with them: "That would mean overthrowing the cabinet. Is that of no concern? Is it really worth taking such a strong stand [if it sets a bad example for the future]?"[58] Toyoda, who had just been summoned to Tokyo, was turned down, and Shimada Shigetarō, commander-in-chief of the Yokosuka Naval Station, was sent for. He arrived in Tokyo on the night of the 17th, but deferred making a definite answer until he had talked with Nagano. After a 30-minute conversation with Nagano the next morning he gave his informal consent. Tōjō had no objections to this recommendation.

Despite this dispute over the new navy minister, Tōjō's cabinet was organized with lightning speed, being completed by the afternoon of the 18th. Just after Tōjō returned to his office from the palace on the 17th, Mutō presented him with a proposed cabinet roster, saying: "This is a cabinet organization plan we [Mutō, Satō, and members of the Military Affairs Section] thought up." Visibly cross, Tōjō dismissed it: "Don't meddle."[59] When forming his cabinet Tōjō tried to rid himself of the army portfolio, and with the aid of Hoshino Naoki, a former president of the Cabinet Planning Board, and Akamatsu Sadao, an Army Ministry secretary, both of whom he had specially sent for, he went so far as to make personal telephone calls asking people to join the cabinet.

The *Asahi Shimbun* reported what Tōjō had said to those close to the Throne at 11 p.m. on the 17th: "I will most certainly endeavor to bring to successful completion the state policies that the entire nation as one body has ordained."[60] And during the subsequent late-night negotiations with Tōgō over his joining the cabinet, Tōjō stated: "Because the mandate has fallen to me and I have maintained a hard-line view on the issue of stationing troops, it is understood that I can persist to the very end with a hard-line attitude on that issue."[61] On the evening of the 18th the new cabinet issued a ringing declaration after its first meeting: "The unshakable national policy of the Empire is to bring the China Incident to a successful conclusion, firmly establish the Greater East Asia Coprosperity Sphere, and contribute to world peace."[62] Such strict adherence to existing state policies, of course, was also possible on the basis of a Kido-style policy of "wiping the slate clean." Given that Tōjō had quite candidly taken a dual stance on war or peace with the United States, one corresponding to Kido's "bow and stern oarlock set-up," it was apparently Tōjō's intention when forming his cabinet to somehow arrange state policy so that outwardly Japan would boldly confront the United States (contrary to Konoe's policy) and inwardly do everything possible not to go to war.[63]

Persuaded by Tōjō's determination and self-confidence, Tōgō

agreed to enter the cabinet. Perhaps he was convinced that this would be the moment to implement the far-reaching perspectives already contained in "The Empire's Foreign Policy toward Europe and the United States after Withdrawing from the League of Nations"[64] adopted in April 1933 soon after he became chief of the Europe and Asia Bureau (see Appendix 8). Having immersed himself in a thorough investigation of relevant documents upon his appointment as foreign minister, moreover, Tōgō discovered documents leading him to believe that the United States was inclined toward war. Before long, therefore, he revised his judgment: as far as he was concerned, Japan would have to make wide-ranging concessions.[65] Herein lay the root of future differences both large and small between Tōjō and himself.

The High Command Opposes Tōjō

From the evening after Tōjō was ordered to form a cabinet until daybreak on the 18th Ishii Akiho, complying with the policy of "wiping the slate clean," drafted eleven questions covering the principal items involved in reexamining the Imperial Conference decision:

1. What will be the outcome of the war in Europe?
2. What are the operational prospects in a war with the United States, Britain, and Holland, in the initial period and over several years? In the event of war, what military measures might the United States and Britain take to utilize the unoccupied areas of China?
3. If we commence war to the south this fall, what attendant phenomena might arise in the north?
4. What is the forecast on ship requisitions and shipping attrition in a war with the United States, Britain, and Holland over a three-year period from the start of hostilities?
5. In this connection, what are the prospects for shipping and the supply and demand of basic commodities for domestic civilian requirements?
6. What will the scale of the Empire's budget be and what is our estimate of our fiscal staying power in the event of war with the United States, Britain, and Holland?
7. If we go to war with the United States, Britain, and Holland, how much cooperation could we get Germany and Italy to promise?
8. Can we limit our opponents to only Holland, or to only Britain and Holland?
9. In the event that war breaks out around March of next year:

What are the stakes in overseas relations?

What is the outlook for the supply and demand of basic commodities?

What are the stakes operationally?

In light of the above, when should we decide to go to war?

In this connection, can we abandon plans for war with the United States, Britain, and Holland and preserve the status quo by stepping up the production of synthetic petroleum, etc.? What are the stakes involved?

10. Is there any prospect that by continuing negotiations with the United States we can achieve our minimum demands, as set forth in the September 6 Imperial Conference decision, within a very short period of time? Is there any possibility of a compromise agreement if we soften our minimum demands to some extent? To what extent? Can the Empire allow this?

In the event that we accept in full the American memorandum of October 2, how will the Empire's international position, above all its position vis-à-vis China, change in comparison with what it was before the Incident?

11. What effect will starting a war against the United States, Britain, and Holland have on the will power of Chungking?

Adopted by the first cabinet meeting that same day, these questions became the agenda for the so-called reexamination of state policy carried out in daily liaison conferences from the 24th on. Because Kido had never formally conveyed the emperor's clean slate message to the high command, however, the military were not bound by it in any way. Moreover, Kido made no reference whatever to the annulment of the Imperial Conference decision; therefore, preparations for war continued as before. Thus it is not surprising that the high command reacted unfavorably when the new cabinet decided to reexamine state policy.

The army's War Guidance Office, when presented with Ishii's agenda, noted that "the high command will make a stab at a reexamination although there really is no room for reexamination."[66] On the 19th the navy's War Guidance Office also expressed its unease: "What does 'reexamination' mean?"[67] And Nagano was prompted to sound off at liaison conferences:

I cannot accept any obstacles being placed in the way of tactical operations. The decision of the Imperial Conference is not open to change. (October 21)

Let's be clear on this: it is incomprehensible why we should conduct a reexamination or the like at this point. (October 23)[68]

On the 20th the Army General Staff attempted to have the Army Ministry call a temporary halt to the Japanese-American negotiations being conducted through Nomura, but opposing views in the ministry were strong. After talking with Oka Takazumi in the Naval Affairs Bureau and Yamamoto Kumaichi, chief of the Foreign Ministry's American Bureau, Mutō disregarded the Army General Staff and cabled Nomura on the 21st: "Although detailed instructions will be cabled later, it being too soon after the formation of the cabinet to do so now, enthusiasm in the new cabinet for a diplomatic adjustment between Japan and the United States, on a fair and just basis, is unchanged from the previous cabinet."[69]

Within the Army General Staff, Vice Chief Tsukada and those under him had all begun reexamining state policy with great irritation and distaste, and this cable gave rise to opinion favoring the overthrow of the new cabinet, with some arguing that the way to do this was to make Tōjō resign his concurrent post as army minister. It took a ruling by Sugiyama in support of Tōjō to finally calm matters down. But such trends in the Army General Staff, which was not under the direction of the army minister, made one-sided power plays by Tōjō and the government impossible, thereafter forcing them to compromise. Moreover, Mutō, who straddled the fence on peace or war, confided to Oka on the 21st:

> Tōjō finds himself in circumstances in which he cannot carry out a war. [Oka assumed this was probably because Tōjō was acting on the emperor's wishes]. Yet the Army General Staff is hardening its position and he is perplexed over how to bring matters under control. He recognizes that it may be necessary for him to change his thinking, resign from office, and go along with the key officers in the Army General Staff [primarily Tanaka].[70]

And Tōjō also confided to Shimada on the 23rd:

> The two hundred thousand souls who died in the China Incident would never forgive me if I were to turn back now. And yet, if it comes to war between Japan and the United States, great numbers of officers and men will have to be sacrificed. I am truly in the dark about what to do.[71]

Once again he indirectly asked the navy for an official statement on no war between Japan and the United States, but once again Shimada and Oka turned a deaf ear. Shimada, however, had corresponded privately with Yamamoto Isoroku and been influenced by Yamamoto's opposition to a war with the United States. On the 22nd he went so far as to tell Sawamoto:

> Diplomatic negotiations will require a considerable amount of time. When and if Navy Chief of Staff [Nagano] opposes this, I will not be able to discharge my official duties. So either I will have to resign or have the chief of staff resign. One of us will have to go.[72]

At least this once he showed that he was different from the indecisive Oikawa.

The liaison conferences between the 24th and the 30th (which occurred daily except for the 26th) met in an atmosphere complicated by antagonism on the part of both high commands, Tōjō's anxiety, Shimada's vacillation, and Tōgō's willingness to make wide-ranging concessions. Based on Ishii's eleven-point memorandum, the so-called reexamination of state policy was supplemented by explanatory documents provided by relevant government offices, in particular on the responsibility of army and navy officers who were, except for Shimada, the same military figures as those at liaison conferences during the previous cabinet; deep down, most of them were strongly opposed to the reexamination itself. One even stated clearly that "an examination of documents and the like at this stage is outrageous."[73]

Under the circumstances, rigged documents premised on the possibility that a war could be prosecuted found their way into the explanatory documents, and it is not surprising that a reexamination of state policy grounded on such documents should wind up back at square one. Thus, the plan for both peace and war ultimately adopted was just as Sugiyama suspected when he asked Tōjō on the morning of November 1: If we go ahead with this plan today, "doesn't it come down to reiterating once again the Imperial Conference decision of September 6?"[74]

The Navy Officially Announces Its Determination to Go to War

Several points should be noted about this six-day process of deliberation. First, the Army General Staff took the position that "first we must resolve on going to war, then we will examine whether we can carry it off in terms of our national strength and set the nation's course so as to be able to do so."[75] As always, the Army General Staff advocated a mind-over-matter approach to peace or war that made light of estimates regarding the nation's matériel strength. For example, Vice Chief-of-Staff Tsukada Osamu made "frantic" statements, "dressing down or pleading with Oka, or dressing down ministers of state."[76] When it came to reviewing the data on national strength, Tsukada nonchalantly ordered his subordinates to "study up on these because I don't understand them very well."[77]

Second, the Army General Staff, insisting on the long-term stationing of troops primarily with a view to ruining the Nomura negotiations, ultimately forced Tōjō to concede. At the liaison conferences of the 29th and 30th, Sugiyama and Tsukada were so adamant in their opposition to withdrawing troops that arguments with Tōgō reached a boiling point. Tōjō resignedly proposed a 25-year period within which to withdraw troops, that being "a way of saying close to eternity."[78] Although many present observed that the United States would not accept 20 or even 10 years, to say nothing of 25, Tsukada was still opposed, arguing that to mention any figure would be an indication of weakness.

Third, naval leaders in both the ministry and the General Staff officially voiced their determination to go to war. When Sawamoto, Itō, Oka, and Fukudome met on the 28th, Sawamoto insisted on achieving a diplomatic solution and Itō also used language suggesting that deep down he was inclined to avoid war. In contrast, Fukudome argued strongly against a genuine "wiping the slate clean" policy as well as against allowing the buck to be passed to the navy:

1. A diplomatic solution will ultimately be a diplomatic about-face, even going to the point of withdrawing from the Tripartite Alliance. That will amount to throwing our lot in with the Anglo-American camp; we will incur the contempt of the Chinese and a great loss of national prestige. Are we prepared to go that far?
2. There must be resolute countermeasures when the navy is held responsible for colliding with the prime minister and army. What about this?[79]

Sawamoto and Itō found this argument difficult to refute and the meeting ended inconclusively.

Shimada's attitude was difficult to fathom. For example, many years before this he had been chief of the First Section (Operations) when the Navy General Staff Regulations were being revised, and he had caved in to pressure from the lower echelons of the Navy General Staff in regard to issues that he and the then Naval Affairs Bureau chief, Terajima Ken, had discussed and agreed upon. Yamamoto Isoroku called him "a simpleton."[80] Another former Naval Affairs Bureau chief, Hori Teikichi, declared it "a well known fact that Shimada takes after Oikawa."[81] Still under Yamamoto's influence, Shimada hinted to Sawamoto on the 22nd that Nagano should be transferred. Then Shimada received a letter from Yamamoto, dated the 24th, stating:

> Considering things from the larger perspective, if a collision between Japan and the United States can be avoided, avoid it. There is no question that at this time we must exercise patience and prudence, perseverance and determination. That will take extraordinary courage and strength.[82]

Nonetheless, on the 30th Shimada summoned Sawamoto and Oka and announced a determination for war:

1. Taking an overall view of the atmosphere during the past several days, the general situation is not easily retrievable. If things are done rashly and badly, great harm will result.
2. Under the present circumstances the United States may try at any moment to gain the advantage of a head start. If that happens, Japan's naval strategy will be fundamentally shattered and chances for victory will vanish.[83]

When Sawamoto argued against him, Shimada replied somewhat irritably: "We must come to a timely resolution; it is very important not to miss the right opportunity."[84] Nagano had been a consistent advocate of war since June. With Shimada now having also come to a determination for war, the leaders of the Navy Ministry and General Staff abandoned Oikawa's evasiveness and came out in support of war. Thereafter the navy focused its efforts primarily on acquiring resources in preparation for war.

When Shimada was summoned to Tokyo on the evening of the 17th and asked to be navy minister, Sawamoto and Oka had briefed him on the state of the navy's war preparations. Having informally agreed on the morning of the 18th to assume office, he called on Tōjō at noon:

> It will be difficult for me to make up my mind without asking you some questions. The first concerns the prompt completion of the navy's military preparations for war. . . . In the likelihood that we press forward on diplomacy with the United States but still arrive at the worst-case scenario, the role of the navy will be of the utmost importance. Might I have your full appreciation on that score? . . . I would like to hear your thoughts on the role of the navy in this eventuality.[85]

Once Tōjō confirmed what Sawamoto and Oka had told him, that the navy's military preparations would be given top priority, Shimada entered the cabinet. Thus, when item 2 in Ishii's memorandum—the operational outlook in a war with the United States, Britain, and Holland—was deliberated on the 24th and 25th, Shimada and Oka did nothing but "state over and over again: give the navy the necessary resources." In subsequent deliberations they merely repeated, "Give us steel, give us appropriations; if you don't, we can't fight a war."[86]

By October 29 the foregone conclusion was reached that there were no "prospects" with regard to Ishii's item 10: the possibility of achieving Japan's minimum demands through negotiations with the United States in a short period without conceding anything. The issue now became how far Japan could go in moderating its conditions. Tōgō concluded that Japan would have to make an about-face. He had previously drawn up the following propositions:

1. With regard to stationing troops, all troops will be withdrawn within five years, even in the special regions.
2. The principle of free trade has spread throughout the world, and this being the case, there are no objections to accepting its application to China as well.
3. Japan will withdraw troops from southern French Indochina.
4. Although we have already made de facto concessions on the Tripartite Pact, there is still room for investigating the problem of terminology in the event that the other problems are solved.[87]

With these points and the results of their deliberations up to that point in mind, Tōgō outlined Plan A (see Appendix 9), which he presented to the Liaison Conference on October 30. General agreement was reached as follows:

1. As regards the Tripartite Pact: no change.
2. Concerning the problem of the Four Principles: Tōgō emphasized that what had been stated to the United States up to now had been unavoidable, and that "an agreement in principle with conditions attached" would also be impossible.
3. Nondiscriminatory treatment in trade with China is acceptable provided that "the principle of nondiscrimination is applied throughout the world."
4. On the withdrawal of troops from French Indochina: no change.
5. On the problem of stationing and withdrawing troops in China: no change. However, as regards the required period for stationing troops, Japan will reply that its goal is around 25 years.[88]

Shimada Makes Steel a Quid Pro Quo

Once scrutiny of each of Ishii's items had been concluded on the 30th, Nagano and Sugiyama insisted on making a decision without delay. But both Kaya and Tōgō hoped for a day's respite, Kaya saying, "let me think it over for a day," and Tōgō that "I want to get my thoughts in order." Tōjō acceded and then, determined that a decision be reached at the Liaison Conference of November 1 two days hence even if it took all night, he announced that a conclusive choice would then be made among three proposals:

Proposal 1: Exert every effort to avoid war and undergo great hardship and privation.

Proposal 2: Determine to go to war immediately and focus political and military strategies to this end.

Proposal 3: Being determined to go to war, continue on with diplomatic measures in an effort to reach a compromise agreement while completing preparations for military operations.[89]

On the 31st Mutō and his subordinates in the Army Ministry adopted Proposal 3, partly as a "political ploy to prompt the navy and the Foreign Ministry along the path to war."[90] At a conference of division chiefs that started in the afternoon and lasted into the night, however, the Army General Staff took the bull by the horns and adopted Proposal 2. It rejected the Army Ministry's proposal on the grounds that "preparations for war and diplomacy are basically incompatible, and war will break out early in December."[91] When Satō Kenryō informed the Army Ministry of this, the ministry's key officials convened; then Tōjō, in his capacity as prime minister, summoned Shimada, Tōgō, Kaya, and Suzuki to join the discussion, which lasted until the dead of night. With the exception of Tōgō, they fell in line behind Proposal 3.

November 1 began with an early morning meeting between Tōjō and Sugiyama. Tōjō insisted that:

As prime minister I want to adopt proposal 3. But even at that I am not confident that a stipulation to the effect that early December is to be the time for initiating military action will obtain the emperor's approval. The high command will not give up its insistence on this, but it will not be easy to get the emperor to consent. And I must give due regard to the emperor, who in his heart of hearts likes to do things openly and above board; now that we are determined to go to war, I think the emperor simply will not tolerate a diplomacy of deception [up to day X].[92]

In response, Sugiyama pressed Tōjō for assurance: "won't there be a lowering of the terms of negotiation with the United States beyond those" set forth in Plan A? He then went on to argue:

> If the negotiations go well it will mean removing the troops [from the southern regions] that have been put in readiness. This will be a problem. We have dispatched 200,000 troops from Japan, and troops from China as well. It will affect morale if, having sent troops to the South Seas, we pull them out without their having done battle.[93]

As army minister, Tōjō had always managed to achieve compromises with the Army General Staff and had never faced a Liaison Conference without having first developed a unified army position. Now, as prime minister and army minister, Tōjō no longer wished to seek prior mutual agreements with Sugiyama that would compromise his position. Both men thus went into the decisive Liaison Conference with differing viewpoints.

The Liaison Conference began at 9 a.m. on the 1st. At the outset Shimada stubbornly insisted on increases of steel and other resources for the navy, repeating the demands he had made when he met with Tōjō the night before. His demand for 1.1 million of the 1.7 million tons of ordinary steel allocated for military use in the fiscal 1942 Matériel Mobilization Plan had astonished Tōjō, who revealed his thoughts to Sugiyama early on the morning of the 1st:

> The navy's insistence on steel and other resources, coming suddenly and at the last moment, is a strong one. I cannot help but have doubts about what their true purpose is. Are they trying to put the blame for not going to war on national strength—that is, on the government— should great resources not be acquired just as the navy desires? Or, now that the army is in a hurry to go to war, is the navy trying to make us approve of what amounts to grabbing resources for naval use? . . . If, as they explained it, they are trying to make the government take cognizance of the navy's critical importance, they are still out of order in presenting these demands just when we are on the verge of a great decision.[94]

That same day the army's War Guidance Office also expressed its uneasiness: "Why the hell are they making this proposal on the night before the very last stage, the holding of the 7th Liaison Conference, and just before the nation comes to a momentous determination?" Undeterred, Shimada reasserted his demands at the Liaison Conference: "If the navy doesn't get more steel, we can't resolve on going to

Table 3.1[95]
SUPPLY AND ALLOCATION OF ORDINARY STEEL
(UNIT: 1000 TONS)

Year	Supply Planned	Actual	Planned Allocations Army	Navy	Civilian
1938	4,725	--	642	533	3,550
1939	6,248	4,096	929	500	4,819
1940	5,502	4,816	740	510	4,252
Increases as per reallocations, second half fiscal 1940		--	180	283	--
1941		4,346	902	1,052	2,862
1942[a]		4,500	790	1,100	2,610

[a] Projected.

war." The navy's demand was ultimately granted: amounts allotted to the army and for civilian use were decreased, and the amount for the navy was upped in one stroke from 850,000–900,000 tons to 1.1 million. Sugiyama then asked Shimada pointedly, "Will you resolve on going to war if you get the steel?" Shimada nodded in assent.[96]

In fact, after this nothing of a problematic nature arose in liaison conferences as far as the navy was concerned. Shimada had already indicated to those in the Navy Ministry on October 30 that he was determined to go to war, and now, judging that the navy had attained its maximum allocation of steel, he probably made his determination to go to war official at this Liaison Conference. Thereafter he firmly advocated stationing troops in China, declared that pessimism about the overall prospects in a war was unwarranted, and even took Tōgō aside in an effort to persuade him in favor of going to war.[97] He had now become a thoroughgoing advocate of war.

However, Cabinet Planning Board President Suzuki Teiichi tried to explain to the Liaison Conference that the total supply of ordinary steel would be only 4.3 million tons even if that for civilian use were kept at a constant 3 million tons, as in his draft explanation for the fiscal 1942 Matériel Mobilization Plan based on the board's research. Nonetheless, following a meeting between the army and the navy, the Liaison Conference raised the total supply of steel from 4.3 million to 4.5 million tons and approved an increase of 300,000 tons for the navy, making a total of 1.1 million tons (see table 3.1). Then the army arranged to share with the navy as much as it could spare of its allotted 790,000 tons. Thereupon Tōjō appealed to Suzuki: "Because the army and navy have made this decision, I would really like to have the Cabinet Planning Board draft a plan around it," and Suzuki caved in to Tōjō's request out of political considerations.[98] Caught up in this one-act farce, Shimada also went along, knowing full well that the approved 300,000 ton increase was in fact largely an exercise in rhetoric and nothing more.

Timing the Breaking-off of Negotiations

It was evening by the time the steel issue was resolved. Tōjō then proceeded to the three options he had put forward before. Tōjō first asked if there were any other options. That being out of the question, the Liaison Conference turned to an examination of option 1, to endure hardship and privation. Nagano made his position clear:

> The basic issue that I would like you to understand and appreciate in particular today is that the time for Japan to go to war against the United States is now. Should we miss this opportunity to go to war it will not present itself again. [The time to fight and win] is now. The chance to go to war will not come later.[99]

Then Suzuki declared his judgment with regard to changes in the nation's material strength:

> Should the present situation continue essentially unchanged, matters will no doubt become extremely disadvantageous seen solely in the light of augmenting the matériel side of our national strength.[100]

To endure hardship and privation would therefore be difficult, both strategically and in terms of the nation's material strength.

Kido's "wipe the slate clean" policy had been formulated immediately after he had rejected arguments for a Higashikuni cabinet, a cabinet that would have revolutionized the nation in order to adhere strictly to a policy of no war with the United States. It was thus a product of Kido's "bow and stern oarlock set-up": let's put Tōjō at the helm whether war can be avoided *or* becomes inevitable—whichever. Accordingly, option 1 was beyond the limits of Kido's policy because it would have meant enduring long-term hardship and privation based solely on the unconditional objective of no war with the United States, putting all thought of "gradual pauperization" aside and regardless of the pros and cons in terms of strategy and in terms of changes in the nation's material strength. From the start, therefore, what was allowable within the limits of that policy was no more than a provisional, no more than a partial enduring of "hardship and privation," and proponents of war and of the simultaneous pursuit of peace as well as war both pointed out the "gradual pauperization" implicit in Kido's policy. From the standpoint of the absolutely no war position, by contrast, "gradual pauperization" posed no obstacles whatsoever, but a Kido-like policy could never have been made so consistent in its logic as to go that far. That is to say, Kido had already foreclosed the option of a literal and thorough-going policy of enduring hardship and privation when he transmitted his "wipe the slate clean" policy to Tōjō in the first place. It is not surprising that this option was consigned to oblivion when the reexamination of state policy concluded; what is surprising is that it took so long.

At this point the discussion turned to choosing between the remaining two options. Sugiyama and Tsukada advocated war, as they had in their confrontation with Tōjō early that morning:

SUGIYAMA: As I have said again and again, early December is the right time to commence operations. Thus the time that remains is one month. It is believed to be all but impossible to adjust relations through diplomatic negotiations during that time, to judge from past experience. Rather, I think it appropriate at this time to resolve to go to war as per the second option, using diplomatic negotiations to justify commencing military operations and to conceal our plans.

TSUKADA: The high command can do nothing unless the two things which are at issue here are first decided on: "to determine on going to war immediately" and "to initiate hostilities early in December." I would like the matter of diplomacy to be resolved after these issues have been decided on. Even if we decide to carry on with diplomacy, I want these two issues resolved first. . . . If we are irresolute at this late hour, I cannot take responsibility for national defense.[101]

Tōgō and Kaya disagreed, insisting on the option of pursuing both peace and war, and Tōjō was adamant in supporting them.

The debate then turned to the question of the precise time that negotiations should be terminated and military operations given sole attention:

TSUKADA: . . . diplomacy must not obstruct operations. . . .

Tōjō: and
Tōgō:

Because we are going to pursue diplomacy and military operations simultaneously, there will be trouble if you do not guarantee that if diplomacy succeeds you will desist from initiating a war.

Tsukada:

That's not possible. After . . . [such and such a date] . . . the supreme command will be thrown into confusion.

Sugiyama
and Nagano:

That will endanger the supreme command.[102]

With that exchange, the confrontation intensified between the government, demanding diplomacy, and the high command, demanding military operations. A 20-minute recess had to be taken, during which Sugiyama and Nagano summoned their Operations Division chiefs, Tanaka and Fukudome. Upon further study, they concluded that continuing diplomatic negotiations until November 30 would not really be a problem for the supreme command, and the conference reconvened.

Tsukada set this time limit with painstaking care:

Tōjō:

Won't December 1 do? Can't we carry on with diplomacy even one day longer?

Tsukada:

Beyond November 30 is absolutely out of the question. . . .

Shimada:

Tsukada, until what time on November 30th? Would midnight be all right?

Tsukada:

Midnight will be fine.[103]

Tsukada based his insistence on the fear that even if diplomatic negotiations were successful after this deadline, subordinate units would not obey an order to cease operations sent after November 30. In fact, army forces for the invasion of Malaya were scheduled to sail from Sanya, Hainan island, on December 4, and the naval task force due to leave Hitokappu Bay on November 26 had been informed that it was to cease operations against Hawaii and return home at any time if diplomatic negotiations were satisfactorily concluded even after November 30. Thus it would have been possible to telegraph orders to all subordinate units of both the army and the navy to cease military operations after midnight on November 30, if only the determination to do so existed. Acceptance by the conference of midnight on November 30 as the deadline was thus a partial victory for Tsukada's pro-war argument.

At a meeting of Army General Staff leaders the evening before, Tsukada had labelled the proposal to pursue both peace and war as

nothing more than a rehash of the earlier Imperial Conference decision, and he had expressed concern that the subsequent sequence
of events would be repeated: Imperial Conference decision, cabinet
dissension over prospects for success, cabinet collapse. Tanaka had
also pointed out that "even if we settle on the proposal to pursue both
peace and war for the time being, we must indicate clearly when we
will determine on going to war and when we will break off diplomatic
negotiations; we must avoid repeating the folly of the previous Imperial Conference decision."[104]

Thus the deadline was set at midnight on November 30 in anticipation that they would resolve to go to war and exercise military force
early in December. This was no longer the uncomplicated option of
pursuing peace and war simultaneously; it was now a compromise
between that option and the option for war that had produced a
proposal which was, so to speak, one-fourth for peace, three-fourths
for war.

December 1: The Final Time for Decision

At 10 p.m. the discussion shifted topics for the fourth time, taking up
what diplomatic negotiations should be undertaken with the United
States until the November 30 deadline. Tōgō suddenly presented a
new plan, Plan B (see Appendix 9), together with Plan A. Tōgō had
already secured agreement to Plan A derived from his October 29
synopsis. Plan B had been drafted by former Foreign Minister Shidehara Kijūrō and by former Ambassador to Britain Yoshida Shigeru as
an expedient to save the situation. Both Grew and British Ambassador Craigie had been sounded out on the plan, and Craigie's response
had been interpreted as being rather favorable.[105] It was therefore
forwarded to Tōgō for his approval. Tōgō made revisions and appended a new clause, Article 4.

However, there had been no prior communication concerning
Plan B with the army and navy. Just that morning Sugiyama had
pressed Tōjō for assurance: "won't there be a lowering of the terms
of negotiation with the United States beyond [Plan A]?" and Tōjō had
given him his firm promise that there would not be.[106] Consequently,
when Plan B was proposed Tōjō was stunned and the high command
went through the roof. Unaware that the military had not been
consulted, Tōgō stuck to Plan B at the conference:

A look at the diplomatic record up to now reveals that we have been
talking past one another; there is scant hope for success if we do no

more than simply keep on going in this manner, so I would like to narrow the issues and dispose only of the South Seas problem, leaving it to Japan to solve the China problem.

It is not appropriate to have the United States intervene in the China problem. Their diplomacy until now has been largely absorbed with reviving the Nine Power Treaty, and I think that has been a foolish approach. As I have said several times, anything like agreement in principle to [Hull's] Four Principles makes no sense.[107]

And he continued his insistence on this in his explanation at the Imperial Conference on December 5:

[Hull's counter revised draft]. . . . is a reaffirmation of the Nine Power Treaty when you view it as a whole. It would reverse the policies the Empire has implemented at enormous sacrifice since the Manchurian Incident . . . , and there is no little concern that it would . . . undermine the Empire's leading position in East Asia.[108]

Sugiyama and Tsukada, who were furious over Plan B, voiced stout opposition:

1. To leave out completely the disposition of the China Incident will bequeath a source of great trouble to the future, even if negotiations are successful.
2. It is doubtful that the necessary petroleum will in fact be forthcoming from the United States on the basis of such a provisional settlement. The United States will retain the power of life and death over Japan; we will eventually have to fight even if a makeshift expedient is resorted to, and by then the opportune moment for going to war will have passed.[109]

Their voices rose as they engaged in a heated exchange with Tōgō, who would not budge from Plan B:

If the conditions [of the Army General Staff] are to amend the section on trade, add "no obstructing a settlement of the China Incident" to Article 4, and eliminate withdrawing troops from southern Indochina, then diplomacy is not possible; these make diplomacy useless.[110]

His words led to a head-on collision with the Army General Staff. There were murmurs that "if the foreign minister opposes going to war he might well be replaced,"[111] resulting in fears that the cabinet might collapse should he resign. Ever the peacemaker, Mutō proposed another recess, of ten minutes, during which Sugiyama and Tsukada left the room to confer with the Army Ministry's Tōjō and Mutō. Upon careful reconsideration, the Army General Staff's Sugiyama and Tsukada reluctantly agreed to soften their demands:

> The judgment has been reached that diplomatic negotiations will not succeed in accordance with Plan B were the condition "no obstructing a settlement of the China Incident" to be added to its provisos. We must also consider the fact that if [the proviso on] transferring troops from southern Indochina is rejected, the foreign minister will resign—that is, there will be a change of government. If that happens the chances are great that the next cabinet will be anti-war, and we will have to take the time to reach a determination on going to war [all over again]. At this point we cannot allow either a change of government or a postponement of the deadline.[112]

For his own part, Tōjō had to accept the Army General Staff's compromise proposal to revise Article 3 of Plan B to provide that Japan and the United States "shall together restore trade relations to what they were prior to the freezing of assets, and the United States will promise to supply Japan with the petroleum it needs," and to accept the expressly added proviso to Article 4 that the United States "shall not take such actions as may hinder efforts toward peace by both Japan and China." Instead of rejecting Plan B outright, the Army General Staff made diplomatic negotiations in accordance with it as difficult as possible without causing a change of government. And the keynote of the compromise, one-fourth for peace, three-fourths for war, was likewise attained. The discussion was now substantially over. With majority support for the following document, the Liaison Conference finally adjourned at 1:30 a.m., November 2.

ESSENTIALS FOR CARRYING OUT THE EMPIRE'S POLICIES[113]

I. The Empire, in order to resolve the present critical situation, to assure its self-preservation and self-defense, and to establish a New Order in Greater East Asia, is now determined to go to war against the United States, Britain, and Holland. The following measures are to be taken:

1. The deadline for initiating military action is to be early December, by which time the army and navy are to complete preparations.
2. Negotiations with the United States are to be carried out in accordance with the attached "Essentials."[114]

3. Cooperation with Germany and Italy is to be strengthened.
4. Close military relations will be established between Japan and Thailand immediately before military action is initiated.

II. If negotiations with the United States are successful by zero hours on December 1, the initiation of military action will be suspended.

When the conference adjourned at 1:30 a.m., Tōgō and Kaya had not been willing to give their immediate consent to this decision and had asked for the remainder of the night to think it over. Kaya subsequently conveyed his acceptance to Tōgō, who indicated to Tōjō at noon that he too agreed with the majority view. Tōgō also secured Tōjō's consent when he proposed that "In the event that the United States evidences interest in Plan A or Plan B, I would be empowered to make further limited concessions—for example, on how long troops would be stationed—in order to bring the negotiations to a successful conclusion, and Tōjō would support me in this."[115] Tōgō thereupon told former Ambassador to Germany Kurusu Saburō, who had been asked once again on the evening of the 3rd to make an emergency visit to the United States, that "in the event that the United States is interested in either Plan A or Plan B, we should consider making some concessions."[116]

The Emperor Seeks Final Assurance

With Kaya and Tōgō having agreed to the "Essentials," that policy became the unanimous decision of the November 1 Liaison Conference. At 5 p.m. Tōjō, standing alongside Sugiyama and Nagano, tearfully gave a full report to the Throne on the Liaison Conference discussion and its conclusion. The emperor remained buried in thought after hearing the report, a sad look on his face; then he made his wishes clear once again:

1. If we are unable to achieve success even though we exhaust all avenues for resolving the situation through negotiations, must we inevitably determine to go to war against the United States and Britain?
2. If the situation is as you describe, perhaps it is unavoidable that we continue preparations for military operations, but in any event I want you to do everything you possibly can to seek a negotiated settlement.[117]

Always of a mind to obey the emperor, instantly and unconditionally, Tōjō told Satō after returning to his office: "Plan B is not a pretext for going to war; I swear to the gods that with this plan I hope to reach an accommodation with the United States whatever it takes."[118] When on November 3 Ishii brought him an explanatory draft for use at the forthcoming informal meeting of the Supreme War Council, Tōjō directed:

> There will be trouble if the "Essentials for Carrying Out the Empire's Policies" is misunderstood. This draft leans toward war. War and diplomacy are fifty-fifty. Go rewrite it.[119]

Here Tōjō boldly put forth a fifty-fifty interpretation different from the one-fourth peace, three-fourths war character of the "Essentials."

On the other hand, the Army General Staff had pressured Tōgō to add unreasonable terms destructive of Plan B to Articles 3 and 4. When questioned by Privy Council President Hara Yoshimichi at the Imperial Conference on the 5th, Tōgō said pessimistically:

> I don't think we will be able to come to an agreement on Plan B either. Take, for example, the matter of withdrawing troops from Indochina. And the United States has not in the past acquiesced on the China Question taken up in Article 4, so I don't think they will give their assent now. Nor do I think the United States will readily assent to item 2 of the notes [on nondiscrimination in trade], for the simple reason that they have been demanding that Japan abide by this. However, I hardly think Japan's grievances are unreasonable. If the United States wishes for peace in the Pacific, and if it realizes that Japan is firmly determined, I think the United States will give more serious thought to our proposals.
>
> Because it comes down to Japan's coercing the United States with military force, it is not impossible that the United States will resist. And we are short of time. . . . Thus there is little expectation of success even if we continue negotiating. Regrettably, there is scant hope that negotiations will succeed. It is difficult to come up with more than a 10 percent chance of success.[120]

In contrast, Tōjō followed Ishii's revised explanation in his reply to the Supreme War Council, which met in the presence of the emperor on the 4th:

> The possibility for success is around 30 percent. . . . Because we think that there is some small chance of achieving our demands, I would like to exert one more effort before we appeal to force as the last resort.[121]

He gave the same answer in responding to a question from Hara at the Imperial Conference on the 5th. And when Kurusu called on him that same evening before setting out for the United States, Tōjō said:

> The United States does not want a war to occur for no good reason. The prospects for success in the negotiations can by no means be judged to be nil. The probability for success should be around 30 percent, for failure around 70 percent.[122]

These statements probably reflect Tōjō's wishful thinking back when he put the odds for war or peace at fifty-fifty. Kurusu too was aware of this, for he explained to Hull at their first meeting on the 17th:

> In his heart of hearts Prime Minister Tōjō hopes for an accord between Japan and the United States and seems to be fastening his hopes on this *to a rather surprising degree*. Among the three issues over which Japan and the United States are deadlocked at present—nondiscrimination in trade, the Tripartite Pact, and the withdrawal of troops—it seems that the prime minister is very hopeful of a solution on the first two. (Author's emphasis) (Nomura dispatch of November 17)[123]

At the Imperial Conference of November 5 Tōjō began by explaining the reasons for proposing the "Essentials for Carrying Out the Empire's Policies." Tōgō then explained the diplomatic issues involved, Suzuki expounded on matters relating to national strength, Kaya spoke on the financial issues, and Sugiyama and Nagano addressed strategic matters. As was customary at Imperial Conferences, Privy Council President Hara posed questions that were answered by those present. The emperor simply listened with an air of dejection. This time the Imperial Conference concluded true to form by adopting the proposed draft without any dissension. Tōgō had confidentially suggested Plan A to Nomura the previous day, explaining that "in effect Plan A comes down to accepting *in toto* the American demands with regard to two of the three pending issues [nondiscrimination in trade and the Tripartite Pact], and we are prepared to make maximum concessions even on the last point, the issue of stationing and withdrawing troops."[124] Then on the 20th he cabled Nomura in regard to Plan B:

> Things having come to such a pass, there is only one conceivable way to resolve matters: with a large view to avoiding the worst contingency by means of a political solution, reach agreement with all possible

dispatch on several absolutely essential items and prevent war from breaking out in the first place.[125]

Nomura was hereby apprised of Tōgō's objective: to allay American misgivings by furnishing proof that Japan would pull back to its position prior to the freezing of assets and that Japan had no intention of advancing any farther south, thereby alleviating a situation verging on crisis. Taking the emperor's wishes to heart, Tōjō had boldly interpreted the "Essentials" just approved by the Imperial Conference as offering equal chances for war or peace, and with that in mind he then had both Plan A and Plan B presented to the United States. The outcome now hinged largely on how they would be received by the United States. First, however, we must briefly explore the blind spots that existed in the reexamination of state policy.

3. Blind Spots in the Reexamination of State Policy: The Navy's Prospects for Victory

The Navy Hopes Against Hope

Needless to say, a war between Japan and the United States would essentially involve a series of engagements in the Pacific for which the navy would be primarily responsible. Within the navy, the Navy Ministry was charged with the task of estimating Japan's matériel strength. From the summer of 1940 on Navy Minister Yoshida Zengo had expressed anxiety about going to war with the United States. His successor, the ever-ambiguous Oikawa Koshirō, managed throughout his tenure to avoid any official statement on the issue. Finally, and in contrast to Oikawa, Navy Minister Shimada Shigetarō had declared at the conclusion of the reexamination of state policy that there was no need for pessimism if an additional 300,000 tons of steel were forthcoming.

The Navy General Staff, on the other hand, was responsible for military operations, and Admiral Nagano, who had been appointed chief of the Navy General Staff in April 1941, had declared at the Liaison Conference of July 21, *prior to* the imposition of a total embargo by the United States:

> There is at this moment a chance to win a war against the United States, but the prospects will diminish as time goes by; by the second half of next year we will hardly be a match for them any longer.

... Please keep in mind that the situation will become progressively disadvantageous with the passage of time.[126]

On September 3 he declared to the Liaison Conference that approved the draft policy to be presented to the Imperial Conference of the 6th:

> As time goes by we will become more and more crippled. When it becomes evident that there are no prospects at all for a diplomatic settlement, we must quickly determine on war. I am convinced that if we strike now we have a chance for victory.[127]

And we saw above (p. 258) that Nagano made the same assertion at the conclusion of the reexamination of state policy. No evidence has been uncovered that Nagano took any pains to explain whether "chances of winning," "prospects for victory," and "triumph" referred chiefly to "first-stage operations," as explained at the September 6 Imperial Conference which we will take up later, or to a Japanese-American war in its entirety, and we can only speculate about this. However, his statement at the Liaison Conference of September 3 would seem to indicate that he was talking primarily about the initial stage of the war: "Even if the war becomes protracted, I believe it will be to our advantage in a protracted war to avail ourselves of the fruits of victory in a blitzkrieg encounter."[128] And on November 1 he told the Liaison Conference:

> The chances are eight or nine out of ten that the war will become protracted. In the event of a protracted war, however, we shall establish during the first and second years the foundations for fighting such a war; during this period there is an assured chance of victory, but after the third year there is no predicting what the outcome will be. This is all I can responsibly answer.[129]

For Nagano, "to say 'I don't know' was the best he could do"[130] about a protracted war lasting more than two years, and in fact "I don't know" is all that he could responsibly undertake to say. In other words, he implied that there was a strong probability of losing and, conversely, little chance of winning.[131] Nagano's operational outlook on overall trends in a war with the United States might therefore be summarized as follows: In the initial stages of the war there would be "prospects of victory," "chances of winning," and "opportunities to strike." If Japan took advantage of the fruits therefrom, it would be

Table 3.2 [132]
JAPAN'S NAVAL STRENGTH
COMPARED TO THAT OF THE UNITED STATES

Ship Type	Japan			United States	
	NUMBER	TONNAGE	RATIO	NUMBER	TONNAGE
Battleships	10	301,400	56%	17	534,300
Aircraft Carriers	10	152,970	94%	8	162,600
Cruisers					
(Heavy)	18	158,800	93%	18	171,200
Cruisers (Light)	20	98,855	62%	19	157,775
Destroyers	112	165,868	69%	172	239,530
Submarines	65	97,900	84%	111	116,621
Total	235	975,793	71%	345	1,382,026

in a better position to cope with a protracted war than if it did not. If the war were prolonged beyond two years, however, it is likely that Japan would lose.

In June 1941 the Navy General Staff commenced studies on operations against the United States, roughly completing them in late August. Their conclusion was that if interceptive operations took place in Japan's home waters "there would be chances of success if we have a naval ratio of at least 50 percent that of the United States," taking into account the effects of the reduction in enemy forces, their exhaustion from trans-Pacific passage, and Japan's geographical advantages. By the end of 1941, moreover, Japan's effective strength overall, including over-age warships, would rise to 70 percent of that of the United States (see table 3.2). This would be more than sufficient to give Japan a fighting chance. However, the situation would be drastically different from 1942 on if both navies completed the construction of ships being built or on the drawing boards up through 1941 (320,000 tons for Japan and 1,900,000 tons for the United States), as shown in table 3.3.

So long as ratios were regarded as the sole criterion for success, military strategies of any promise would quickly become impossible of realization after April 1943. The general picture becomes even more stark when forecasts of annual aircraft production are added to this, as table 3.4 reveals.

To judge from naval ratios, the natural conclusion to be reached was that defeat was very likely and there was little chance for victory, that "there is little hope of success after the first two years; we cannot make plans beyond two years."[133] Despite this, Nagano insisted on saying "I don't know" about the long-term outcome because he was

Table 3.3 [134]

RATIOS OF JAPAN'S WARSHIPS TO U.S. WARSHIPS,
1942–1944

Year	Excluding Over-age Ships	Including Over-age Ships
1942	65%	76%
1943	50%	60%
1944	30%	30%

Table 3.4 [135]

JAPAN'S NAVAL AIRCRAFT COMPARED TO U.S.
AIRCRAFT, 1942–1944

Year	Japan	U.S.
1942	4,000	47,900
1943	8,000	85,000
1944	12,000	over 100,000

gambling on sheer luck in operational matters. In his view the fortunes of war were unpredictable; victory involved one thing and defeat another, therefore defeat was by no means certain; you could not know until you tried, and you might win as many as one bout out of five; unless you had the courage to run risks you would have no chance of success. [136]

The Navy General Staff Counts on "Ratioism" for Success

Had Nagano rested his case on cold facts, allowing nothing for luck, common sense would have led him to the conclusion that Japan had little chance of success in a war with the United States. From the very beginning, however, Nagano declined to make any of the necessary explanations about armaments and operations, and government leaders could not help feeling that they were proceeding with their investigation on the basis of guesswork. [137] After the Liaison Conference adjourned early on November 2, Tōgō threw in the towel, having no choice but to accept Nagano's forecast because he found himself in a position where he could no longer argue with the navy's chief of staff. Yet on the day a conclusion was reached, [138] Tōgō did venture a sound rebuttal:

When war breaks out, the United States will construct submarines in large numbers and actively deploy them on a wide scale. It is appropriate, therefore, to calculate the attrition of Japan's shipping during the second year at a higher tonnage than during the first.[139]

Nagano responded that there was "no need for worry whatsoever." When Kaya asked pointedly on that same day, "If a forecast can be made for the first two years, why not come up with a rough prediction for the third and following years?"[140] Nagano avoided a frank "rough prediction" that there was "no chance of success" by saying evasively, "I don't know." Had Nagano presented the anticipated shifts in naval ratios (see table 3.3) to the Liaison Conference as a consideration in the reexamination of state policy, it is unlikely that his argument in favor of trusting the war's outcome to lady luck would have withstood the common sense arguments made by Tōgō and Kaya. In fact, Nagano's refusal, on the pretext of military secrecy, to allow any substantial appraisal of the chances for victory[141] did meet with sound criticism from those in the navy who knew the real situation. Okada Keisuke, for example, charged: "Nagano says we must go ahead and do it even though we shall lose; this does not stand to reason."[142]

At the London Naval Conference of 1930 the Navy General Staff had firmly insisted on three principles: 1) an overall 70 percent ratio in auxiliary ships vis-à-vis the United States; 2) a 70 percent ratio in heavy cruisers; and 3) retention of existing submarine strength (78,000 tons). The resulting treaty was violently opposed by the Navy General Staff, which in 1936 abrogated in one stroke the London Treaty as well as the Washington Naval Treaty of 1922 (stipulating a 60 percent capital ship ratio with the United States). Overly preoccupied with conferences on naval limitations ever since the Washington Conference, the Navy General Staff seemed to ignore all considerations except the issue of naval ratios, the focal question around which discussions of naval treaties revolved. The view came to prevail within the Navy General Staff that theoretically there would be virtually no problem in going to war with the United States so long as Japan maintained a 70 percent ratio vis-à-vis the United States in capital ships, heavy cruisers, and total auxiliary vessels, and a submarine strength of 80,000 tons. In the autumn of 1941, excluding over-age warships, these conditions had all been met, and the Navy General Staff counted on "ratioism" for success in the initial stages of the war.

Whether treaties of naval limitation existed or not, however, once a state of belligerency came into being, any ratio restrictions on naval construction would surely cease to exist. Inevitably, the United States, vastly superior to Japan in national strength, would promptly set about building an overwhelmingly powerful navy, and in the judgement of Inoue Shigeyoshi, "only the superior navy would benefit from the formidable law of n². "¹⁴³ To estimate chances of success on the basis of ratioism was nothing more than to indulge in a daydream which was bound to be shattered from the moment hostilities commenced. In short, the debate over Japan's relative military strength vis-à-vis the United States at the outset of hostilities was of such a nature that it could not be a factor of any decisive bearing on the overall outcome of a war between Japan and the United States no matter what the ratios. Even though the ratios existing at the outbreak of war could not in themselves assure victory at sea against a major power, the Navy General Staff had been consistently so ridden by "ratio neurosis" (Inoue Shigeyoshi) ever since the Washington Conference that it sought in the existing ratios chances for victory in the initial stages of the war.¹⁴⁴ And the Navy General Staff seems to have taken the liberty of adding lady luck into the equation as well.¹⁴⁵

Consider, for example, the process of revising the "Outline of Strategy and Plan of Operations" to accord with the third National Defense Policy of 1936. The Navy General Staff officers involved at that time—Vice Chief Shimada, Operations Division Chief Kondō, and Operations Section Chief Fukudome—planned exclusively for decisive battles at the outset of operations against the United States; they made no specific investigations into a war of endurance that might ensue. Embracing the illusion that national defense could be assured by initial operations, they tended to ignore the fact that the essence of a war with the United States lay in subsequent operations.¹⁴⁶ And by "initial operations" they simply assumed that once hostilities began the United States fleet would sally forth immediately for a sudden and decisive one-sided sumo bout. War games against the United States were conducted exclusively on this assumption, and when the commander of the Red (United States) Fleet refused to allow his forces to sally forth, the war games referee would be called on to compel him to attack so that things would turn out according to plan. Prudent admirals, however, could not fail to see that the trump card of interceptive operations had been played for thirty years but the outcome had always been rigged, that however often war games were repeated, the Blue (Japanese) forces stood no chance of winning.¹⁴⁷ In his "Memorandum on Armaments" drafted on January 7, 1941, for example, Admiral Yamamoto made explicit the views he had expressed to Oikawa in November 1940. The memorandum reads in part:

> Up to now studies regarding operational policies have focused on fair and square interceptive operations. As I read the results of repeated war games, the Imperial Navy has not once achieved a great victory. It has been the usual practice to stop a war game whenever there was concern that it might lead to "gradual pauperization" if it were continued.[148]

Here was another argument vindicating Yamamoto's policy of avoiding war with the United States. For admirals not obsessed with the illusion of "ratioism," Japan ultimately had no chance of victory despite all the effort that had gone into operational plans, war games, and naval maneuvers over the almost forty years since the Battle of the Japan Sea. The question thus boiled down to one point: would naval leaders face this historical conclusion head on and accept it? Yonai and Yamamoto did; Nagano would not.

Nagano's Operational Plans

The closest Nagano came to revealing the full particulars of the operational plans he entertained was in his explanation at the Imperial Conference of September 6:

> As to our forecast of how naval operations are likely to go, we recognize that the probability is very high that the United States will from the outset plan on a protracted war. Therefore, it is necessary for the Empire to brace itself for a long war. If they were to plan on a blitzkrieg encounter and send out their main naval forces, challenging us to a quick war, this would be just what we hope for. Today, with the war in Europe still in progress, the naval forces that Britain is capable of sending to the Far East will be considerably limited. Accordingly, in the event we were to intercept even the combined British-American navy in the area of the ocean we anticipate, and bearing in mind other factors such as the use of aircraft, we are convinced that our chances of victory are high. However, *even if the Empire should win a victory in this decisive battle, we will not thereby be able to bring the war to a conclusion.* It is anticipated that thereafter the United States will attempt to turn the war into a protracted conflict, utilizing its impregnable position and its superiority in industrial power and natural resources.
> The Empire *does not have the means to break the enemy by offensive operations and make them give up their will to fight.* Moreover, *because we are*

short of resources at home, we strongly desire to avoid a protracted war. However, if we become involved in a protracted war, the first and foremost means for assuring that we would be able to bear this burden will be to occupy the enemy's important strategic points and resource areas quickly at the beginning of the war, solidifying our operational position and at the same time obtaining essential commodities from areas now under the enemy's sway. *If this first stage of our operations is carried out properly,* the Empire will have secured strategic points in the southwest Pacific and be able to establish an impregnable position, *laying the basis for protracted operations,* even if the United States should proceed with its military preparations as scheduled. What follows will depend to a large extent on overall national strength—including various elements, tangible and intangible—and on developments in the world situation.

Thus the outcome of a protracted war *will depend to a large extent on the success or failure of first-stage operations.* . . . (Author's emphasis)[149]

Before leaving for the Imperial Conference Nagano had told Fukudome, "Today I am going to state exactly what I believe and speak solely on my own individual responsibility, so I intend to proceed to the palace without listening to anything you and the others have to say." And after the conference was over, he turned to Fukudome and declared, "I stuck to my opinion from first to the last."[150] That was also the extent of Nagano's understanding of the responsibility he bore for his explanation at the Imperial Conference. In his plan for conducting a protracted war, Japan's national power and military strength would be enhanced rather than reduced if Japan were first to establish an impregnable position in the natural resource areas to the south and then, protected by this impregnable position, continue to obtain needed resources from those areas. It was also his view that "the United States will attempt to turn the war into a protracted conflict," that Japan "does not have the means to break the enemy by offensive operations and make them give up their will to fight," and further that Japan is "short of resources at home." Therefore, such a "plan" for a protracted war, regardless of who conceived it, was in fact the only rational plan left to Japan for guidance in a war with the United States. The foremost strategic requisites for the concrete success of such a plan were: 1) the establishment of an impregnable position in the natural resource areas to the south, and 2) a guarantee that resources from the southern areas would be delivered to Japan by sea. However, the actual strategies that Nagano chose were largely irrelevant to these requisites.

Time Runs Out for Establishing an Impregnable Position

In itself, occupying natural resource areas to the south would be a relatively easy task, for it would involve taking on colonial troops and the weak naval forces of the United States, Britain, and Holland. The real problem would come after these areas had been occupied, when Japan would have to establish strategic positions completely invulnerable to American counterattacks by sea and air—in other words, the problem was to make these areas into impregnable fortresses within a sphere of absolute security. Inoue Shigeyoshi, who a month before had been appointed commander of the Fourth Fleet (charged with defending the mandated islands in the South Seas), discovered when he took up his command that not even minimum fortifications had been built on the islands.[151] This situation remained virtually unchanged right up to the outbreak of war in December. Early in 1942 the Navy General Staff was forced to admit:

> When we entered the war, land and sea facilities—above all in [the mandated islands of] the South Seas (facilities for aircraft, defenses, and communication; fuel storage areas; submarine bases; harbors)—still remained incomplete. . . . Inadequate elements in the annual plan for preparations to dispatch forces are: . . . b) lack of awareness of the importance of land bases for aircraft; c) lack of awareness of the importance of anti-aircraft defense forces; . . . g) inadequate judgment regarding the form naval operations would take.[152]

Air power, along with supporting facilities, was to be the mainstay for maintaining an impregnable position, and the fourth supplementary program, currently being carried out, was a radical program designed to more than double, in the five short years from 1939 to 1943, the air power created since the advent of naval air forces twenty years before. In August 1941 it had been decided to move up the completion date by one year, to the end of 1942, and this program was now being pursued in earnest.

The Operations Section of the Navy General Staff now began to argue that in order to establish an impregnable position Japan would have to shoot down every American plane raiding Japanese bases in the south. It would not be enough simply to maintain the requisite land-based air forces. What was needed was air power that would be equal to a protracted war of attrition against the air forces of the United States. By July 1940 the conclusion was therefore reached

Table 3.5

JAPAN'S CUMULATIVE AIR POWER, PLANNED AND ACTUAL
1939–1941*

	Land-Based Planes	Carrier-Based Planes	Total
Air power in being (programs 1–3)	827	1090	1917
Air power planned in program 4	1478	174	1652
Cumulative air power anticipated upon completion of program 4	2305	1264	3569
Actual air power (as of the end of Dec. 1941)	908**	1354	2262

*Compiled from JDA Archives.
**Standard aircraft only; fighter planes as of the end of December 1941 are included in the figure for carrier-based planes.

that the fourth supplementary program would have to be expanded more than four-fold. In the spring of 1941 a general agreement was reached between the Navy Ministry and General Staff that as soon as there was any prospect of obtaining the necessary budget and matériel, this program, albeit somewhat trimmed down, should be undertaken in installments as the fifth supplementary program. Given the nation's resources, however, implementation of this fifth program proved exceedingly difficult, and all that could be completed of the program before the outbreak of the war was a mere 17 air training units. In fact, as table 3.5 indicates, Japan plunged into war with the *fourth* program uncompleted.

Not surprisingly, staff officers in charge of naval aviation in the Operations Section came crying to Fukudome in early September, complaining that war with the United States was impossible, that there was no hope for ultimate victory in air operations against the United States when the fourth program had not even been completed, to say nothing of starting on the fifth.[153] On September 29 Yamamoto sent Nagano the following prophetic warning:

> As I have been telling you for some time, my own conviction is that we need a thousand combat planes, and a thousand land-based attack planes. Right now, the Combined Fleet has only 300 combat planes. Two hundred planes will be required for defense of the home islands,

and around 200 additional planes on standby will also be needed The prospect is that during operations in the south 650 planes will be lost. In addition, considerable damage will be incurred in noncombat situations. If we do not take sufficient compensatory action, it will be difficult to continue [the war after operations in the south are over].[154]

This means that when Nagano gave his explanation to the liaison conferences in September, the conditions for establishing an impregnable position in the natural resource areas of the south were nowhere in sight.

Convoy Operations Are Neglected

Guaranteeing delivery of commodities from the south meant convoy operations to protect vessels engaged in the transportation of goods between the South Seas and Japan. Navy Minister Yoshida had worried about this problem back in the summer of 1940, and on July 29, 1941, the Cabinet Planning Board presented the government and the high command with a memorandum, "Matériel Mobilization Requirements for the Empire's Prosecution of War," in which it was sternly pointed out:

If by any chance we were to wage an armed conflict in the South Seas under present conditions, the result would be that our shipping losses may well exceed our building capacity if we do not at once secure complete command of the sea and air in at least the southwest Pacific. . . . Should we not do so, our nation's overall productivity will decline further and further. Unless all conceivable measures are decisively taken in advance to meet this situation, there will be extremely serious repercussions.[155]

If transport vessels were sunk in transit, not only would goods from the south not reach Japan but also, if the tonnage of vessels sunk surpassed that of ships being built, eventually Japan would have no ships to transport goods from the south. Anyone with sound common sense was bound to cross-examine the Navy General Staff about this; and it was only natural that Hara Yoshimichi sought guarantees on this matter at the two Imperial Conferences of September 6 and November 5. On both occasions, Nagano replied with complete composure:

For every 10 vessels (4 in the Atlantic and 6 in the Pacific) the United States has, Japan has 7.5. Surface vessels in the Far East can be easily destroyed. If underwater vessels [submarines] should escape, we shall bring them under control. Merchant ship losses have been fully studied by the army, navy, and the Cabinet Planning Board, and the outlook is good. (September 6) [156]

... we shall exhaust every means available to protect our sea lanes, because they involve Japan's very existence. I think losses will be considerable each year, but assuming that we can protect and augment our sea lanes, I do not think casualties will interfere with Japan's shipping. (November 5) [157]

As we have already seen, Foreign Minister Tōgō made perfect sense when he pointed out that the United States would engage in extensive submarine construction that would lead to higher shipping losses during the war's second year, and Nagano, taking refuge in military secrecy, refused to respond.[158] Then, on November 4, the emperor had asked whether it would "be possible to obtain and transport oil without hindrance when faced with attacks by planes and submarines based in Australia" and what measures would be taken to deal with the problem.[159] Even this query failed to make Nagano reconsider his position.

In late November Admiral Kobayashi Seizō pointed out in his memorandum to Navy Minister Shimada:

It is three thousand miles to the southern regions. Enemy submarines and planes will constantly obstruct our transport over such long distances. Will our navy have the capacity to protect these sea lanes while engaging the enemy in battle? From what I know, our naval forces are bound to be unprepared in this regard.[160]

It cannot be denied that convoy operations were in fact made secondary to fleet organization, countermeasures, structures, training. Convoy strength at the outbreak of the war was limited to four coast guard ships and 25 submarine chasers. During the first year of the war not a single coast guard ship or plane for convoying purposes was added. Not until the latter half of the second year were 14 coast guard ships of the *Etorofu* class and 8 of the *Mikura* class built; the completion of 18 T-type destroyers had to wait until the third year of the war.

In terms of structure, no strong central organization existed to control convoy operations; rather, a weak system prevailed under which each naval station and each fleet planned and implemented convoys on its own. Even with regard to drill and implementation, direct convoy was limited to important fleets, and the situation overall

TABLE 3.6
ANTICIPATED VS. ACTUAL LOSSES

Year of War	Anticipated Losses (Tons)	Actual Losses (Tons)
1	800,000	1,250,000
2	600,000	2,560,000
3	700,000	3,480,000
4	——	1,500,000

was jury-rigged by setting up designated sea routes and ports of refuge. These measures were behind the times and a far cry from what the British navy had implemented even during World War I, not to speak of the patrolling and transport convoying then being carried out in the Atlantic against German submarines by the British and American navies.

On August 19 the Navy General Staff expressed its "confidence" to the Army General Staff:

Where South Seas operations are concerned, it would seem that shipping can be largely guaranteed. We may safely anticipate losses at around 10 percent and annual ship construction at 500,000 tons.[161]

Calculated on the basis of actual losses in World War I, the Navy General Staff presented to the Liaison Conference anticipated shipping losses for which it would take official responsibility, but as the comparison in table 3.6 reveals, actual losses were far greater:[162]

As it turned out, losses during the first several months of the war were slight and below estimate because American submarines suffered from an extreme shortage of torpedoes and those they had were seriously defective. The Japanese navy should at least have taken lessons from the wartime experience of the Royal Navy in the First World War and made needed military preparations based on operational plans for protecting maritime traffic during this interim, instead of making much of temporary imperfections on the part of the U. S. Navy and being optimistic about the future of Japan's maritime transport. But the fact of the matter was that because plans and preparations remained wedded to Nagano-style rhetoric, this precious period during which losses were fewer than anticipated was squandered by inaction. When the American navy rallied, the Japanese navy's estimates quickly turned into daydreams, and shipping for civilian requirements began a downward trajectory to zero. As with everything else, Nagano's explanation in regard to guaranteed delivery of resources from the south by sea proved to be empty rhetoric.

Inoue's Plan for New Armaments Is Turned Down

What would a concrete strategy to achieve Nagano's idea of securing an impregnable position in the south look like? Let us give careful attention to the "Plans for New Armaments" submitted to Navy Minister Oikawa by Inoue in his official capacity as chief of the Naval Aviation Bureau in June 1941, the main points of which are as follows:

1. In this day of highly developed aircraft, there will be no such things as decisive battles between main fleets in the wars that occur from now on.
2. There is no need to build capital ships and the like, which cost vast sums of money. However numerous the enemy's capital ships, they can all be sunk if we have sufficient air power.
3. Air bases on land are absolutely unsinkable aircraft carriers. The aircraft carrier is convenient to use because of its mobility, but it is extremely vulnerable. Therefore, the mainstay of naval air power must be land-based air power.
4. *In a war with the United States, land bases will be the mainstay of our military capacity for national defense,* and islands scattered in the Pacific are extremely important god-given treasures.
5. I declare categorically that a war with the United States will of necessity revolve around military struggles for these bases. In other words, primary operations will consist of landing operations and defensive campaigns against them.
6. Therefore, it is important above all to maintain the military capability of these bases, and for this reason *their fortification* must be speedily carried out *before anything else.*
7. Accordingly, air power must be consolidated on *the principle that land-based air power comes first;* battleships, cruisers, and the like can be sacrificed to this end.
8. Next, for Japan to survive and keep on fighting, it is *extremely important to make maritime traffic secure;* therefore, it is *necessary that the full military strength [convoy capability] needed for this be made second in priority.*
9. Because submarines can be used to defend bases, to protect sea-going commerce, as well as to attack, their perfection must be considered third in priority. (Author's emphasis)[163]

Inoue's memorandum broke free from "ratioism" and keeping up with American naval power in terms of naval ratios. Inoue went back to the drawing boards and rationally examined what a war with the United States in the Pacific would look like, how to win in such a conflict, and what was needed to do so. His memorandum was so profoundly insightful that it all but predicted how the war would turn out. Yet Nagano did nothing to rebut Inoue's memorandum, nor did he adopt any of its recommendations. On the contrary, according to Enomoto Shigeharu, Inoue was "treated as a nuisance" by Nagano and Navy Minister Oikawa, who colluded to have him shipped out as commander-in-chief of the Fourth Fleet in August.

Nagano had consistently avoided any forecast of what would happen after two years of warfare by saying "I don't know." But insofar as he was obsessed with "ratioism," he must have calculated that Japan stood no chance of victory from the third year on, and it may be inferred from the fact that he had tacked on the qualifying phrase "even if the United States should proceed with military preparations as scheduled" that he sought a way out of this predicament in a rational plan for staging a protracted war. However, this plan he took such pains over was itself nothing but a castle built of sand, given that strategically there was virtually no concrete basis for establishing an impregnable position in the resource areas of the south or for guaranteeing delivery by sea of resources from the south. His explanation at the September 6 Imperial Conference had come close to being a grand exercise in rhetoric. In any case, it would seem that Nagano kept on clamoring for war principally because he banked first on the British-German war situation and second on lady luck, trusting in the fortunes of war promised by Yamamoto's military tactics.

Taking Advantage of the British-German War at Sea

The Liaison Conference of November 13 took up a "Draft Proposal for Hastening the End of the War against the United States, Britain, Holland, and Chiang." Following the rhetoric of laying the basis for a long-term war, the proposal declared: "The Empire will engage in a quick war . . . and will secure those areas producing vital materials as well as the main lines of communication, thereby completing arrangements for long-term self-sufficiency." It then went on to add new items not contained in Nagano's earlier explanation at the Imperial Conference:

At the appropriate time, we shall use every means available to lure in the main fleet of the United States and annihilate it.

Cooperating together, Japan, Germany, and Italy will first contrive to have Britain surrender.

We shall endeavor to have Germany and Italy adopt the following policies:

a) To carry out military operations in the Near East, North Africa, and the Suez, and at the same time take steps against India.

b) To strengthen the blockade of Britain.

c) To carry out the invasion of the British Isles when conditions permit.[164]

At the meeting of the Supreme War Council held on November 4 in the presence of the emperor, Nagano had replied:

... we consider Britain to be the vulnerable point of the allied British-American forces. In other words, if sea communications are cut off, Britain will weaken and find it difficult to continue the war. The most expedient way is to starve Britain into surrendering. If prior to this the German invasion of the British Isles succeeds, it will be all the more advantageous. What we must focus on is forcing Britain to the point of unavoidable submission and putting pressure on Britain and the United States, whose destinies are intertwined.[165]

When Yokoi Tadao, naval attaché in Germany, had reported on the general situation in April and May of 1941, however, he had appended a note clearly stating that German forces were in no position to invade the British Isles.[166] Moreover, Foreign Minister Tōgō had stated with regard to the conclusion reached by the reexamination of state policy:

Under existing circumstances, it is difficult to foresee a German invasion of the British Isles. ... It is questionable whether or not Britain can be brought to its knees through a blockade of the British Isles. ... There are a number of doubts about our future in a protracted war.[167]

Nonetheless, the vice chief of the Navy General Staff, Itō Seiichi, went ahead and directed Yokoi to make explicit in the original Japanese draft of the Japanese-German military pact that Germany would invade the British Isles even if the pact were under negotiation at the outbreak of war with the United States. To make sure that Yokoi did this Itō telephoned him in Germany: "You can change the language somewhat, but don't you dare delete the invasion of the British

Isles."[168] That is the extent to which Nagano and Itō depended on Germany's attacking Britain, or rather counted on a turnaround in the war situation that Japan could take advantage of.

In reality, however, the situation in Europe since the spring of 1941 had by no means been as favorable to Germany as Nagano hoped it would be. Not only had the planned invasion been abandoned in September 1940, but the effectiveness of the German war on commerce in the Atlantic had declined sharply from July 1941, as the monthly totals of American, British, and neutral tonnage sunk from April to December reveal:[169]

April	May	June	July	August
260,000	350,000	310,000	60,000	70,000

September	October	November	December
210,000	180,000	90,000	70,000

Chiefly because of shortages of warships for escort duty since 1940, Britain had been unable to adopt a system of continuous convoying in the Atlantic. In May 1941, with the aid of the Canadian navy, Britain was able to establish an advance base at Saint John's, Newfoundland, and new convoy forces were organized for deployment from this base. On May 22 Erich Raeder, commander-in-chief of the German navy, was compelled to report to Hitler:

> The enemy has adopted a very flexible convoy system, combined with a far-reaching and excellent direction finding network. The reports are evaluated very rapidly for the purpose of convoy control. Enemy defence of convoys has been strengthened; a close watch of the area west of Britain is being kept by air reconnaissance, anti-submarine groups, surface forces, and single ships.[170]

In July continuous convoying in the north Atlantic was provided not only for fleets bound for the British Isles but also for those sailing from them. At the same time, aerial escort by long-range aircraft with antisubmarine weapons continued to make progress. The danger to German submarines from the air had increased so markedly that they chose to operate in an 800 nautical mile gap between Iceland and Newfoundland where airplanes from neither could reach them.

The first large-scale convoy sea battle between Britain and Germany took place from June 23 to 27, when 10 German submarines launched an attack on British Convoy HX 133 south of Greenland

and were counterattacked by 13 British escort warships, with support from two convoys bound for the United States. The battle ended roughly in a draw, with the British losing three merchant vessels and the Germans two submarines. That battle marked the turning point in the war on commerce in the Atlantic.

The Atlantic Conference between Roosevelt and Churchill in August had the important consequence of de facto participation in the war by the United States navy. Roosevelt ordered the navy to shoot German submarines on sight in a zone extending all the way to Iceland. On the 11th he declared that American naval protection of the Atlantic sea lanes would extend to eastern Iceland and that the United States would defend by force of arms half the distance covered by convoys bound for Britain. On the 16th Convoy HX 150 departed under escort by the United States navy, which convoyed it to a rendezvous point south of Iceland in the heart of the Atlantic at 22° west longitude. At the same time, United States long-range army and navy aircraft began aerial escorts, one group operating from Newfoundland in cooperation with the Canadian air force, another operating from Iceland in cooperation with the British coastal air force. These measures drastically reduced the 800-mile gap in which German submarines had been operating, and in October Britain's shipping losses began to decline, a trend that became more marked and sustained after November. It appeared that Britain had at last been able to bring the destruction of its commerce by the German navy under control to a very large extent.[171]

Nagano, however, did not draw a single lesson for Japan's southern resource problem from the British navy's accomplishments in convoying since World War I. On the contrary, in November 1941 he still pursued the fantasy, far removed from reality, that Japan could take advantage of German success: "If sea communications are cut off, Britain will weaken and find it difficult to continue the war."[172]

Actual developments in the war in the Atlantic were of course top secret matters between the belligerents at the time, and Tokyo could hardly have been fully apprised of them. As always, only one-sided and optimistic propaganda was broadcast to Japan from Germany. Even though Japan stood at the crossroad between war and peace, however, Nagano did nothing to rectify the navy's traditional neglect of its Intelligence Division; much less did he strengthen it in terms of personnel, equipment, and overseas postings. Leaving this deficiency unremedied and setting aside a thorough investigation into the European war from a comprehensive naval point of view, Nagano was never able to come up with viable strategic recommendations on Japan's behalf.

Nagano Advocates War Without a Strategy

In May 1941 Admiral Yamamoto had proposed an attack on Pearl Harbor. On September 12 he completed war games on the attack and the following day held a briefing. On October 19 he renewed his proposal to Navy Vice Chief Itō, and on the 20th Nagano decided to adopt it. From the outset Yamamoto's plan for a series of decisive encounters, starting with an attack on Pearl Harbor, was not necessarily incompatible with Nagano's plan for laying the basis for a protracted war by achieving an impregnable position in and ensuring sea-borne transport of resources from the South Seas. On November 30, 1940, Yamamoto himself had told the then chief of the Navy General Staff, Prince Fushimi, "If a war breaks out with the United States, the navy will have to put all its strength into interceptive operations, so . . . massive sea-borne supplies might be *momentarily* interrupted" (author's emphasis).[173] In other words, following an attack on Pearl Harbor at the outset of the war, the way would still be definitely open for the chief of the Navy General Staff to engage in decisive battles within the strategy of preparing for a long-term war. Heeding the experience of the British navy since World War I, he could put the entire strength of the navy into two structures: into the Combined Fleet and into convoy squadrons directly controlled by the Navy General Staff. But Nagano did not do this, and here one perceives the impracticality—the breakdown of rhetoric, so to speak—in Nagano's plan for a long-term war: even after the attack on Pearl Harbor he continued to commit the navy's entire strength and its deployment to the Combined Fleet, turning to Yamamoto as the only hope in all-out decisive naval battles. In fact, when prior to the outbreak of the war he had been confronted with Yamamoto's commitment to a positive offensive strategy, Nagano simply shelved the task of reconciling it with his own plan for a protracted war and, resorting to a characteristic political solution, took up Yamamoto's plan wholeheartedly: "If Yamamoto has so much confidence, I'll let him have a go at it."[174]

Thus Nagano's strategy shifted from victory based on "ratioism" to the rhetoric of preparing the basis for a protracted war, and then to acceptance of Yamamoto's plan. And those present at the Liaison Conference of November 1 were given pause about Nagano's sense of responsibility when he came up with a statement that made him appear to be merely a bystander:

> Starting from the "Outline of Measures toward French Indochina and Thailand" in January this year we have now moved ahead to the point of going to war [with the United States]. Today this is all but irreversible. We have come to the end of our rope.[175]

Prior to this, on October 7, Navy Vice Minister Sawamoto Yorio had been concerned about Nagano's attitude, and he and Oikawa had called on the elders of the navy about it. Admiral Okada Keisuke responded that "with determination domestic problems can be easily handled; at this time we have to be most cautious about getting into a war." Admiral Yonai Mitsumasa agreed:

> Is there no way to avoid succumbing to the enemy if the United States does not come to the attack and [as a result] the war turns into one of endurance? We must not decide on everything out of fear of "gradual pauperization." Various other circumstances must be taken into account. . . . There are also a number of issues that time will probably resolve. We must be extremely wary about getting into a war too hastily. . . . We must make every effort to avoid risking a war at this time.

When Admirals Kobayashi Seizō and Sakonji Seizō (the former vice navy minister) visited Nagano around October 16 under personal instructions from Okada and Yonai, Nagano responded in "abusive language":

> That Okada is the source of false rumors. The man is misrepresenting public opinion. We have gathered accurate information from all quarters and are making decisions for the future on the basis of such information. A person who bandies about such irresponsible talk is a real pain.[176]

Yamamoto's Forecast

On September 29 Yamamoto requested a conference with Nagano. He stated bluntly, not as the commander-in-chief of the Combined Fleet but "as an admiral and as an objective observer," that:

> It is obvious that a war between Japan and the United States will become protracted. So long as the war continues to Japan's advantage,

the United States will not give up the fight. As a result, our resources will be depleted over the course of several years of fighting and we shall face enormous difficulties in replacing damaged fleets and ordnance. In the end, we shall not be able to stand up to them. The commanders of the First, Second, Third, and Fourth Fleets are virtually unanimous on this.[177]

But a Nagano who advocated war without a strategy would have none of this. By a strange turn of fate Yamamoto now found himself having to take charge of a war against the United States, knowing that "in the end we shall not be able stand up to them." On October 11 he revealed his inner anguish to his old friend Hori Teikichi, former chief of the Naval Affairs Bureau:

I must admit that we have now gotten into a worst-case scenario. My present position is indeed a strange one; my only recourse is to come to a firm resolution precisely and diametrically contrary to my own personal view and push on in that contrary direction.[178]

On the 14th he wrote to Shimada Shigetarō:

After more than four exhausting years of operations in China, we are now considering simultaneous operations against the United States, Britain, and China, and then operations against Russia as well. It is the height of folly to try and hold out in a war of endurance demanding self-reliance and self-defense for over ten years and covering an area several times larger than German operations in Europe. If we have the audacity to do this—nay, if we are compelled by the drift of events to do so—we the fleet commanders see absolutely no prospect of victory through ordinary naval operations. The upshot is that we have got ourselves into a pretty fix which will require that we combine the strategies employed in the battles of Okehazama, Hiyodorigoe, and Kawanakajima.[179]

On his last visit to Tokyo on December 1, Yamamoto categorically stated to Shimada and Nagano that he "was determined to proceed with offensive operations; there is no chance of victory with such deployments as those termed 'fleet in being [preserving the fleet].' "[180] The Pearl Harbor attack was a concrete implementation of this strategy, which aimed at seeing what decisive encounters would accomplish in the initial stages of the war given the difficulty of bringing off the plan for early interceptive operations because of the unlikelihood that the United States fleet would mount an early attack. In other words, this was a positive strategy to deal with the changes in Japanese-U.S. naval ratios, discussed above, to which the decisive early battle strategy would lead and to postpone a worsening of those ratios. Once war broke out with the United States, Yamamoto firmly believed that decisive fleet encounters had to be induced during the first year of the war no matter what. First, a crippling blow had to be dealt the American fleet at Pearl Harbor; then it had to be crushed. Operations would have to be undertaken with particular care to prevent a great gap from developing in Japan's naval ratio with the United States. Just before setting out for the Battle of Midway he revealed his inner thoughts to members of the Navy General Staff: "Ultimately, there is no choice but to force a decisive fleet encounter. If we set out from here to do that and we both go to the bottom of the Pacific in a double suicide, things will be calm and peaceful on the high seas for some time." [181]

However, when Yamamoto insisted on attacking Pearl Harbor, he met with "considerable opposition from both the Tokyo authorities and the operating units (excluding the aviators). By objecting that even if successful it would be no more than a side operation and not amount to much, and should it fail it would be disastrous, they made me very upset at the time." Yamamoto retorted that, "although there are various uncertainties and difficulties in this operation, a war against Britain and the United States in and of itself poses the fundamental difficulty." [182] As a matter of fact, even if the Pearl Harbor attack did succeed, "the fundamental difficulty" of conducting operations against the United States would indeed be hard for Yamamoto to overcome. In the fall of 1940 Yamamoto had bluntly told Konoe that "if I am told 'go at it,' you will see me run wild for half a year, maybe a year. But I have no confidence whatsoever when it comes to two years, three years." [183] After the war broke out he acknowledged: "Whatever happens, I would like to carry through on first stage operations until the enemy recovers, to work our way up to the point of readiness for protracted war *if only in appearance*" (author's emphasis). [184] There would be no change in Yamamoto's outlook: he would run wild for a year, and readiness for a protracted war would be "only in appearance." He had been compelled against his judgment to fight a war that he was convinced Japan had no chance of winning, and as he predicted, he and all of Japan's naval forces would fight the good fight—and perish.

4. Blind Spots in the Reexamination of State Policy: War Guidance Policy

Suzuki Advocates War

The production of synthetic oil constituted the focal point of the program to expand productivity that had been started in 1938 with a view to making Japan economically independent of the United States and Britain. Since the outset of the Sino-Japanese War, the demand for steel products necessary to equip plant facilities for that purpose competed with the urgent need for munitions. High-pressure reaction cylinders, which were the main components of plant machinery, and various tubing, which constituted the ordinary components of that machinery, became equally difficult to obtain. Thus, synthetic oil production met with stumbling blocks virtually from the moment it was undertaken. In addition, vast new supplies of coal were needed as raw material, and the coal had to be of specified quality, which meant that supplies were extremely difficult to guarantee. Given the Sino-Japanese War and the southern advance policy, requirements regarding location, shipment, and labor would also be hard to meet.

At the same time, friction arose between the army and the navy over technological problems: the army regarded them as insoluble domestically and insisted on importing technology from Germany, whereas the navy insisted to the end on finding technical solutions on its own. When no political solution could be reached between them, the project met with further delay. In June 1940 the navy had concluded that it had come a step closer to the successful production of synthetic oil at Mitsui's Ōmuta mines, and it stopped purchasing high-pressure reaction cylinders from Germany. A year later Japan finally arranged to take advantage of the Japanese-German trade agreement of 1941 by importing everything from Germany—technology, licenses, complete mobile units, large numbers of high-pressure reaction cylinders, high-powered presses, and other necessary steel products. But this turned to naught when war broke out between Germany and the Soviet Union. By the time Japan began its reexamination of state policy in late October 1941, the situation was as follows:

1) It could hardly be said that the technology involved had been fully worked out, and numerous uncertainties still lay ahead.

2) In addition, the acquisition of components for high-pressure reaction cylinders, of presses, steel products, coal, shipping facilities, and labor competed frontally with urgently needed munitions. To

Table 3.7[185]
SYNTHETIC OIL PRODUCTION, PLANNED AND ACTUAL
(THOUSANDS OF TONS)

	Ordinary Gasoline		Crude Oil	
	1940	1941	1940	1941
Plant Capacity				
Planned	133.55	168.5	937	984
Actual	40.4	49.3	984	984
Production				
Goal	76	290	886	850
Planned	87	16.6	683.7	205
Actual	7.8	10.8	336	238

move ahead with a dramatic increase in synthetic oil production, armaments would have to be sacrificed, particularly the completion of naval armaments.

3) Finally, it was impossible to meet the demand for quality petroleum, especially aviation gasoline, with synthetic oil.[186]

As Table 3.7 shows, the actual results of synthetic oil production for 1940 and 1941 were far below what was planned. At the Liaison Conference on October 28, Rear Admiral Hoshina Zenshirō, chief of the Naval Armaments Bureau, evaluated this situation and expressed his strong opposition to a plan to produce 4 million tons of synthetic oil per year: "If we do this, as much as half of the navy's armament program will be postponed. . . . And there is another side to it: the oil problem cannot be solved merely by producing synthetic oil."[187] The fundamental question the navy faced at the time was how to overcome the conflicting claims for munitions. Insofar as the focus of the current matériel mobilization plan was not switched from munitions to synthetic oil production—in other words, insofar as there were no plans to reduce munitions as well as ease international tensions—synthetic oil production was bound to suffer the same fate it had suffered during the third Konoe cabinet. In the summer of 1941 that cabinet's decision to produce synthetic oil had come into immediate contradiction with its decision to give priority to munitions in that year's matériel mobilization plan, and without the natural resources to back it up, the cabinet's decision on synthetic oil wound up as mere rhetoric.

And that is indeed what happened during the reexamination of state policy in the fall of 1941. The fact was that a successful plan to produce synthetic oil would be next to impossible unless tensions between Japan and the United States were eased completely and a policy of absolutely no war adopted. Such a policy, however, was not possible for the Tōjō cabinet because it was confined by a Kido-style "wipe the slate clean" policy even on synthetic oil production; and because it confronted the problem hesitantly and tentatively, fearing the "gradual pauperization" that lay ahead, it was loath to commit all the resources needed to produce synthetic oil. It is therefore not surprising that Suzuki Teiichi, head of the Cabinet Planning Board, made the following explanation at the Imperial Conference on November 5:

> Should we seek to increase our synthetic oil capacity by 5.2 million kiloliters, we will require 2.25 million tons of steel, 1,000 tons of cobalt, 30 million tons of coal, the expenditure of 3.8 billion yen, 380,000 coal miners, and a minimum construction period of six months for low-temperature carbonization plants and about two years for synthetic hydrogenolysis plants. Therefore, we will need more than three years to complete all plants.
>
> If we examine closely the foregoing conditions, as well as the domestic engineering skills necessary for their completion—particularly the ability to manufacture high-pressure reaction cylinders, tubes, and the like—we must conclude that it is well-nigh impossible to achieve self-sufficiency in liquid fuels in a short period of time by depending on synthetic oil alone. It is estimated that even if we take drastic measures, at least seven years will be required.
>
> Consequently, if we go forward with our national policy of depending solely on synthetic oil, it will sooner or later cause very serious defects in our national defense. This is extremely dangerous, given a world torn by wars and a situation in which we are moving forward with the prosecution of the China Incident.[188]

Largely from his investigation into synthetic oil production, Suzuki reached the general conclusion "that if the situation continues to be the same as it is at present, it will be extremely disadvantageous from the point of view of building up the matériel side of national power, if nothing else," and he insisted that from a matériel standpoint the so-called policy of "hardship and privation" would be difficult to sustain. Similarly, at the conclusive Liaison Conference of November 1, he asserted that "there is the danger that with one false step the anti-war argument will bring on a fragmentation of national views and dull the people's minds."[189] Once again he endeavored to win Kaya and Tōgō over: "Were we to go to war, . . . there would be no worry about matériel in 1941 and 1942; in terms of resources, 1943 will be a better year if we have gone to war. . . . It is better to go to war now." [190] On what estimates of the nation's matériel strength did Suzuki base his argument for war?

The Cabinet Planning Board Sets Three Conditions

With the formation of the Tōjō cabinet, the General Affairs Office for Matériel Mobilization of the Cabinet Planning Board was informally directed to "estimate the nation's matériel strength for next year and the year following and draw up a comparative chart, anticipating that Japan would start a war with the United States and Britain sometime . . . between December this year and March next year." The Office set to work on October 22. Because they were unable to obtain any data from the military, the following hypotheses were based on their own assumptions:

1. Of the 6.5 million tons of shipping (counting ships over 100 tons) on hand, vessels to be requisitioned by the military at the outbreak of war would total 2.6 million tons for the army and 1.6 million tons for the navy.
2. The navy would continue to requisition 1.6 million tons on a regular basis, but the army would gradually reduce its requisitions and after seven months discharge 900,000 tons.
3. The ratio between ships lost and ships newly constructed will be . . . 700,000 tons to 400,000 tons during the first year, . . . 600,000 tons for both during the second year, . . . 400,000 tons and 800,000 tons respectively for the third year.

On the basis of these assumptions, on November 2 the General Affairs Office put forward the following objective:

If we can maintain on a regular basis a minimum of 3 million tons of shipping for matériel mobilization, we should somehow be able to make good the basic figures in this year's matériel mobilization. On this basis we should be able to secure a base of 1.9 million tons of oil for civilian use and the production of 4.3 million tons of steel. [191]

For four months from June 1940, starting in the waning days of the Yonai cabinet, the Office had raised levels of imports paid for with foreign currency for each period of the Matériel Mobilization Plan, fearing that the United States might tighten its trade embargo against Japan. The Office had also altered the figures for ad hoc imports paid for out of gold reserves held by the Bank of Japan:

1. June 4: 100 million yen for scrap iron, electrolytic copper, and aviation gasoline.
2. August 9: 20 million yen for electrolytic copper, tin, and nickel, and 163 million yen for special steel, electrolytic copper, and aviation gasoline.
3. September 24: 128 million yen for electrolytic copper, tin, manganese, aviation gasoline, and high-grade machine oil.

As a result of these emergency imports, costing more than 400 million yen, the quantities in storage around October 1940 had risen to: 950,000 tons of scrap iron, 10,000 tons of special steel, 210,000 tons of manganese ore, 80,000 tons of copper, 60,000 tons of lead, 20,000 tons of zinc, 280,000 tons of category A petroleum, 220,000 tons of category B petroleum, and 200,000 tons of aviation gasoline.[192] In 1942, after deducting quantities consumed on the basis of the 1941 Matériel Mobilization Plan adopted by the cabinet on August 22, 1941, special stockpiles were to include, as a percentage of those in 1941: electrolytic copper, 27,000 tons (21%); lead, 50,000 tons (68%); zinc, 10,000 tons (12%); mercury, 180 tons (32%); high-grade asbestos, 360 tons (17%); ordinary asbestos, 5,500 tons (39%); high-grade mica, 90 tons (82%); wool, 236,000 bails (115%); Manila hemp, 1,700 tons (7%); carbon black, 400 tons (6%); and castor beans, 9,800 tons (30%).[193] The issue faced by the wartime Matériel Mobilization Plan was this: setting aside domestic production, how would these stockpiles be distributed and expended when war broke out and imports from areas other than the yen block were cut off? It was self-evident that the longer resource strangulation and the decline of national power continued, the greater would be Japan's "gradual pauperization" and the greater the depletion of its stockpiles; even without incurring enemy raids from abroad, Japan would perforce die a beggar's death.

The solution to this dilemma was of course to ensure that resources would continue to flow to Japan from the South Seas and elsewhere by regularly commissioning ships to maintain the minimum of 3 million tons needed for matériel mobilization. Such a plan would depend largely on anticipated shipping losses after the war started. To exaggerate, shipping losses would decide whether or not Japan would "die a beggar's death." In his written explanation about changes in the estimates of national strength, Suzuki concluded, "I am convinced that to maintain and augment our national strength, it will be more advantageous to make use of the certain fruits of battle in the initial stages of the war and vigorously undertake necessary measures in all fields than to sit tight and wait for the enemy to put pressure on us."[194] But he also explained that his forecast was subject to the following conditions:

First, *so long as it is possible* to maintain a constant minimum of 3 million gross tons of shipping for civilian use, it will be possible to secure the quantities of supplies called for in the Matériel Mobilization Plan for fiscal 1941, except for some materials.

That is, except for some materials, at least 3 million gross tons of shipping are needed in order to secure matériel from the Zone of Self-Support [Japan, Manchuria, and China] and the first Supplementary Zone [French Indochina and Thailand] to the extent set out in the Matériel Mobilization Plan for fiscal 1941. We judge that on average it will be possible to transport as much as 4.8 to 5 million tons per month with this tonnage, taking into account a decline from wartime operations of from 15 to 20 percent. The above transportation capacity is equal to the average of 5 million tons of matériel actually transported in the first half of the fiscal 1941 Matériel Mobilization Plan.

Second, *if* the yearly loss in shipping is *estimated to be* between 800,000 and 1 million gross tons, the maintenance of the 3 million tons of shipping mentioned above should be possible if we can obtain an annual average of about 600,000 gross tons of new construction. . . .

Fourth, in order to maintain the shipping needed for production, it will be *necessary to follow the plan* agreed upon among the army, navy, and the Cabinet Planning Board when it comes to the scheduled tonnage of shipping needed in particular for southern operations.

That is, the scheduled tonnage of shipping needed specifically for southern operations is as follows (in gross tons):

Army

First month	2,100,000
Second month	2,100,000
Third month	2,100,000
Fourth month	2,100,000
Fifth month	1,700,000
Sixth month	1,650,000
Seventh month	1,500,000
From the eighth month on	1,000,000

Navy

Each month 1.8 million gross tons, including small vessels, as follows:

Tankers	270,000
Fishing boats	94,000
Freight-passenger boats	336,000
Freighters	1,100,000

Because it is estimated that during southern operations fiscal 1942 shipping for civilian purposes for a given period of time will bottom out at a little less than 1.6 million gross tons and cargo at around 2.6 million tons, it is anticipated that quantities of steel in that period will drop to as little as 3.8 million tons on an annual calculation, and that quantities of other important matériel will decline by as much as 15 percent.

Consequently, steel production in 1941 will amount to around 4.5 million tons as against the 4.76 million tons in the plan. (Author's emphasis) [195]

By so carefully insisting on such crucial conditions in his explanation about changes in estimates of the nation's matériel strength, Suzuki was passing the buck to the high command. Even the matter of oil supplies was made a problem for the high command to examine. And he avoided responsibility by saying such things as: "I was told that it would be fine if I simply read the explanation aloud, tacking on the phrase 'according to the high command's investigation,' so that is exactly what I did." [196] On these grounds he fanned the argument for war, saying that wholly as a matter of general principle Japan had better go to war now.

At the Imperial Conference, which focused on the oil question, Suzuki ignored the work of the Cabinet Planning Board on that issue and merely recited from the briefs prepared by the military, thus abandoning any effort to reach an independent judgment on this particular issue. Around November 13, however, Army Chief of Staff Sugiyama left both the government and the navy breathless when he reported to the Throne that there was "no worry about the oil problem [prospects of supply and demand]." [197] Because Sugiyama's report concerned matters properly under the government's jurisdiction, the emperor questioned Tōjō about its contents. On the 20th Tōjō ordered Suzuki to investigate, and Suzuki in turn ordered the General Affairs Office for Matériel Mobilization to make an immediate investigation. Even then Suzuki did not disclose to his staff members the military's figures on the prospects of supply and demand that he had recited at the Imperial Conference of November 5. The General Affairs Office began its investigation and then approached the Army Ministry's War Preparations Section for information. On the 21st the latter replied: "Sugiyama's report to the Throne is correct. We shall send you documents such as copies of the report to the Throne. We want you to make the conclusions of the Cabinet Planning Board tally with Sugiyama's report to the Throne." [198] On the other hand, the Navy Ministry's Armaments Bureau informed the Office:

> We know nothing about Sugiyama's report to the Throne. The navy has not presented any figures to the army nor has it in any way consulted with the army concerning the storage of oil, its consumption, and the quantities scheduled to be obtained from southern regions mentioned in the report to the Throne. The amount of oil stored is top secret military information; there has been no communication between the Navy General Staff [and the Armaments Bureau] about the quantities scheduled to be obtained.[199]

The General Affairs Office's investigation was completed on the 23rd. The following day the Army Ministry's War Preparations Section enjoined: "The army is determined to go to war. We want you to write the conclusion of the opinion you present to the Throne in strong language."[200] Suzuki had received the Office's report that same day but was uncertain as to what value he should attach to it. The arrival of the Hull note on the 26th, however, convinced him that diplomatic negotiations had become hopeless, and on the afternoon of the 27th he drafted a pro-war opinion which he attached to his report to the Throne of the 28th. In effect, Suzuki went along with and confirmed Sugiyama's earlier report to the Throne.

The Three Conditions Are Ignored

As we have seen, the changes in the estimates of the nation's matériel strength on which Suzuki based his advocacy of war were made possible in the first place on three assumptions: 1) that only between 800,000 and 1 million tons of shipping would be lost annually; 2) that the military had to follow the plan agreed upon with the Cabinet Planning Board regarding the scheduled tonnage of shipping to be requisitioned; and 3) that it would be possible to maintain on a regular basis a minimum of 3 million tons of shipping for civilian use. If the army and navy general staffs had neither the intention nor the ability to fulfill these conditions in the process of prosecuting a war against the United States, Suzuki's argument would collapse immediately.

There is no record that, at this Imperial Conference or at the liaison conferences which reexamined state policy, the two high commands objected to the conditions presented by Suzuki or to having the buck passed to them. Upon returning to his office on the 29th, for example, Tsukada ordered the War Guidance Office to "study up on" the data for estimating national strength, "because I don't understand them very well," which suggests that both general staffs let Suzuki's conditions go in one ear and out the other. Furthermore, given Suzuki's disposition to evade responsibility on the oil question, there is also reason to doubt how sincere he was in making his case for them. The likelihood is that Suzuki stated these conditions perfunctorily, being satisfied merely to pass the buck to the army and navy general staffs, and with it the sole responsibility for abiding by them once war broke out. From the start neither high command appeared to have any inclination to listen seriously to the explanations given by Suzuki, a person lacking in independent judgment.

By their very nature, however, these three conditions constituted precisely the perimeters that the government had given to the high commands for war guidance, perimeters based on the minimum levels of matériel needed to maintain Japan's national strength and enable it to continue a war. Neither high command had opposed the conditions; therefore, it follows that each had given its guarantee to the government before going to war that together they would keep the scale of any war within those perimeters and would follow them after war broke out, thereby maintaining the minimum levels of matériel needed to continue the war.

More concretely, the government demanded that the high command give it a written promise that the scale of warfare and guidance over military operations once the war began would without fail take place within these perimeters and that under no circumstance would hostilities be conducted, or the war situation be allowed to develop, in such a way as to undermine these conditions. To this the high command officially agreed at the Imperial Conference. If they were to ignore these perimeters once war broke out, not only would they be violating an official pledge to the government, but the minimum levels of matériel strength needed to sustain the war would also be instantly undermined.[201] It is highly doubtful that the high command ever gave careful consideration to Suzuki's three conditions, or that it decided on going to war with the United States determined, or even expecting, to adhere to these perimeters in guiding the war and controlling its magnitude. More likely, they cherished plans for a large-scale war that ignored Japan's national strength and their official pledge. Doubtless they made light of the situation, certain that once the war started they would be able to drag the government along, however grudgingly, in the direction they desired, regardless of their official pledge.

Table 3.8a[202]
STATUS OF SHIPS DISCHARGED, MARCH—JULY 1942 (ARMY)

1942	Agreed upon Shipping Tonnage[a]	Agreed upon Discharge Schedule[a]	Notified for Discharge[a]	Usable Mobilized Shipping in Each Respective Month[a]	Resulting Decline in Supply Capability from That Stipulated in the Matériel Mobilization Plan[b]
March	2,100,000	—	—	—	—
April	1,700,000	400,000	0	0	−770,000
May	1,600,000	50,000	182,000	120,000	−635,000
June	1,500,000	150,000	60,000	0	−795,000
Subtotal	—	600,000	242,000	187,600	—
July	1,000,000	500,000[c]	—	—	—
Total	—	1,100,000	—	—	—

[a] Gross tons
[b] Tons.
[c] Supplementary requisition request of 200,000 grow tons made.

Let us examine the facts of the situation. The ability to guarantee a sustained minimum civilian shipping capacity of 3 million tons, given there could be no rapid increase in shipbuilding capacity, would depend on giving top priority to military operations that would keep shipping losses at 800,000 to 1 million tons annually. However, it has already been noted that Nagano's plans for maritime transport of resources from the southern regions were nothing more than empty rhetoric, given the status of structures, fleet organization, counter-measures, and training. Convoy operations were regarded as completely secondary in importance at that time, and under such circumstances it was inconceivable that military operations geared to limits on shipping losses would be given top priority. The conclusion seems inescapable that Nagano had made light of the official pledge given at the Imperial Conference. Thus, no efforts whatsoever were made to keep to the jointly agreed-upon official pledge on shipping losses, or to the schedule for discharging obsolete vessels, as Tables 3.8a and 3.8b show. Consequently, the planned transport of 500,000 tons of cargo per month or 6 million tons per year fell to 3.86 million tons in the first fiscal year, somewhat over half the bare minimum envisaged in the Matériel Mobilization Plan. Table 3.9 shows the status of cargo shipping for civilian use during 1942.[203] Any correspondence between actual war guidance and the Matériel Mobilization Plan collapsed at this point, foreshadowing as early as the first year of the war

Table 3.8b[202]
STATUS OF SHIPS DISCHARGED, MARCH–JULY 1942 (Navy)*

1942	Agreed Upon Discharge Schedule[a]	Notified for Discharge[a]	Usable Mobilized Shipping in each Respective Month[a]	Resulting Decline in Supply Capability from that Stipulated in the Matériel Mobilization Plan[b]
March	80,000	0	0	——
April	——	0	0	−150,000
May	——	76,000	0	−150,000
June	——	0	44,800	−70,000
Subtotal	——	——	——	——
July	——	——	——	——
Total	——	——	——	——

* See fn 202.
[a] Gross tons.
[b] Tons.

Japan's eventual defeat from its basic matériel incapacity to sustain a war.

This being the case for civilian cargo shipping, Table 3.10 reveals the actual quantities of oil available after the war started, in comparison with the high command's projections which Suzuki was made to read at the Imperial Conference. The transport of oil by sea from the southern regions—of key importance in calculating the supply and demand of oil—collapsed because of tanker losses resulting from inattention to convoy operations. The high command thus ignored its official pledge with grave consequences for the conduct of the war in terms of oil supplies, particularly from the southern regions, as table 3.10 reveals. Even if the total projected quantities for both military and civilian use had amounted to those planned for originally—5.2 million tons in the first year, 5 million in the second, and 4.75 million in the third—the projected amount in storage at the end of the third year would have totalled no more than 2.1 million kiloliters, a quantity almost exactly offset by the actual deficit in oil for military use of 2.06 million kiloliters at the end of the third year, as shown in table 3.10.[204] From these oil figures it is clear that Japan would not be able to engage in military operations from its home islands, to say nothing of producing oil for military and civilian requirements, from the fourth year on. In fact, the actual need for oil rose greatly over the original estimates—for example, the navy

Table 3.9[205]

CARGO SHIPPING, JANUARY-NOVEMBER, 1942

	Cargo Shipping for Civilian Use (Gross Tons)	Cargo Capacity for Civilian Use (Tons)
January	1,730,000	2,210,000
February	1,700,000	2,160,000
March	1,700,000	2,140,000
April	———	3,470,000
May	———	3,020,000
June	———	3,190,000
July	———	3,700,000
August	2,300,000	3,500,000
September	2,300,000	3,400,000
October	2,300,000	———

November	Supplementary requisition request	
	Army	Navy
	200,000	150,000
December	1,760,000	———

Table 3.10

OIL SUPPLIES FOR MILITARY USE, 1941–1943*

	1st Year	2nd Year	3rd Year	Total
Domestic Crude Petroleum				
Projected production	250,000	200,000	300,000	750,000
Actual	262,000	274,000	254,000	790,000
Balance	12,000	74,000	-46,000	40,000
Synthetic Oil				
Projected production	300,000	400,000	500,000	1,200,000
Actual	240,000	272,000	219,000	731,000
Balance	-60,000	-128,000	-281,000	469,000
Oil from Southern Regions				
Projected imports	300,000	2,000,000	4,500,000	6,800,000
Actual	1,489,000	2,746,000	1,330,000	5,565,000
Balance	1,189,000	746,000	-2,170,000	-1,235,000
Total				
Projected supplies	850,000	2,600,000	5,300,000	8,750,000
Actual	1,991,000	3,292,000	1,403,000	6,686,000
Balance	1,141,000	692,000	-3,897,000	-2,064,000

*Compiled from JDA Archives.

needed 50 percent more crude oil and over 100 percent more aviation gasoline—and therefore the offset would occur even earlier than the third year.

Since July 1941 Japan had been faced with a virtual worldwide boycott spearheaded by the United States. Given its high dependence on foreign trade, how Japan would conduct warfare after war broke out would logically be determined by the acquisition of resources required to sustain the war. A policy for guiding the war would necessarily come down to this one basic consideration, and consequently any reexamination of state policy on the assumption that war would break out ought to have focused exclusively on whether such a policy could be produced. Despite this, Suzuki took a pro-war stance in order to avoid personal responsibility and simply read aloud a prepared text, with its apparent conditions, and talked about oil problems as a proxy for others. Though they acceded to the three conditions, the two supreme commands still cherished the idea of a large-scale war, apart from those conditions and with no connection to the nation's strength, and essentially ignored the text Suzuki presented.

Thus, in their reexamination of state policy the government and the high command frittered away the one and only opportunity to clarify a policy to guide the war in its first stages and failed to give anything but the most superficial consideration to the key issue of matériel strength. Once that happened, there was no possibility that they would be able to set up a policy to guide them throughout a war against the United States. The "reexamination of state policy" having been concluded, the November 15 Liaison Conference adopted the "Draft Proposal for Hastening the End of the War Against the United States, Britain, Holland and Chiang," but that document was nothing more than rhetoric added to rhetoric. Japan plunged into war with the United States without with any policy whatsoever for guiding such a war.

5 Hull's Ultimatum

Tokyo Rejects Nomura's Plan

The day before the Konoe cabinet fell, Roosevelt wrote to Churchill, "you and I have two months of respite in the Far East."[206] Churchill replied on November 5: "When we talked about this at Placentia you spoke of gaining time, and this policy has been brilliantly successful so far."[207] Both men, particularly Roosevelt, evidently intended to continue to play for time. Roosevelt accepted the "Estimate Concerning Far Eastern Situation" of November 5 sent to him by Chief of Staff General George C. Marshall and Chief of Naval Operations Admiral Harold R. Stark, which urged a cautious policy toward Japan and concentration on defeating Germany,[208] and on the 6th informed Stimson that when and if Kurusu Saburō, Japan's new special emissary, arrived, he might propose to him "a truce in which there would be no [troop] movement or armament for six months and then if the Japanese and Chinese had not settled their arrangement in that meanwhile, we could go on on the same basis."[209] Of course, Stimson promptly objected, but Roosevelt appears to have already suggested this to Hull as well. At his meeting with Nomura on November 10, Roosevelt caught Nomura's attention when he said:

> ... a so-called *modus vivendi* was necessary in order for the people to live and stated that this term might be translated as "method of living," or the like. While it is not at all clear what this means, we must follow up and ascertain beforehand whether it means a provisional agreement. (Nomura dispatch of November 10)[210]

The previous evening Nomura had called on Postmaster General Walker, who had confided in the ambassador:

> Prefacing his remarks by saying "In all seriousness and just between the two of us, I swear to God that I am telling this only to you because of our close relationship," he went on to say: "The United States government has acquired reliable information that Japan will go into action shortly. The United States government continues to believe that your meeting with the president on Monday or Kurusu's coming to the United States will have no effect whatever on the overall situation. My "boss" (the president) believes this information, as does the secretary of state." (Nomura dispatch of November 10)[211]

Walker's comments were rather naive observations from the sidelines, and Roosevelt had already revealed his thinking to Harold Balfour, the British undersecretary of state for air, who called on him on the 9th:

> His present Japanese policy is one of stalling and holding off. If during the next few weeks this policy looks likely to succeed for some months ahead, or alternatively, if the President can sign up for peace with

Japan so as to ensure no sudden hostilities then he will feel able at once
to direct a further diversion of heavy bombers to U.K.

On the other hand the Japanese situation may blow up in the very
near future. . . .[212]

Roosevelt's meeting with Balfour focused on the question of how
many heavy bombers were to be supplied to Britain. The president's
playing for time vis-à-vis Japan was of course the other side of the
coin of his policy of positive assistance to Britain.

In preparation for his first meeting with Kurusu on the 17th,
Roosevelt had already sent Hull a memorandum entitled "Six
Months," which he had pencilled himself, and at that first meeting
with Kurusu, which Nomura also attended, he alluded to point 4 of
his memorandum:

> In regard to the China problem, the difficulty of withdrawing troops
> has come to my attention, but the United States does not desire to
> intervene or mediate in the Sino-Japanese dispute. I don't know
> whether such a term exists in the diplomatic lexicon, but we are only
> attempting to become an introducer. (Nomura dispatch of November
> 17)[213]

When Nomura and Kurusu called on Walker later that evening,
Walker intimated that the president had suddenly changed his mind
again as the result of a conversation he had just had with Walker:

> The President is very desirous of an understanding between Japan and
> the United States. In his latest speech he showed that he entertained
> no ill will towards Japan. I would call that to your attention. Now the
> great majority of the cabinet members, with two exceptions, in princi-
> ple approve of a Japanese American understanding. If Japan would
> now do something real, such as evacuating French Indo-China, show-
> ing her peaceful intentions, the way would be open for us to furnish
> you with oil and it would probably lead to the reestablishment of
> normal trade relations. The Secretary of State cannot bring public
> opinion in line so long as you do not take some real and definite steps
> to reassure the Americans.[214]

With Walker's now optimistic assessment as well as the meeting with
Roosevelt in mind, Nomura incorporated Walker's suggestions into a
proposal which he submitted on his own initiative when he met with
Hull on the 18th:

If we both continue to build up our military strength, we shall one day become involved in a lamentable catastrophe. There would be no end to fighting on the basis of high-minded idealism, but at the present time there is first of all the need to reduce tensions by bringing things back to the situation which existed before the implementation of the freeze order. Namely, in return for Japan's withdrawal of troops from southern French Indochina, the United States will rescind the freeze order. If at any rate we relieve the atmosphere by doing this, there would be no need to send warships to Singapore, or to reinforce military installations in the Philippines. It would be desirable to pursue further talks on this basis. (Nomura dispatch of November 18)[215]

Kurusu also reported to Tokyo in the same dispatch:

According to Ambassador Nomura's and my own observations, the president outwardly maintains an impassive attitude, but it is evident that at this time he has considerable enthusiasm for a Japanese-American accord; to conclude hastily that this is a delaying tactic and immediately take irreversible actions, simply because he does not swallow our proposals whole, is something we must be on utmost guard against at present.

For the U.S. [some indication of a return to conditions which existed prior to July 24] is the quid pro quo. And Plan B. . . . by itself, in light of the course of negotiations up to now, probably would not be acceptable. It is desirable at this time to be prepared beforehand to demonstrate our good faith at least to the extent of beginning our withdrawal of troops from southern French Indochina.[216]

Nomura's proposal was in line with Roosevelt's thinking. Walsh, who was in contact with Walker, visited the Japanese embassy on the morning of the 19th and said

that according to information that he had obtained, the United States would announce the lifting of the oil embargo at the same time that [Japan] announced its intention to withdraw troops from southern French Indochina, and availing itself of that opportunity, would transmit its intention to decide on steps toward the resolution of pending issues; he then extended congratulations to me [Kurusu] for the success of my mission.[217]

That evening Nomura and Kurusu visited Walker, who gave them roughly the same information. Walker even let fly with a joke: "The Admiral should be well aware of the difference between petroleum for military use and petroleum for civilian use."[218]

From the vantage point of leaders in Tokyo, the Nomura proposal reduced Plan B to only two points: item 3 and item 1 of the reference notes (see Appendix 9). Given that Plan B was an agreement barely salvaged at the end of heated debates between Tōgō on one side and Sugiyama and Tsukada on the other, and confirmed by an Imperial Conference, Tokyo would hardly be amenable to unilateral changes made in Washington. When informed of Nomura's proposal, Tōjō was critical: "It will be awkward if those at the other end present proposals of their own." Tōgō therefore called Nomura to task by return telegram on the 20th: "In light of the delicate domestic situation, it is most regrettable that you as ambassador have put forward a proposal of your own, as per your telegram, without consulting us beforehand." Despairing over an agreement based on Plan A, Tōgō also directed Nomura "to say that you are in receipt of corrected instructions from us regarding your personal proposal . . . and to submit Plan B at your next meeting."[219] Nomura therefore resubmitted Plan B in its entirety at his meeting with Hull on the 20th. By this time Roosevelt's "Six Months" proposal, the Morgenthau proposal, and the Far Eastern Division's proposals for both a comprehensive and a provisional agreement had all been set forth by the United States. Plan B resembled the Far Eastern Division's proposed provisional agreement on many points; thus on its face there was nothing reprehensible in it for the State Department, the army, or the navy. For them, it was a more than suitable plan, either as the basis for a stopgap arrangement or as a scheme for gaining time.[220]

Hull's Proposal for a Modus Vivendi Is Abandoned

Plan B also provided a stimulus to bring together the scattered ideas in the various American proposals.[221] The U.S. response was drafted on the 22nd, and a final draft was completed by the 25th. At their meeting on the morning of the 25th Hull showed the final draft to Stimson and Knox, proposing to hand it to the Japanese that day or the next.[222] A "war council" was convened at the White House at 1:30 p.m. that afternoon, attended by Roosevelt, Hull, Stimson, and Knox with the addition of the two chiefs of staff. The consensus was that the final draft should be presented to the Japanese as a counterproposal to Plan B.[223] But when evening arrived, Hull "abandoned or . . . practically abandoned" the idea.[224]

Around 9:30 the next morning, Stimson called Hull and then Roosevelt to ask whether the president had received army reports that a convoy of ten to thirteen 10,000-ton-class ships (carrying around 50,000 troops) had been sighted south of Taiwan. Roosevelt "fairly blew up—jumped into the air, so to speak, and said he hadn't seen it and that that changed the whole situation because it was evidence of bad faith on the part of the Japanese."[225] By this time Roosevelt may have personally made up his mind to abandon his "Six Months" plan, preferring war with Japan to looking on idly while Japanese attacks mounted against Dutch and British possessions in Southeast Asia.

Hull had been lukewarm from the outset to the proposal for a tentative agreement and had objected strongly when on or around the 10th Nomura had tried to bring up the subject of a modus vivendi that did not deal in depth with the China problem. Rather than seizing on the proposal for a tentative agreement, although it would be equally effective in buying time, Hull apparently decided to utilize the gambit of direct talks between Japan and China, an approach that also appealed to the Japanese. Taking advantage of Plan A, which Nomura had presented on November 7 under instructions from Tōgō, Hull suddenly proposed an idea that had just occurred to him:

> If China's highest authorities pledged China's sincere friendship and trust to Japan and its citizens and desired the restoration of friendly relations between China and Japan, what would Japan think? I have not yet broached this with the Chinese, so this is entirely my own individual opinion, but if something like this should take place, it would set a fine example for peace in the Pacific and have a favorable effect on the world. I would like you to transmit these thoughts to the Japanese government and sound out their views. (Nomura dispatch of November 7)[226]

Somewhat doubtful, Nomura observed in his report that "it is reasonable to presume that it will probably be of no avail to solicit the intentions of the Chinese any longer." Tōgō replied immediately that Hull's statement

> could be construed as intending to leave the China problem, which has been a stumbling block in the Japanese-American negotiations, to direct negotiations between Japan and China. Therefore, it could be understood as intending to have Chiang Kai-shek propose to us that peace consultations be begun. If such is the case, this is to be appreciated as an effective means of contributing to the promotion of peace between Japan and China, and the Imperial Government would certainly welcome this. The government's view on this will be cabled

separately in a follow-up telegram, but in the meantime please ascertain what effect this proposal has on negotiations between Japan and the United States, the connection thereto.[227]

Tōgō's hopes were aroused to such an extent that the next day he issued Nomura further instructions:

If at this juncture the U.S. government intends to mediate between the Japanese and Chinese governments along the lines Secretary Hull indicated in regard to a Sino-Japanese peace, and to leave the details of the peace terms to direct consultations between the Japanese and Chinese, this in effect accords with what the Imperial Government has hoped for from the beginning. By taking advantage of Hull's suggestions, we will be able to exclude for the time being the issue of withdrawing troops stationed in China from our current negotiations. This would naturally result in promoting a negotiated accord between Japan and the United States. At the same time, it would allow us to carry on Sino-Japanese peace negotiations without American interference.

In taking advantage of the above proposal it is of course necessary to have the United States furnish a promise or avowal that it will not make peace between Japan and China a condition for reaching an accord through Japanese-U.S. negotiations, nor, with regard to the China problem, will it interfere with a Sino-Japanese peace (this includes bringing activities in support of Chiang to a halt)—and to make it perfectly clear that an agreement between Japan and the United States is to be promptly signed and implemented.[228]

In light of Hull's sudden proposal, Tōgō cannot be faulted for adopting such an interpretation.[229] Nomura and his assistant, Wakasugi Kaname, pressed Hull at their meeting on the 12th:

Is the import of this that Sino-Japanese relations should be left to Japan and China, and that agreement on the remaining problems between Japan and the United States is possible? We would like to know a little more concretely at this point about how you will secure China's "pledge" on this. Or is Secretary Hull of a mind to leave this to direct negotiations between Japan and China? Then again, is it the intention of the U.S. to secure a pledge from China and have it sent on to Japan? Or is it the intention of the U.S. to pursue this as part of a trinational conference among the U.S., Japan, and China? Is the intention to get China to participate in this conference at a [certain] stage and have them make the above "pledge?"

In response Hull merely

intimated obliquely his having the intention of mediating between Japan and China depending on the conditions, bringing up the example that when participants in a two-man dispute find it difficult to confer with each other they could do so through the good offices of any number of persons. (Nomura dispatch of November 13)[230]

It seemed to Nomura that "Hull has no clear and definite plan in mind regarding how to go about it." Hence, matters reverted once again to what they had been before Hull's proposal of the 7th. U.S. records regarding this incident are inaccurate, but there is no evidence to suggest that Hull had consulted the Chinese before he made his proposal. In essence, Hull went further than simply buying time; he succeeded only in confusing matters, instilling false hopes in the Japanese and causing subsequent disappointment.[231]

Having thus turned one of the three pending issues to his advantage, Hull then took up the Tripartite Pact, making new demands that went beyond the scope of the talks. On the 16th, Nomura reported, Hull

> repeated his desire that [the Tripartite Pact] be terminated or become a dead letter. When Wakasugi closed in by asking whether it was the United States' position that an agreement between Japan and the United States was impossible unless Japan withdrew from the Tripartite Alliance, he repeated in effect that since a mutual agreement on peace and a military alliance were contradictory, he hoped that for the sake of a mutual agreement between Japan and the United States the treaty of alliance would become a dead letter.[232]

In his meeting with Roosevelt on the 17th, Kurusu declared:

> Japan has obligations with regard to the Tripartite Pact of Alliance; moreover, it has its honor as a Great Power. It would be impossible to do anything to violate the pact, and I cannot imagine that the United States, which has long advocated respect for international treaties, would desire this. . . . If at this time we were somehow able to reach some kind of major understanding between Japan and the United States in regard to the Pacific, as the president has suggested, this would naturally "outshine" [steal the light from] the Tripartite Pact. In that case I think your apprehensions over the applications of the alliance pact will naturally melt away. (Nomura dispatch of November 17)[233]

Although these views were reiterated to Hull the following day, Hull persisted in believing that the Tripartite Pact was incompatible with a

Japanese-American understanding, and when he received Plan B on the 20th he again affirmed to Nomura that:

As long as ineradicable suspicions associated with the Tripartite Pact exist in the minds of the American people, it will be extremely difficult for the United States to abandon its policy of supporting Chiang Kai-shek. Changing our policy of supporting Chiang would be just as difficult as abandoning our policy of supporting Britain.[234]

Far from mediating peace between Japan and China, Hull invoked the Tripartite Pact to justify vigorous assistance to China. With respect to nondiscrimination in trade, Hull's oral statement of the 15th was also a frontal rejection of the Japanese proposal.

From about the 18th, his utterances to Nomura became extremely hard-line and consistently so, "giving indications that he was shoving all three pending problems to the fore and pressing for an across-the-board acceptance of the American proposal:"[235]

... he frankly did not know whether anything could be done in the matter of reaching a satisfactory agreement with Japan; that we can go so far but rather than go beyond a certain point it would be better for us to stand and take the consequences . . . .
. . . if the Japanese could not do anything now on those three points . . . he could only leave to Japan what Japan could do. (November 18)[236]
. . . . all we can do is to stand firm on our basic principles. (November 19)[237]
. . . [Japan] should not have to be paid to come back to a lawful course. . . .
. . . unless the Japanese were able to do a little there was no use in talking. (November 22)[238]

While taking a firmer and firmer line since the beginning of November, Hull had also succeeded in buying time. Then on the morning of the 26th he assured himself that Roosevelt had abandoned the proposal for a modus vivendi, and without consulting the army and navy or sounding out the envoys of Britain, Australia, Holland, and China, who had been summoned on the 22nd and again on the 24th, Hull informed Roosevelt alone that he intended to summon Nomura and Kurusu, hand them the so-called Hull Note, and at the same time retract the proposal for a modus vivendi. Roosevelt concurred on the spot. The situation faced by the Japanese ambassadors now switched suddenly from consideration of the fortnight-old modus vivendi to dealing with a "Hull Note" that would be handed to them without the army or navy having seen it. Did Nomura's premonition of the difficulties that Plan B would encounter result from these same trends in Hull's thinking that Walker had also noted when Nomura visited him on the 25th?[239]

Neither the secretary of war nor the secretary of the navy knew anything about Hull's sudden decision to hand over the note. Stimson learned of the note only after Nomura's telegram about it was decoded, and when Stimson called Roosevelt and Hull to ascertain its contents and to seek their views regarding what emergency measures the army and navy should take, Hull made it clear that "I have washed my hands of it [the dispute with Japan] and it is now in the hands of you and Knox—the Army and the Navy."[240]

Envoys Stationed in Japan Support the Proposal for a Modus Vivendi

On the other hand, the American, British, and Australian envoys in Tokyo all favored a modus vivendi. When Craigie called on Tōgō on October 29, Tōgō told him:

> The American attitude has in any event a tendency to be too theoretical. The negotiations between Japan and the U.S. at present hold no prospect for an accord and the situation gives extreme cause for alarm. If negotiations fail, I cannot guarantee that we will not see an unexpected state of affairs develop. . . . At this time, it would be appropriate for Great Britain to work for an improvement in the relations among the three nations of Japan, Britain, and the United States and for the preservation of world peace. (Tōgō dispatch of November 3)[241]

Craigie "promised to raise the matter promptly with his government and took his leave." Having at the same time received a similar communication from Yoshida Shigeru, Craigie reported to his government that "this indirect request for British intervention was genuine, and not intended primarily to make trouble between us and the United States."[242] Completely unaware that the Liaison Conference had approved both Plans A and B on November 2, Grew reported to Washington on November 3:

> If the fiber and temper of the Japanese people are kept in mind, the view that war probably would be averted, though there might be some

risk of war, by progressively imposing drastic economic measures is an uncertain and dangerous hypothesis upon which to base considered United States policy and measures. War would not be averted by such a course, if it is taken, in the opinion of the Embassy. . . .

. . . There should be no compromise with principles, though methods may be flexible.[243]

Grew, however, had omitted from this report his views that the State Department's approach was too far-reaching and too rigid, that there was too much deliberation of general principles, and that there was insufficient flexibility in dealing with the concrete issues that separated Japan and the United States.[244]

It was characteristic of Hornbeck to include in his memorandum of the 5th sarcastic refutations of Grew's earnest report,[245] but the British government also instructed Craigie to reply to Tōgō that "we also wanted a general settlement, but that we saw no advantage in entering upon negotiations until the principles of an agreement had been decided, and that we were content to leave these preliminary discussions to the United States."[246] And in a communication to the United States government around the 19th, the British government conveyed via Ambassador Lord Halifax its concurrence with Hull's hard-line policy of making no concessions whatsoever except in return for definite (that is, submissive) actions by the Japanese. On the 25th it responded again with a hard-line argument in connection with Hull's conference with the envoys of concerned countries. On or about November 29, London expressed apprehension regarding the modus vivendi itself. In short, the British government from the start adopted an even more hard-line posture than did the U.S. Department of State's Far Eastern Division.[247]

This hard-line posture emanated primarily from Churchill. A month earlier Churchill had become optimistic about the Far Eastern situation, as shown by his October 25 dispatch to Australian Prime Minister John Curtin:

I am still inclined to think that Japan will not run into war with A.B.C.D. (American-British-Chinese-Dutch) Powers unless or until Russia is decisively broken. Perhaps even then they will wait for the promised invasion of the British Isles in the spring. Russian resistance is still strong, especially in front of Moscow, and winter is now near.[248]

But the Australian government did not share his optimism and took a more flexible attitude toward reports from its envoys. On November

22 the Australian chargé d'affaires in Tokyo reported, "The [Japanese] government's attitude all goes to confirm the view that they are genuinely anxious to secure agreement with the United States and to avoid at present anything that might prejudice discussions in Washington."[249] Richard Casey, Australia's minister in Washington, reported to Canberra after meeting again with Hull on the 24: "It was the first time for months . . . that countries other than the United States had anything tangible to work on and, although the proposal [Plan B] was unacceptable in itself it might, with modification, be made acceptable to all parties."[250] Based on these reports, Minister of External Affairs Herbert Evatt decided that every possible effort should be made to avoid a rupture in the talks between Japan and the United States, that "the Japanese are clearly anxious to avoid war themselves," and that the "rigid" American attitude was driving Japan into a war of desperation. He believed strongly that Hull should not reject the Japanese proposal outright but should make counterproposals and reach a temporary agreement.[251]

On the 25th, therefore, he instructed Casey to pursue discreetly the chance to intervene in the conversations, his primary concern being to prevent the talks from breaking down. On the 26th he repeated the suggestion that, since Japan's advance into French Indochina had occasioned economic restrictions against Japan, those restrictions might be lessened in return for Japanese withdrawal of troops from French Indochina, provided that Japan gave a general guarantee against advancing into other regions and entered into an understanding to negotiate a subsequent Pacific accord at a later time. "On the whole this would be a Japanese diplomatic retreat," Evatt instructed, "but it should be possible to give Japan a chance to retreat without inflicting unnecessary humiliation."[252]

In accordance with Evatt's instructions, Casey called on Hull on the 29th "and made some reference to the possibility that he might cause Kurusu to call on him, at which time he would discuss the pros and cons of the present relations . . . and wind up by suggesting that Australia would be glad to act as mediator or something of the sort." Hull dismissed the suggestion with the declaration that "the diplomatic stage was over and that nothing would come of a move of that kind."[253] Nonetheless, on the 30th Casey called on Kurusu and offered to arrange a meeting with Halifax. Soon after taking his leave, however, Casey sent word that the meeting was off, probably because Halifax objected. At a cabinet meeting on December 1 the Australian government reiterated its view that a further endeavor should be made to encourage the establishment of a modus vivendi between the

United States and Japan that would be satisfactory to China as well as to the other countries concerned.[254]

A Virtual Ultimatum

Roosevelt and Hull, however, were no longer troubled by Britain's optimistic hard-line argument or by Australia's argument for caution. When he handed his note to Nomura and Kurusu on the 26th, Hull "made no rebuttals of any force" against the displeasure expressed by both ambassadors, nor did he give any further explanation. His attitude made it plain that discussion would be useless, and the two ambassadors found themselves with no place to turn.[255] Finally they asked:

> As ambassadors earnestly desiring a bilateral accord between Japan and the United States, we have grave doubts as to whether transmitting this as is to our government is a step we should take. . . . Does this mean that the United States considers there to be no room for considerations beyond this proposal? In light of the president's having recently said among his friends that there is no "final word," can we arrange for a meeting?

In an almost cavalier fashion Hull "agreed to arrange this even though he appeared disinclined to do so,"[256] and Nomura and Kurusu met with Roosevelt the following day. Roosevelt appeared calm and unhurried, assuming his usual open and friendly attitude, but he gave no indication that he was prepared to reconsider the Hull Note, and the two ambassadors' efforts to achieve a turnaround in the deadlocked situation by having the U.S. reconsider its position ultimately ended in failure.[257]

As if to chastise them, Hull then held an unusually long press conference in which he gave a one-sided and detailed description of how the talks had gone since spring that year. Referring to impending actions by the Japanese military in French Indochina, he declared that future developments would depend on decisions by the military extremists in Japan. As demonstrated by his subsequent testimony that "we had no serious thought that Japan would accept our proposal [the Hull Note],"[258] if the abandonment of the proposal for a modus vivendi marked the point of no return with Japan as far as Hull was concerned, this press conference constituted the point of no return with domestic public opinion.

Word that such a point had been reached had already been sent out. On the 26th Roosevelt telegraphed High Commissioner of the

Philippines Francis B. Sayre that "I consider it possible that this . . . Japanese aggression might cause an outbreak of hostilities between the United States and Japan."[259] Unaware that the Hull Note had been delivered, Admiral Stark telegraphed a warning to commanders of the Asiatic and Pacific fleets on the 27th: "This dispatch is to be considered a war warning. Negotiations with Japan . . . have ceased and an aggressive move by Japan is expected within the next few days."[260]

Hull himself first informed Halifax on the 29th that "the diplomatic part of our relations with Japan was virtually over and that the matter will now go to the officials of the Army and the Navy with whom I have talked and to whom I have given my views."[261] He then conveyed this to Casey. On December 1 Hull met with Nomura and Kurusu, declaring that:

> there was a limit beyond which we cannot go further and . . . one of these days we may reach a point when we cannot keep on [with conversations] as we are. . . .
> . . . he [Hull—trans.] has practically exhausted himself here, . . . the American people are going to assume that there is real danger to this country in the situation, and . . . there is nothing he can do to prevent it.[262]

Both Hull and Roosevelt were fully aware that by delivering the Hull Note, which they had no intention of reconsidering, they had crossed the point of no return, at home and abroad. Regardless of its wording, that note was to be taken as notification of the termination of diplomatic negotiations; in terms of conventional diplomatic wisdom this was virtually an ultimatum without a deadline for responding. The issue for the United States now turned solely on when and how war against Japan would commence.

Tōgō's cable of the 20th, decoded that same day, contained instructions that since Plan B "is the Imperial Government's final proposal, there is absolutely no room for concessions. Unless we get American consent to it there is nothing we can do but rupture negotiations."[263] Tōgō's cable of the 22nd, decoded that day, instructed that all procedures relating to the agreement had to be completed by the 29th: "Further changes as far as this date is concerned are absolutely impossible. After that date things are going to develop automatically, and that is that."[264]

Hull himself later testified that "I realized that there was very little possibility that the Japanese would accept a modus vivendi except such as [Plan B]."[265] Therefore, he had no reason to expect that Japan would accept the Hull Note, replete with the most extreme and uncompromising demands proposed by the United States since that spring.[266] Moreover, in making the extremely grave decision to abandon the proposed modus vivendi and deliver the note, Hull had been utterly arbitrary in his behavior, almost devil-may-care; he consulted neither the military nor the envoys of other countries concerned. That was the result of his having "had so little confidence in the practical value" of the note.[267]

Therefore, although the Hull Note was in fact an ultimatum, it was presented in the form of another American proposal in an endeavor, solely for the sake of posterity, not to tarnish the American record and to allow the United States to avoid the stigma of having rejected Plan B without offering any kind of counterproposal.[268] Hull attempted to make the note serve as a substitute, so to speak, for an ultimatum.

The Japanese High Command Fears That Negotiations Will Be Successful

The high commands of both the army and navy were from the beginning strongly opposed to pursuing both peace and war simultaneously. Then on November 1 Navy Minister Shimada also announced the ministry's determination to go to war. Not only was Tōjō alone in adhering to the "one-fourth peace, three-fourths war" decision of the November 5 Imperial Conference; but also, in his unconditional submission to the emperor, he went so far as to interpret this as meaning a fifty-fifty chance for either peace or war. No sooner had the Tōjō cabinet been formed than controversy arose within the Army General Staff over "whether the army minister has integrity" (October 20 and November 1), and whether he "is an apostate" (November 1); by November 2 it had come to the point of "a surge of no confidence voices" against Tōjō.[269] Standing alone among the four top military leaders, Tōjō gradually succumbed to the pressure of widespread pro-war arguments in both the Army General Staff and the Army Ministry—for example, from Military Affairs Section Chief Satō Kenryō. After the 5th he began to deviate from his position of unconditional submission to the emperor's wishes.

Immediately after the draft for the Imperial Conference had been approved at the Liaison Conference of the 2nd, the Army General Staff, without a second thought, sent Mutō a pointed question via

Operations Division Chief Tanaka Shin'ichi: "If agreed upon, won't Plan B interfere with national defense initiatives?" Even after the Imperial Conference decision, the Army General Staff persisted in its pro-war stance, some hoping "and praying that Tōjō would not be an apostate" (November 7) when it came to Kurusu's mission. "Some prayed that Kurusu's plane would crash; Operations Section Chief Hattori Takushirō, Europe-America Section Chief Amano Masakazu, and the War Guidance Office shared the same feelings" (November 10). Although "fearing that Plan B might be successful" (November 13), they took comfort from Article 4 of Plan B calling for the termination of American support to Chiang that Sugiyama and Tsukada had appended in return for the Army General Staff's assent to Plan B, predicting that "despite Plan B, negotiations will not succeed" (November 10), that "because of this demand, there is no doubt that negotiations will soon break down" (November 20).[270] "Due to this, the negotiations will finally break down. That's great, just great!" (November 21).[271]

The Army General Staff was still deeply "concerned that diplomacy would succeed," and on November 14 they set about studying "guaranteed terms" should Plan B be accepted. On the 17th the War Guidance Office generated a proposal and sent it on to the Army Ministry's Military Affairs Section which, in consultation with the navy, drafted a "plan regarding measures to be taken henceforth in the negotiations between Japan and the United States." Military Affairs Bureau Chief Mutō then presented the plan to Tōjō and Tōgō. Under the guise of "guarantees" should plan B be accepted, it aimed at sabotaging the plan by adding the following new and problematic conditions:

1. At the time an agreement is reached on Plan A or Plan B, we ask to be supplied with petroleum in the amount of 6 million tons annually from the United States, 1.5 million tons of which is to be aviation gasoline, and 4 million tons annually from the Dutch East Indies, all to be in equal monthly allotments.
2. If the negotiated accord is not implemented within a week after it is reached, war against the United States, Britain, and Holland will be initiated.
3. If the United States and Britain comply but Holland does not follow suit, the necessary troops will be sent to the Dutch East Indies to make good on the guarantee.[272]

Fully aware that some further concessions would have to be made if either Plan A or Plan B were to succeed, Tōjō and Tōgō steadily refused to consent to burdening Plan B with additional conditions in complete disregard of the Imperial Conference decision, and Tōgō immediately ordered that they be withdrawn. Sugiyama nonetheless insisted on bringing up the issue again at the Liaison Conference on November 26:

> I think that negotiations based on Plan B will not succeed. But in case they should, if concrete guarantees for the future are not attached when they succeed: 1) there is the danger that we shall not be able to meet the aspirations of the Empire after an agreement is reached; 2) if an agreement is reached, there is the danger that for the sake of concrete arrangements opportunities will be postponed and we shall miss them.[273]

In the end, Tōgō agreed to the following compromise:

> For the time being, petroleum [imports] for next year will be set at the following amounts, to be increased incrementally:
> 4 million tons from the U.S. (including aviation gasoline); 2 million tons from the Dutch Indies (ditto).
> Telegram the above amounts immediately to Ambassador Nomura.
> Note: In the last fiscal year 3.3 million tons were imported [from the United States] and 1.8 million tons were demanded by Yoshizawa Kenkichi [from the Dutch East Indies].[274]

That same day instructions were accordingly issued to Nomura. The compromise decision dumbfounded the Foreign Ministry's America Bureau chief, Yamamoto Kumaichi, who commented sarcastically to Ishii Akiho of the Military Affairs Section that "if the military could go so far as to put forward such a plan, they might just as well have come right out and said that 'if we go to war we're going to win.' "[275] And while they continued to pursue their schemes to wreck the negotiations, the Army General Staff "prayed that December 1 [the deadline for breaking off negotiations] would come as soon as possible" (November 17), and "that things would come to a rupture" (November 23).[276] In the midst of all this, on November 27, the Hull Note arrived.

Tōjō Is Cornered Into Making a Decision

Relying on Tōgō's account,[277] let us now compare the main points of the Hull Note of November 26 with Hull's revised counterproposal of June 21, the first United States proposal:

1. The November 26 proposal newly advocates a multilateral nonaggression pact, which has no counterpart in the June 21 draft.
2. The November 26 proposal newly advocates a multilateral nonaggression pact regarding French Indochina, which has no counterpart in the June 21 draft.
3. "Reinvestigate hereafter the terms and timing of the withdrawal of Japanese forces from China" (June 21 proposal) has been amended to read "immediate and unconditional withdrawal of Japanese forces and police from China and French Indochina" (November 26 proposal).
4. "Amicable negotiations regarding Manchukuo" (June 21 proposal) has been amended to read "will not acknowledge any Chinese government other than the Chiang Kai-shek regime" (November 26 proposal).
5. "Japan publicly promises, as its understanding of the Tripartite Pact, not to invoke it against actions of self-defense by the United States" (June 21 draft) has been amended to read "abrogation of the Tripartite Pact" (November 26 proposal).
6. The November 26 proposal insists *de novo* that Japan renounce its extraterritorial rights, its concessions, and its Boxer Protocol rights in China, demands with no counterpart in the June 21 proposal.

The Hull Note made new demands or exceeded those made since the spring, completely ignoring the negotiations over the preceding six months. When he received the note Kurusu immediately objected to point one:

> Japan has had extremely bitter experiences with this kind of collective framework since the Washington Conference. As an attempt to enforce a Nine Power Treaty type of framework, this proposal would entail that our country gain absolutely nothing from the present incident of four years standing, and that cannot possibly be tolerated.

With regard to the fourth point, Nomura charged:

> Talks involving such matters as the recognition of the Chungking regime are completely out of the question. Our country can never abandon the Nanking government. . . . It is virtually tantamount to pleading with us to apologize to Chungking for the China problem. The president's recent references to "an introducer" could not have been made with anything like that in mind.[278]

The Hull Note, Charles Beard later wrote, revealed the "maximum terms of an American policy for the whole Orient."[279] According to

Herbert Feis, the aim of the first item was, in effect, to revalidate the Nine Power Treaty.[280] In Tōgō's judgment, the Hull Note conflated the Tripartite Pact and economic issues with both Nine Power Treaty concepts and an extension and application of the Stimson doctrine to China, French Indochina, and the entire Far East.[281] He also suspected that Hull had deliberately presented terms that would be difficult for Japan to accept in a form that would be difficult to accept. Overcome with despair, he instantly lost the zeal with which he had fought the high command tooth and nail up to that point. Solely concerned to avoid war, however, he shut his eyes and tried to swallow the Hull Note whole, but awakened to the fact that it stuck in his throat and simply would not go down.[282]

After November 5 Tōjō had gradually given in to the pro-war advocates, but based on his tacit understanding with Tōgō he still made room for certain concessions so that Plan A or Plan B might succeed. When he was asked after the war about the circumstances surrounding the proposed modus vivendi in the United States, he replied:

If they had only listened to Plan B, [the attack on Pearl Harbor] certainly would not have occurred. Nor would that have occurred if the United States did not go all the way but just met us halfway on Plan B. What I am trying to say [is that if the United States had adopted any one of the provisions of Plan B, it would have thereby avoided the attack on Pearl Harbor]. That is, I believe that if the United States had come forth in a conciliatory spirit, the terms could have been mitigated. . . . As the result [of presenting Plan B] we would have had to wait and see what moves the United States would make. After that it would become a problem of feeling things out. . . . In the event that the United States came forward with a proposal for a tentative arrangement [a modus vivendi], I think that the situation would have changed considerably.[283]

When Satō Kenryō asked him a similar question shortly before the attack on Pearl Harbor, Tōjō sighed: "If such a reply would only come."[284] What actually arrived, however, was the Hull Note, which bore not the slightest resemblance to Plan B, and at the Liaison Conference which began at 2 p.m. on November 27 over which he presided, Tōjō reached the following basic conclusions:

1. The U.S. memorandum of November 26 is clearly an ultimatum to Japan.
2. This memorandum cannot be accepted by our country; and the United States, knowing that Japan could not accept these condi-

320 THE DECISION FOR WAR

tions, still communicated them to us. Moreover, this has been done with the intimate understanding of the countries concerned.

3. Judging from the above, and from recent events—particularly steps, utterances, and acts toward Japan and what is to be deduced therefrom—it seems that the U.S. has already resolved on war against Japan.[285]

In this way both Tōjō and Tōgō, who had been prepared to retreat to some extent from Plan A or B and had up to that point opposed the arguments for war, caved in. Arguments for a 50–50, or even a 25–75 chance for peace or war disintegrated, and the Liaison Conference, visibly disappointed,[286] for the first time lined up behind war.

The Command to Initiate Operations Is Issued

The Army General Staff was concerned that war preparations, which had been geared from the start to action in early December, would be thrown into confusion in the event that the U.S. accepted Plan B for the sole purpose of buying time. Should the United States later revert to a hard-line policy, concerns over the Soviet Union would make southern operations difficult for the army, and the navy would find it harder to prosecute a war against the United States in terms of naval ratios and fuel. In short, the Army General Staff had been concerned all along that Japan would lose its "national defense initiative" and then be unable to avoid humiliation; it therefore worked to block an accord based on Plan B.[287] Thus it greeted the Hull Note, which buried Plan B, with a sense of relief: "This must be divine grace; this makes it easy for the Empire to cross the Rubicon and determine on going to war. That's great, just great!"[288] Tōgō observed that advocates of war in the military appeared to feel "relieved because of this."[289] And Grew testified after the war that: "it has always been my belief that it was about the time of [Japan's] receipt of Mr. Hull's memorandum . . . that the button [setting off the war] was pushed."[290] Ambassador Craigie expressed the view that in this ultimatum

> the decision on the American side not to proceed with . . . counter proposals [to Plan B] was "unfortunate." . . .
> . . . [Japan's] decision [for war] would at least have been postponed if [Plan B] had been accepted as a basis of negotiations. . . . the "final reply" [Hull Note] of the United States Government to Japan was in terms which the latter was certain to reject. . . . the Japanese decision to go to war was taken on or about November 27 [when it was received].[291]

On the 29th the Liaison Conference decided without debate on the draft proposed for the Imperial Conference. True to form, the Imperial Conference, convened on December 1, acquiesced in that decision, which was captioned "On Initiating War against the United States, Britain and Holland:"

> Negotiations with the United States based on the "Essentials for Carrying Out the Empire's Policies" approved on November 5 have finally proven unsuccessful. The Empire will go to war against the United States, Britain, and Holland.

Tōjō made the opening statement:

> On the basis of the November 5 Imperial Conference decision, the army and navy have endeavored to complete operational preparations, while the government has exhausted every means at its disposal and made every effort to reach an adjustment in diplomatic relations with the United States. Not only has the United States not conceded an inch in its original demands; under the American-British-Dutch-Chinese alliance, it has appended new conditions—such as demanding the unconditional and total withdrawal of troops from China, the repudiation of the Nanking government, and the transformation of the Tripartite Pact between Japan, Germany, and Italy into a dead letter—and has importuned the Empire for unilateral concessions. If the Empire were to submit to these, not only would the Empire lose its authority and be unable to anticipate concluding the China Incident; the very existence of the Empire would also be placed in jeopardy. It has become clear that the Empire's demands cannot possibly be achieved through diplomatic means. At the same time, the United States, Britain, Holland, China and other countries have stepped up their economic and military pressure. From the viewpoint of our nation's power, and also from the important standpoint of operations, we have reached a situation that simply does not allow us to proceed as we have been. Moreover, strategic requirements in particular do not allow for any further extensions of the deadline. As things now stand, the Empire has come to the point where going to war against the United States, Britain, and Holland is inevitable for the sake of resolving the present crisis and achieving self-preservation and self-defense.

Having heard this, Tōgō then asserted:

> As for the present American offer, should it be accepted the Empire's international position would decline to a point even lower than that prior to the Manchurian Incident, and we should recognize that our existence cannot but be put in jeopardy as well. Namely,

322 THE DECISION FOR WAR

1. China under the rule of Chiang Kai-shek will become increasingly dependent upon Britain and the United States, the Empire will lose its credibility with the National Government of China, Japanese-Chinese friendship will be damaged far into the future, and in due course our complete withdrawal from the continent will be made inevitable. As a result, the position of Manchukuo as well will necessarily be affected. In this way our means for bringing the China Incident to a successful conclusion will be undermined to the very core.

2. Britain and the United States will come to reign as leaders over these regions, the authority of the Empire will be cast to the ground, our position as a stabilizing force will be destroyed, and our great task of constructing a New Order in East Asia will collapse in mid-course.

3. The Tripartite Pact will become nothing more than a dead letter, and the Empire will lose credibility overseas.

4. The attempt to control the Empire by forming a collective organization that would also include the Soviet Union will increase our worries to the north.

5. Although their call for nondiscrimination in trade and other such principles should not necessarily be.rejected, the intent from the start to apply them only to the Pacific region is in the last analysis nothing more than a means for Britain and the United States to carry out self-serving policies; they will pose major obstacles for us in acquiring vital materials.

In short, it would be terribly difficult for us to approve the above proposal. I am compelled to say that even if we continue further negotiations based on the above proposal, in particular to get the United States to withdraw that proposal in its entirety, it will be virtually impossible for us to realize our demands, and that's that.[292]

First Tōgō then Tōjō had stood alone in their steadfast opposition to the advocates of war, and the Hull Note deprived them of the slender grounds for a compromise proposal. On the other hand, the note boosted the spirits of the war advocates, who felt that their assessment of the United States had been confirmed: "You saw that, didn't you?" In other words, it unified the government and the high command and drove them to go to war.

Immediately after the decision for war was sanctioned by the Imperial Conference, the two chiefs of staff jointly reported to the Throne that "we therefore wish to issue an order to the front-line forces of the army and fleets of the navy to launch operations"; they then respectfully requested that the emperor sanction orders to commence attack operations. The next day, December 2, they again jointly reported to the Throne and sought imperial sanction to commence operations on December 8, Japan time:

> The primary reasons for scheduling December 8 as the date to initiate military action have to do with the phase of the moon and the day of the week. In order for the army and navy to implement the first air strike with ease and make it effective, a moonlit night between midnight and sunrise with the moon about 20 days old would be appropriate. A Sunday would be best for the naval task force's air attack on Hawaii: relatively high numbers of warships will be berthed at Pearl Harbor, Sunday being a day of rest and recreation. Therefore we have selected December 8, a Sunday in Hawaii, with the moon 19 days old. Of course, the 8th will be a Monday in the Far East, but we have put the emphasis on a surprise attack by the task force.
>
> In light of the fact that the American attitude in the diplomatic negotiations between Japan and the United States has recently become remarkably hard-line, it can be inferred that the United States has begun in earnest to prepare for war with Japan. Britain has from the beginning taken extremely strict precautions regarding the Empire's movements, and it can be concluded that its naval warships have been placed on emergency standby.
>
> Therefore, a preemptive strike against us by Britain and/or the United States prior to December 8 could happen. However, moving up the date for initiating military action would not only be difficult in terms of army cargo ship operations and navy task force movements, but it is also to be expected that confusion among the various units would result. Therefore, we humbly ask you to approve an imperial command authorizing the initiation of military action against the United States and Britain on December 8 as initially planned.[293]

Admiral Yamamato was immediately informed that the emperor had sanctioned the attack, and at 5:30 p.m. he telegraphed the task force bound for Pearl Harbor: "Commencement of hostilities set for December 8. Carry out attack as planned." The arrow initiating war with the United States had finally been let fly from the bowstring and could no longer be retrieved.

Problems of method and timing aside, if by delivering the Hull Note Roosevelt and Hull aimed to propel Japanese-American relations from the diplomatic stage onto the stage of war, they certainly hit the bull's-eye.

324 THE DECISION FOR WAR

6 Japan's Ultimatum

The Senior Statesmen and Government Confer

In despair over the Hull Note, the Liaison Conference decided on the 29th to go to war with the United States. But even at this late hour some outside the conference continued to assert that war could still be avoided, pointing in support of their argument to the blind spots in the reexamination of state policy. As the result of his meeting with Prince-of-the-Blood Takamatsu Nobuhito, who was serving in the navy, the emperor disclosed to Kido on the 30th his impression that "the navy seems to have its hands full and would like to avoid war between Japan and the United States if it could, but what's really going on?" [294]

At Kido's suggestion, Shimada and Nagano came to the palace after 3:30 p.m. and were asked by the emperor:

I think it will become a protracted war, but will you go ahead anyway? Do each of you, as minister and as chief of staff, believe that everything will be all right?

In response, both men replied:

The training of the fleet has been thorough and the *commander-in-chief* [Yamamoto] *possesses sufficient confidence. Sufficient preparations in* both men and *material having been made,* he awaits your command. (Author's emphasis)

His cross-examination having yielded nothing further, the emperor informed Kido shortly after 6:30 p.m. that, "since both [Shimada and Nagano] replied with considerable confidence when I inquired about the matter just a while ago, tell the prime minister to proceed as planned." [295] Prince Takamatsu's daring intervention collapsed in the face of Shimada's and Nagano's ultimately evasive comments concerning the navy's prospects for victory.

The emperor also asked Tōjō on the 26th whether the Senior Statesmen had assented, given that it was essential for the nation to be completely unified if war occurred. He suggested that the Senior Statesmen might attend the December 1 Imperial Conference. Tōjō replied that the November 27 Liaison Conference had discussed this and he thought that it would not be appropriate to have the Senior Statesmen attend the Imperial Conference; it would blur the lines of responsibility if the Senior Statesmen, who unlike those in the government and high command were not constitutionally responsible for advising and assisting the Throne, took part in a decision with those who were. When the emperor then recommended that Tōjō confer with the Senior Statesmen in his presence, it was decided that Tōjō would gather the Senior Statesmen at the palace for consultation, at which time each would submit his individual views to the emperor. The conference convened at 9:30 a.m. on the 29th, and it was former prime ministers Wakatsuki Reijirō and Okada Keisuke who were the most reluctant to acquiesce in the government's position. When it came time to serve lunch at noon, the emperor ordered that the discussion continue until it was completed, but at close to one o'clock the Senior Statesmen requested a break for lunch. After dining with the emperor, each of the Senior Statesmen presented his views to the Throne from 2 to 3 p.m., with only Tōjō in attendance. Wakatsuki and Okada remained unconvinced:

WAKATSUKI: Even though we don't have to worry about the spiritual strength of our people, there is a need to study carefully whether or not they can endure a protracted war from the standpoint of commodities. Although there was an explanation by the government about this during the morning, I worry about it.

OKADA: I am extremely concerned whether there are sufficient prospects for success as far as our capacity to supply commodities is concerned. Although there was an explanation by the government a while ago, I am still not convinced.

Yonai Mitsumasa also agreed: "I ask that you be careful not to plunge into sudden pauperization in attempting to avoid gradual pauperization."[296] The discussion continued until 4 o'clock, but Wakatsuki at least returned home unpersuaded.[297] On November 19 Nomura had also strongly advised Tōjō: "From my vantage point, it could not be more inopportune to venture forth further into a great war of protracted length at a time when, following on the heels of the Manchurian Incident, the nation's strength has been exhausted by over four years of the China Incident."[298] The misgivings of Wakatsuki, Okada, Yonai, Nomura and others concerning assessments of Japan's material strength and the navy's prospects for victory, the blind spots in the reexamination of state policy, could never be dispelled.

As noted above (pp. 258-59), the enduring of great hardship and privation to be carried out within Kido's framework for "wiping the slate clean" was no more than provisional and partial and meant only that Japan would be in trouble if in the future it underwent gradual pauperization and lost its "national defense initiative." The arguments by Wakatsuki, Okada, and Nomura suggested that because the chances for success were extremely questionable as far as assessments of the nation's material strength were concerned, there was no alternative but to endure great hardship and privation, utterly and completely, by not going to war with the United States. And Yonai's assertion implied "better gradual pauperization than sudden pauperization." Thus, all of these men had already gone beyond the framework for "wiping the slate clean" that Kido had imposed on the Tōjō cabinet. From the very start, the Tōjō cabinet was confined within that framework and very much indisposed to going through with an absolutely no war policy that would put up with such gradual pauperization. Above all, Kido himself had always opposed an absolutely no war policy that would tolerate revolutionary changes.

In Washington, Kurusu exhausted every means at his disposal and then played his trump cards: the extension of the deadline for breaking off diplomatic negotiations and a personal exchange of telegrams between the two heads of state. In his November 26 report to Tokyo he argued:

> As related in successive telegrams, there is almost no prospect of gaining approval for Plan B in its entirety. On the one hand, the deadline is fast approaching, and as things now stand, there will regretfully be no alternative but to break off negotiations. My ineffectiveness overwhelms me with shame. As the only means of breaking the deadlock at this time, and I am utterly overwhelmed with trepidation in suggesting this, I would first like to have President Roosevelt telegraph His Majesty his desire for bilateral cooperation between Japan and the United States with the objective of preserving peace in the Pacific. (Awaiting the emperor's intentions, I shall negotiate to the utmost of my ability.) Then, by seeking a personal telegram from the emperor in response to this, we shall clear the air and at the same time gain a period of grace for the present. While bearing in mind the possibility that Britain and the United States may attempt a protective occupation of the Dutch East Indies, I think it appropriate for us to make the first move by proposing the establishment of neutral states which will include French Indochina, the Dutch East Indies, and Thailand (as you are aware, President Roosevelt proposed neutrality for French Indochina and Thailand in September of this year). Although there is the view that a rupture in the current negotiations will not necessarily mean the outbreak of war between Japan and the United States, a British-American

advance into French Indochina could be anticipated following a rupture as noted above, and ultimately a collision with Britain and the United States owing to an attack on our part would be inevitable. It is highly questionable whether Germany will agree to activate its obligations under Article 3 of the [Tripartite—trans.] Pact and there will be no alternative but to defer a resolution of the Sino-Japanese Incident until at least the end of the current world war. Since this telegram may be the last report of my views, I earnestly desire your response one way or the other by immediate return telegram once you have shown it at least to Privy Seal Kido.[299]

Kido refused his approval, giving Kurusu's proposal hardly any more consideration than he had previously given to the Hull Note when he argued that "domestic strife would result if we were to try to reach a settlement on the basis of such a proposal."[300] After the outbreak of war, Koga Mineichi remarked: "History shows that countries do not perish from internal strife; those responsible at the time should have fought off the outbreak of war with unfaltering determination and without fearing domestic strife."[301] Ever since the argument for a Higashikuni cabinet surfaced, Kido consistently steered clear of an absolutely no war policy if it remotely risked the possibility of domestic strife: war would be preferable to that.

Timing Japan's Ultimatum

The problems of the navy's prospects for victory and of assessing the material strength of the nation brought up outside the liaison conferences were thus buried once and for all; the Liaison Conference's decision of November 29 to go to war could no longer be overturned, and only the necessary formalities remained to be determined. At that conference Nagano, Itō, Shimada, and Oka, on behalf of the navy, insisted that "we still have some leeway, so carry on with diplomacy as if we were waging war; sacrifice diplomacy to waging war." Tōgō thought this somewhat strange and retorted: "Well, when the hell are you going to start the war?" Bowing to the inevitable, Nagano lowered his voice and revealed for the first time, "December 8." To which Tōgō replied, "Right. Can't I tell our people over there about our decision?"[302]

Ever since the Hull Note had arrived, Tōgō had held the view that because Japan would be going to war this time for self-preservation there was no need for prior notification, and his response to Nagano may well have reflected this view. In his report of the 27th, however, Nomura had dwelt on the need to give prior notification that negotiations were to be terminated. The emperor had also warned Tōjō immediately after the Imperial Conference of December 1 to be careful not to initiate an attack before final notification was delivered; he too regarded the issuing of a final notification as only natural.[303] Therefore, Tōgō changed his mind and decided to eliminate any room for future controversy by issuing a final notification.[304] At the Liaison Conference of December 4 he said:

> I would like to convey in our final diplomatic note to the United States that diplomatic relations are abandoned and severed, relating in full the U.S. position, Japan's attitude thereto, and the substance of the Imperial Rescript declaring war. . . .
> Once we say this [to the United States], there's nothing further to be said. If we rework this draft severing diplomatic relations, cable it tomorrow afternoon, the 5th, and it [arrives] on the 6th, I think that will be just the right day for delivering it.[305]

Tōgō then read the draft of the final notification. Itō proposed that it be delivered in Washington at 12:30 p.m. on the 7th (7 a.m. in Hawaii). It was therefore decided that the draft, along the lines proposed, would be entrusted to Tōgō but that he would decide on the time of transmission and delivery in consultation with the high command so as to meet their requirements.

The navy's Oka Takazumi then asked America Bureau Chief Yamamoto Kumaichi whether this notice severing diplomatic negotiations would constitute an ultimatum; Yamamoto affirmed that it would. The draft was then referred to the Navy Ministry, where the Naval Affairs Bureau argued that Japan's intent to go to war should be more clearly stated, and with Oka's concurrence the phrase, "the Empire reserves the freedom of action it deems necessary," was appended to the end of the draft. But when Oka showed this revised draft to Tōgō, Tōgō replied that the "Foreign Ministry's original plan will suffice," and Oka withdrew the revision. "If the Foreign Minister says it will suffice," he told Ishikawa, "then it will suffice, won't it?"[306] Tōgō would appear to have consistently taken the position that notification that negotiations were severed would also serve as notification that war had begun. For example, on December 10, after the war started, Tōgō declared in instructions to embassies and consular offices abroad: "It is the usual practice not to give a clear expression of one's intention to exercise military force in a notification severing diplomatic negotiations, and it would be considered rather strange to expect a clear expression in this regard."[307]

Itō, however, deemed it necessary to postpone the time of delivery to 1 p.m., and since the Army General Staff had no objections, Itō and Tanaka Shin'ichi (deputizing for Vice Chief Tanabe Moritake who was in western Japan) called on Tōgō on the afternoon of the 5th to request his consent to postponing the time of delivery for thirty minutes. Tōgō asked Itō whether "the hour" of 1 p.m. "left some time [to deliver the notification] before commencing a hostile act."[308] When Itō replied affirmatively, Tōgō consented to their request. At the Liaison Conference of the 6th Itō reported that the time of delivery had been changed to 1 p.m. (7:30 a.m. in Hawaii). Endorsing this change, the Liaison Conference also set the time of transmission at 4 a.m. on the 7th (Tokyo time).

Why did Itō change his initial proposal to deliver the notification at 12:30 p.m.? He had calculated a margin of one hour before the scheduled time for the attack on Pearl Harbor to begin (8 a.m. Hawaii time, 1:30 p.m. Washington time), but subsequently realized that, on the basis of past experience with maneuvers, actual execution was commonly delayed by about 20 minutes when large-scale forces were involved. Given that it was highly likely that the attack would begin 20 minutes late (1:50 p.m. Washington time, 8:20 a.m. Hawaii time), 1 o'clock would allow an acceptable margin of 50 minutes to deliver the notification. If delivered at 12:30, however, the margin of 1 hour and 20 minutes would be excessive. In any case, why a 30-minute postponement was needed, to say nothing of how Itō arrived at that figure, was never explained to Tōgō, to the Liaison Conference, or even to the Navy Ministry.

Surprise Attack or Straightforward Attack?

Yamamoto had obtained authorization from Nagano on October 20 for strike operations against Pearl Harbor, and on November 5 he was ordered to advance to the staging area:

NAVY ORDER NO. 1
November 5, 1941
    By Imperial Order, Chief of the Navy General Staff Nagano Osami directs Commander-in-Chief of the Combined Fleet Yamamoto as follows:

1. The Empire, for the sake of survival and self-preservation, antici-
    pates going to war against the United States, Britain, and Holland

in early December and has determined to complete all operational preparations.

2. The Commander-in-Chief of the Combined Fleet shall implement the necessary operational preparations.

3. The Chief of the Navy General Staff shall give instructions regarding details.

NAVY DIRECTIVE NO. 1

November 5, 1941

Chief of the Navy General Staff Nagano Osami directs Commander-in-Chief of the Combined Fleet Yamamoto as follows:

1. In preparation for the inevitable eventuality of war against the United States, Britain, and Holland in early December, the Combined Fleet shall, at the appropriate time and with the required forces, advance to the staging area prior to the commencement of operations.

2. In making this advance, a strict lookout against an unexpected attack shall be maintained.

3. Operational guidelines in the event of war with the United States, Britain, and Holland follow under separate cover.

Yamamoto thereupon issued Combined Fleet Order No. 1. But still hoping for a last-minute diplomatic agreement, he declared that "in the event of a major change in the situation, there is a chance that 'Preparations for War No. 1' may be reinstated in place of 'Preparations for War No. 2' [deployment for operations at sea]." And when the leadership of the Combined Fleet took up operational preliminaries at Iwakuni in mid-November, Yamamoto personally gave verbal instructions on this point. On the 17th he gathered the ships' captains, officers, and crews of the task force and personally gave strict orders that the entire task force was to turn back in the event that diplomatic negotiations succeeded and a pull-back was ordered:

> The military has been fostered for one hundred years solely for the purpose of preserving peace. Therefore, no matter what difficulties arise, I want that order above all to be obeyed, absolutely and without question.[309]

On November 21 Yamamoto was ordered to deploy for an advance to the standby area:

NAVY ORDER NO. 5

November 21, 1941

By Imperial Order, Chief of the Navy General Staff Nagano Osami orders Commander-in-Chief of the Combined Fleet Yamamoto as follows:

1. The Commander-in-Chief of the Combined Fleet shall at the appropriate time have those forces necessary for the execution of operations proceed to the standby area at sea.
2. In the event that the Commander-in-Chief of the Combined Fleet is challenged by forces of the United States, Britain, or Holland while conducting operational preparations he may exercise force in self-defense.
3. The Chief of the Navy General Staff shall give instructions regarding details.

Simultaneously, Nagano instructed Yamamoto that "the Commander-in-Chief of the Combined Fleet shall, if Japanese-American negotiations succeed, immediately assemble the task force and return." And he made arrangements to ensure that in such an eventuality both the Navy General Staff and the Combined Fleet would recall the task force over several air waves, demanding encoded responses. However, when on December 1 the Imperial Conference gave final approval to the decision to go to war, the following order was issued:

NAVY ORDER NO. 9

December 1, 1941

By Imperial Order, Chief of the Navy General Staff Nagano Osami orders Commander-in-Chief of the Combined Fleet Yamamoto as follows:

1. The Empire has determined to go to war with the United States, Britain, and Holland in early December.
2. The Commander-in-Chief of the Combined Fleet shall destroy enemy fleets and air forces in the Far East, and if enemy fleets come to the attack he shall intercept and destroy them.
3. The Commander-in-Chief of the Combined Fleet, in cooperation with the Supreme Commander of Southern Forces, shall immediately capture the key bases of the United States, Britain, and Holland in East Asia, and shall occupy and secure essential areas in the south.
4. The Commander-in-Chief of the Combined Fleet shall cooperate in the operations of the fleet in the China theater as need arises.
5. Orders follow on when to initiate military actions as per the above.

Then on the 2nd Navy Order No. 12 set the date on which Japan would go to war: "The Commander-in-Chief of the Combined Fleet shall, as per Navy Order No. 9, initiate military action on or after December 8."

In accordance with Navy Order No. 5 the task force had set sail from Hitokappu Bay on the island of Etorofu at 6 a.m. on November 26, prior to the Imperial Conference, and was underway for Pearl Harbor. At 5:30 p.m. on December 2 the Combined Fleet, on the basis of Navy Order No. 12, wired the task force the coded message, "1208: climb Mount Niitaka," meaning "December 8 has been set as the day to go to war; attack as planned." The task force having been informed that the decision to go to war had been made, that there would be no need to return home, and that X-day was the 8th, its attack on Pearl Harbor now became firmly operational.[310]

On November 1 Tōjō had told Sugiyama, "Since the emperor likes to do things openly and aboveboard, I think he will not hear of carrying on with deception."[311] After the Imperial Conference of December 1 the emperor himself had warned Tōjō more than once against attacking without notification. When Nagano went to the palace on behalf of the navy, he reported to the Throne that "I will take care to prosecute the war openly and aboveboard in all respects so that we will not be criticized from any quarter."[312] On the 7th Nagano gathered together Navy General Staff officers of the status of section chief and above and told them that "there must be no behavior such as to invite reproach from future generations." Yamamoto, on his final visit to Tokyo, had cautioned, "the war is to be carried on fairly, and prior notification will certainly be given."[313] And as the first reports of the Pearl Harbor attack were being received, he inquired of his staff officers in the operations room of the flagship, "Prior notification was received before the attack began, wasn't it?"[314]

If the task force's attack on Pearl Harbor had been carried out as scheduled, it would have taken place thirty minutes after notification had been delivered in Washington. Yamamoto was fully prepared to execute that attack after notification—that is, in full awareness that the United States would be poised for a counterattack after receiving final notification. However, even though under international law the attack would have been lawful once notification had occurred, the U.S. land warfare manual published in 1914 and the British land warfare manual published in 1936 both acknowledged that it was possible for an attack to become a surprise attack tactically when it was advantaged by the opponent's being unprepared. If Pearl Harbor were attacked following notification, and if the United States had completed preparations to fight back based on that notification, the attack would have been carried out under conditions in which Japan's plans had been fully disclosed (a straightforward attack). But if Japan were advantaged by the United States' being unprepared, it could be taken as a surprise attack.

Yamamoto had written in his "Memorandum Regarding War Preparations" of January 7, 1941, that "on a moonlit night or at dawn the enemy is to be attacked straightforwardly (or by surprise) with our entire air power in hopes of annihilating its forces." In other words, he took the position that in principle it was to be a straightforward attack, which would become a surprise attack only in the event that the United States was unprepared. Either way, one premise was considered self-evident: the attack would occur after notification had been received.

The following practical issues were also involved:

1. The patrol radius of the U.S. air force based in Hawaii extended to 500–600 nautical miles, and it was necessary to add another 40 miles or so to this for good visibility allowing detection of a large task force.
2. Because of the range of the task force's flight units, the flight patterns of the fighter planes, and other factors, the aircraft could not be launched from the aircraft carriers until the task force approached within 230 nautical miles north of Pearl Harbor.
3. A formation speed for the task force above an average of 24 knots was not possible.

The plan was therefore to increase speed to an average of 24 knots, change course and head south at around 35° latitude at 7 a.m. on December 7, Tokyo time (11:30 a.m., December 6, Hawaii time), and to launch planes from the aircraft carriers 30 minutes after daybreak (1:30 a.m. Tokyo time; 6 a.m. Hawaii time) on the day of the attack. This entailed entering the 600-mile patrol radius of the U.S. air force after 11 a.m. on December 7 (3:30 p.m., December 6, Hawaii time), and the 500-nautical mile patrol radius of the U.S. air force after 3 p.m., (7:30 p.m., December 6, Hawaii time). The task force might be spotted a day earlier depending upon the deployment of U.S. patrols, a possibility raised during map exercises conducted in September. But even then, the task force was to continue south and carry out its assault the following day so long as it did not suffer such a great blow that its mission would be difficult to accomplish. Even in the fortunate event that they were not spotted the day before, Japan's reconnaissance planes would enter Hawaiian air space about 30 minutes before the scheduled time of attack (7:30 a.m., December 7, Hawaii time), and it was also likely that the attack squadrons would themselves be picked up by American patrols; in either case, the assumption was that this would be a straightforward attack because it would have been detected by the United States approximately an hour before the attack was to commence.

Thus, the attack had been planned in anticipation that it would be a straightforward attack detected either the day before or no later than one hour beforehand. Orders concerning the attack had been issued in preparation for both a straightforward attack and a surprise attack, but basically it was neither planned nor implemented with any expectation that it would be a surprise attack, much less a surprise attack without notification. In the event, it turned out to be a surprise attack without notification. It became a surprise attack arising from blunders on the part of the United States; it became a surprise attack without notification arising from blunders on the part of Japan.

The Strange Attitude of U.S. Military Leaders

Japan began transmitting the lengthy text of the notification breaking off negotiations at 8:30 p.m. on December 6, Japan time. By the evening of December 5 the United States had finished decoding parts 1–13, which were delivered to Hull, Stimson, and Knox by 8:30 p.m. But no warning whatever was transmitted that evening to front-line areas such as Hawaii and the Philippines. The decoded text of the remaining Part 14 was delivered to Stark's office at 9:30 a.m. on the 7th; the decoded text of Tōgō's dispatch of the 7th–"Will the Ambassador please submit . . . our reply [in person] to the United States at 1:00 p.m. . . . "—was delivered to Stark's office at 10:30 a.m.[315]

Stark arrived at his office sometime between 8:30 a.m. and 11:30 a.m. but took no steps to send out a warning. Then Marshall arrived at his office at 11:25, read the decoded text, and at 11:30 a.m. telephoned Stark about sending out a warning. Stark replied that to do so would risk confusing the commanders on the scene. Marshall nonetheless wrote out a message and at 11:40 again telephoned Stark. This time Stark concurred with sending the telegram, appending the sentence, "Show this to your Naval officers." But he still did not send out his own warning.[316] Nor did he use his secret desktop telephone (scrambler) which allowed direct communication with Hawaii, or the FBI radio, or the navy's radio: he entrusted the transmission to commercial wire services.[317] Furthermore, the transmission was handled as routine, not as most urgent, top priority, and therefore it did not arrive in Hawaii until just after the air attack had commenced.

A radar station had been set up in Hawaii on the top of Opana at the northernmost point of the island of Oahu, but it customarily ceased operations at 7 a.m. It so happened that the truck that was to relieve the radar technician, Private George Elliott, Signal Corps, Aircraft Warning, and his assistant, Private Joseph L. Lockhard, was a bit late in arriving; the radar had therefore been kept in operation after 7:00 to train Private Lockhard. At 7:02 Lockhard spotted an air squadron of probably more than 50 planes, a larger number than he had ever spotted before, approaching from the northwest at 137 miles north, 3 degrees east.[318] Their report to the Information Center at first elicited no response. The switchboard operator who finally answered said "there was nobody around there. . . . [Private Elliott asked him to—trans.] get somebody that would know what to do and pass on the information, and have him take care of it." Lieutenant Kermit Tyler, who happened to be on hand, was informed by the switchboard operator and telephoned the radar station, telling them "forget it. . . . Don't worry about it. . . . "[319]

Elliott and Lockhard continued to track the squadron by radar until 7:39, when it had closed to 20 nautical miles. Then, because the radar waves were blocked by mountains and they could no longer track it, they turned the radar off at 7:40 and began to go down the hill.[320] That was precisely five minutes before the air raid began. These were the circumstances in Washington and Hawaii that allowed the assault to become a surprise attack.

The Embassy's Executive Staff: Undisciplined and Derelict

The Liaison Conference of the 6th approved 1:00 p.m. (Washington time) on December 7 as the time for delivering the notification severing diplomatic negotiations. Subsequently the timing was altered slightly, and the text of the notification was divided into parts transmitted from 8:30 p.m. on the 6th to 4 p.m. on the 7th. Figure 3.1 below indicates the times of their transmission; the times by which Kameyama Kazuji, chief of the Foreign Ministry's Telegraph Section, estimated they would be decoded by the Japanese embassy in Washington; what actually transpired in the Japanese embassy in Washing-

Figure 3.1

TIMING OF DISPATCHES NOTIFYING THE UNITED STATES THAT DIPLOMATIC RELATIONS HAD BEEN SERVICED

	Time of Transmission by the Foreign Ministry	Time of Transmission by the Tokyo Central Telegraph Office	Kameyama's Estimated Times for Completion of Decoding	Reception and Processing in the Japanese Embassy in Washington	Times of Interception by the U.S.	Distribution of the Decoded Messages by the U.S.
Tōgō Dispatch No. 901 "Regarding the transmission of the memorandum to U.S"	2030, Dec. 6–0020, Dec. 7			Dec. 6, a.m.	0715, Dec. 6	1400, Dec. 6 (Department of the Navy)
Main text of the notification Parts 1–13		0150, Dec. 7	2130, Dec. 6	Arrived after 1200, Dec. 6. Decoding completed at 2300, Dec. 6; *clean copy not prepared.*	0803–1152, Dec. 6	Dec. 6: 2030 (Departments of the Army, Navy) 2130 (President)
Part 14	1600, Dec. 7	Dec. 7: 1700 (via Mackey) 1800 (via RCA)	1100, Dec. 7	Arrived *before 0900, Dec. 7; decoding not begun immediately. Decoded between 1000–1230;* clean copy prepared between 1100–1350	0305–0310, Dec. 7	Dec. 7: 0930 (Navy Department) 1000 (President)
Tōgō Dispatch No. 907 "Regarding the time designated for delivering the memorandum"	1730, Dec. 7	Dec. 7 1828 (via RCA) 1830 (via Mackey)		Decoding completed 1100, Dec. 7	0437, Dec. 7	1030, Dec. 7 (Department of the Navy) ˙
	Tokyo time	Tokyo time	Washington time	Washington time	Washington time	Washington time

ton; and the times of their interception and decoding by the United States.[321]

Let us focus chiefly on the question of why the Japanese embassy was derelict in its decoding and its preparation of clean copies, disregarding why the United States was so prompt in doing so. During the morning of the 6th, the embassy had received Tōgō's Dispatch No. 901, which stated:

1. With regard to the U.S. proposals of November 26, the government, as the result of exhaustive cabinet deliberations, has agreed on a memorandum (in English) to the United States.
2. Partly because the memorandum is lengthy, you will probably not receive it in its entirety until tomorrow. But because the present situation is extremely delicate, your having received it should be kept strictly confidential for the time being.
3. Although we shall send a separate follow-up telegram as to when to present the above memorandum to the United States, you will please refine the wording and complete all other advance preparations beforehand, so as to be able to deliver it to the United States whenever so directed once the separate telegram is received.[322]

Dispatch No. 904 subsequently instructed: "Though this really does not need mentioning, you are not under any circumstances to employ 'typists' or the like in preparing this memorandum."[323] Hence, to ensure that these very important instructions calling for extraordinary precautions were faithfully adhered to, the embassy staff had to be ready to decode each part of this lengthy notification as it was received, immediately preparing clean copies of each. To comply with the directive prohibiting the use of typists meant that the executive staff themselves would have to use English-language typewriters with which they were unfamiliar, because that was the only way it could be done.[324]

Each telegram was supposed to be decoded as it was received and a clean copy prepared; therefore, Telegraph Section Chief Kameyama naturally assumed that the entire text would be decoded and turned into clean copy almost simultaneously. But this is not what actually happened. Although the text up to Part 13 was delayed about one hour and a half beyond Kameyama's forecast, decoding had been completed by 11 p.m. on the 6th. But by the time that portion was submitted to the secretary's office by the intelligence and telegraph sections, Counselor Iguchi Sadao and the three secretaries—Okumura Katsuzō, Matsudaira Kōtō, and Terasaki Hidenari—had all gone out for the evening. As a result, not a single hand was turned that evening to preparing clean copies, let alone to putting the finishing touches on what had been decoded by the telegraph section. Moreover, in accordance with Iguchi's instructions for the evening, telegraph section personnel had gone home at dawn, leaving only one person on duty; arrangements for decoding were therefore severely reduced. When Sanematsu Yuzuru, the naval attaché, arrived at the embassy around 9 a.m. on the 7th, he discovered the office door mail box so crammed with incoming telegrams that the lid would not shut. He personally sorted the telegrams and took them into the office, but no one had yet arrived for work. Telegraph section personnel came in sometime after 9:30 and at 10 o'clock set to work on the decoding.[325] The three secretaries arrived shortly thereafter, but only Okumura sat down at a typewriter to put parts 1–13, which had been decoded the previous evening, into document form and then into clean copy. The telegraph section had finished decoding part 14, which had arrived that morning, and delivered it to the secretary's office at 12:30, but Okumura was still preparing a clean copy of parts 1–13 and did not complete a clean copy of the entire text, including Part 14, until 1:50.

In the meantime, Tōgō's Dispatch No. 907, specifying 1 o'clock for delivery of the notification, had been decoded by 11:00 a.m. and a 1 o'clock meeting with Hull was immediately arranged by telephone. But under the circumstances, at 12:30 a postponement to 1:45 had to be requested. In fact, Nomura and Kurusu did not arrive at the State Department until 2:05 and were then kept waiting in an anteroom until 2:20 when they finally met with Hull. The attack on Pearl Harbor had begun an hour earlier at 1:20 (7:50 a.m. Hawaii time), and Hull had been duly informed around 2:00: he had kept the two ambassadors waiting for an additional 15 minutes so that he could confirm it.[326] In the meeting that followed, Hull took the position that the United States had been attacked without prior notification, whereas the two ambassadors, who knew nothing at all about any attack, could only stand silently by and absorb Hull's self-righteous tirade: "In all my fifty years of public service I have never seen a document that was more crowded with infamous falsehoods and distortions—infamous falsehoods and distortions on a scale so huge that I never imagined until today that any Government on this planet was capable of uttering them."[327]

Competition for influence and recognition among the three embassy secretaries had been worrisome to all concerned Japanese residents at the time.[328] Because Minister Wakasugi Kaname and Counselor Iguchi exerted little control over them, the teamwork among the executive staff of the embassy had been extremely poor. When pressure mounted, it was standard Foreign Ministry operating procedure to have two or three embassy staff on night duty to decode telegrams; those of consequence would be circulated even in the dead of night. Tōgō and other officials had long been trained to follow such procedures.[329] How, then, could such unbelievable violations of instructions, indiscipline, and dereliction of duty occur at this critical juncture between peace and war? The lack of teamwork at fault here was corroborated by Nomura, who immediately complained that "they just won't do anything for you" whenever he visited his old haunts, the naval attachés' office.[330]

There was to be a margin of only 50 minutes between the delivery of notification and the commencement of the attack: the theoretical 30 minutes plus Itō's forecast of a 20-minute delay in carrying out the attack. On the pretext of military secrecy, however, Itō had divulged none of this to Tōgō, and he avoided consulting with Tōgō to arrive at a margin that was reasonable or adequate. Itō's secretiveness and self-righteousness, classically that of the "able-bureaucrat," undeniably contributed to the fiasco because it led him to a forecast that erred in the opposite direction: the attack actually took place 10 minutes earlier, and the margin was therefore shaved to a scant 20 minutes.

At the very instant that the assault was becoming a surprise attack as the result of blunders on the part of the United States, the surprise attack became a surprise attack without notification as the result of blunders on the part of Japan.

Roosevelt Tries to Provoke Japan Into Firing the First Shot

In the autumn of the previous year Roosevelt, in a speech during his campaign for a third term as president, repeatedly pledged that "we will not go to war unless we are attacked." Nonetheless, after his meeting at sea with Churchill in August 1941, he plunged rapidly into an undeclared war against the German navy, without notification either breaking off diplomatic relations or initiating war. This contradiction was exposed by the U.S.S. *Greer* incident in September and the U.S.S. *Kearny* incident in October. When Roosevelt explained that on each occasion the United States had been attacked, Congress initially countered with considerable skepticism and resistance.

It was under these circumstances that Secretary of War Stimson, the ringleader of the hard-liners within the cabinet, wrote in his diary on October 16: " . . . we face the delicate question of the diplomatic fencing to be done so as to be sure that Japan was put in the wrong and made the first bad move—overt move."[331] His intent was to improve the artifices of undeclared war and ensure that the first blow was struck *overtly* by Japan in the Pacific so that the kind of contradictions with U.S. public pledges that had been so blatantly exposed in the Atlantic would not occur. The entry in Stimson's diary for the 25th illustrates that Roosevelt too had adopted this stance. In his testimony after the war Stimson elaborated further: "In spite of the risk involved . . . in letting the Japanese fire the first shot, we realized that in order to have the full support of the American people it was desirable to make sure that the Japanese be the ones to do this so that there should remain no doubt in anyone's mind as to who were the aggressors."[332]

The day after the Hull Note was delivered, Major General Walter C. Short and officers under him in Hawaii were issued the following order: "If hostilities cannot be avoided the United States desires that Japan commit the first overt act Period."[333] This order, Marshall testified, "was a direct instruction from the President."[334] Brigadier General Leonard T. Gerow, chief of the War Plans Division, testified that Roosevelt "had definitely stated that he wanted Japan to commit the first overt act." Marshall even testified further that "governmental policy on our part [was to make] certain that the overt act should not be attributed to the United States, because of the state of the public mind at the time."[335]

Meanwhile, the Hull Note was delivered to the two ambassadors by the secretary of state, who was involved with these artifices. It can fairly be concluded that the Hull Note went beyond being simply an ultimatum; it included within it an intent to provoke Japan to strike the first blow.

Roosevelt's Stratagem

As December began there was still a clear disparity between the unanimous view of the cabinet and trends in Congress, the organs of public opinion, and the public itself. Even though an attack on Japan, even in Southeast Asia, would have violated his own campaign pledges, Roosevelt came forward with a positive offensive against Japan on December 1.

The day before, Lord Halifax, acting on orders from London, had made the following representations to the State Department:

There are important indications that Japan is about to attack Thailand and that this attack will include a sea-borne expedition to seize strategic points in the Kra isthmus. . . .

[British] Commander-in-Chief, Far East, has asked for permission to move into Kra isthmus, if air reconnaissance establishes the fact that escorted Japanese ships are approaching the coast of Thailand, and he asks for an immediate decision. . . .

It looks . . . as though, to ensure the defense of Singapore and for wider reasons, we might have to take the proposed action to forestall the Japanese.

Please make sure to get United States support for our plan.[336]

After a brief respite, Roosevelt returned to Washington on December 1 and met with Hull and Stark before noon; he then summoned Halifax in the afternoon. With Harry Hopkins at his side, Roosevelt told Halifax that in the event of a direct attack by Japan on British or Dutch possessions, "we should obviously all be together," and therefore that if Britain were to take action to defend the Kra isthmus following a Japanese attack on Thailand, Britain could anticipate aid from the United States, although that aid might not materialize for several days. Roosevelt further suggested that if Britain were to offer resistance to a Japanese attack against or infiltration of Thailand, Britain should make a public pledge to the Thai government that it would respect and guarantee the complete sovereignty and independence of Thailand into the future. And he stated that although the United States constitution would not allow the president to extend such a guarantee, Britain could count on assistance from the United States in its protection of Thailand.[337]

Going still further, Roosevelt desired clarification regarding "various unclear eventualities" such as:

1. What if Japanese troop reinforcements did not reach French Indochina?
2. What if Japanese troop reinforcements did reach French Indochina?
3. What if Japan invaded Thailand but did not attack the Kra isthmus?
4. What if Japan went no further than to demand concessions from Thailand of the kind that would be "dangerously detrimental to the general position"?

Roosevelt alluded to the positive intentions of the United States government and encouraged Britain to make clear its intentions as far as these eventualities were concerned. Summing up, Halifax reported that "he thought the United States would support whatever action we might take in any of these cases."[338]

At his meeting with Halifax on the evening of the 3rd, Roosevelt stated that United States support meant armed support and agreed with the British plan for lead operations in the Kra isthmus in the event that Japan attacked Thailand. Halifax reported that he was firmly convinced that Britain could rely on U.S. armed support in the event that Britain commenced such operations. Totally reassured, the British government instructed Halifax to express its very deep appreciation of Roosevelt's response, which was duly conveyed on the evening of the 4th.[339] As a result, the British government on the 5th informed each of the Dominion governments that:

> it had now received an assurance of armed support from the United States (a) if Britain found it necessary either to forestall a Japanese landing in the Kra Isthmus or to occupy part of the Isthmus as a counter to the Japanese violation of any other part of Thailand; (b) if the Japanese attacked the Netherlands East Indies and Britain at once went to the support of the Netherlands; (c) if the Japanese attacked British territory.[340]

British Air Chief Marshal Sir Robert Brooke-Popham, in command of the Royal Air Force and British Army Forces in Malaya, also received notification from the British War Department that "we have ... received assurance of American armed support" in such circumstances.[341]

Nomura had learned of these developments and on the 3rd reported: "Judging from all indications, we feel that some joint military action between Great Britain and the United States, with or without a declaration of war, is a definite certainty in the event of an occupation of Thailand."[342]

Churchill, who had a deep knowledge of the United States, shared his insights with Stanley Bruce, the Australian high commissioner in London: "American opinion would react favourably to a war which America had entered in defence of her own interests but would be inclined to be antagonistic to the idea of entering a war into which Britain had already entered and for the purpose of coming to the assistance of Britain."[343]

In order to resolve the contradiction between his pledge to Britain to enter a war against Japan and his campaign promise to the American people, Roosevelt apparently planned to pursue a stratagem that would make Japan fire the first overt shot. To this end a concrete plan was drafted to manufacture an incident *off the coast of French Indochina* that would cause Japan to fire on the Stars and Stripes and sink one or two U.S. warships. It appears that once he received Halifax's request on the 30th, Roosevelt had summoned Hull and Stark to refine the plan prior to his meeting with Halifax on the 1st. As a result, Stark sent the following orders to Admiral Thomas C. Hart, commander-in-chief of the Asiatic Fleet:

> President directs that the following be done as soon as possible and within two days if possible after receipt this despatch. Charter 3 small vessels to form a "defensive information patrol." Minimum require-ments to establish identity as U.S. men-of-war are command by a naval officer and to mount a small gun and 1 machine gun would suffice. Filipino crews may be employed with minimum number naval ratings to accomplish purpose which is to observe and report by radio Japanese movements in West China Sea and Gulf of Siam. One vessel to be stationed between Hainan and Hue one vessel off the Indo-China coast between Camranh Bay and Cape St. Jacques and one vessel off Pointe de Camau. Use of Isabel authorized by president as one of the three but not other naval vessels. Report measures taken to carry out presi-dents views.[344]

Stark then added the further order that "*Isabel* may be replaced by chartered vessels at your discretion."[345] The *Isabel* was a refurbished yacht that had been taken out of commission by the navy, an old vessel that was occasionally used by the chief of the Asiatic Fleet. The other two were to be small boats requisitioned locally. In reality, to create a "defensive information patrol" with such vessels was almost meaningless. Conditions at the time were such that the Asiatic Fleet was already obtaining ample information from frequent air patrols based in Manila. Nor had the navy promoted such a plan. Later Admiral Ingersoll testified that "Stark would not have done this un-less he had been told [by the president]."[346]

Stark had already sent a letter on July 28 to Commander-in-Chief of the Pacific Fleet Husband E. Kimmel, which stated that: "I very much suppose that we would follow a course of action [in the Pacific also] similar to the one we are now pursuing in the Atlantic as a [nominal] neutral."[347] The question may therefore be posed whether Roosevelt planned to deploy, this time right in the middle of the Pacific sea lanes used by Japan to convoy troops to the south, a "defensive information patrol," such as had already been used in the

Atlantic to touch off an undeclared war with Germany, in order to provoke Japan into firing the first overt shot.

But the three ships used were pathetic to the point of being useless, and U.S. combat capacity, as revealed in the *Greer* and *Kearney* incidents in the Atlantic, was so attenuated that if an overt attack did occur it would necessarily be a *unilateral* action on Japan's part. Yet Roosevelt's pledge to Halifax on the afternoon of the 1st was surely related to his anticipation that such a stratagem would succeed.

When at 9:30 p.m. on the 6th he received the first 13 parts of the decoded text of Japan's notification severing negotiations, Roosevelt remarked, "This means war." He ignored Hopkins's protest that "since war was undoubtedly going to come at the convenience of the Japanese, it was too bad that we could not strike the first blow and prevent any sort of surprise."[348] Despite having received the decoded text by 8:30 p.m., Hull, Stimson, and Knox did no more than make arrangements over the telephone to meet at 10 a.m. the following day. In short, the leaders of the U.S. government did nothing that night. Nor were any warnings wired to the front lines. Perhaps this had some connection with their anticipation that a stratagem of enticing Japan to fire first would bear fruit.

This unusual tranquility carried over into the following morning. Marshall went out for a canter, Stark strolled in his garden, and Roosevelt thought he would work on his stamp collection for the first time in a long spell. On the surface, U.S. government leaders appeared unconcerned. At 10 a.m. Roosevelt was handed the decoded text of Part 14, which concluded:

> Thus, the hope of the Imperial Government to adjust Japanese-American relations and to maintain and secure peace in the Pacific through cooperation with the Government of the United States has finally been lost. It is therefore with regret that the Imperial Government herewith notifies the Government of the United States that in view of the attitude of the Government of the United States it has no choice but to acknowledge that it is not possible to reach an accord even if negotiations were to continue hereafter.[349]

But Roosevelt merely said, "It looks like the Japanese are going to break off negotiations."[350] He telephoned no one during the remainder of the morning, and no one bothered to telephone him that morning, even after the meeting between Hull, Stimson, and Knox, which began at 10:30.

Marshall finally arrived at his office around 11:20, read the decoded text of Part 14, and after two discussions with Stark issued a warning to Hawaii after 12 noon, deliberately sending it via a commercial wire service. Marshall later testified that he avoided emergency measures at the time because he feared they would precipitate an overt act by the United States against Japan.[351]

Roosevelt Is Rescued from His Moral Predicament

Navy Secretary Knox was in a meeting with Stark and War Plans Director Richmond Kelly Turner when the first reports of the attack on Hawaii reached the Navy Department at 1:50 p.m. (8:20 a.m. Hawaii time). "My God, this can't be true," he cried out, "this must mean the Philippines."[352] He immediately informed Roosevelt, who reacted more calmly and remarked candidly to Hopkins: "if this action of Japan's were true it would take the matter entirely *out of his own hands*, because the Japanese *had made the decision for him*" (author's emphasis).[353]

A timely warning had not been sent to Hawaii in the expectation either that the stratagem would not succeed or that the stratagem would succeed off the coast of French Indochina. As a result, Japan's assault turned into a surprise attack, and the U.S. Pacific Fleet suddenly sustained "the greatest military . . . disaster in our Nation's history."[354] Whatever stratagem Roosevelt might have been planning, Japan had now gone forward on its own and made an overt attack.

This completely unforeseen act by the Japanese in one stroke not only freed Roosevelt from his campaign promise but also enabled him to dig himself out of the moral predicament between that campaign promise and his pledge to Britain, a dilemma he had found himself in since the start of December. More than anything else, a sense of relief would hold sway over Roosevelt from that day forward.

At 4 p.m., Hull, Stimson, Knox, Marshall, Stark, and Hopkins were summoned for a cabinet war conference. In his entry for that day, Hopkins wrote: "The conference met in not too tense an atmosphere because I think that *all of us believed that . . . sooner or later we were bound to be in the war* and that *Japan had given us an opportunity*" (author's emphasis).[355] After 10 p.m. Roosevelt summoned the leaders of both parties and told them, "Well, we were attacked. There is no question about that."[356] Newspaper reporters who met with him after midnight noted that Roosevelt "was completely relaxed," as if a great burden had at last been taken off his mind. And in a telephone conversation with Churchill that day, Roosevelt remarked, "They have attacked us at Pearl Harbour. We are all in the same boat now."[357] Here again one can perceive his sense of relief at being rescued from a moral predicament and allowed to carry out his pledge to Britain unimpeded. Some six weeks later, on January 24, Hopkins wrote:

> I recall . . . it always disturbed him because [Roosevelt] really thought that the tactics of the Japanese would be to avoid a conflict with us; that they would not attack either the Philippines or Hawaii but would move on Thailand, French Indochina. . . .
> . . . Hence his great relief at the method [of starting the war] that Japan used.[358]

But perhaps it was the observations of the only woman in his cabinet, Secretary of Labor Frances Perkins, that most touched what was in Roosevelt's heart. Perkins later recollected his appearance at the cabinet meeting held from 8:30 p.m. to 9:30 p.m.: "in spite of the terrible blow to his pride, to his faith in the Navy and its ships, and to his confidence in the American Intelligence Service . . . he had, nevertheless, a much calmer air. His *terrible moral problem had been resolved by the event*" (author's emphasis).[359]

At a press conference on December 2 Roosevelt had had to avoid responding when asked "if the Japanese marched into Thailand what would the United States . . . do?"[360] But now the moral predicament had been lifted from him at one stroke by the "irony of the situation."[361]

In his telegram of November 27 Nomura had carefully reported to Tokyo:

> In the event that we engage in some kind of independent action after the deadline but without having somehow wound up the present negotiations, there is the danger that the United States . . . will proclaim that we willfully commenced preplanned action despite the ongoing negotiations and will attempt to put the blame for rupturing the negotiations on us. In fact, as can be inferred from repeated instances of their having mentioned that negotiations had been suspended because of our occupation of French Indochina, if we were suddenly to engage in independent action without any indication of our intent to break off the current negotiations, there is the danger that this would be *used for counterpropaganda* in the above manner. Not only that. Careful consideration is needed because our honor as a Great Power is at stake as well. . . . I believe that the best policy might be for the government at its own discretion . . . to make clear in an appropriate way that the current negotiations are at an end. *Of course, it is desirable in that event*

that we make concurrent representations, your having informed us confidentially beforehand. (Author's emphasis)[362]

Influenced by this report, Tōgō decided to have the notification severing negotiations delivered in Washington. Once this decision was made, he took every precaution to ensure that the notification was transmitted at the appropriate time and that instructions were sent in advance by separate telegram detailing the arrangements for preparing and delivering the notification. Ironically, however, Nomura's intention was betrayed by his direct subordinates. Had he been able to deliver the notification at 1 p.m. as Tōgō had instructed, it would have been very difficult, technically speaking, for the United States to engage in propaganda about being attacked without notification. In any case, the shock of the surprise attack on Pearl Harbor and such propaganda instantly swept the American people up in a tidal wave of hostility. The indiscipline and dereliction of duty on the part of the embassy executive staff resulted in "one of the costliest mistakes ever committed by the Japanese government or its agents."[363]

On December 8 an imperial proclamation of war was issued by Japan, and on the same day the U.S. Congress sanctioned U.S. entry into the war. On May 22 Hitler had stated to Grand Admiral Erich Raeder:

It is unmistakable that the U.S. Government is disappointed about this cautious attitude on the part of Germany [in avoiding military clashes on the high seas], since one of the most important factors in preparing the American people for entry into the war is thus eliminated.[364]

As the result of such extreme patience on Hitler's part, Roosevelt continued to find it hard to manufacture a cause for going to war, a *casus belli,* in the Atlantic, despite his unprecedented and wholesale disregard for international law. It was in the Pacific that Roosevelt was presented with a dramatic cause for going to war amply sufficient to put before Congress and the American people.

The European war was essentially a British-German war, but Germany's march into the Soviet Union entangled Britain in that war as well. With war declared between Japan and the United States, the United States and Germany were also now at war; the war in Europe had literally become a world war. The struggle between Japan and the United States was only one phase of that world war, and its future course was bound to be fundamentally constrained by trends in the total war.

Appendixes

Appendix 1

The concluding sections to Parts I and II of Iwakuro Hideo's telegram of April 17, 1941, to army officials in Tokyo.*

I

...

As related above, the actual situation within U.S. circles is one of firm resolve. Upon further reflection, we can by no means simply conclude that the struggle for supremacy between Germany and Britain will result in German victory. Should Germany fail in its showdown with Britain, that would of course be the worst-case scenario, in which event it would avail the Empire if peace were quickly restored in the West and the Empire were left alone in the Far East. It is still conceivable that even if Germany succeeds in invading Britain in the near future, the "Anglo-Saxon" powers led by the United States will obstruct the Empire's path for a considerable length of time. If we compare the damage the Empire would sustain to that the United States would absorb over such a lengthy period, the outcome is simply not open to debate. Not only that; the Empire will be put in the most disadvantageous position possible, that of being plundered by third powers. In light of the above considerations I am convinced that the sure and right policy for the sake of the Empire's accomplishing its state policies is to take advantage of the United States for the time being. It is my judgment that now is not the opportune time to pursue those policies. Although there might be plans to deal with matters in light of the outcome of a showdown between Germany and Britain, it is hopeless to expect that they could succeed given the dangers I have mentioned before. This judgment of the situation is the unanimous view of our officials stationed here. Based on this judgment and under the leadership of the ambassador since early April, army, navy, and Foreign Ministry officials have been working in complete concert on a policy to resolve issues between Japan and the United States and, at the same time, have been sounding out the ideas of the ministers of state. The result of efforts to procure a concrete draft that has any possibility of being implemented is the rough draft, as reported in the cable to the Foreign Ministry (*quod vide*).

II

...

Clandestine maneuvers began in earnest from the evening of April 5. Because ground-breaking maneuvers by Ikawa had already achieved considerable progress, matters moved forward very smoothly. Having been able on the 8th to produce a first rough draft from an American draft in which our

TSM: Bekkan, p. 393.

demands had been largely incorporated, on the 9th the ambassador, in concert with army and navy officials, looked it over again, drew up a second rough draft, and sounded out American ideas on it [this sentence is a fabrication by Iwakuro]. Because at this juncture the American side appeared largely satisfied, we proposed to proceed to the discussion stage between the ambassador and Hull. At the first conversation between the ambassador and Hull on the 14th both disclosed that they knew about the clandestine maneuvers and began their discussions by immediately taking up the provisions of the second rough draft. Given the hour of the day they arranged to meet again and then parted (for details please see the Foreign Ministry cable). The second conversation between the ambassador and Hull took place on the 16th. Although the second rough draft, that reported in the cable to the Foreign Ministry, has been approved by Roosevelt and is quite authoritative, Hull did propose to Ambassador Nomura at their meeting on the 16th that he would first like to know the views of the government in Tokyo because the United States would be put in an untenable position if the draft were rejected by the Japanese government. It was confirmed that unless there were a great change in the situation the Japanese government would approve its main features with a declaration of intention within a day or two.

Appendix 2

"Opinion Regarding Ambassador Nomura's Proposal" (Meeting of bureau and division chiefs, army and navy ministries and general staffs, at the Naval Club [Suikōsha], April 21, 1941)*

What the United States plans to do by means of this draft proposal is to seize world leadership as well as complete its military preparations, calculating to change the direction of, and to rescue itself from the wretched state of the domestic and foreign policies it has implemented by taking advantage of the Empire's weaknesses, preventing our forceful advance to the south, and then augmenting its aid to Britain, thereby weakening the Axis alliance.

In response, the Empire should seize the opportunity to turn this American scheme to its own advantage. By adopting the gist of this draft proposal, the Empire should plan to bring the China Incident to a successful conclusion and restore and sustain its national strength. Furthermore, it is necessary to obtain for ourselves a major voice in the establishment of world peace. It is our desire to dispose of the matter at hand by giving consideration to the following items based on the above evaluation:

1. Allow no obstacles to stand in the way of achieving the aims of our holy war—that is, not to make it impossible to firmly establish the Greater East Asia Coprosperity Sphere, which is the goal of the current Sino-Japanese incident, and not to be indecisive about the Empire's just demands on China, both material and spiritual.
2. Allow nothing to damage international faith in the Empire—that is,

*TSM: Bekkan, pp. 408–409.

neither shall the good will created by the previously concluded Tripartite Alliance be violated, nor shall it be made easy for the United States to augment its aid to Britain or to participate in the war.

3. Allow no restraints to be put on the defense of the Empire—that is, in order for us to deal with future changes in the international situation as they concern the Pacific, no restraints are to be put on our freedom of national defense.

4. The Empire shall put its heart and soul into creating a lasting world peace in cooperation with the United States, first by establishing peace in the Pacific and then by directing its efforts to restoring peace in Europe.

Appendix 3

Matsuoka's telegram to Ōshima of June 9, 1941*

Although I imagine that this minister's resolve and manner of negotiating with regard to Japanese-U.S. negotiations are already all but fully known to Führer Hitler and Foreign Minister Ribbentrop, please convey immediately the following points to Foreign Minister Ribbentrop, however redundant they may be:

1. It is beyond a shadow of doubt that Roosevelt's true intentions are basically to bring about fissures in the Tripartite Pact and, by giving the American people the impression that Japan will on no account enter the war when the United States and Germany collide, to turn to such extreme measures as convoying.

2. It is equally beyond a shadow of doubt that by such measures he will try to get Germany to attack first, and by employing pettifogging techniques he will then insist that it was not the United States that started the war, thereby making it easy to obtain a declaration of war from Congress; at the same time, he will strongly try to impress on the American people that the United States, having been attacked, was inevitably put on the defensive and was acting solely for the sake of defense.

3. What this minister has believed from the very start is that Roosevelt resolved on participating in the war long before this. Today that is obvious. All he is doing at this point is thinking through the points raised in items 1) and 2) above; participation in the war is merely a matter of time.

4. Although it is conceivable that he may have abandoned his previous idea of extending patrols to Greenland, President Roosevelt may just have resolved on coming up with a plan to revoke or revise the neutrality law, begin shipping war materials in American vessels, and convoy them with American warships (namely, he might be giving some consideration to legalization in terms of public international law). When he sets about repealing or revising the neutrality law, that will be the time his resolve comes out in the open.

*JFM, *Keii,* pp. 108–110.

5. Based on the above observations and with firm determination, this minister will exert every effort to prevent any further onslaughts by the United States. While identifying completely with the thinking of both Germany and Italy on this point, however, I am deeply concerned over how long my efforts can in fact be effective. Compared to this, the idea of getting the United States out of China is of no more than secondary importance. Should there be any concern about an adjustment in Japanese-American relations that departs from the above two points, nothing could be further from the mind of this minister; on this point Führer Hitler and Foreign Minister Ribbentrop may rest assured.

Appendix 4

Essential points of the First Committee position paper, "The Position to Be Taken by the Imperial Navy under the Present Circumstances," of June 5, 1941*

...

Part One: Evaluation of the Situation

I. Basic terms for evaluating the situation.

1. Given the great fluctuations in the present world situation, every policy the Empire implements must ultimately be based on the national strength the Empire itself possesses; firmly establishing the footing that is absolutely indispensable for its self-preservation and self-defense must be the Empire's objective. The reason for the Empire's mapping out the means for self-preservation and self-defense is therewith to strengthen its own power and thereby avoid error in deciding on peace or war in response to fluctuations in the world situation.

2. The situations the Empire confronts are at the stage of "close contest," so to speak, and the time has arrived for us promptly to make clear our resolve on whether it is to be peace or war. Moreover, the Imperial Navy, and it alone, holds the ultimate key in deciding on war or peace. Therefore, the Imperial Navy must decide on its fundamental policies first of all by basing them on its own evaluation of the situation.

II. The state of affairs with regard to resources.

...

As for wartime requisites, especially matériel, the Empire will in large measure firmly establish the means for self-preservation in terms of armaments and expansion of production if supplies from Thailand, French Indochina, and the Dutch East Indies can be guaranteed. Therefore, it might be neces-

---

*JDA Archives. For the full text, with the exception of "Part Four: Evaluation of the Situation Regarding Resources," see *TSM: Bekkan*, pp. 427–440; that source gives no reason why "Part Four" was omitted—trans.

sary to guarantee supplies by using armed force against Thailand, French Indochina—and the Dutch East Indies should that be unavoidable for self-preservation. As things stand at present, acquisitions to the extent permitted under economic agreements currently in force are inadequate, and it is necessary to devise measures promptly for increasing the quantity of acquisitions within a setting of armed force.

...

III. An examination of strategic conditions in the Far East.

...

Although there are no signs as yet of military advances by Britain and the United States into Thailand and French Indochina, we will decide our course of action in French Indochina as we calculate the comparative strength of the Empire vis-à-vis that of Britain and the United States. But if the Empire does not come up in short order with a policy that has a real grasp of the situation, it is to be feared that in the face of an international crisis the Empire will be counterattacked, suddenly and unexpectedly. If we are indeed to establish an invincible position, we must first commit ourselves on French Indochina.

With regard to matters in Thailand, many areas are under British control as far as general trends in that country are concerned, although at least the regime in office is pro-Japanese. Therefore, if we do not go ahead and get the upper hand of Britain and the United States, we will not even be able to make forecasts on when sudden changes might occur. In short, if the Empire does not advance into Thailand and Indochina, the way will be paved in both areas for Britain and the United States to steal a march on us.

...

It is clear that trends in the Dutch East Indies today move in virtual unison with actions taken by Britain and the United States; we will not be able to achieve our economic demands by ordinary measures. What is worse, the current state of affairs in the Dutch East Indies shows signs of a movement toward a military alliance with Britain and the United States. What the Dutch East Indies most fears is the exercise of force by the Empire. Therefore, it would be very effective in terms of implementing the Empire's Dutch East Indies policy for the Empire to assume such a stance. From the above point of view it is of vital importance for the Empire to advance its military foothold in French Indochina and Thailand.

...

IV. An examination of the international situation.

1. At this juncture the general trends of the war in Europe are, militarily, for landing operations against Britain and for operations to close (cap-

ture) the Suez Canal, and, politically, for war to break out between the United States and Germany and for a decision to be made on peace or war between Germany and the Soviet Union.

While these four key factors are interconnected, what the Empire must be most concerned about in terms of deciding its course of action are the two trends involving landing operations against Britain and the outbreak of war between the United States and Germany. That is, landing operations against Britain will decide whether peace will be made or whether there will be a war of endurance; the outbreak of war between the United States and Germany will be the key factor in whether Japan participates in the war or not.

2. The opportunity to carry out landing operations against Britain will depend on four key factors: operations to close the Suez Canal, the outbreak of war between the United States and Germany, preparations for landing operations, plus the weather. [In the margins Oka (?) wrote: "And will also depend on how effective anti-blockade operations are"]. As things stand at present, because the weather and landing preparations can be judged virtually when it becomes appropriate to take action, the issue boils down to four questions: whether landing operations should be at the end of operations in the Suez area or whether they should be conducted in parallel with those operations, and whether to execute landings prior to the possible outbreak of war between the United States and Germany and prior to the United States' augmenting its actions in support of Britain (the implementation of all-out convoying, having American ships enter British seaports) or to do so after a state of war between the United States and Germany has developed.

Suez operations should occur after a compromise between Germany and the Soviet Union is reached; it is not necessary for the Empire to come up with a plan to deal with this immediately.

Therefore, the point that the Empire must be most concerned with is whether landings are carried out before the United States implements its policy of augmenting aid to Britain and/or before a state of war between the United States and Germany develops. In either case, if Britain is compelled to submit, that will give rise to circumstances in which peace is swiftly concluded or the British government moves to another territory. A war of endurance after the British government moves to another territory would be the most painful blow for the Empire; it is highly likely that joint attacks by Britain and the United States will be directed against the Far East, and the Empire will find itself in a position where it would have had to have established a firm foothold beforehand to counter them.

...

9. Trends in the United States. It is inevitable that the American position toward Germany will intensify in the direction of supporting Britain. The problematic issue here is whether the United States, even after Germany carries out landing operations against Britain (on the premise that these will surely succeed), will still concentrate all its strength in the

Atlantic region, or whether it will react by concentrating its main forces in the Pacific and Far East region. It is our judgment that as long as Britain does not submit and as long as the British government's place of exile remains in the western hemisphere, the chances are great that the United States will lean toward concentrating its main forces in the Atlantic, but if that is not the case then the chances are great that the United States will concentrate its main forces in the Pacific.

...

Part Two: Policies the Imperial Navy Should Adopt

I. Fundamentals.

Matters the Imperial Navy should consider fundamental in thinking about the various policies it should adopt under current conditions are as follows:

...

2. While making clear the limits that the Empire can put up with in terms of self-preservation and self-defense, we must make manifest our clear and firm resolve with regard to the exercise of armed force in the event those limits are exceeded, and we shall bring to completion all preparations accordingly. Note [a postscript by Ishikawa?]: If we vacillate and miss this opportunity, national strength will gradually decline; and when at long last we resolve to find a way out of our fatal situation, we will have already lost our power to make a comeback; when we try to rise up we will not be able to do so. Herein lies the necessity for making our resolve perfectly clear from this day forth.

...

II. Attitude on changes in the European situation.

1   The Empire is hopeful that Germany's efforts to reduce Britain will be protracted and that the United States will be deeply engrossed in Europe's problems.
To this end:
    1. It is absolutely essential to strengthen the Tripartite Axis.
    2. We should continue adjusting relations with the United States without losing patience and facilitate United States involvement in Europe. But the precondition for this is the suppression of domestic dissension and strife. Therefore, if we lack confidence in domestic countermeasures, efforts to adjust relations with the United State should be discontinued.

2. In the event that Germany does carry out landing operations against Britain, the Empire must set to work on countermeasures immediately thereafter.

...

If it is anticipated that the government will flee to another territory after landings:

1. We must secure such strategic positions as are necessary for self-defense, because it is inevitable that Britain and the United States will advance into the Far East—that is, will step up their pressure on Japan. In this case, securing both Thailand and French Indochina is a must; we must also make preparations to secure needed portions of the Dutch East Indies as well should that prove necessary.

2. As stated previously with regard to the China Incident, we shall take steps to block completely all actions by third countries in support of Chiang Kai-shek.

3. We need to devise measures to guarantee supplies of essential resources—politically and diplomatically of course, but militarily as well—in order to wage a greatly drawn-out war and to break away completely from dependence on Britain and the United States. The minimum territories necessary to do this are: all of Thailand, all of French Indochina, and the Dutch East Indies (Borneo, Celebes, New Guinea).

...

IV. Stance on the N-maneuvers [Draft Understanding between Japan and the United States].

1. We hope that the N-maneuvers will succeed on the condition that no restrictions are placed on the Empire's exercise of armed force in the south and on the condition that the United States is not permitted to intervene in peace negotiations with regard to terminating the China Incident. However, if the Empire rules out the issue of establishing peace between Japan and China, no absolute need for deliberately seeking an adjustment in relations with the United States is deemed to exist.

2. Should it be ascertained beforehand that Chiang Kai-shek will make demands for wholesale American guarantees regarding the conditions for peace between Japan and China, that will necessarily result in arguments between Japan and the United States over a Sino-Japanese peace. Because a war pitting Japan against the United States and China will inevitably arise in the near future as the result of collaboration between the United States and Chiang Kai-shek, the Empire must take strict precautions against this. The Empire should only request of the United States that Japan and China promptly suspend hostilities under an American guarantee.

3. Should N-maneuvers succeed, it is to be very much feared that as far as

the domestic situation is concerned there will be a precipitate return to dependence on Britain and the United States, enormously upsetting our building of a national defense state structure, our controlled economy policies, etc. Therefore, it is necessary to draft and have ready emergency legislation in advance. Severe countermeasures against reactionary political forces rearing up against the navy and army are of particularly crucial importance.

4. In the event that a state of war between the United States and Germany erupts even though N-maneuvers succeed, the Empire is released from its obligation to abide by those maneuvers.

・・・

VI. Resolve regarding the exercise of armed force.

The Imperial Navy must resolve without delay to exercise armed force in the following instances:

1. Should the United States (Britain) and Holland shut off oil supplies;
2. Should the Dutch East Indies, Thailand, and French Indochina place a total embargo on rubber, rice, tin, and/or nickel;
3. Should French Indochina and Thailand reject such military cooperation as the Empire deems necessary for self-defense;
4. Should military reinforcements in the Far East by the United States, Britain and Holland reach a strategically unacceptable level;
5. Should Britain and the United States impede the Empire's military operations after it invokes its right of belligerency against China;
6. Should Britain and the United States initiate military operations in Thailand.

VII. Conclusions.

1. It is necessary for the Imperial Navy, at this critical juncture in the Empire's destiny, to make clear immediately its resolve to go to war (including war against the United States) so as not to upset the Empire's implementation of its policies and to face up boldly to all countermeasures.

・・・

2. It is necessary not to lose any time in resolutely carrying out military advances in Thailand and French Indochina.
3. It is necessary to drive home in all quarters of the nation the Imperial Navy's evaluation of the situation (in terms of resources, strategies, and international conditions).

・・・

Attached Document [interim plan?]

・・・

Part Two: Domestic Conditions.

I. Latest trends in the army.

We have collated information from all concerned sections and the following points must be heeded by the navy:

•••

4. In regard to implementing policies toward the South Seas: We conclude in regard to the Japanese-American scheme that the army's bottom line is to put an absolute stop to any forceful moves into the south at this time. This is given expression in the following two kinds of thinking on its part:

   1. The top echelons of the navy—including the navy minister, chief of the Naval Affairs Bureau, chief and vice chief of the Navy General Staff—are resolved on opposing absolutely an advance into the South Seas under any circumstances (a total embargo on oil and other commodities or provocation by the United States), and the existence of such resolve has been confirmed by acts and utterances at meetings, etc., at the time the general principles for implementing policies in the South Seas were agreed upon and thereafter, right up to the present. Consequently, the argument by officials in the Navy Ministry and General Staff that preparations must be made is nothing more than hot air. Therefore, even though military forces had been readied for the South Seas should worse come to worst, now they are setting about the liquidation of these forces because they think that today such forces are completely useless.

   2. According to studies by the Cabinet Planning Board, the army itself, and others, it would be more than extremely difficult to enlarge the war front beyond what it is today; therefore, any and all advances into the South Seas should be called off.

•••

5. In regard to the N-maneuvers, and problems with the United States, the view of the Army Ministry and General Staff at first was that it was possible to separate Britain and the United States and that Britain and the United States were by no means united together in the Far East. Consequently, the argument for capturing Singapore was relatively fervent (primarily for the purpose of strategic collaboration with Germany). But just recently the army has adopted the navy's judgment of the situation and acknowledged that Britain and the United States are united; the army has also perceived that capturing Singapore would be extremely difficult and is pressing for the abandonment of an advance into the South Seas.

•••

II. General trends within the nation.

Among the general trends in such areas as politics, economics, etc., the following will affect our navy:

1. The effect of the maneuvers. N-maneuvers have already been leaked to the public and this gambit has been stirring up one wave after another within the country, with the result that the public will be ensnared by American trickery. However, the one point among the recently occurring phenomena of which the Imperial Navy must be mindful is the observation that, lacking confidence in its military preparations, the navy is itself taking the lead in making desperate efforts to adjust relations with the United States.

The point here is that in terms of the future expansion of military preparations the Imperial Navy must take every precaution against the emergence of the biased argument, arising from this observation, that it is inconceivable that the navy should forget its duty to demonstrate the utility of military preparations by becoming obsessed with political and diplomatic maneuvers outside its proper domain in order to acquire a massive military budget, declaring all the while that it is making firm preparations for war with the United States.

···

Part Three: Evaluation of the International Situation

···

II. At this juncture the general trends in the showdown between Germany and Britain are, militarily, for landing operations against Britain and for operations to close (capture) the Suez Canal, and, politically, for war to break out between the United States and Germany and for a decision to be made on peace or war between Germany and the Soviet Union.

Although the war to destroy commerce in the Atlantic and trends in France and the countries of the Near East will have their affect, they are not fundamental factors in determining the large picture. Operations to close the Suez Canal (by occupation or by bombing and mining) are not only possible but virtually inevitable. The more important factor that will decide how things go is the timing of operations to close the Suez Canal in relation to landing operations against Britain. Britain is making life-or-death efforts to induce the United States to join in the war; Germany is increasing the severity of its war to destroy commerce in the Atlantic and is, as reports indicate, completing preparations and stepping up actions for landing operations—and the weather is improving as well; Japan is taking positive steps to adjust Japanese-U.S.

relations; the Soviet Union is accepting German demands. All these factors combined make it highly likely that the schedule for landing operations against Britain will be moved up. If in particular Germany's landing forces are able to secure some air bases in portions of the British Isles, the Straits of Dover supply route will be made secure; interception by British naval power would become all but impossible— on the contrary, it is far more likely that such action would bring about the suicide of the British navy. . . . It is our judgment that as far as Germany's relations with the Soviet Union are concerned, reports indicate that the chances are slim that war will break out, given the Soviet Union's temporizing concessions.

...

Part Four: Evaluation of the Situation Regarding Resources.

...

XI. The problem of transport ships and shipping. Losses (rate of wartime losses) will be 20%; an example from the history of previous wars is the actual experience of Britain: 10% [figures provided by Fujii Shigeru of the Naval Affairs Bureau, Second Section?].

Part Five: The Positions and Countermeasures the Navy Should Adopt.

I. Resolve on peace or war. Given the current situation, the Imperial Navy must make clear its resolve to go to war (including war against the United States) and base all decisions about preparations to be made and positions to be taken on that policy.

...

II. We must make it our policy to limit the exercise of armed force (including military pressure) to Thailand and the Dutch East Indies. Should it prove unavoidable, we anticipate expanding the exercise of armed force into British possessions.

III. Regarding the fundamentals of foreign policy:

1. Although N-maneuvers are to continue, we must promote hard-line diplomacy, one having military force as its setting, toward Thailand, French Indochina and the Dutch East Indies as well as Britain, without regard for those maneuvers.

2. It is our intention to break off N-maneuvers as the occasion calls

for, depending on the progress of this hard-line diplomacy.

3. Should we meet with embargoes by the United States, embargoes by the Dutch East Indies, or resistance by Thailand and French Indochina, we shall immediately dispose of all diplomatic matters by resolving to invoke military force.

4. We must avoid implementing diplomatic policies such as would bring about a virtual abandonment of the Tripartite Alliance.

IV. Guiding those within the navy. We must press home the idea that war is inevitable.

V. Position toward those outside the navy.

...

2. Position toward the government and the army. We must induce them in the direction of resolving to go to war.

...

Appendix 5

Two sections of the "Desiderata Bearing on the Empire's Prosecution of War from the Standpoint of the Mobilization of Matériel," July 29, 1941, are as follows: *

1) Basic limitations on the Empire's prosecution of a war.

"If the Empire maintains its present productivity and the consumption of resources approximates in large measure that of the 1940 resource mobilization, we will be able to appreciate just how enormous imports still are today from outside our self-defense zone and our first supply zone [Thailand and French Indochina]. We must pay particular attention to the fact, moreover, that such imports all come from British and American spheres of influence. Because of this we must be prepared for the very grave results that will ensue should we incur a substantial, across-the-board rupture of economic relations with Britain and the United States. In such an eventuality, the Empire's . . . capacity to prosecute a war will rely primarily on the productivity of the self-defense and first supply zones and on existing stocks; thereafter it will chiefly depend on expanding new productivity by making use of the fruits of war. . . . Given such total wars as exist today, there is virtually no hope of final victory unless we stand ready from first to last for protracted war based on self-sustaining productivity [relying on stocks is not possible]. . . ."

---

*See TSM: *Bekkan*, p. 499. The full "Desiderata" are to be found in *ibid.*, pp. 498–500—trans.

2 Considerations on when to commence military operations and on their guidance.

"As far as the most important raw materials needed by the Empire are concerned, our inquiry into the time between acquiring the fruits of war and the securing of new production as that relates to existing stocks (excluding stocks directly held by the military) reveals that it will be necessary to acquire new production within the following periods of time for the following items:
Nickel and nickel ore, about 2 months;
Manganese ore, about 4 months;
Pitch coke, about 4 months;
Manila hemp, about 1 month;
First-grade crude oil, about 4 months;
Second-grade crude oil, about 6 months;
Aviation gasoline, about 15 months;
Ordinary gasoline, about 2½ months;
Heavy crude, about 1½ months;
Ordinary machine oil, about 2½ months;
Light fuel oil, about ⅓ of a month;
Kerosene, about 1 month;
Machine lubricants, about 3 months;
Castor oil, about 6 months
In other words, it is necessary, when and if Britain and the United States . . . rupture economic relations fully, that the conditions for newly acquiring such items be firmly established within the respective times stated from the time those items are embargoed. Consequently, in planning to acquire them by military force . . . operations must also be conducted with this firmly in mind."

Appendix 6

"Essentials for Carrying Out the Empire's Policies," adopted by the Imperial Conference of September 6, 1941.*
    In view of the critical situation at present, in particular the offensives that such nations as the United States, Britain and Holland are taking against Japan, the situation in the Soviet Union, and the resiliency of the Empire's national strength, we shall carry out the policies toward the south contained in the "Outline of National Policies in View of the Changing Situation" as follows:

1. To achieve self-preservation and self-defense, the Empire shall complete preparations for war by the approximate deadline of late October, based on the resolve not to flinch from war with the United States (Britain and Holland).
2. Concurrently, the Empire shall strive to obtain its demands by ex-

*TSM, 7:248–49; TSM: Bekkan, pp. 510–11.

hausting all possible diplomatic means vis-à-vis the United States and Britain.

The minimum objectives the Empire shall achieve in negotiations with the United States (Britain) and the limits on what the Empire can agree to therein are set forth in the Supplement.

3. In the event that by early October there is still no prospect of obtaining our demands through diplomatic negotiations, we shall immediately resolve to go to war with the United States (Britain, Holland).

Policies other than that toward the south shall be carried out in accordance with established national policies. In particular, every effort shall be made not to cause the United States and the Soviet Union to form a united front against Japan.

Supplement

Minimum objectives that the Empire shall achieve in negotiations with the United States (Britain) and the limits on what the Empire can agree to therein.

Part One: Minimum objectives that the Empire shall achieve in negotiations with the United States (Britain):

1. The United States and Britain shall not interfere with or obstruct the Empire's settlement of the China Incident.

    a) They shall not obstruct the Empire's plans to settle the Incident in conformance with the "Fundamental Treaty between Japan and China" and with the "Trinational Joint Declaration by Japan, Manchukuo, and China."

    b) They shall close the Burma Road, and they shall not provide military, political, or economic support to the Chiang regime.
    Note: The above shall not disturb the Empire's claims made heretofore in N-maneuvers regarding the settlement of the China Incident. In particular, we shall hold fast to the Empire's right to station troops under new arrangements between Japan and China. There is, however, no obstacle to affirming in principle that we are prepared to withdraw troops other than those dispatched to China to prosecute the China Incident pursuant to its resolution.
    There is no obstacle to affirming that American and British economic activities in China will not be restricted so long as they are conducted on an equitable basis.

2. The United States and Britain shall not engage in actions in the Far East that threaten the national defense of the Empire.

    a) They shall not acquire military rights or interests in Thailand, the Dutch East Indies, China, and the Soviet Far Eastern territories.

    b) They shall not expand or strengthen their military forces in the Far East beyond current levels.

Note: Demands to dissolve the special relation between Japan and French Indochina based on agreements between Japan and France shall not be countenanced.

3. The United States and Britain shall cooperate in the Empire's acquisition of required commodities.

a) They shall restore commerce with the Empire and shall also supply the Empire with commodities from their territories in the southwest Pacific that are critical to the Empire's self-preservation.
b) They shall contribute amicably to economic cooperation among the Empire, Thailand, and the Dutch East Indies.

Part Two: Limits on what the Empire can agree to. In the event that the Empire's demands indicated in Part One are met:

1. The Empire will not use French Indochina as a base to advance militarily into neighboring areas other than China.
Note: In the event that questions arise concerning the Empire's attitude toward the Soviet Union, we shall reply that there will be no cause for action on our part as long as the USSR observes the Soviet-Japanese Neutrality Pact and does not engage in actions that violate the spirit of that pact, such as menacing Japan and Manchukuo.
2. The Empire is prepared to withdraw troops from French Indochina after a just peace has been established in the Far East.
3. The Empire is prepared to guarantee the neutrality of the Philippines.

Addendum

Japanese and American attitudes toward the European war will be governed by conceptions of protection and self-defense. Japan's interpretation of the Tripartite Pact and actions pursuant thereto in the event that the United States enters the European war will be made with complete autonomy.

Note: The above in no way alters the Empire's obligations under the Tripartite Pact.

Appendix 7

Explanation attached to "On the turning point between politics and war and the moment for deciding on whether there are prospects for success in diplomatic negotiations," September 24, 1941*

I. Although this matter has already been settled by an Imperial Conference, we herewith express once again the views of the high command in hopes of troubling the government to give them the utmost regard, given that since that Imperial Conference diplomatic negotiations have not progressed as swiftly as anticipated and now, with scarcely

*Tomioka, "Taiheiyō sensō," 2:92–94.

any time remaining, operational requirements are becoming more and more pressing.

II. From the standpoint of war guidance, it is beyond dispute that the durability of the Empire's war resources and the resiliency of national strength attendant upon that durability will have the greatest effect on military operations. And it is also self-evident that one day's procrastination will produce operational disadvantages several times greater because of advances in war preparations against Japan and the like by nations under the leadership of the United States.

It is necessary to give particularly serious consideration to the obstacles posed by weather, which bear so greatly on operations. And in view of the northern question, it is absolutely essential that military operations in the South Seas be substantially completed during the winter season (by the middle of March). At this point we consider mid-November to be the latest allowable date for initiating military operations in the South Seas.

The above is the united view of the high commands, both army and navy.

III. From this standpoint, the high commands, both army and navy, have inaugurated operational preparations so as to be basically ready to commence hostilities in early November. As far as the army's operational preparations are concerned, those preparations considered essential are the provisional formation of units mobilized in the home islands and the transfer of forces now engaged in operations in Manchuria and China. These preparations will be activated in roughly two stages: before resolving to commence hostilities, and thereafter. The first stage was officially announced previously, and the troop transfers began on September 23; for the most part troops will arrive on station in south China and Taiwan between mid and late October. Insofar as possible, these measures have been designed so as not to provoke rival nations during the period scheduled for diplomatic negotiations nor to pose problems for those negotiations. The units to be activated next will form the main component in the preparation for military operations to follow; they will start being transferred from around October 15 and be strategically deployed throughout the region, including southern French Indochina. The movements of these units will of course be in accordance with imperial commands based on the resolution to commence hostilities.

As far as the navy's operational preparations are concerned, task forces will be readied by mid-October. The command to deploy them over an extensive area in order to commence military operations cannot be issued without a resolution to commence hostilities being finalized.

Thus the situation is such that we must resolve to commence hostilities in mid-October at the latest in order to start military operations in mid-November.

From what has been related above, and in light of overall war guidance along with considerations of operational guidance and operational preparations vis-à-vis the South Seas, we consider it crucial to decide on October 15 at the latest whether it will be politics or war. Diplomatic negotiations must be conducted with this requirement deeply in mind.

Appendix 8

Provisions regarding the United States in "The Empire's Foreign Policy toward Europe and the United States after Withdrawing from the League of Nations," April 1933*

1. Supposing that war were to break out now between Japan and the United States and even that our side were successful, it is clear that this alone would not be a mortal blow and cause them to surrender immediately. It would be difficult on our part to capture Hawaii or to mount an offensive against the United States proper. Therefore, other than achieving partial victories in the Far East there is essentially little to be gained by going outside the Far East. Not only that; it is to be greatly feared that as the inevitable result of doing so a war of endurance disadvantageous to us will unfold and that such a war will be protracted.

2. Moreover, given such international relations as exist at present, it is extremely difficult even to conceive of a war involving only the United States. It is difficult to foresee trends advantageous to us in the postures of such nations as France, to say nothing of Britain, in that eventuality, and it is to be greatly feared that if we do move this will provoke joint actions by these nations.

Appendix 9

"Essentials for Negotiations with the United States," attached to the "Essentials for Carrying Out the Empire's Policies," adopted by the Imperial Conference of November 5, 1941†

We shall seek a negotiated agreement with the United States, taking up negotiations as per Plan A or Plan B below, both of which moderate the language on important pending matters.

Plan A

The most important pending matters in negotiations between Japan and the United States are: 1) the stationing and withdrawal of troops in China and French Indochina; 2) nondiscriminatory trade in China; 3) interpretation and observance of the Tripartite Pact; and 4) the Four Principles. These matters are to be moderated to the following extent:

1) The stationing and withdrawal of troops in China.

Setting aside for the moment our reasons for stationing troops, we shall moderate our stance to the following extent, considering that the United

---

* Tōgō, *Jidai no ichimen,* pp. 65–66.

† The author's footnote containing plans A and B omitted 4) in Plan A and erroneously compounded language in both 3) and 4) in his 3) of Plan A. See *TSM: Bekkan,* p. 571. I have followed *TSM: Bekkan,* pp. 571–72, in translating this appendix—trans.

States has (a) attached great importance to the stationing of troops for an indeterminate period of time, (b) objected to the inclusion of this item in the terms for a peace settlement, and (c) called for a clearer expression of intent regarding the withdrawal of troops:

> Japanese forces dispatched to China because of the China Incident shall occupy designated areas of north China and Mongolia and Hainan island for as long as is necessary after peace is concluded between Japan and China. The evacuation of other forces shall commence the minute peace is concluded, in accordance with separate arrangements made between Japan and China, and shall be completed within two years.
> Note: Should the United States ask what "for as long as is necessary" means, we shall reply to the effect that our goal is roughly 25 years.

2) The stationing and withdrawal of troops in French Indochina.
The United States entertains misgivings that Japan has territorial ambitions in French Indochina and is attempting to make it into a base for military advances into adjacent territories. In recognition of this, we shall moderate our stance to the following extent:

> The Japanese government respects the territorial sovereignty of French Indochina. Japanese troops currently dispatched to French Indochina will be immediately evacuated upon the settlement of the China Incident or upon the establishment of a just peace in the Far East.

3) Nondiscriminatory treatment in trade with China.
In the event that there is no prospect of securing complete agreement to our previous proposal of September 25, we shall deal with this issue on the basis of the following proposal:

> The Japanese government acknowledges that the principle of nondiscrimination will be applied in the entire Pacific region and China as well, insofar as that principle is applied throughout the world.

4) Interpretation and observance of the Tripartite Pact.
We shall respond on this matter by making it even clearer that we have no intention of unduly broadening our interpretation of the right of self defense; that as far as interpreting and observing the Tripartite Pact is concerned, the Japanese government will act on its own discretion, as we have frequently elaborated before; and that we think that the United States already understands this fully.

5) As for what the United States calls its four principles, we shall avoid with all our might their inclusion in anything formally agreed to between Japan and the United States (whether that be the Draft Understanding or other declarations).

Plan B

1) Both Japan and the United States shall promise not to make any advances by military force into Southeast Asia and the South Pacific region, other than French Indochina.

2) The governments of Japan and the United States shall cooperate together so as to guarantee the procurement of necessary resources from the Dutch East Indies.

3) The governments of Japan and the United States shall together restore trade relations to what they were prior to the freezing of assets, and the United States will promise to supply Japan with the petroleum it needs.

4) The United States government shall not engage in such actions as may hinder efforts toward peace by Japan and China.

Notes

1) If it is necessary to do so, there is no objection to promising that if the present agreement is concluded, Japanese forces now stationed in southern Indochina are prepared, with the approval of the French government, to transfer to northern French Indochina, and that these Japanese forces will withdraw from French Indochina upon settlement of the China Incident or the establishment of a just peace in the Pacific region.

2) If it is also necessary to do so, additional insertions may be made to the provisions regarding nondiscriminatory treatment in trade and those regarding interpretation and observance of the Tripartite Pact in the existing proposals (last plans).

Notes

Introduction

1. The most recent English-language bibliography of Japanese scholarship on Japan's modern foreign relations up to the end of the Allied Occupation of Japan is Sadao Asada's *Japan and the World, 1853–1952: A Bibliographical Guide to Japanese Scholarship in Foreign Relations* (1989). The Introduction, chapter 1, and chapters 4–7 bear directly on the Pacific War and its background. The *Guide* cites articles, books, and documentary collections published up to 1986; an effort was made to include works published up to November 1987. Asada's volume supplements and updates James William Morley, ed., *Japan's Foreign Policy, 1868–1941: A Research Guide* (1974), which includes works in Japanese, English, and other western languages. A thoughtful and penetrating essay on Japanese scholarship of the 1930s and early 1940s on Japan's foreign relations between 1931 and 1941 is provided by Mitani Taichirō in *Pearl Harbor as History: Japanese-American Relations 1931–1941*, edited by Dorothy Borg and Shumpei Okamoto (1973), pp. 575–94. Saburō Ienaga's *The Pacific War: World War II and the Japanese, 1931–1945* (1978), a translation by Frank Baldwin of Ienaga's *Taiheiyō sensō* (1968), contains a pointed and critical examination of Japanese sources (pp. 247–56). A judicious "Bibliographical Essay" on both Japanese and English language studies is to be found in Akira Iriye's excellent study, *The Origins of the Second World War in Asia and the Pacific* (1987), pp. 187–90.

The most comprehensive and up-to-date bibliography of English language sources on the Pacific War is John J. Sbrega, *The War against Japan, 1941–1945: An Annotated Bibliography* (1989). Containing 5,259 references to articles, books, and documentary collections published up to December 31, 1987, Sbrega's bibliography includes very useful author and subject indexes.

Much has been published since 1987 on the Pearl Harbor attack. Japan bashing was in full swing in the mid- and late-1980s, and 1991 marked the fiftieth anniversary of the attack. It is beyond the scope of this introductory essay to evaluate all the studies that have appeared since 1987 that bear directly and indirectly on the Pearl Harbor attack, much less to deal with popular press coverage of the fiftieth anniversary in Japan and the United States. Reference to more recent scholarship will be made only as is deemed necessary in placing the volume translated here in a critical scholarly and historical context.

2. Asada, *Japan and the World*, p. 224.

3. *Ibid.*, p. 225.

4. See volume two of the series of selected translations from *Taiheiyō sensō e no michi*, given the covering title in English *Japan's Road to the Pacific War*: James William Morley, ed., *The China Quagmire: Japan's Expansion on the Asian Continent, 1933–1941*, pp. 233–86.

5. James William Morley, ed., *The Fateful Choice: Japan's Advance into Southeast Asia, 1939–1941*, pp. 156–57. The Burma Road, opened in the fall of 1938 and accounting for another 31 percent of supplies to China, was closed for a period after July 1940. *Ibid.*, pp. 156–58.

6. *Ibid.*, pp. 287–95.

7. Morley, *China Quagmire*, pp. 237, 262–67.

8. Asada, *Japan and the World*, p. 225.

9. For comprehensive studies that give more pessimistic evaluations of the chances for avoiding the Pacific war than does Tsunoda, see Michael A. Barnhart, *Japan Prepares for Total War: The Search for Economic Security, 1919–1941* and Stephen E. Pelz, *Race to Pearl Harbor: The Failure of the Second London Naval Conference and the Onset of World War II*.

10. Ienaga, *The Pacific War*, p. 253. Ienaga toned down his criticism in the second edition of his book (1986). While arguing that the positive attitude toward the war taken by Kamikawa Hikomatsu and Tsunoda Jun plagued the series and posed serious problems in historical interpretation, Ienaga pointed out that the series was enormously useful if used as a resource collection. And he added that using the series as a "hostile witness" gave more persuasive power to his argument than using works by authors who shared his thinking. Ienaga Saburō, *Taiheiyō sensō: daini han* (The Pacific War: Second Edition), p. 417.

11. Morley, *Japan Erupts;* Morley, *China Quagmire*.

12. Morley, *Japan Erupts*, pp. 148–52.

13. *Ibid.*, p. 166.

14. *Ibid.*, p. 146. Utsunomiya was born in 1861.

15. *Ibid.*, p. 143. Born in 1889, Ishiwara died on August 15, 1949.

16. Ienaga, *The Pacific War*, p. 20.

17. *Ibid.*, pp. 22–23.

18. Asada, *Japan and the World*, p. 52; Ienaga, *The Pacific War, passim;* Borg and Okamoto, *Pearl Harbor as History*, pp. 459–549.

19. Ienaga, *The Pacific War*, p. 29.

20. Pelz, *Race to Pearl Harbor*, Chs. 3–4.

21. Borg and Okamoto, *Pearl Harbor as History*, p. 323.

22. *Ibid.*, p. 338.

23. *Ibid.*, pp. 459–486.

24. *Ibid.*, p. 480.

25. For a decisive analysis of how unproductive America's tough stance was see Chihiro Hosoya, "Miscalculations in Deterrent Policy: Japanese-U.S. Relations, 1938–1941," pp. 97–115, and his "Characteristics of the Foreign Policy Decision-Making System in Japan," pp. 353–69.

26. In "Going to War: Who Delayed the Final Note?" Hata Ikuhiko has taken exception to the argument that Japan's embassy staff was derelict. The way the notification breaking off negotiations was sent and the content of the notification itself were such that the embassy staff could hardly have known the urgency of the notification. Hata points out that the crucial 14th part concluding the lengthy notification

... ended with the weak assertion: "The Japanese Government regrets to notify hereby the American Government that in view of the attitude of the American Government it cannot but consider that it is impossible to reach an agreement through further negotiations."

The note clearly is not a declaration of war, and it does not contain language warning of independent Japanese action. Drafted originally in English—not Japanese—to avert any mistranslation before it was handed over, it conveys on the surface only a decision to break off negotiations. (p. 57)

27. This is not the place to discuss the "conspiracy" theories of revisionists who argue that President Roosevelt knew of the Pearl Harbor attack plan beforehand. I am indebted to Joe Devlin for an A.N.E. video tape that presents the case that Roosevelt could not help but have known. Nor is this the place to discuss conspiracy theories claiming that Roosevelt maneuvered Japan into "firing the first" shot, which Tsunoda endorses with his usual ambiguity (pp. 578–92). Roosevelt and other key leaders *could* have known about the imminent attack on Pearl Harbor, but the enormous amount of "noise" about Japanese movements coming into Washington from all quarters made such certain knowledge all but impossible. Japan was moving south, and an attack on Singapore, Malaya, the Philippines, and/or the Dutch East Indies seemed the most likely. As Tsunoda notes, when the attack on Pearl Harbor occurred, Navy Secretary Frank Knox exclaimed, "My God, this can't be true, this must mean the Philippines" (p. 588).

28. See my *Palace and Politics in Prewar Japan*, pp. 171–82. For a judicious and penetrating discussion of the institutional constraints on the emperor as well as the constraints imposed upon the emperor by himself and Kido, see Stephen S. Large's excellent study, *Emperor Hirohito and Shōwa Japan: A Political Biography*, particularly Chs. 4–5.

29. U.S. Department of State, *Papers Relating to the Foreign Relations of the United States: Japan, 1931–141*, 2:656–61.

30. *Ibid.*, pp. 768–70.

31. Borg and Okamoto, *Pearl Harbor as History*, p. 516.

32. *Ibid.*, p. 580.

33. *Ibid.*, p. 581.

34. Chihiro Hosoya, "Twenty-Five Years after Pearl Harbor: A New Look at Japan's Decision for War," p. 58. For an enlightening analysis of the thought and behavior of Japan's army leaders in 1940–41, see Hatano Sumio, *Bakuryō-tachi no Shinjuwan* (The Army Leadership's Pearl Harbor).

35. Titus, *Palace and Politics*, pp. 156–70, 252–55, 264–65.

36. Asada, *Japan and the World*, p. 325.

37. Edward S. Miller, *War Plan ORANGE*, pp. 1–8, 19–30.

38. *Kodansha Encyclopedia of Japan*, 7:174; Sakai Saburō, *Shōwa Kenkyūkai: aru chishikijin shūdan no kiseki* (The Shōwa Kenkyūkai: A Gathering of Men of Knowledge), pp. 177–82, 378, 381; Muroga Sadanobu, *Shōwa Juku: danatsu no arashi no naka demo, jiyū no akari o mamori tsuzuketa hitotsu no juku ga atta* (Amidst the Storm of Oppression There Was One School That Preserved the Light of Freedom: The Shōwa Juku).

39. "Shōwa Tennō no dokuhaku hachijikan" (The Shōwa Emperor's Eight-Hour Soliloquy), p. 100.

40. Iriye, *Origins*, p. 2.

41. John W. Dower, *War without Mercy: Race and Power in the Pacific War*, p. 148.

42. Barnhart, *Japan Prepares*, p. 17.

43. Akira Iriye, "The Failure of Economic Expansion: 1918–1931," p. 237.

44. *Ibid.*, p. 238.
45. *Ibid.*, p. 239.
46. *Ibid.*, pp. 241–43.
47. Pelz, *Race to Pearl Harbor*, p. 1.
48. Dower, *War without Mercy*, p. 298.
49. Leslie Connors, *The Emperor's Adviser: Saionji Kinmochi and Pre-War Japanese Politics*, p. 9.
50. Harada Kumao, *Saionji kō to seikyoku* (Prince Saionji and the Political Situation), 1:17–18.
51. Pelz, *Race to Pearl Harbor*, p. 74.
52. Borg and Okamoto, *Pearl Harbor as History*, p. 244.
53. Pelz, *Race to Pearl Harbor*, p. 178.
54. Iriye, *Origins*, p. 90.
55. Barnhart, *Japan Prepares*, p. 106.

1. Confusion Arising from a Draft Understanding

1. *Encylopaedia Britannica* (1959), 16: 304.
2. U.S., Department of State, *Foreign Relations of the United States: Diplomatic Papers, 1940* (hereafter cited as *FR, 1940*), 4: 598.
3. William L. Langer and S. Everett Gleason, *The Undeclared War, 1940–1941*, p. 7.
4. *FR, 1940*, 4: 171.
5. Joseph C. Grew, *Turbulent Era: A Diplomatic Record of Forty Years, 1904–1945*, 2: 1231.
6. According to the State Department, it was drafted by Hornbeck's assistant Alger Hiss on January 16 and sent to Roosevelt for signature on the 19th. Langer and Gleason, however, say that it was "drafted by Hornbeck," and this is evidently the author's authority. U.S., Department of State, *Foreign Relations of the United States: Diplomatic Papers, 1941* (hereafter cited as *FR, 1941*), 4: 6, n. 15; Langer and Gleason, *Undeclared War*, p. 320, n. 73–trans.
7. *FR, 1940*, 4: 469.
8. Langer and Gleason, *Undeclared War*, p. 320.
9. *FR, 1941*, 4: 7–8.
10. *FR, 1940*, 4: 121.
11. *Ibid.*, p. 160.
12. *Ibid.*, p. 369.
13. *Ibid.*, p. 168.
14. William L. Langer and S. Everett Gleason, *The Challenge to Isolation, 1937–1940*, p. 579.
15. Robert E. Sherwood, *Roosevelt and Hopkins: An Intimate History*, p. 405.
16. *FR, 1941*, 4: 151.
17. *FR, 1941*, 5: 77.
18. U.S., Department of State, *Papers Relating to the Foreign Relations of the United States: Japan, 1931–1941* (hereafter cited as *FR, Japan*), 1: 880.
19. *Ibid.*, 2: 227.
20. Langer and Gleason, *Undeclared War*, p. 298.
21. *Ibid.*, p. 44.

22. U.S., Department of State, *Peace and War: U.S. Foreign Policy, 1931–1941*, pp. 603, 604, 601—trans.

23. *Tōkyō Asahi shimbun* (evening edition), December 19, 1940; *FR, Japan*, 2: 125.

24. *Tōkyō Asahi shimbun*, January 21, 1941. For the *Tokyo Gazette* translation of this quote, see S. Shepard Jones & Denys P. Myers, eds., *Documents on American Foreign Relations*, 3: 266. The author has misquoted the source, mistaking "mid-Pacific" for "mid-Atlantic," and I have made the correction accordingly—trans.

25. *Tōkyō Asahi shimbun*, January 27, 1941.

26. Japan, Foreign Ministry (hereafter cited as JFM), *Nihon gaikō nempyō narabi ni shuyō bunsho* (Chronology and Major Documents of Japanese Foreign Relations), 2: 478–79.

27. JFM, *Nichi-Bei kōshō shiryō: Kiroku no bu* (Source Materials on Japanese—American Negotiations: Documents Volume) (hereafter cited as JFM, *Kiroku*), p. 3.

28. JFM Archives; Hata Shunroku, *Hata Shunroku nikki* (The Diary of Hata Shunroku), p. 286.

29. U.S., Department of State, *Documents on German Foreign Policy, Series D (1937–45)* (hereafter cited as *DGFP*), 12: 456.

30. Japan, National Defense Agency, Military History Office Archives (hereafter cited as JDA Archives); Sanbō Honbu (Army General Staff), comp., *Sugiyama memo* (The Sugiyama Memoranda), 1:174.

31. Interview with Ōshima Hiroshi, March 10, 1962.

32. Nihon Kokusai Seiji Gakkai, Taiheiyō Sensō Gen'in Kenkyūbu (Japan Association on International Relations, Study Group on the Causes of the Pacific War), ed., *Taiheiyō sensō e no michi: Bekkan shiryō hen* (The Road to the Pacific War: Supplementary Volume of Documents) (hereafter cited as *TSM: Bekkan*), p. 363.

33. Ibid., p. 384.

34. *FR, 1941*, 4: 924.

35. *DGFP*, 12: 407–409.

36. *FR, 1941*, 4: 933.

37. *Tōkyō Asahi shimbun* (evening edition), December 19, 1940; *FR, Japan*, 2: 125.

38. Saitō Yoshie affidavit, Exhibit 3143, in *Kyokutō Kokusai Gunji Saiban Kōhan Kiroku* (Records of the International Military Tribunal for the Far East), in Japan, Justice Ministry (hereafter cited as JJM), War Crimes Materials Office (hereafter cited as IMTFE Records); Saitō Yoshie, *Azamukareta rekishi: Matsuoka to Sangoku Dōmei no rimen* (History Deceived: The Inside Story of Matsuoka and the Tripartite Pact), p. 30.

39. Ōhashi Chūichi letter to Kiyose Ichirō, dated October 12, 1946.

40. Interview with Matsuoka Kin'ichirō, April 30, 1962. The eldest son of Matsuoka Yōsuke, Matsuoka Kin'ichirō was a former executive vice president of Asahi Television—trans.

41. *FR, 1941*, 4: 113.

42. Ibid., p. 922.

43. Ibid., p. 933–34.

44. Ibid., p. 937.
45. Telegram of May 10, 1941, in JFM, *Kiroku,* p. 45.
46. JFM Archives. Roy Howard was a well known journalist and a personal friend of Matsuoka—trans.
47. Kase Toshikazu shuki (Kase Toshikazu Memoir).
48. Fukai Eigo, *Sūmitsuin jūyō giji oboegaki* (Notes on Important Sessions of the Privy Council), p. 142.
49. Harada Kumao, *Saionji kō to seikyoku* (Prince Saionji and the Political Situation), 8: 330.
50. Ibid., p. 378.
51. Ibid., p. 363.
52. Nomura Kichisaburō, *Beikoku ni tsukai shite: Nichi-Bei kōshō no kaiko* (Ambassador to the United States: Reminiscences of the Japanese-American Negotiations), p. 13.
53. JJM Archives.
54. Harada, *Saionji kō,* 8: 378.
55. Kiba Kōsuke, ed., *Nomura Kichisaburō,* p. 421.
56. Nomura, *Beikoku,* p. 17.
57. Ibid., pp. 12–13.
58. Ibid., pp. 15–17.
59. Ibid., pp. 19–21.
60. Harada, *Saionji kō,* 8: 388.
61. Nomura, *Beikoku,* p. 17.
62. JDA Archives.
63. *FR, 1941,* 4: 332.
64. Nomura, *Beikoku,* p. 185.
65. JJM Archives.
66. Interview with Shiba Katsuo, March 25, 1961.
67. Kichisaburo Nomura, "Stepping Stones to War," *U.S. Naval Institute Proceedings,* September 1951, p. 929.
68. Kiba, *Nomura,* p. 422.
69. Yamamoto Isoroku letter to Shimada Shigetarō, dated December 10, 1940, in Imperial Navy records and documents.
70. Kiba, *Nomura,* p. 422.
71. Joseph C. Grew, *Ten Years in Japan,* p. 357.
72. *TSM: Bekkan,* pp. 394–95.
73. Ibid., p. 395.
74. Ibid., p. 423. For the full text of the "Working Analysis," see R.J.C. Butow, *The John Doe Associates: Backdoor Diplomacy for Peace, 1941,* pp. 323–33—trans.
75. JDA Archives.
76. *FR, 1941,* 4: 123.
77. *FR, Japan,* 2: 333; *FR, 1941,* 4: 135–36, 154–55.
78. Interview with Takagi Sōkichi, April 4, 1962.
79. Walsh affidavit, Exhibit 3143, IMTFE Records.
80. Telegram of July 11, 1941, in JFM, *Kiroku,* p. 97.
81. *TSM: Bekkan,* p. 403–404.
82. JFM Archives.

83. Walsh affidavit, IMTFE Records, Langer and Gleason, *Undeclared War*, p. 321.

84. *FR, 1941*, 4: 14–16.

85. Ibid., 4: 17–18.

86. Ibid., pp. 51–52.

87. Ibid., p. 52.

88. JFM Archives.

89. *FR, 1941*, 4: 54.

90. Ibid., pp. 63–64.

91. Ibid., p. 69.

92. Ibid., pp. 73–74.

93. Ibid., pp. 95–96.

94. Ibid., pp. 96–97.

95. Ibid., pp. 100, 106, 101–102, 101, 16, 102, 107—trans.

96. Ibid., p. 96.

97. *TSM: Bekkan*, p. 389.

98. *FR, 1941*, 4: 63, 69–70, 74, 97.

99. Ibid., pp. 63, 70.

100. Ibid., p. 116.

101. JFM Archives.

102. Ibid.

103. Ibid.

104. JDA Archives; Morishima Morito, *Shinjuwan, Risubon, Tōkyō: zoku ichi gaikōkan no kaisō* (Pearl Harbor, Lisbon, Tokyo: A Diplomat's Memoirs, Continued), p. 61.

105. JDA Archives.

106. *FR, 1941*, 4: 53.

107. JDA Archives.

108. *FR, 1941*, 4: 70.

109. Ibid., p. 116.

110. Ibid., p. 53.

111. Langer and Gleason, *Undeclared War*, p. 468.

112. *FR, 1941*, 4: 111–12.

113. Original in quotes was in English—trans.

114. *TSM: Bekkan*, p. 404.

115. JDA Archives.

116. *FR, 1941*, 4: 119.

117. Ibid., p. 135.

118. *FR, Japan*, 2: 398–402. Quotations were taken by the author from this source as well as from *FR, 1941*, 4: 106, 101—trans.

119. *FR, 1941*, 4: 132–34.

120. *TSM: Bekkan*, p. 408.

121. JDA Archives.

122. Interview with Iwakuro Hideo, February 4, 1961.

123. JDA Archives.

124. JFM, *Kiroku*, pp. 9–10.

125. *TSM: Bekkan*, pp. 392–94; for the omitted portions of Parts I and II of this telegram see Appendix 1.

126. Nomura, *Beikoku*, p. 26.

127. *DGFP*, 12: 154.

128. Interview with Sanematsu Yuzuru, May 7, 1961. Sanematsu graduated from the Japanese naval academy in 1923 and was posted as naval attaché to Washington in September 1940; he returned to Japan in August 1942—trans.

129. JFM, *Kiroku*, p. 24.

130. Ibid., pp. 30–31.

131. JDA Archives.

132. Iwakuro interview.

133. *TSM: Bekkan*, p. 412.

134. Telegram No. 277, May 8, 1941.

135. *FR, 1941*, 4: 122.

136. Ibid., pp. 124–25.

137. Ibid., p. 142.

138. Langer and Gleason, *Undeclared War*, p. 493.

139. *FR, 1941*, 4: 55.

140. Ibid., pp. 62–63.

141. Ibid., p. 142.

142. Ibid., pp. 152–53.

143. *FR, Japan*, 2: 389.

144. *FR, 1941*, 4: 76.

145. *FR, Japan*, 2: 407, 409.

146. Ibid., pp. 406–10.

147. JFM Archives.

148. JFM, *Kiroku*, p. 44.

149. JDA Archives.

150. *TSM: Bekkan*, p. 477.

151. JFM, *Kiroku*, p. 40.

152. *TSM: Bekkan*, p. 422–23 (The proposal Iwakuro refers to was the one modified by American counterproposals of May 31). The numbering is the author's—trans.

153. Ibid., p. 584.

154. Sanematsu interview.

155. Interview with Nishiura Susumu, August 22, 1962. A 1921 graduate of the Japanese army academy, Nishiura became a member of the Military Section, Military Affairs Bureau, in March 1937; in October 1941 he was appointed secretary to the army minister—trans.

156. Satō Kenryō, *Tōjō Hideki to Taiheiyō sensō* (Tōjō Hideki and the Pacific War), pp. 171–75.

157. JDA Archives.

158. Ibid.

159. Ibid.

160. *TSM: Bekkan*, p. 390. Item 7 was omitted by the author. The Konoe Declaration referred to in item 3 was issued January 16, 1938, and stated in effect that Japan would no longer deal with the Nationalist government of Chiang Kai-shek. See Tōkyō Daigaku Bungakubu, Kokushi Kenkyūshitsu (Tokyo University Faculty of Letters, Japanese History Office), *Nihon kindaishi jiten* (Dictionary of Modern Japanese History), pp. 205–206—trans.

161. JDA Archives.
162. Ibid.
163. Ibid.
164. Ibid.
165. *TSM: Bekkan*, pp. 408–409.
166. *FR, 1941*, 4: 958.
167. Interview with Shiba Katsuo, April 8, 1961.
168. Ibid.
169. Interview with Onoda Sutejirō, October 14, 1961. Onoda graduated from the Japanese naval academy in 1920. In 1940 he was a member of the First Division, Navy General Staff, after serving briefly as an adjutant in the Navy Ministry—trans.
170. JJM Archives.
171. Interview with Inoue Shigeyoshi, November 8, 1961.
172. Ibid., and Shiba interview.
173. Nomura, *Beikoku*, p. 52.
174. JDA Archives.
175. Tomita Kenji, *Haisen Nihon no uchigawa: Konoe kō no omoide* (Inside Defeated Japan: Recollections of Prince Konoe), p. 130.
176. *Tōkyō Asahi shimbun*, April 12, 1941.
177. Papers of Konoe Fumimaro.
178. Ibid.
179. JFM, *Kiroku*, pp. 27–28.
180. Kido Kōichi, *Kido Kōichi nikki* (Diary of Kido Kōichi) (hereafter cited as *Kido nikki*), 2: 870.
181. Interview with Ōhashi Chūichi, September 30, 1961.
182. Tomita, *Haisen Nihon*, p. 135.
183. Ōhashi Chūichi, *Taiheiyō sensō yuraiki* (Origins of the Pacific War), pp. 110–17; Saitō, *Azamukareta rekishi*, pp. 177, 217.
184. *FR, 1941*, 4: 127.
185. Iwakuro interview.
186. *DGFP*, 11: 907.
187. Ibid., 12: 391–92.
188. Ibid., pp. 456–57.
189. *FR, 1941*, 5: 152.
190. *Kido nikki*, entry of June 30, 1941, 2: 886–87.
191. Ōhashi interview.
192. JDA Archives.
193. Ibid.
194. Ibid. A slightly different version appears in *TSM: Bekkan*, p. 421—trans.
195. Ibid., p. 457.
196. JDA Archives.
197. *TSM: Bekkan*, p. 414. The quotation has been slightly altered by the author—trans.
198. Ibid., p. 416.
199. Ibid., pp. 414–15.
200. JFM Archives.
201. *DGFP*, 12: 724.

202. JFM, *Kiroku*, p. 32.

203. Nomura, *Beikoku*, p. 53.

204. JFM, *Kiroku*, pp. 33–37.

205. Yabe Teiji, ed., *Konoe Fumimaro*, 2: 269. See also *FR, Japan*, 2: 412—trans.

206. JFM, *Nichi-Bei kōshō shiryo: Keii no bu* (Source Materials on Japanese-American Negotiations: History Volume), (hereafter cited as JFM, *Keii*), p. 37.

207. JFM, *Kiroku*, pp. 58–59.

208. Ibid., p. 59.

209. Matsuoka to Nomura, May 15, 1941, Ibid., p. 60.

210. *FR, Japan*, 2: 145–46; *FR, 1941*, 4: 235.

211. *FR, 1941*, 4: 238.

212. Konoe papers. On May 4 Otto Tolischus wrote that Matsuoka "told Walter Duranty in an interview that if America became involved in hostilities with Germany, Japan would feel bound in loyalty and honor to fight against the United States, and that this would apply even to patrol-boat clashes." Otto D. Tolischus, *Tokyo Record*, p. 115. Walter Duranty (1884–1957) was a prominent correspondent with the *New York Times* until 1940. See S.J. Taylor, *Stalin's Apologist: Walter Duranty, The New York Time's Man in Moscow*—trans.

213. JFM, *Kiroku*, pp. 47–57. See *FR, Japan*, 2: 420–25, for the English version of the revised draft and Japanese comments on it—trans.

214. Nomura, *Beikoku*, p. 53.

215. JFM, *Kiroku*, p. 105.

216. Ibid., p. 26.

217. *TSM: Bekkan*, p. 475. See also *FR, Japan*, 2: 425—trans.

218. *TSM: Bekkan*, pp. 388–89.

219. JDA Archives.

220. Ibid.

221. JFM, *Kiroku*, pp. 37–39.

222. Konoe papers.

223. *DGFP*, 12: 724.

224. Ibid., p. 749–50.

225. Ibid., p. 755.

226. *TSM: Bekkan*, p. 415–16.

227. JFM, *Keii*, p. 40.

228. Konoe papers.

229. JFM Archives? Citation missing—trans.

230. JFM, *Kiroku*, pp. 46–47. See *DGFP*, 12: 777–80 for a more elaborate English version—trans.

231. JDA Archives.

232. JFM, *Kiroku*, p. 3.

233. JFM, *Keii*, pp. 99–100.

234. Japan, Army General Staff, War Guidance Office, "*Daihon'ei Kimitsu sensō nisshi*" (Confidential War Diary of the Imperial Headquarters), in JDA Archives (hereafter cited as AGS, "Kimitsu nisshi").

235. Ibid., dated May 12, 1941.

236. Ibid.

237. Ibid.

238. Konoe Fumimaro, *Heiwa e no doryoku: Konoe Fumimaro shuki* (My Struggle for Peace: The Memoirs of Konoe Fumimaro), p. 50.

239. Ibid., p. 55.

240. Nomura, *Beikoku*, p. 49.

241. JFM, *Kiroku*, p. 44.

242. Konoe papers.

243. *FR, Japan*, 2: 434.

244. Nomura, *Beikoku*, p. 59.

245. *FR, Japan*, 2: 441.

246. Ibid., p. 361.

247. *FR, 1941*, 4: 228–32.

248. Ibid., p. 194.

249. Ibid., p. 214.

250. Ibid., p. 162.

251. Ibid., p. 213.

252. Ibid., p. 263.

253. Langer and Gleason, *Undeclared War*, p. 493.

254. June 6, in *FR, Japan*, 2: 466.

255. Ibid., p. 417.

256. Nomura, *Beikoku*, p. 55.

257. *FR, Japan*, 2: 413.

258. Ibid., p. 418.

259. Ibid., p. 440.

260. Ibid., pp. 416–17.

261. Ibid., p. 434.

262. Ibid., P. 455.

263. Ibid., p. 413.

264. Ibid., p. 454.

265. Nomura, *Beikoku*, p. 60; JDA Archives.

266. Nomura, *Beikoku*, p. 60.

267. Ibid., p. 63.

268. Konoe papers.

269. JFM, *Kiroku*, p. 39.

270. Ibid., p. 42.

271. *FR, Japan*, 2: 332.

272. *FR, 1941*, 4: 210.

273. *DGFP*, 12: 661.

274. *FR, 1941*, 4: 198, 209.

275. Ibid., p. 200.

276. Herbert Feis, *The Road to Pearl Harbor: The Coming of the War between the United States and Japan*, pp. 203–204.

277. JFM, *Kiroku*, pp. 87–91. See also *FR, Japan*, 2: 485–86, from which the English translation is taken—trans.

278. Ibid., p. 484.

279. Ibid., p. 493.

280. *FR, 1941*, 4: 263.

281. Konoe, *Heiwa e no doryoku*, p. 61.

282. JFM, *Nihon gaikō nempyō*, 2: 522. See also *DGFP*, 12: 820–21, 847—trans.

283. JFM, *Nihon gaikō nempyō*, pp. 523–26.

284. JFM, *Kiroku*, p. 45.

285. JDA Archives.

286. JFM, *Keii*, pp. 108–10; see Appendix 3.

287. Konoe, *Heiwa e no doryoku*, pp. 54–55.

288. *DGFP*, 12: 724.

289. Ibid., p. 809.

290. Ibid., p. 848.

291. JDA Archives.

292. Ibid. There is no record of a Liaison Conference being held on June 22—trans.

2. Leaning Toward War

1. Harada, *Saionji kō*, 8:161, 126. The author has slightly altered the original source here—trans.

2. Ogata Taketora, *Ichi gunjin no shōgai: Kaisō no Yonai Mitsumasa* (The Life of a Military Man: Reminiscences of Yonai Mitsumasa), p. 219.

3. Letter from Yamamoto Isoroku to Koga Mineichi, dated January 23, 1941, Imperial Navy Records. Given the date of this letter, it is presumed that Yamamoto was giving Koga a record of the positions he had taken from late 1940 to the time the letter was written—trans.

4. Ibid.

5. Ibid.

6. Letter from Yamamoto Isoroku to Hori Teikichi, dated February 6, 1941, Imperial Navy Records.

7. JJM Archives.

8. Interview with Fukudome Shigeru, August 12, 1961.

9. JJM Archives.

10. *Kido nikki*, 2: 895.

11. JJM Archives.

12. Konoe papers.

13. Onoda interview.

14. Interview with Takada Toshitane, December 5, 1961.

15. The First Committee was one of three ad hoc committees set up in November 1940 on the recommendation of Takada Toshitane. All three were staffed by personnel from both the Navy General Staff and the Navy Ministry. The first dealt with policy, the second with military preparations, the third with public opinion. The First Committee was of particular importance and was comprised of four officers: Takada Toshitane, First Section chief in the Naval Affairs Bureau; Ishikawa Shingo, Second Section chief in this same bureau; Ōno Takeji, chief of the War Guidance Office in the Navy General Staff; and Tomioka Sadatoshi, Operations Section chief, Navy General Staff. See James William Morley, ed., *The Fateful Choice: Japan's Advance into Southeast Asia, 1939–1941*, pp. 281–82; and Nihon Kindai Shiryō

Kenkyūkai (Modern Japanese History Archival Research Society), comp., *Nihon rikukaigun no seido-soshiki-jinji* (The Institutions, Organization, and Personnel of the Japanese Army and Navy), pp. 84–85, 103, 106, 231 (hereafter cited as *Nihon rikukaigun*)—trans.

16. *TSM: Bekkan*, p. 497.

17. With the exception of Hashimoto Shōzō, chief of the Armaments Bureau's Fleet Mobilization Section in the Navy Ministry, and Kurihara Etsuzō, chief of the Mobilization Section in the Navy General Staff, the membership of the Second Committee overlapped that of the First Committee.

18. Ibid., pp. 427–40 (see Appendix 4).

19. Shiba interview.

20. Fukudome interview.

21. Interview with Miyo Kazunari, December 10, 1961. A 1923 graduate of the Japanese army academy, Miyo Kazunari (Tatsukichi) served at staff headquarters for the 3rd Air Force then became First Section chief, First Division, Navy General Staff in October 1939—trans.

22. Shiba, Onoda, and Takada interviews.

23. Tomioka Sadatoshi "Taiheiyō sensō Nihon kaigun senshi" (The Japanese Navy in the Pacific War), 2:30.

24. Takada interview.

25. JJM Archives.

26. JDA Archives.

27. Fukudome interview.

28. Onoda interview.

29. JDA Archives; Itō Takashi and Nomura Minoru, eds., *Kaigun taishō Kobayashi Seizō oboegaki* (The Memoranda of Admiral Kobayashi Seizō), p. 102.

30. JDA Archives; Sanbō Honbu, *Sugiyama memo*, 1:220.

31. Letter from Yamamoto Isoroku to Shimada Shigetarō, December 10, 1940, Imperial Navy Records.

32. Interview with Inoue Shigeyoshi, November 5, 1961.

33. Ibid.

34. *TSM: Bekkan*, p. 388.

35. Nomura, *Beikoku*, p. 49.

36. Stephen W. Roskill, *White Ensign: The British Navy at War, 1939–1945*, pp. 90–94. In using this citation Tsunoda mistook "escort vessels *not yet equipped* with sonar and radar" for "vessels *equipped* with sonar and radar," and the text has been corrected accordingly—trans.

37. "Ishii Akiho taisa kaisōroku" (Memoirs of Colonel Ishii Akiho), in JDA Archives (hereafter cited as Ishii memoirs).

38. Ibid.

39. JDA Archives.

40. Ibid.

41. Ibid.

42. Ibid.

43. Ibid.

44. Ibid.

45. Ibid.

46. AGS, "Kimitsu nisshi."
47. Ibid.
48. *TSM: Bekkan*, pp. 386–87.
49. JDA Archives.
50. AGS, "Kimitsu nisshi."
51. *TSM: Bekkan*, pp. 424, 426.
52. AGS, "Kimitsu nisshi."
53. Ishii memoirs.
54. AGS, "Kimitsu nisshi."
55. Konoe papers.
56. Kōseishō Engokyoku (Welfare Ministry, Relief Bureau), ed., "Kaisen made no kokusaku no keii, shūsen kettei no keii oyobi kaigun daijin kōtetsu kankei bunsho" (Documents Pertaining to State Policymaking up to the Beginning of the War, How It Was Decided to End the War, and Replacing the Navy Minister), in JDA Archives (hereafter cited as "Kaisen made no kokusaku."
57. Shiba interview.
58. AGS, "Kimitsu nisshi."
59. JDA Archives.
60. *TSM: Bekkan*, p. 467. For a slightly different English version, see Nobutake Ike, *Japan's Decision for War: Records of the 1941 Policy Conferences*, pp. 78–79—trans.
61. *TSM: Bekkan*, pp. 464–66; Sanbō Honbu, *Sugiyama Memo*, 1:256–59.
62. "Yōhei jikō ni kansuru jōbunsho (sono ichi)" (Report to the Throne on Tactical Matters—Part 1), in JDA Archives.
63. AGS, "Kimitsu nisshi."
64. Ibid.
65. Ibid.
66. Ibid.
67. Interview with Tanaka Shin'ichi, January 30, 1960.
68. AGS, "Kimitsu nisshi."
69. Interview with Satō Kenryō, March 26, 1960.
70. Satō, *Tōjō*, pp. 189–90.
71. AGS, "Kimitsu nisshi."
72. JDA Archives. Material in parentheses is in the original document as cited by the author, but no mention is made of who sent this report to whom—trans.
73. Interview with Ōshima Hiroshi, February 7, 1960.
74. Asahi Shimbunsha (Asahi News), ed., *Kindai Nihon no gaikō* (The Diplomacy of Modern Japan), p. 77.
75. *FR, 1941*, 4:933.
76. Fukai, *Sūmitsuin*, p. 148.
77. Ōshima interview; Interview with Yokoi Tadao, July 8, 1961.
78. Ōshima interview.
79. Asahi, *Kindai Nihon no gaikō*, p. 76.
80. Ōhashi interview.
81. *DGFP*, 12:536–37.

82. Shidehara Heiwa Zaidan (Shidehara Peace Foundation), ed., *Shidehara Kijūrō*, pp. 517–19.

83. *DGFP*, 12:536.

84. Ōhashi interview.

85. *Tōkyō Asahi shimbun*, April 23, 1941.

86. *Kido nikki*, 2:879.

87. *TSM: Bekkan*, p. 445; Sanbō Honbu, *Sugiyama memo*, 1:226.

88. *TSM: Bekkan*, p. 458.

89. Konoe, *Heiwa e no doryoku*, p. 58.

90. *DGFP*, 12:725.

91. Exhibit 795, IMTFE Records.

92. Exhibit 793, Ibid.

93. *FR, 1941*, 4:996.

94. Fukai, *Sūmitsuin*, p. 149.

95. Yabe, *Konoe*, 2:270.

96. JDA Archives.

97. AGS, "Kimitsu nisshi."

98. Interview with Doi Akio, January 20, 1962.

99. *TSM: Bekkan*, p. 460; Sanbō Honbu, *Sugiyama memo*, 1:249.

100. Interview with Nakanishi Toshinori (Toshikazu), June 27, 1962. Born in 1894, Nakanishi graduated from Tokyo Imperial University (law) in 1918 and immediately joined the South Manchuria Railway. He became a director in 1936, leaving the SMR in 1940 to join the foreign Ministry. He accompanied Foreign Minister Matsuoka to Germany and the USSR in 1941—trans.

101. JDA Archives; Sanbō Honbu, *Sugiyama memo*, 1:221, 244, 246, 249.

102. *TSM: Bekkan*, p. 444; Sanbō Honbu, *Sugiyama memo*, 1: 223.

103. *TSM: Bekkan*, pp. 457–458; Sanbō Honbu, *Sugiyama memo*, 1:244.

104. *DGFP*, 12:420.

105. *TSM: Bekkan*, p. 457; Sanbō Honbu, *Sugiyama memo*, 1:244.

106. JDA Archives; Sanbō Honbu, *Sugiyama memo*, 1:248–49.

107. *FR, 1941*, 4:989.

108. Ishii memoirs.

109. Konoe papers.

110. Fukai, *Sūmitsuin*, p. 204. Itō Nobufumi was head of the Cabinet Information Bureau. With "faultless French" and "faultless English" (Tolischus, *Tokyo Record*, p. 58), he frequently hosted foreign correspondents and diplomats at gala parties in 1941, seeking to allay fears about "Japan's real intentions" (Ibid., p. 174)—trans.

111. JDA Archives.

112. *Kido nikki*, 2:883.

113. Nomura, *Beikoku*, p. 120.

114. JFM, *Keii*, p. 112.

115. Konoe papers.

116. Nomura, *Beikoku*, p. 185.

117. *Kido nikki*, 2:884.

118. *FR, Japan*, 2:503.

119. Ibid., p. 504.

120. Ibid., p. 510.

121. Ibid., p. 513. On July 7 the U.S. government had announced its intention to station forces in Iceland, which was within Germany's maritime defense zone.

122. JFM, *Keii*, pp. 133–36.

123. JFM, *Kiroku*, p. 98.

124. *TSM: Bekkan*, p. 472; Sanbō Honbu, *Sugiyama memo*, 1:269.

125. JFM, *Keii*, pp. 141–42.

126. JDA Archives. *TSM: Bekkan* relies on this same source for its record of the July 12 Liaison Conference (pp. 472–74), and these exact words by Matsuoka are cited (p. 474) as a response to Navy Minister Oikawa, not Sugiyama. According to the *TSM: Bekkan* record, both the navy's Oikawa and the army's Sugiyama fought with Matsuoka over "room for negotiation" during the July 12 Liaison Conference—trans.

127. *TSM: Bekkan*, pp. 471–72.

128. Tōgō Shigenori, *Jidai no ichimen* (One View of an Era), p. 152.

129. JFM, *Kiroku*, pp. 100–102; Sanbō Honbu, *Sugiyama memo*, 1:101.

130. *TSM: Bekkan*. p. 476.

131. Ibid., p. 475.

132. Konoe, *Heiwa e no doryoku*, p. 67.

133. These words do not appear in the June 20 entry cited by Tsunoda (*Kido nikki*, 2:883), which reads: "Prince Konoe came over at 5:50. He talked confidentially about various problems, such as having difficulty in grasping the foreign minister's views, just as the international situation was becoming tense over rumors of war between Germany and the Soviet Union, etc. He said it might even come to the point of holding the cabinet responsible, but I stated that such an issue as holding the cabinet responsible was not at stake. . . ."—trans.

134. Kido Kōichi affidavit, Exhibit 3340, IMTFE Records. To "assume responsibility" in this context meant for Konoe and his cabinet to resign—trans.

135. *Kido nikki*, 2:890.

136. Tomita, *Haisen Nihon*, p. 60.

137. Shiba interview, April 8, 1961.

138. *TSM: Bekkan*, pp. 480–81. See also Ike, *Japan's Decision for War*, pp. 105–106. The author leaves out the names of Tatekawa, ambassador to the USSR, Nomura, ambassador to the United States, and Horikiri Zenbei, ambassador to Italy, who were also sent special word by Toyoda "to carry on as before." The omission is not unimportant, because all four ambassadors were taking somewhat different courses, and "carry on as before" meant that they could and would continue to do so—trans.

139. JFM Archives.

140. Ibid.

141. JDA Archives. As quoted, this fragment lacks context. Apparently, the complaint by the Army General Staff here is that the army was not fully consulted when the third Konoe cabinet was formed, and therefore the army

could not exercise a "voice" in its composition and policies. At this time in Japan's history, "voice" amounted to a veto power—trans.

142. Ibid.

143. *TSM: Bekkan*, p. 482.

144. Konoe papers.

145. Ibid.

146. JDA Archives; Sanbō Honbu, *Sugiyama memo*, 1:285.

147. JDA Archives.

148. Ibid.

149. Heinz Guderian, *Panzer Leader*, translated from the German by Constantine Fitzgibbon, pp. 188–190.

150. JDA Archives.

151. Ishii memoirs.

152. Tanaka Shin'ichi, *Taisen totsu'nyū no shinsō* (The Truth about the Plunge into the Pacific War), p. 35.

153. *TSM: Bekkan*, pp. 487–88.

154. JDA Archives; Sanbō Honbu, *Sugiyama memo*, 1:288–89.

155. *TSM: Bekkan*, p. 488.

156. JFM, *Kiroku*, pp. 144–48. For the English version handed to the secretary of state by Ambassador Nomura on August 6, one that varies from the text here translated, see *FR, Japan*, 2:549–50—trans.

157. There were two Imperial Guard divisions in 1941. Although the author indicates "Imperial Guard Division(s) it was apparently only the 2nd that was mobilized into the 25th Army. The 25th Army was formed on June 26, 1941. See *Nihon rikukaigun*, pp. 402, 403—trans.

158. JFM, *Nihon gaikō nempyō*, 2:532.

159. *TSM: Bekkan*, p. 500 (see also Appendix 5).

160. Konoe papers. For a rearranged version of this citation see *TSM: Bekkan*, p. 504—trans.

161. JJM Archives; "Kaisen made no kokusaku."

162. *TSM: Bekkan*, p. 474; Sanbō Honbu, *Sugiyama memo*, 1:272.

163. Tanaka, *Taisen*, p. 87; JDA Archives. For a slightly different version, see *TSM: Bekkan*, p. 481—trans.

164. JDA Archives; Itō and Nomura, *Kaigun taishō Kobayashi*, pp. 92–93. In the sentence before this quote the author wrote that Nagano had advocated war with the United States "even before . . . a total embargo by the United States (the 26th Japan time)." The embargo was ordered on August 2, not July 26, Japan time. Japanese assets were frozen on the 26th, and I have changed the text accordingly. The same applies to the sentence following the quote—trans.

165. *Kido nikki*, 2:895–96.

166. *FR, 1941*, 5:223.

167. Higashikuni Naruhiko, *Ichi kōzoku no sensō nikki* (The War Diary of One Member of the Imperial Family), p. 71.

168. Tanaka, *Taisen*, p. 65. Sugiyama was using a baseball metaphor here—trans.

169. JFM, *Kiroku*, pp. 123–24.

170. JDA Archives.
171. Ibid.
172. Doi and Satō interviews.
173. JDA Archives.
174. "Tanaka Shin'ichi chūjō gyōmu nisshi "(The On-Duty Diary of Lieutenant General Tanaka Shin'ichi), in JDA Archives (hereafter cited as Tanaka diary).
175. JDA Archives.
176. Ibid.
177. Ibid.
178. Ibid.
179. Ibid. Attending the meeting were the services' Operations Section chiefs, high-ranking officers of those sections, and the chiefs of the army and navy War Guidance offices.
180. Ibid.
181. Ibid.
182. Ibid.
183. Ibid.
184. Ibid.
185. Interview with Kawai Iwao, May 13, 1961. A 1919 graduate of the Japanese naval academy, Kawai served at staff headquarters, 2nd Fleet, in 1936; in 1940 he was a member of staff, 4th Fleet—trans.
186. JDA Archives; Sanbō Honbu, Sugiyama memo, 1:378. For a slightly different version see TSM: Bekkan, p. 553—trans.
187. JDA Archives; Itō and Nomura, Kaigun taishō Kobayashi, pp. 95–100.
188. Ibid. The inadequacy of the navy's preparations was pointed out by naval air chief Inoue Shigeyoshi and ship procurement chief Toyoda Soemu.
189. Ibid.
190. Ibid.
191. Ibid. At this time Yamamoto was commander of the Combined Fleet. Prior to this he had been vice navy minister—trans.
192. See Appendix 6 for a translation of the "Essentials," which the author had placed in the text—trans.
193. JDA Archives. For the full text of this document, see TSM: Bekkan, pp. 517–23. For an English translation of the Bekkan text, which varies somewhat from my translation of the portions cited by the author, see Ike, Japan's Decision for War, pp. 152–63—trans.
194. Fukudome interview.
195. JDA Archives; Sanbō Honbu, Sugiyama memo, 1:322.
196. Hattori Takushirō, Dai Tōa sensō zenshi (A History of the Greater East Asia War), 1:177.
197. Kido nikki, 2:905; Kido Kōichi affidavit, Exhibit 3340, IMTFE Records.
198. JDA Archives.
199. Ibid. For a slightly different version see TSM: Bekkan, pp. 509–10—trans.
200. JDA Archives; Sanbō Honbu, Sugiyama memo, 1:311. It is interesting that the official record of this conference, as given in TSM: Bekkan, pp. 508–

23, simply notes that "at the conclusion there were special words from His Majesty. (They are contained in the Record of Imperial Questions [omitted].)"—trans.

201. *Kido nikki*, 2:905.
202. Ibid., 2:901. The author left out the chief of the Navy General Staff, whom I duly restored as in the source cited—trans.
203. Ibid., 2:905.
204. Satō, *Tōjō*, p. 206.
205. Ishii memoirs.
206. Yabe, *Konoe*, 2:363.
207. Suzuki Teiichi affidavit, Exhibit 3605, IMTFE Records.
208. JDA Archives.
209. Kido Nikki Kenkyūkai, ed., *Kido Kōichi kankei bunsho* (Documents concerning Kido Kōichi), p. 483 (hereafter cited as *Kido bunsho*). The original source cited by the author, Kido's diary entry for October 17, 1941 (Kido, 2:917), does not contain this statement. It is included in a copy of the transcript of the meeting Kido obtained from the Board of Chamberlains Internal Records Division in 1946 for the purposes of the trials. *Kido bunsho*, p. 488—trans.
210. AGS, "Kimitsu nisshi."
211. *FR, 1941*, 4:355.
212. Konoe, *Heiwa e do doryoku*, pp. 72–74.
213. Tanaka, *Taisen*, p. 93.
214. Satō, *Tōjō*, p. 202.
215. JDA Archives; Konoe Fumimaro, *Ushinawareshi seiji* (The Politics That Failed), p. 105.
216. Satō, *Tōjō*, p. 199.
217. JFM, *Kiroku*, pp. 149–50.
218. Ibid., p. 162.
219. Ibid.
220. *FR, Japan*, 2:547–48.
221. JFM, *Kiroku*, pp. 148–49.
222. *FR, 1941*, 1:346.
223. Langer and Gleason, *Undeclared War*, p. 659.
224. JFM, *Kiroku*, pp. 152–53.
225. Winston S. Churchill, *The Grand Alliance*, p. 593.
226. Paul Hasluck, *The Government and the People, 1939–1941*, p. 534.
227. Langer and Gleason, *Undeclared War*, p. 696, citing the Stimson diary entry of August 19.
228. *FR, 1941*, 4:410, citing Hull's August 30 conversation with British Chargé d'Affaires Ronald Campbell.
229. JFM, *Kiroku*, pp. 172–80. This section has been slightly altered to conform with *FR, Japan*, 2:556–59, which contains the texts of an "Oral Statement" and a "Statement" handed to Nomura that day. The *FR* text of the "Statement" has been used as the translation of the Japanese source cited by the author—trans.
230. JFM, *Kiroku*, pp. 167–68.
231. Nomura, *Beikoku*, p. 96.

232. Langer and Gleason, *Undeclared War*, p. 697.

233. JFM, *Kiroku*, pp. 197–98.

234. Ibid., p. 209.

235. Ibid., p. 211.

236. *FR, Japan*, 2:572.

237. Nomura dispatch of the 28th, JFM, *Kiroku*, p. 213.

238. Ibid., pp. 214–15.

239. Langer and Gleason, *Undeclared War*, p. 697.

240. *FR, Japan*, 2:565, 602–603; *FR, 1941*, 4:382–83. In the passages from the August 18 dispatch the author quotes parts of two separate sentences as if they were one sentence—trans.

241. *FR, 1941*, 4:399, 414, 419, 427–28.

242. Ibid., p. 420.

243. Nomura dispatch of September 3, JFM, *Kiroku*, pp. 232–33.

244. Ibid., p. 242. For the English version of this passage, see *FR, Japan*, 2:591—trans.

245. Nomura, *Beikoku*, p. 71.

246. JFM, *Kiroku*, p. 149.

247. Ibid., p. 151.

248. Ibid., pp. 152–53.

249. Ibid., p. 157.

250. Ibid., pp. 180–82.

251. Nomura, *Beikoku*, pp. 188–89.

252. Ibid., p. 80.

253. Ibid., pp. 81–82.

254. JFM, *Kiroku*, p. 181.

255. *FR, Japan*, 2:604–606; Grew, *Turbulent Era*, 2:1329.

256. *FR, 1941*, 4:487. A slightly different version appears in *FR, Japan*, 2:648–49—trans.

257. *FR, 1941*, 4:488. A slightly different version appears in *FR, Japan*, 2:650—trans.

258. Exhibit 2908, IMTFE Records.

259. JJM Archives.

260. JDA Archives.

261. Ishii memoirs.

262. Ishikawa Shingo, *Shinjuwan made no keii: Kaisen no shinsō* (To Pearl Harbor: The Truth about the Outbreak of the War), p. 309.

263. JDA Archives. Presumably, Konoe would be "coaxed along" by Roosevelt—trans.

264. Grew, *Turbulent Era*, 2:1272–73, 1330 n. 65.

265. Ibid., p. 1333.

266. There is no mention of Toyoda's introducing this new proposal in the *TSM: Bekkan* record of the September 3 Liaison Conference (pp. 507–508), although such a proposal was indeed made. See n. 268—trans.

267. JFM, *Kiroku*, pp. 242–44.

268. Ibid., p. 246. For the full and somewhat different English version of Toyoda's proposal, including the two pledges presented by the author, see *FR, Japan*, 2:608. In Tsunoda's original text it appears that these two pledges

were in the August 5 "Plan." No mention is made of Japan's withdrawing troops from China or of Japan's attitude toward the war in Europe in the August 5 "Plan." Reference to the August 5 "Plan" in the original has therefore been deleted—trans.

269. Ibid., pp. 248–49. The English "meet" is used in the Japanese original—trans.

270. JDA Archives; Sanbō Honbu, *Sugiyama memo*, 1:334.

271. Shigemitsu had returned to Japan in June 1941 after serving for two and a half years as ambassador to Britain—trans.

272. *TSM: Bekkan*, pp. 528, 527.

273. JFM, *Kiroku*, p. 213.

274. U.S. Congress, Joint Committee on the Investigation of the Pearl Harbor Attack, *Hearings before the Joint Committee on the Investigation of the Pearl Harbor Attack*, part 12, p. 68 (hereafter cited as *Pearl Harbor Hearings*).

275. Ibid., p. 72.

276. JFM, *Kiroku*, pp. 293–94.

277. Elliott Roosevelt, ed., *F.D.R., His Personal Letters, 1928–1945*, 2:1217.

278. Nomura, *Beikoku*, p. 125.

279. JFM, *Kiroku*, pp. 327–41. Also *FR, Japan*, 2:660—trans.

280. Nomura, *Beikoku*, p. 125.

281. *FR, Japan*, 2:665.

282. Tracy B. Kittredge, "United States Defense Policy and Strategy; 1941," *U.S. News and World Report*, Vol. 37, No. 23 (December 3, 1954), p. 112.

283. Feis, *Road to Pearl Harbor*, p. 275.

284. *Kido nikki*, 2:909.

285. Satō, *Tōjō*, p. 201.

286. *TSM: Bekkan*, p. 489.

287. The author's figures here, wherever they were derived, bear little relation to the figures in table 2.2. For example, the total tonnage requisitioned in table 2.2 from the end of June to the end of August 1941, is 497,000 tons, and the tonnage from the end of June to the end of September is 760,000 tons; neither conforms to the 784,000 claimed for July-September 1941—trans.

288. AGS, "Kimitsu nisshi."

289. Ibid.

290. Tanaka diary.

291. Ishii memoirs.

292. For the "explanation" attached to this "proposal" see Appendix 7. The source of the "proposal" appears to be the same as that for the "explanation"; see Appendix 7—trans.

293. JDA Archives; Sanbō Honbu, *Sugiyama memo*, 1:340.

294. Tanaka, *Taisen*, p. 103.

295. AGS, "Kimitsu nisshi."

296. Ishikawa, *Shinjuwan*, p. 319.

297. AGS, "Kimitsu nisshi."

298. JFM, *Kiroku*, p. 317.

299. AGS, "Kimitsu nisshi."

394 2. LEANING TOWARD WAR

300. JJM Archives.
301. JFM, *Kiroku*, pp. 341–43. The word "deadlock" in English is used in the telegram—trans.
302. Tanaka, *Taisen*, p. 103; JDA Archives.
303. Tanaka, *Taisen*, p. 104; JDA Archives.
304. Shiba interview.
305. Tsunoda here cites *Kido nikki*, 2:906–07. However, regarding Tōjō's meeting with the emperor that day Kido records only the following: "At 10:30 a.m. Army Minister Tōjō came to my office after his audience; I heard about the results of investigations into preparations for war with the United States, etc." I was unable to locate the quote in *Kido bunsho*—trans.
306. AGS, "Kimitsu nisshi."
307. JJM Archives.
308. Ishii memoirs.
309. AGS, "Kimitsu nisshi."
310. Ibid.
311. JJM Archives.
312. AGS, "Kimitsu nisshi."
313. Tanaka, *Taisen*, p. 105.
314. Tomioka, "Taiheiyō sensō," 2:95–96.
315. AGS, "Kimitsu nisshi"; Ishii memoirs.
316. Tanaka, *Taisen*, pp. 105–108; JDA and JJM Archives.
317. AGS, "Kimitsu nisshi."
318. Ibid.
319. JJM Archives.
320. Tanaka, *Taisen*, pp. 109–110.
321. JJM Archives.
322. AGS, "Kimitsu nisshi."
323. Shiba interview; JDA Archives.
324. *Kido nikki*, 2:913. This statement by Fushimi is not in the source cited. Kido notes only that the emperor "was painfully disappointed" over Fushimi's "extreme radicalism regarding U.S.-Japan problems . . . when Prince Fushimi had an audience with him the other day." I was unable to locate the quote in *Kido bunsho*—trans.
325. Ishii memoirs.
326. JFM, *Kiroku*, p. 232.
327. Ibid., p. 343.
328. Tōgō, *Jidai no ichimen*, p. 151.
329. *Kido bunsho*, p. 483.
330. Ishii memoirs.
331. Takada interview.
332. JJM Archives.
333. Tomita, *Haisen Nihon*, p. 185; Tomita Kenji affidavit, Exhibit 3467, IMTFE Records; Tomita Defense Exhibit (not submitted) 2264, Ibid.
334. JJM Archives.
335. Tomita affidavit, IMTFE Records.
336. Ibid.
337. Shiba interview, April 8, 1961.
338. Satō, *Tōjō*, pp. 209–210.

339. JDA Archives; Sanbo Honbu, *Sugiyama memo,* 1·315–47. For yet another version, see *TSM: Bekkan,* pp. 531–32—trans.
340. Tomita, *Haisen Nihon,* pp. 185–186.
341. JDA Archives; Itō and Nomura, *Kaigun taishō Kobayashi,* p. 105.
342. JJM Archives.
343. Toyoda Soemu, *Saigo no teikoku kaigun* (The Last Imperial Navy), p. 65.
344. Kido affidavit, IMTFE Records.
345. See *Kido bunsho,* p. 485, for an almost identical version of this quotation, and pp. 485–88 for the entire Konoe message. Apparently the author uses the Kido Kōichi affidavit for this as well as the previous quotation—trans.
346. JDA Archives. For a somewhat different version, see *TSM: Bekkan,* pp. 533, 534–35—trans.
347. *TSM: Bekkan,* p. 535.
348. Tomita, *Haisen Nihon,* p. 188; Tomita Defense Exhibit (not submitted), IMTFE Records.
349. JDA Archives; Itō and Nomura, *Kaigun taishō Kobayashi,* pp. 103–104. Known as the Seiyōkai's "naval expert," Uchida Nobuya (or Shinya) was a prominent party politician and shipping magnate who was a member of the House of Representatives from 1924 to 1946, and again in 1952. He was minister of railways, 1934–36, and briefly minister of agriculture and commerce under Tōjō in 1944—trans.
350. JDA Archives; Itō and Nomura, *Kaigun taishō Kobayashi,* pp. 103–104.
351. Mutō Akira affidavit, Exhibit 3554, IMTFE Records; Satō, *Tōjō,* p. 209.

3. The Decision for War

1. *TSM: Bekkan,* p. 535; Sanbō honbu, *Sugiyama memo,* 1:351.
2. Exhibit 2250, IMTFE Records; Tanaka, *Taisen,* p. 123.
3. Suzuki affidavit, IMTFE Records.
4. Ibid.
5. Ibid.
6. Ibid.
7. Ibid.
8. Ibid.
9. *Kido nikki,* 2:915.
10. Ibid.
11. Suzuki affidavit, IMTFE Records.
12. Ibid.
13. *Kido nikki,* 2:915–16.
14. Exhibit 1148, IMTFE Records.
15. Ibid.
16. Higashikuni, *Ichi kōzoku,* p. 89.
17. *Kido nikki,* 2:916.
18. Satō, *Tōjō,* p. 223.

19. Higashikuni Naruhiko affidavit, Exhibit 3604, IMTFE Records.
20. Konoe papers.
21. *Kido nikki*, 2:916.
22. Suzuki affidavit, IMTFE Records.
23. Kido affidavit, *ibid.*
24. Exhibit 1148, *ibid.*
25. Harada, *Saionji kō*, 8:358.
26. *Tōkyō Asahi shimbun*, October 16, 1941.
27. Higashikuni, *Ichi kōzoku*, pp. 54–55.
28. *Kido nikki*, entry of July 31, 1941, 2:895–96.
29. Ibid., 2:896.
30. Matsudaira Yasumasa affidavit, Defense Evidence 2503 (not submitted), IMTFE Records.
31. JDA Archives; Itō and Nomura, *Kaigun taishō Kobayashi*, p. 105.
32. Matsudaira Yasumasa affidavit.
33. Sakuta Takatarō, *Tennō to Kido* (The Emperor and Kido), pp. 168–69. Kido makes no mention of this telephone call in his diary: *Kido nikki*, 2:917—trans.
34. *Kido bunsho*, pp. 481, 484. The numbering is by the author—trans.
35. Satō, *Tōjō*, pp. 223–24.
36. *Kido bunsho*, p. 482.
37. Ibid., p. 481.
38. Ibid., p. 483.
39. Ibid., p. 484.
40. Wakatsuki Reijirō, *Kofūan kaikoroku*, (Reminiscences from a Moss-grown Hermitage), p. 418; Yabe, *Konoe*, 2:403; Okada Keisuke, *Okada Keisuke kaikoroku* (Reminiscences of Okada Keisuke), p. 200; Hirota Kōki Defense Materials, IMTFE Records.
41. Tomita, *Haisen Nihon*, p. 195.
42. AGS, "Kimitsu nisshi."
43. Ibid.
44. Ibid., entry for October 17, 1941.
45. Ishii memoirs.
46. Satō, *Tōjō*, p. 224.
47. Akamatsu Sadao affidavit, Defense Evidence 2265 (not submitted), IMTFE Records. A 1922 graduate of the Japanese army academy, Akamatsu became secretary to the army minister and prime minister in October 1941—trans.
48. Ishii memoirs.
49. *Kido nikki*, 2:917.
50. *Kido bunsho*, p. 491—trans.
51. This is a carefully worded misrepresentation. The position of lord keeper of the privy seal was not a government office and therefore was not mentioned in the Meiji Constitution; there would naturally be no provision therein for the privy seal to advise and assist the emperor. The office of lord keeper of the privy seal, a palace office, was established by Imperial House Ordinance (Kōshitsurei) No. 4 of November 1, 1907, based on the Imperial House Law enacted concurrently with the Meiji Constitution and having the same efficacy as the constitution. That ordinance stipulated that the privy

seal shall "advise and assist the emperor in regular attendance," as had the first provisions regarding the privy seal's office enacted in December 1885. If anything, the privy seal had even more authority to advise and assist the emperor than did ministers of state, given the dual constitutional nature of Japan's prewar political system. See Tōyama Shigeki and Adachi Yoshiko, *Kindai Nihon seiji hikkei* (Manual of Modern Japanese Politics), p. 113; also David A. Titus, *Palace and Politics in Prewar Japan*, pp. 171–82, 246–74—trans.

52. Hirota Kōki Defense Materials, IMTFE Records.
53. Satō interview.
54. JJM Archives.
55. Sakuta, *Tennō*, pp. 168–169.
56. Hirota Kōki Defense Materials, IMTFE Records.
57. No source is given by the author for this statement of the emperor's wishes. Kido makes no such statement of the emperor's wishes either in his diary or his *bunsho*. There are no words to this effect in his posthumously published "Shōwa Tennō no dokuhaku hachijikan" (The Shōwa Emperor's Eight-Hour Soliloquy), *Bungei shunjū* (1990), 12:100–145. The author is apparently paraphrasing what he thought the emperor would have said had he been free to do so, and there are ample grounds for such a position in the above sources—trans.
58. JJM Archives.
59. Satō, *Tōjō*, p. 229.
60. *Tōkyō Asahi shimbun* (extra), October 18, 1941.
61. Tōgō, *Jidai no ichimen*, p. 147.
62. *Tōkyō Asahi shimbun*, October 19, 1941.
63. Ishii memoirs.
64. Tōgō, *Jidai no ichimen*, pp. 65–66. See Appendix 8—trans.
65. Ibid., p. 199.
66. AGS, "Kimitsu nisshi."
67. Ibid.
68. Ibid.
69. JFM, *Kiroku*, p. 381.
70. JJM Archives.
71. Ibid.
72. Ibid.
73. Ibid.
74. Ishii memoirs.
75. AGS, "Kimitsu nisshi."
76. Ibid.
77. Ibid.
78. *TSM: Bekkan*, p. 542.
79. JJM Archives.
80. Inoue interview.
81. JDA Archives.
82. Imperial Navy Records.
83. JJM Archives.
84. Ibid.
85. Ibid.

86. AGS, "Kimitsu nisshi"; Sanbō honbu, *Sugiyama memo*, 1:354.

87. JDA Archives.

88. The author gives no source for these items agreed to, but a version appears in *TSM: Bekkan*, p. 542, that is similar in meaning—trans.

89. The author once again gives no source for these three options advanced by Tōjō. For a different and clearer version of the options, see *TSM: Bekkan*, p. 543—trans.

90. AGS, "Kimitsu nisshi."

91. Ibid.

92. Ibid.; Sanbō honbu, *Sugiyama memo*, 1:371–72.

93. Ibid.

94. *TSM: Bekkan*, pp. 548–49.

95. No source for this data is given by the author. The "planned allocations" figures for 1941 here add up to a planned supply figure of 4,816, not 4,346—trans.

96. AGS, "Kimitsu nisshi," entries for November 1 and November 2.

97. Tōgō, *Jidai no ichimen*, pp. 206, 211, 214.

98. JDA Archives.

99. Tōgō, *Jidai no ichimen*, p. 213; JDA Archives.

100. JDA Archives. With the exception of one verb form, this is exactly what Suzuki reported to the Imperial Conference of November 5. See *TSM: Bekkan*, p. 578—trans.

101. JDA Archives; Kaya Okinori, "Kaisen no shinsō" (The Truth about the Outbreak of the War), *Yosan* (Budget), Vol. 31, April, p. 38.

102. *TSM: Bekkan*, pp. 550–51.

103. Ibid., p. 551.

104. Tanaka, *Taisen*, p. 153.

105. Kurusu Saburō, *Nichi-Bei gaikō hiwa: waga gaikōshi* (A Confidential Account of Japanese-American Diplomacy: My Diplomatic History), p. 92.

106. See *TSM: Bekkan*, p. 549, for words to this effect—trans.

107. JDA Archives; Sanbō honbu, *Sugiyama memo*, 1:376. A differently worded record of Tōgō's statement appears in *TSM: Bekkan*, p. 551—trans.

108. *TSM: Bekkan*, p. 573.

109. JDA Archives. A quite different version of the official record, and citing only Tsukada, appears in *TSM: Bekkan*, pp. 551–52—trans.

110. *TSM: Bekkan*, p. 552.

111. Tōgō, *Jidai no ichimen*, p. 214.

112. JDA Archives; Sanbō honbu, *Sugiyama memo*, 1:377.

113. *TSM: Bekkan*, pp. 571–72.

114. See Appendix 9.

115. Tōgō, *Jidai no ichimen*, pp. 207, 216; interview with Nishi Haruhiko, July 20, 1960.

116. Tōgō, *Jidai no ichimen*, p. 223.

117. Tōjō Hideki affidavit, Exhibit 3655, IMTFE Records.

118. Ishii memoirs.

119. Ibid.

120. *TSM: Bekkan*, p. 567.

121. Ibid., p. 560.

122. JJM Archives.

123. JFM, *Kiroku*, p. 448.
124. Ibid., p. 389.
125. Ibid., p. 468.
126. *TSM: Bekkan*, p. 481.
127. JDA Archives. A slightly different version appears in *TSM: Bekkan*, p. 507—trans.
128. JDA Archives. The author mistakenly dates this Liaison Conference as September 2; there was no Liaison Conference on that day. The record of the September 3 Liaison Conference gives a different version of Nagano's statement. See *TSM: Bekkan*, p. 507—trans.
129. JDA Archives. A different account is given in *TSM: Bekkan*, p. 550—trans.
130. Fukudome Shigeru, *Kaigun no hansei* (A Self-Examination by the Navy), pp. 81–82, 84–85.
131. Fukudome interview.
132. JDA Archives.
133. JDA Archives.
134. Tomioka, "Taiheiyō sensō," 2:174–75.
135. Ibid. The author seems to compare the numbers of Japanese naval aircraft with the total number of U.S. aircraft. Moreover, the numbers for Japanese naval aircraft, in tidy increments of 4,000 from 1942 to 1944, appear to be fictional even at the forecast level—trans.
136. Fukudome, *Kaigun no hansei*, pp. 81–82 and 84–85; Kawai interview; JDA Archives.
137. Tōgō, *Jidai no ichimen*, p. 203; Kaya, "Kaisen," pp. 37–38.
138. Tōgō, *Jidai no ichimen*, p. 215.
139. Ibid., p. 203.
140. JDA Archives; Sanbō honbu, *Sugiyama memo*, 1:373.
141. Tōgō, *Jidai no ichimen*, p. 215.
142. Okada, *Kaikoroku*, p. 203.
143. This refers to one of Lanchester's equations. "*Lethality* increases much more rapidly with every troop unit than it does with every unit of extra *efficiency* per troop unit. The exact scale of the statistical relationship is largely irrelevant; Lanchester called it a 'square law' meaning that the lethality increased by the square of the number of troops, but by a much lower proportion as the capacity of each troop increased." "Lanchester was an engineer who, during the First World War, produced a series of mathematical analyses of [weapon systems] and their relationship to manpower." David Robertson, *Guide to Modern Defense and Strategy*, p. 176—trans.
144. Inoue interview.
145. The author's argument here is misleading, because he confuses the navy's arguments about ratios in the initial stages of war with those that would arise in a prolonged war. Those like Nagano suggested that Japan would have a favorable ratio in terms of Lanchester's equation if the U.S. fleet could be provoked to attack while Japan had an overall ratio of 70 percent because the ratio would increase as a result of trans-Pacific attrition, possibly giving Japan the ratio advantage. A "ratio neurosis" in any case is certainly justified; that is precisely what Lanchester's n^2 is all about—trans.

146. Shimanuki Takeji, "Nihon no kokubō hōshin: Yōhei kōryō" (Japan's National Defense Policy: Tactical Principles), *Kokubō*, November 1961, p. 81.

147. Takagi interview.

148. Imperial Navy Records; the full text is given in JDA, *Senshi sōsho: Daihon'ei rikugunbu, Dai Tōa sensō kaisen keii* (War History Series: The Imperial Headquarters Army, Circumstances Leading to the Outbreak of the Greater East Asian War), 2:144–47.

149. The author gives no citation for this lengthy quote, which is contained in *TSM: Bekkan*, p. 512—trans.

150. Fukudome Shigeru, *Shikan Shinjuwan kōgeki* (An Historical View of the Attack on Pearl Harbor), p. 118.

151. Inoue and Kawai interviews.

152. JDA Archives.

153. Miyo and Kawai interviews.

154. JJM Archives.

155. *TSM: Bekkan*, p. 500.

156. Tomioka, "Taiheiyō sensō," 2:104.

157. *TSM: Bekkan*, pp. 568–69.

158. Evidently the author forgot what he wrote on page 271 regarding Nagano's response, which was, "no need for worry whatsoever"—trans.

159. *Kido nikki* 2:921. According to this source, which the author mistakenly dates as November 14, this question was directed at Kido, not Nagano; two days earlier Tōjō and the two chiefs of staff had reported to the Throne, but Kido reports nothing of what transpired—trans.

160. JDA Archives; Itō and Nomura, *Kaigun taishō Kobayashi*, p. 111.

161. AGS, "Kimitsu nisshi."

162. Fukudome, *Kaigun no hansei*, p. 245; Satō, *Tōjō*, p. 250.

163. Inoue interview.

164. For this text, as quoted by the author and approved verbatim by the November 15 Liaison Conference, see *TSM: Bekkan*, p. 585—trans.

165. JDA Archives; Sanbō honbu, *Sugiyama memo*; 1:396. See also *TSM: Bekkan*, p. 561—trans.

166. Yokoi interview.

167. JDA Archives; Sanbō honbu, *Sugiyama memo*, 1:383.

168. Yokoi interview.

169. Hans-Adolf Jacobsen and Jurgen Rohwer, *Entscheidungsschlachten des zweiten Weltkrieges* (Decisive Battles of World War II), p. 335.

170. Anthony Martienssen, *Hitler and His Admirals*, p. 105.

171. Roskill, *White Ensign*, pp. 127–47.

172. JDA Archives? The author gives no source for this quote—trans.

173. Yamamoto Isoroku letter to Shimada Shigetarō, December 10, 1940, Imperial Navy Records.

174. Onoda interview.

175. JJM Archives. The author uses the expression "meeting of the leaders" rather than Liaison Conference here. I have changed it because other than Tōjō's· early morning meeting with Sugiyama there could hardly have been another top-level meeting in addition to the marathon Liaison Conference that day. Nagano's statement does not appear in the official record of that conference—trans.

176. Okada Taishō Kiroku Hensankai (Association for the Compilation of the Archives of Admiral Okada), *Okada Keisuke den* (A Biography of Okada Keisuke), pp. 363–65, 368.

177. JJM Archives.

178. Imperial Navy Records.

179. Ibid. The battle of Okehazama was a surprise attack that occurred in 1560; the battle of Hiyodorigoe (1184) involved an attack through a dangerous pass; Kawanakajima was a series of haphazard forays and indecisive engagements that occurred in 1553, 1555, 1557 and 1561—trans.

180. Fukudome, *Kaigun no hansei*, p. 129.

181. Onoda interview.

182. Yamamoto Isoroku letter to Koga Mineichi, January 2, 1942, Imperial Navy Records.

183. Yabe, *Konoe*, 2:162.

184. Yamamoto Isoroku letter to Ogata Taketora, January 9, 1942, cited in Ogata, *Ichi gunjin*, p. 13.

185. JDA Archives.

186. JDA Archives; Sanbō honbu, *Sugiyama memo*, 1:359–61, 369.

187. Ibid.; Sanbō honbu, *Sugiyama memo*, 1:360. See also *TSM: Bekkan*, p. 541, for words to the same effect, although this *Bekkan* document seems to have mislabeled the office and does not mention the name of the officer—trans.

188. *TSM: Bekkan*, pp. 577–78—trans.

189. Tanaka, *Taisen*, p. 149.

190. *TSM: Bekkan*, p. 550.

191. JDA Archives.

192. Ibid. The last 3 items did not include stocks held by the military.

193. *TSM: Bekkan*, p. 505.

194. This is an abbreviated and doctored quotation from Suzuki's explanation to the November 5 Imperial Conference; see *TSM: Bekkan*, pp. 576–77—trans.

195. JDA Archives. This is directly quoted from Suzuki's written explanation at the November 5 Imperial Conference; see *TSM: Bekkan*, pp. 574–75—trans.

196. JDA Archives.

197. Ibid.

198. Ibid.

199. Ibid.

200. Ibid.

201. The author gives no source for this demand by the government and the high command's agreement to it. Neither it nor any official agreement to the three conditions appears in the November 5 Imperial Conference record. See *TSM: Bekkan*, pp. 564–80—trans.

202. JDA Archives. This table reveals the chaotic nature of the archives, the author's mind, or both—trans.

203. This sentence was added by the translator, but it does little to clarify the author's purpose in putting in the table.

204. The author is unclear about quantities for military use and those for civilian use. Table 3.10 actually refers to oil only for military use, and the *total*

projected quantities are for both military and civilian use (5.2 million, 5 million, and 4.75 million). This is not clear from the author's presentation and I have clarified this in the text. He also has "tons" as the unit, whereas the unit is kiloliters in the Imperial Conference record, and he has 4. 85 million for the third year while the record has 4. 75 million. See *TSM: Bekkan,* p. 576—trans.

205. JDA Archives.

206. Letter of October 15, 1941, in Roosevelt, *F.D.R. Letters,* p. 1223—trans.

207. Churchill, *Grand Alliance,* p. 592.

208. Langer and Gleason, *Undeclared War,* pp. 844–47. At this point the author refers the reader to a later portion of the text written by Fukuda Shigeo. I have altered the author's sentence here to make clear what the November 5 "Memorandum" to Roosevelt was about—trans.

209. *Pearl Harbor Hearings,* 11:5420.

210. JFM, *Kiroku,* pp. 403–404. See also *FR, Japan,* 2:718—trans.

211. JFM, *Kiroku,* p. 400.

212. Sherwood, *Roosevelt and Hopkins,* p. 420.

213. JFM, *Kiroku,* p. 449. "Intervene," "mediate," and "introducer" are in English in Nomura's dispatch—trans.

214. *Pearl Harbor Hearings,* 12:154.

215. JFM, *Kiroku,* p. 453.

216. Ibid., pp. 455–56.

217. JJM Archives.

218. Kurusu, *Nichi-Bei gaikō,* p. 134.

219. JFM, *Kiroku,* p. 467.

220. Langer and Gleason, *Undeclared War,* pp. 880–83.

221. Ibid.

222. *Pearl Harbor Hearings,* 3:1095; Henry L. Stimson and McGeorge Bundy, *On Active Service in Peace and War,* p. 389.

223. Kittredge, "U.S. Defense Policy," p. 116.

224. *FR, 1941,* 4:669.

225. *Pearl Harbor Hearings, Investigation of the Pearl Harbor Attack: Report,* p. 379; Langer and Gleason, *Undeclared War,* p. 892.

226. JFM, *Kiroku,* p. 399. For Hull's version of his statement, see *The Memoirs of Cordell Hull,* 2:1058; for the U.S. Navy's translation of this part of the dispatch see *Pearl Harbor Hearings,* 12:106—trans.

227. JFM, *Kiroku,* pp. 399–400. For the U.S. Navy's translation of this dispatch of November 9, see *Pearl Harbor Hearings,* 12:106—trans.

228. JFM, *Kiroku,* p. 405. For the U.S. Navy's translation of Tōgō's dispatch of November 10 see *Pearl Harbor Hearings,* 12:107–108—trans.

229. Langer and Gleason, *Undeclared War,* pp. 861–62.

230. JFM, *Kiroku,* pp. 411–12.

231. Langer and Gleason, *Undeclared War,* pp. 861–62.

232. JFM, *Kiroku,* p. 431.

233. Ibid., pp. 449–50.

234. Ibid., pp. 470–71.

235. Tōgō, *Jidai no ichimen,* p. 229.

236. *FR, Japan,* 2:745, 749.
237. Ibid., p. 753.
238. Ibid., p. 761.
239. Nomura, *Beikoku,* p. 152.
240. *Pearl Harbor Hearings,* 11:5434–35.
241. JFM, *Kiroku,* p. 384.
242. Sir Llewellyn Woodward, *British Foreign Policy in the Second World War,* p. 178.
243. *FR, Japan,* 2:703–704.
244. Langer and Gleason, *Undeclared War,* pp. 849–50.
245. *FR, Japan,* 4:569.
246. Woodward, *British Foreign Policy,* p. 178.
247. Ibid., pp. 179, 181, 185.
248. Churchill, *Grand Alliance,* p. 590; Hasluck, *Government and People,* p. 553.
249. Ibid., pp. 549–50, n. 2.
250. Ibid., p. 549.
251. Ibid.
252. Ibid., pp. 549–50.
253. *FR, Japan,* 4:687.
254. Hasluck, *Government and People,* p. 553.
255. Kurusu, *Nichi-Bei gaikō,* p. 147.
256. JFM, *Kiroku,* p. 489.
257. Kurusu, *Nichi-Bei gaiko,* p. 153; Langer and Gleason, *Undeclared War,* p. 907.
258. *Pearl Harbor Hearings,* 11:5392; Langer and Gleason, *Undeclared War,* p. 893.
259. Churchill, *Grand Alliance,* p. 598.
260. *Pearl Harbor Hearings,* 5:2124.
261. *FR, 1941,* 4:686–87.
262. *FR, Japan,* 2:773, 777.
263. JFM, *Kiroku,* p. 467.
264. Ibid., pp. 478–79.
265. *Pearl Harbor Hearings,* 3:1311.
266. Langer and Gleason, *Undeclared War,* pp. 898, 901.
267. Ibid., p. 898.
268. Ibid., pp. 896, 898.
269. AGS, "Kimitsu nisshi."
270. Ibid.
271. JDA Archives.
272. AGS, "Kimitsu nisshi."
273. JDA Archives; Sanbō honbu, *Sugiyama memo,* 1:532.
274. Ibid. Foreign minister from January to May 1932, Yoshizawa Kenkichi was appointed head of the trade mission to the Dutch East Indies on November 28, 1940—trans.
275. JDA Archives.
276. AGS, "Kimitsu nisshi."
277. Tōgō, *Jidai no ichimen,* p. 239.

278. JFM, *Kiroku*, pp. 488–89.
279. Charles A. Beard, *President Roosevelt and the Coming of the War*, p. 238.
280. Feis, *Road to Pearl Harbor*, p. 321.
281. Tōgō, *Jidai no ichimen*, p. 245.
282. Ibid., pp. 238, 249.
283. *Steno Records* (in Japanese), No. 347, pp. 9–11, IMTFE Records.
284. JDA Archives.
285. Shiobara Tokisaburō, *Tōjō memo: kakute tennō wa sukuwareta* (The Tōjō Memo: Thus Was the Emperor Saved), p. 94. The transcript of the November 27 Liaison Conference makes no mention of these conclusions by Tōjō—trans.
286. Tōgō, *Jidai no ichimen*, p. 239.
287. Tanaka, *Taisen*, pp. 158–59.
288. AGS, "Kimitsu nisshi."
289. JDA Archives.
290. *Pearl Harbor Hearings*, 2:576.
291. Woodward, *British Foreign Policy*, p. 189.
292. Although the author gives no source for these statements by Tōjō and Tōgō, they appear in the record of the December 1 Imperial Conference; see *TSM: Bekkan*, pp. 596, 600—trans.
293. The author gives no source for this remarkable passage, which proves that the emperor knew about the planned surprise attack on Pearl Harbor at least 6 days before it occurred. I am grateful to Asada Sadao for locating a source for this quotation in *Senshi sōsho*, 5:519—trans.
294. *Kido nikki*, 2:928.
295. Ibid.
296. Ibid., pp. 926–27.
297. Wakatsuki, *Kofūan*, p. 421.
298. JFM, *Kiroku*, pp. 458–59.
299. Ibid., pp. 482–83.
300. Tōgō, *Jidai no ichimen*, pp. 272, 233.
301. Fukudome, *Shikan*, p. 128.
302. Tōgō, *Jidai no ichimen*, p. 256; JDA Archives.
303. Tōjō Hideki interrogation, Exhibit 1201A, IMTFE Records.
304. JJM Archives.
305. JDA Archives; Sanbō honbu, *Sugiyama memo*, 1:563–64. For a slightly different wording, see *TSM: Bekkan*, p. 610—trans.
306. JJM Archives.
307. JFM, *Keii*, p. 298.
308. Tanabe Moritake affidavit, Exhibit 3633, IMTFE Records.
309. Genda Minoru, "Higeki: Shinjuwan kōgeki" (A Tragedy: The Attack on Pearl Harbor), *Bungei shunjū*, December 1962, p. 210.
310. JDA Archives? The author gives no sources for the various orders issued—trans.
311. JDA Archives; Tōjō Hideki interrogation, Exhibit 1201A, IMTFE Records; Sanbō honbu, *Sugiyama memo*, 1:371.
312. JJM Archives.

313. Ibid.

314. Ibid.

315. *Pearl Harbor Hearings*, 9:3990, 4523–24; 11:5393. The author's citations give neither the times nor the quotation. For the quotation see *ibid.*, 12:248—trans.

316. Ibid., 3:1109, 1111; 5:2132–33.

317. Ibid., 3:1288–89.

318. Ibid., 10:5028, 5036–37; 27:520, 522, 531–32; 32:478, 482–83.

319. Ibid., 10:5031–32, 5045; 27:521, 568–70; 33:349.

320. Ibid., 10:5033, 5037, 5046; 27:521, 533; 32:479, 489, 490.

321. Ibid., 8:3557–58; 9:3990, 3997, 4006–4007, 4523–24, 4512–13; 10:4660–64; 11:5393; 12:248; 14:1414–16; Kameyama Kazuji affidavit, *IMTFE* Exhibit 2964, IMTFE Records; Yōki Shiroji affidavit, Exhibit 2967, *ibid.* Upon graduating from Tokyo Imperial University in 1927, Yōki entered the Foreign Ministry, becoming First Section chief, America Bureau, in 1940. A Russian language specialist, Kameyama entered the Foreign Ministry in 1921; after serving in China, Germany, Manchuria, and the Soviet Union, he became a counselor to the Soviet embassy in 1942—trans.

322. JFM, *Kiroku*, p. 534.

323. Ibid., p. 550.

324. Butow, *Tōjō*, p. 381.

325. Sanematsu interview.

326. *Pearl Harbor Hearings*, 2:607; *FR, Japan*, 2:786.

327. *FR, Japan*, 2:786–87.

328. Morishima, *Shinjuwan*, p. 61.

329. Tōgō, *Jidai no ichimen*, p. 267.

330. Sanematsu interview.

331. Langer and Gleason, *Undeclared War*, p. 730.

332. *Pearl Harbor Hearings*, 11:5421.

333. Ibid., 14:1328.

334. Ibid., 3:1310.

335. Harry Elmer Barnes, *Perpetual War for Perpetual Peace*, pp. 353, 355; *Pearl Harbor Hearings*, 39:85, 7:2935.

336. *FR, 1941*, 5:360.

337. Woodward, *British Foreign Policy*, pp. 186–87.

338. Ibid.

339. Ibid.

340. Hasluck, *Government and People*, pp. 555–56.

341. *Pearl Harbor Hearings*, 10:5082–83.

342. Ibid., 12:227.

343. Hasluck, *Government and People*, p. 544.

344. *Pearl Harbor Hearings*, 14:1407.

345. Ibid., 5:2417.

346. Ibid., 9:4252–53.

347. Kittredge, "U.S. Defense Policy," p. 112.

348. *Pearl Harbor Hearings*, 19:4663.

349. For a slightly different English version see *ibid.*, 12:245—trans.

350. Ibid., 11:5283.

351. William H. Stanley and Arthur A. Ageton, *Admiral Ambassador to Russia*, p. 85.

352. *Pearl Harbor Hearings, Investigation of the Pearl Harbor Attack: Report*, p. 439.

353. Sherwood, *Roosevelt and Hopkins*, p. 431.

354. *Pearl Harbor Hearings, Investigation of the Pearl Harbor Attack: Report*, p. 65.

355. Sherwood, *Roosevelt and Hopkins*, p. 431.

356. *Pearl Harbor Hearings*, 19:3505.

357. Churchill, *Grand Alliance*, p. 605.

358. Sherwood, *Roosevelt and Hopkins*, p. 428.

359. Frances Perkins, *The Roosevelt I Knew*, pp. 379–80.

360. *Pearl Harbor Hearings*, 19:3664–65.

361. Hasluck, *Government and People*, p. 555.

362. The author does not give a source for this quotation. Something similar, dated November 26, was intercepted and translated November 29, 1941. See *Pearl Harbor Hearings*, 12:183—trans.

363. Butow, *Tōjō*, p. 379.

364. U.S. Office of Naval Intelligence, trans., *The Fuehrer Conferences on Matters Dealing with the German Navy, 1939–1945*, p. 69.

Glossary

Glossary

Abe Nobuyuki 阿部信行
Akamatsu Sadao 赤松貞雄
Amano Masakazu 天野正一
Anami Korechika 阿南惟幾
Arima Yoriyasu 有馬頼寧
Arita Hachirō 有田八郎
Banzai Ichirō 坂西一良
Chang Tso-lin 張作霖
Chiang Kai-shek (Chieh-shih) 蔣介石
Ch'ien Yung-ming 錢永銘
Doi Akio 土居明夫
Doihara Kenji 土肥原賢次
Enomoto Shigeharu 榎本重治
Fujii Shigeru 藤井茂
Fukudome Shigeru 福留繁
Fushimi-no-miya Hiroyasu, Prince 伏見宮博恭
Gotō Ryūnosuke 後藤隆之助
Hamaguchi Osachi 浜口雄幸
Hara Takashi 原敬
Hara Yoshimichi 原嘉道
Harada Kumao 原田熊雄
Hashimoto Shōzō 橋本象造
Hasunuma Shigeru 蓮沼蕃
Hata Shunroku 畑俊六
Hattori Takushirō 服部卓四郎
Hayashi Senjūrō 林銑十郎
Higashikuni-no-miya Naruhiko, Prince 東久邇宮稔彦
Hiraide Hideo 平出英夫
Hiranuma Kiichirō 平沼騏一郎
Hirata Noboru 平田昇
Hirota Kōki 広田弘毅
Hori Teikichi 堀悌吉
Horikiri Zembei 堀切善兵衛
Horinouchi Kensuke 堀内謙介
Hoshina Zenshirō 保科善四郎
Hoshino Naoki 星野直樹
Hu Shih 胡適
Iguchi Sadao 井口貞夫
Ikawa Tadao 井川忠雄
Inoue Shigeyoshi 井上成美

Ishii Akiho 石井秋穂
Ishikawa Shingo 石川信吾
Isoda Saburō 磯田三郎
Itō Nobufumi 伊藤述史
Itō Seiichi 伊藤整一
Iwakuro Hideo 岩畔豪雄
Kabayama Aisuke 樺山愛輔
Kameyama Kazuji 亀山一二
Kase Toshikazu 加瀬俊一
Katō Sotomatsu 加藤外松
Kawada Isao 河田烈
Kawai Iwao 川井巌
Kaya Okinori 賀屋興宣
Kido Kōichi 木戸幸一
Kimura Heitarō 木村兵太郎
Kobayashi Seizō 小林躋造
Koga Mineichi 古賀峯一
Kondō Nobutake 近藤信竹
Konoe Fumimaro 近衛文麿
Kurihara Etsuzō 栗原悦蔵
Kurusu Saburō 来栖三郎
Lin Sen 林森
Mabuchi Itsuo 馬淵逸雄
Maeda Minoru 前田稔
Makino Nobuaki (Shinken) 牧野伸顕
Matsudaira Kōtō 松平康東
Matsudaira Yasumasa 松平康昌
Matsumoto Shigeharu 松本重治
Matsuoka Kin'ichirō 松岡謹一郎
Matsuoka Yōsuke 松岡洋右
Miki Kiyoshi 三木清
Miyo Kazunari 三代一就 (Tatsukichi 辰吉)
Mutō Akira 武藤章
Nagai Yatsuji 永井八津次
Nagano Osami 永野修身
Nakanishi Toshinori (Toshikazu) 中西敏憲
Ninomiya Yoshikiyo 二宮義清
Nishi Haruhiko 西春彦
Nishiura Susumu 西浦進
Nishiyama Tsutomu 西山勉
Nomura Kichisaburō 野村吉三郎
Nomura Naokuni 野村直邦

Ogata Taketora 緒方竹虎
Ōhashi Chūichi 大橋忠一
Oikawa Koshirō 及川古志郎
Oka Takazumi 岡敬純
Okada Keisuke 岡田啓介
Okamoto Kiyotomi 岡本清福
Okumura Katsuzō 奥村勝蔵
Ōno Takeji 大野竹二
Onoda Sutejirō 小野田捨二郎
Ōshima Hiroshi 大島浩
Ozaki Hotsumi 尾崎秀実
Rōyama Masamichi 蠟山政道
Saionji Kimmochi 西園寺公望
Saitō Makoto 斎藤実
Saitō Takao 斎藤隆夫
Saitō Yoshie 斎藤良衛
Sakamoto Mizuo 阪本瑞男
Sakonji Seizō 左近司政三
Sanada Jōichirō 真田穣一郎
Sanematsu Yuzuru 実松譲
Satō Kenryō 佐藤賢了
Satomi Kishio 里見岸雄
Sawamoto Yorio 沢本頼雄
Shiba Katsuo 芝勝男
Shidehara Kijūrō 幣原喜重郎
Shigemitsu Mamoru 重光葵
Shimada Shigetarō 嶋田繁太郎
Suetsugu Nobumasa 末次信正
Sugiyama Gen (Hajime) 杉山元
Suzuki Teiichi 鈴木貞一
Takada Toshitane 高田利種
Takagi Sokichi 高木惣吉
Takamatsu-no-miya Nobuhito, Prince 高松宮宣仁
Takarabe Takeshi 財部彪
Tanabe Moritake 田辺盛武
Tanaka Shin'ichi 田中新一
Tatekawa Yoshitsugu 建川美次
Terajima Ken 寺島健
Terasaki Hidenari 寺崎英成
Terasaki Tarō 寺崎太郎
Tōgō Shigenori 東郷茂徳
Tōjō Hideki 東条英機

Tomioka Sadatoshi 富岡定俊
Tomita Kenji 富田健治
Toyoda Soemu 豊田副武
Toyoda Teijirō 豊田貞次郎
Tsukada Osamu 塚田攻
Uchida Nobuya (Shin'ya) 内田信也
Uchida Yasuya 内田康哉
Ugaki Kazushige (Kazunari) 宇垣一成
Ugaki Matome 宇垣纒
Umezu Yoshijirō 梅津美治郎
Ushiba Tomohiko 牛場友彦
Utsunomiya Tarō 宇都宮太郎
Wakamatsu Tadakazu (Tadaichi) 若松只一
Wakasugi Kaname 若杉要
Wakatsuki Reijirō 若槻礼次郎
Wang Ching-wei 汪精衛
Yamamoto Isoroku 山本五十六
Yamamoto Kumaichi 山本熊一
Yokoi Tadao 横井忠雄
Yokoyama Ichirō 横山一郎
Yonai Mitsumasa 米内光政
Yoshida Shigeru 吉田茂
Yoshida Zengo 吉田善吾
Yoshizawa Kenkichi 芳沢謙吉
Yuasa Kurahei 湯浅倉平
Yūki Shirōji 結城司郎次

Bibliography

Bibliography

I. Archives

Hirota Kōki 広田弘毅 Defense Materials, in the Shidehara Heiwa Bunko 幣原平和文庫 (Shidehara Peace Collection), National Diet Library, Tokyo.

Japan, Foreign Ministry Archives. Cited as JFM Archives.

Japan, Imperial Navy Records, held in the JDA Archives.

Japan, Justice Ministry Archives. Cited as JJM Archives.

Japan, Justice Ministry, War Crimes Materials Office. "Sempan kankei shiryō" 戦犯関係資料 (Materials Relating to War Crimes).

―――. "Kyokutō Kokusai Gunji Saiban kōhan kiroku 極東国際軍事裁判公判記録 (Records of the International Military for the Far East). Cited as IMTFE Records.

Japan, National Defense Agency, Military History Office Archives. Cited as JDA Archives. These contain the Kōseishō Engokyoku 厚生省援護局 (Welfare Ministry, Relief Bureau), ed. "Kaisen made no kokusaku no keii, shūsen kettei no keii oyobi kaigun daijin kōtetsu kankei bunsho." 開戦までの国策の経緯終戦決定の経緯及び海軍大臣更送関係文書 (Documents Pertaining to state Policymaking up to the Beginning of the War, How It Was Decided to End the War, and Replacing the Navy Minister), in JDA Archives. Cited as Welfare Ministry Documents.

Kase Toshikazu shuki 加瀬俊一 (Kase Toshikazu Memoir), 3 vols. (1946), held in JDA Archives. Vol. 1, "Nichi-Bei ryōkaian settō no sai no Matsuoka Gaisō no taido ni tsuite" 日米諒解案接到の際の松岡外相の態度について (Concerning Foreign Minister Matsuoka's Attitude upon Receipt of the Draft Japanese-American Understanding).

Papers of Konoe Fumimaro 近衛文麿, held in the Yōmei Bunko 陽明文庫, the private library of the Konoe family, Kyoto.

II. Interviews

Doi Akio 土居明夫, former Army General Staff Operations Section chief, January 20, 1962.

Fukudome Shigeru 福留繁, former Navy General Staff Operations Division chief, August 12, 1961.

Inoue Shigeyoshi 井上成美, former chief of Naval Aviation Headquarters, commander of Fourth Fleet, and acting vice navy minister, November 5 and 8, 1961.

Iwakuro Hideo 岩畔豪雄, former Army Ministry Military Section chief and army special envoy to Washington, February 4, 1961.

Kawai Iwao 川井巌, former member of Navy General Staff Operations Section, May 13, 1961.

Matsuoka Kin'ichirō 松岡謹一郎, eldest son of Matsuoka Yōsuke and former executive vice president of Asahi TV, April 30, 1962.

Miyo Kazunari 三代一就, former member of Navy General Staff Operations Section, December 10, 1960.

Nakanishi Toshinori 中西敏憲, former South Manchuria Railway director and Foreign Ministry official, June 27, 1962.

Nishi Haruhiko 西春彦, former Japanese minister to the USSR, July 20, 1960.

Nishiura Susumu 西浦進, former senior officer of Army Ministry Military Affairs Section, August 22, 1962.

Ōhashi Chūichi 大橋忠一, former vice foreign minister, September 30, 1961.

Onoda Sutejirō 小野田捨二郎, former member of First Division, Navy General Staff, October 14, 1961.

Ōshima Hiroshi 大島浩, former ambassador to Germany, February 7, 1960, and March 10, 1962.

Sanematsu Yuzuru 実松譲, former naval attaché in Washington, and secretary to Navy Minister Yonai, May 7, 1961.

Satō Kenryō 佐藤賢了, former Army Ministry Military Affairs Section chief, March 26, 1960.

Shiba Katsuo 芝勝男, former member of First Section, Naval Affairs Bureau, Navy Ministry, March 25 and April 8, 1961.

Takada Toshitane 高田利種, former chief of First Section, Naval Affairs Bureau, Navy Ministry, December 5, 1961.

Takagi Sōkichi 高木惣吉, Rear Admiral and former Navy Ministry Research Section chief, April 4, 1962.

Tanaka Shin'ichi 田中新一, former Army General Staff Operations Division chief, January 30, 1960.

Yokoi Tadao 横井忠雄, former member of Navy General Staff, July 8, 1961.

III. *Published Works and Major Unpublished Materials Cited*

Asada, Sadao, ed. *Japan and the World, 1853–1952: A Bibliographical Guide to Japanese Scholarship in Foreign Relations*. New York: Columbia University Press, 1989.

Asahi Shimbunsha. 朝日新聞社 (Asahi News), ed. *Kindai Nihon no gaikō* 近代日本の外交 (The Diplomacy of Modern Japan). Tokyo: Asahi Shimbunsha, 1962.

Barnhart, Michael. *Japan Prepares for Total War: The Search for Economic Security, 1919–1941*. Ithaca and London: Cornell University Press, 1987.

Barnes, Harry Elmer, ed. *Perpetual War for Perpetual Peace*. Caldwell, Idaho: Caxton Printers, 1953.

Borg, Dorothy, and Shumpei Okamoto, eds. *Pearl Harbor As History: Japanese-American Relations, 1931–1941*. New York and London: Columbia University Press, 1973.

Beard, Charles A. *President Roosevelt and the Coming of the War, 1941: A Study in Appearances and Realities*. New Haven: Yale University Press, 1948.

Butow, Robert J.C. *The John Doe Associates: Backdoor Diplomacy for Peace, 1941*. Stanford: Stanford University Press, 1974.

———. *Tōjō and the Coming of the War*. Princeton: Princeton University Press, 1961; reissued by Stanford University Press, 1969.

Churchill, Winston S. *The Grand Alliance*. Vol. 3 of *The Second World War*. Boston: Houghton Mifflin, 1950.

Connors, Leslie. *The Emperor's Adviser: Saionji Kinmochi and Pre-War Japanese Politics.* London: Croom Helm, and Nissan Institute for Japanese Studies, University of Oxford, 1987.

Conroy, Hilary, and Harry Wray, eds. *Pearl Harbor Reexamined: Prologue to the Pacific War.* Honolulu: University of Hawaii Press, 1990.

Dower, John W. *War without Mercy: Race and Power in the Pacific War.* New York: Pantheon Books, 1986.

Encyclopedia Britannica. Chicago: Encyclopaedia Britannica, 1959.

Feis, Herbert. *The Road to Pearl Harbor: The Coming of the War between the United States and Japan.* Princeton: Princeton University Press, 1950; paperback, New York: Atheneum, 1964.

Fukai Eigo 深井英五. *Sūmitsuin jūyō giji oboegaki* 枢密院重要議事覚書 (Notes on Important Sessions of the Privy Council). Tokyo: Iwanami Shoten, 1953.

Fukudome Shigeru 福留繁. *Kaigun no hansei* 海軍の反省 (A Self-examination by the Navy). Tokyo: Nihon Shuppan Kyōdō Kabushiki Kaisha, 1951.

———. *Shikan Shinjuwan kōgeki* 史観真珠湾攻撃 (A Historical View of the Attack on Pearl Harbor). Tokyo: Ajiasha, 1955.

Genda Minoru 源田実. "Higeki: Shinjuwan kōgeki" 悲劇・真珠湾攻撃 (A Tragedy: The Attack on Pearl Harbor), *Bungei shunjū* 文芸春秋, December 1962, pp. 198–212.

Grew, Joseph C. *Ten Years in Japan.* New York: Simon and Schuster, 1944.

———. *Turbulent Era: A Diplomatic Record of Forty Years, 1904–1945.* Edited by Walter Johnson assisted by Nancy Harrison Hooker. 2 vols. Boston: Houghton Mifflin, 1952.

Guderian, Heinz. *Panzer Leader.* Translated from the German by Constantine Fitzgibbon. New York: Dutton, 1952.

Harada Kumao 原田熊雄. *Saionji kō to seikyoku* 西園寺公と政局 (Prince Saionji and the Political Situation). 8 vols and supplementary volume of documents: *Bekkan* 別巻. Tokyo: Iwanami Shoten, 1950–52, 1956.

Hasluck, Paul. *The Government and the People, 1939–1941.* Series 4, Civil Vol. 1 of *Australia in the War, 1939–1945.* Canberra: Australian War Memorial, 1952.

Hata Ikuhiko. "Going to War: Who Delayed the Final Note?", *Japan Echo*, Vol. 19, No. 1 (Spring 1992), pp. 53–63.

Hata Shunroku 畑俊六. *Hata Shunroku nikki* 畑俊六日記 (The Diary of Hata Shunroku). Tokyo: Misuzu Shobō, 1981.

Hatano Sumio 波多野澄雄. *Bakuryō-tachi no Shinjuwan* 幕僚たちの真珠湾 (The Pearl Harbor of the Army Staff Officers.) Tokyo: Asahi Shimbunsha, 1991.

Hattori Takushirō 服部卓四郎. *Dai Tōa sensō zenshi* 大東亜戦争全史 (A History of the Greater East Asia War). 8 vols. Tokyo: Masu Shobō, 1953–56.

Heinrichs, Waldo H., Jr. *American Ambassador: Joseph C. Grew and the Development of the United States Diplomatic Tradition.* Boston: Little, Brown, 1966.

———. *Threshhold of War: Franklin D. Roosevelt and American Entry into World War II.* New York: Oxford University Press, 1988.

Higashikuni Naruhiko 東久邇稔彦. *Ichi kōzoku no sensō nikki* 一皇族の戦争日記 (The War Diary of One Member of the Imperial Family). Tokyo: Shūhōsha, 1957.

Hosoya Chihiro. "Characteristics of the Foreign Policy Decision-Making System in Japan," *World Politics*, Vol. 26, No. 3 (April 1974), pp. 353–69.

──────. "Miscalculations in Deterrent Policy: Japanese-U.S. Relations, 1938–1941," *Journal of Peace Research* (No. 2, 1968), pp. 97–115.

──────. "Twenty-Five Years after Pearl Harbor: A New Look at Japan's Decision for War," in Grant K. Goodman, comp. *Imperial Japan: A Reassessment* (Occasional Papers of the East Asian Institute, Columbia University). New York: The East Asian Institute of Columbia University, 1967.

Hull, Cordell. *The Memoirs of Cordell Hull.* 2 vols. New York: Macmillan, 1948.

Ienaga, Saburō. *The Pacific War: World War II and the Japanese, 1931–1945.* Translated by Frank Baldwin. New York: Pantheon Books, 1978.

Ienaga Saburô 家永三郎. *Taiheiyō sensō: daini han* 太平洋戦争第二版 (The Pacific War: Second Edition). Tokyo: Iwanami Shoten, 1986.

Ike, Nobutake. *Japan's Decision for War: Records of the 1941 Policy Conferences.* Stanford: Stanford University Press, 1967.

Iriye, Akira. "The Failure of Economic Expansion: 1918–1931," in Silberman, Bernard S., and H.D. Harootunian, eds. *Japan in Crisis: Essays on Taishō Democracy.* Princeton: Princeton University Press, 1974.

──────. *The Origins of the Second World War in Asia and the Pacific.* London and New York: Longman, 1987.

"Ishii Akiho taisa kaisōroku" 石井秋穂大佐回想録 (Memoirs of Colonel Ishii Ahiho). Kōseishō, Hikiage Engokyoku 厚生省引揚援護局 (Welfare Ministry, Repatriation Relief Bureau), 1958, in JDA Archives. Cited as Ishii Memoirs.

Ishigawa Shingo 石川信吾. *Shinjuwan made no keii: kaisen no shinsō.* 真珠湾まで の経緯・開戦の真相 (To Pearl Harbor: The Truth about the Outbreak of the War). Tokyo: Jiji Tsūshinsha, 1960.

Itō Takashi 伊藤隆 and Nomura Minoru 野村実, eds. *Kaigun taishō Kobayashi Seizō oboegaki* 海軍大将小林躋造覚書 (Admiral Kobayashi Seizō Memoranda). Tokyo: Yamakawa Shuppansha, 1984.

Jacobsen, Hans-Adolf and Jurgen Rohwer. *Entscheidungsschlachten des zweiten Weltkrieges* (Decisive Battles of World War II). Frankfurt: Bernard and Graefe, 1960.

Japan, Army General Staff, War Guidance Office. "Daihon'ei kimitsu sensō nisshi" 大本営機密戦争日誌 (Confidential War Diary of the Imperial Headquarters). In JDA Archives. Cited as AGS, "Kimitsu nisshi."

Japan, Foreign Ministry. *Nichi-Bei kōshō shiryō: Keii no bu* 日米交渉資料・経緯の部 (Source Materials on Japanese-American Negotiations: History Volume). Tokyo: Hara Shobō, 1978. Cited as JFM, *Keii.*

──────. *Nichi-Bei kōshō shiryō: Kiroku no bu* 日米交渉資料・記録の部 (Source Materials on Japanese-American Negotiations: Documents Volume). Tokyo: Hara Shobō, 1978. Cited as JFM, *Kiroku.*

──────. *Nihon gaikō nempyō narabi ni shuyō bunsho* 日本外交年表竝主要文書 (Chronology and Major Documents of Japanese Foreign Relations). 2 vols. Tokyo: Hara Shobō, 1966; first published 1955.

Japan, National Defense Agency. *Senshi sōsho: Daihon'ei rikugunbu, Dai Tōa sensō kaisen keii.* 戦史叢書・大本営陸軍部大東亜戦争開戦経緯 (War History Series: The Imperial Headquarters Army, Circumstances Leading to the Outbreak of the Greater East Asian War). 5 vols. Tokyo: Asagumo Shimbunsha, 1973–74.

Jones, S. Shepard and Denys P. Myers, eds. *Documents on American Foreign Relations.* Boston: World Peace Foundation, 1941.

Kaya Okinori 賀屋興宣. "*Kaisen no shinsō*" 開戦の真相 (The Truth about the Outbreak of the War). *Yosan* 予算 (Budget), Vol. 31 (April).

Kiba Kōsuke 木場浩介, ed. *Nomura Kichisaburō* 野村吉三郎 Tokyo: Nomura Kichisaburō Denki Kankōkai, 1961.

Kido Kōichi Nikki Kenkyūkai 木戸幸一日記研究会 (Kido Diary Study Group), comps. *Kido Kōichi Nikki* 木戸幸一日記 (Diary of Kido Kōichi). 2 vols. Tokyo: Tōkyō Daigaku Shuppankai, 1966. Cited as *Kido nikki.*

―――. *Kido Kōichi kankei bunsho* 木戸幸一関係文書 (Documents Concerning Kido Kōichi). Tokyo: Tōkyō Daigaku Shuppankai, 1966. Cited as *Kido bunsho.*

Kittredge, Tracy B. "United States Defense Policy and Strategy; 1941," *U.S. News and World Report,* Vol. 37, No. 23 (December 3, 1954), pp. 53–63, 110–39.

Kodansha Encyclopedia of Japan. Tokyo and New York: Kodansha and Kodansha International/USA, 1983, Vol. 7.

Konoe Fumimaro 近衛文麿. *Heiwa e no doryoku* 平和への努力 (My Struggle for Peace). Tokyo: Nihon Dempō Tsūshinsha, 1946.

―――. *Ushinawareshi seiji* 失はれし政治 (The Politics That Failed). Tokyo: Asahi Shimbunsha, 1946.

Kurusu Saburō 来栖三郎. *Nichi-Bei gaikō hiwa: waga gaikōshi* 日米外交秘話・わが外交史 (A Confidential Account of Japanese-American Diplomacy: My Diplomatic History). Tokyo: Sōgensha, 1952.

Langer, William L. and S. Everett Gleason. *The Challenge to Isolation, 1937–1940.* New York: Harper, 1952.

―――. *The Undeclared War, 1940–1941.* New York: Harper, 1953.

Large, Stephen S. *Emperor Hirohito and Shōwa Japan: A Political Biography.* London and New York: Routledge, 1992.

Lu, David J., ed. *Perspectives on Japan's External Relations: Views from America, A Festschrift in Honor of Dr. Tsunoda Jun.* Bucknell University: Center for Japanese Studies, 1982.

Martienssen, Anthony. *Hitler and His Admirals.* New York: E.P. Dutton, 1949.

Matsumoto Shigeharu 松本重治, Oka Yoshitake 岡義武, Nishi Haruhiko 西春彦, Kawagoe Shigeru 川越茂, and Kase Toshikazu 加瀬俊一. *Kindai Nihon no gaikō* 近代日本の外交 (The Diplomacy of Modern Japan). Tokyo: Asahi Shimbunsha, 1962.

Miller, Edward S. *War Plan ORANGE.* Annapolis: Naval Institute Press, 1991.

Morishima Morito 森島守人. *Shunjuwan Risubon Tōkyō: zoku ichi gaikōkan no kaisō* 真珠湾リスボン東京・続一外交官の回想 (Pearl Harbor, Lisbon, Tokyo: A Diplomat's Memoirs Continued). Tokyo: Iwanami Shoten, 1959.

Morley, James William ed. *The China Quagmire: Japan's Expansion on the Asian Continent, 1933–1941.* New York: Columbia University Press, 1983.

——. *The Fateful Choice: Japan's Advance into Southeast Asia, 1939–1941*. New York: Columbia University Press, 1980.

——. *Japan Erupts: The London Naval Conference and the Manchurian Incident, 1928–1932*. New York: Columbia University Press, 1984.

——. *Japan's Foreign Policy, 1868–1941: A Research Guide*. New York and London: Columbia University Press, 1974.

Muroga Sadanobu 室賀定信. *Shōwa Juku: Danatsu no arashi no naka demo, jiyū no akari o mamoritsuzuketa hitotsu no juku ga atta* 昭和塾・弾圧の嵐の中でも自由の灯を守りつづけたひとつの塾があった (Amidst the Storm of Oppression There Was One School That Preserved the Light of Freedom: The Shōwa Juku). Tokyo: Nihon Keizai Shimbun, 1978.

Nihon Kindai Shiryō Kenkyūkai 日本近代資料研究会 (Modern Japanese History Archival Research Society), comp. *Nihon rikukaigun no seido-soshiki-jinji* 日本陸海軍の制度・組織・人事 (The Institutions, Organization, and Personnel of the Japanese Army and Navy). Tokyo: Tōkyō Daigaku Shuppankai, 1972. Cited as *Nihon rikukaigun*.

Nihon Kokusai Seiji Gakkai, Taiheiyō Sensō Gen'in Kenkyūbu 日本国際政治学会太平洋戦争原因研究部 (Japan Association on International Relations, Study Group on the Causes of the Pacific War), ed. *Taiheiyō sensō e no michi: Bekkan shiryō hen* 太平洋戦争への道別巻資料編 (The Road to the Pacific War: Supplementary Volume of Documents). Tokyo: Asahi Shimbunsha, 1963. Cited as *TSM: Bekkan*.

Nomura Kichisaburō 野村吉三郎. *Beikoku ni tsukai shite: Nichi-Bei kōshō no kaiko* 米国に使して・日米交渉の回顧 (Ambassador to the United States: Reminiscences of the Japanese-American Negotiations). Tokyo: Iwanami Shoten, 1946.

——. "Stepping Stones to War," *U.S. Naval Institute Proceedings*, September 1951.

Ogata Taketora 緒方竹虎. *Ichi gunjin no shōgai: kaisō no Yonai Mitsumasa* 一軍人の生涯・回想の米内光政 (The Life of a Military Man: Reminiscences of Yonai Mitsumasa). Tokyo: Bungei Shunjū Shinsha, 1955.

Ōhashi Chūichi 大橋忠一. *Taiheiyō sensō yuraiki* 太平洋戦争由来記 (Origins of the Pacific War). Tokyo: Kaname Shobō, 1952.

Okada Keisuke 岡田啓介. *Okada Keisuke kaikoroku* 岡田啓介回顧録 (Reminiscences of Okada Keisuke). Tokyo: Mainichi Shimbunsha, 1950.

Okada Taishō Kiroku Hensankai 岡田大将記録編纂会 (Association for the Compilation of the Archives of Admiral Okada). *Okada Keisuke* 岡田啓介. Tokyo: Okada Taishō Kiroku Hensankai, 1956.

Pelz, Stephen E. *Race to Pearl Harbor: The Failure of the Second London Naval Conference and the Onset of World War II*. Cambridge: Harvard University Press, 1974.

Perkins, Frances. *The Roosevelt I Knew*. New York: Viking, 1947.

Robertson, David. *Guide to Modern Defense and Strategy*. Detroit: Gale Research, 1987.

Roosevelt, Elliott, ed. *F.D.R.: His Personal Letters, 1928–1945*. 2 vols. New York: Duell, Sloan and Pearce, 1950.

Roskill, Stephen W. *White Ensign: The British Navy at War, 1939–1945*. Annapolis: United States Naval Institute, 1960.

Saitō Yoshie 斉藤良衛. *Azamukareta rekishi: Matsuoka to Sangoku Dōmei no rimen* 欺かれた歴史・松岡と三国同盟の裏面 (History Deceived: The Inside Story of Matsuoka and the Tripartite Pact). Tokyo: Yomiuri Shimbunsha, 1955.

Sakai Saburō 酒井三郎. Shōwa Kenkyūkai: Aru chishikijin shūdan no kiseki 昭和研究会・ある知識人集団の軌跡 (The Shōwa Kenkyūkai: A Gathering of Men of Knowledge). Tokyo: TBS Britannica, 1979.

Sakuta Takatarō 作田高太郎. *Tennō to Kido* 天皇と木戸 (The Emperor and Kido). Tokyo: Heibonsha, 1948.

Sanbō Honbu 参謀本部 (Army General Staff). *Sugiyama memo* 杉山メモ (The Sugiyama Memoranda). 2 vols. Tokyo: Hara Shobō, 1967. Cited as *Sugiyama memo*.

Satō Kenryō 佐藤賢了. *Tōjō Hideki to Taiheiyō sensō* 東条英機と太平洋戦争 (Tōjō Hideki and the Pacific War). Tokyo: Bungei Shunjū Shinsha, 1960.

Sbrega, John J. *The War against Japan, 1941–1945: An Annotated Bibliography*. New York and London: Garland Publishing, 1989.

Sherwood, Robert E. *Roosevelt and Hopkins: An Intimate History*. New York: Harper, 1948.

Shidehara Heiwa Zaidan 幣原平和財団 (Shidehara Peace Foundation), ed. *Shidehara Kijūrō* 幣原喜重郎. Tokyo: Shidehara Heiwa Zaidan, 1955.

Shimanuki Takeji 島貫武治. "Nihon no kokubō hōshin: Yōhei kōryō" 日本の国防方針・用兵綱領 (Japan's National Defense Policy: Tactical Principals), *Kokubō* 国防 (National Defense), November 1961, pp. 66–82.

Shiobara Tokisaburō 塩原時三郎. *Tōjō memo: kakute tennō wa sukuwareta* 東条メモ・かくて天皇は救われた (The Tōjō Memo: Thus Was the Emperor Saved). Tokyo: Handobukkusha, 1952.

"Shōwa Tennō no dokuhaku hachijikan" 昭和天皇の独白八時間 (The Shōwa Emperor's Eight-Hour Soliloquy), *Bungei Shunjū*, 文芸春秋, Vol. 12 (1990), pp. 100–145.

Stanley, William H. and Arthur A. Ageton. *Admiral Ambassador to Russia*. Chicago: Henry Regnery, 1955.

Stimson, Henry L. and McGeorge Bundy. *On Active Service in Peace and War*. New York: Harper, 1948.

Tanaka Shin'ichi 田中新一. *Taisen totsu'nyū no shinsō* 大戦突入の真相 (The Truth about the Plunge into the Pacific War). Tokyo: Gengensha, 1955.

———. "Tanaka Shin'ichi chūjo gyōmu nisshi" 田中新一中将業務日誌 (The On-Duty Diary of Lieutenant General Tanaka Shin'ichi). JDA Archives. Cited as Tanaka diary.

Titus, David A. *Palace and Politics in Prewar Japan*. New York: Columbia University Press, 1974.

Tōgō Shigenori 東郷茂徳. *Jidai no ichimen* 時代の一面 (One View of an Era). Tokyo: Kaizōsha, 1952.

Tōkyō Daigaku Bungakubu, Kokushi Kenkyūshitsu 東京大学文学部国史研究室 (Tokyo University Faculty of Letters, Japanese History Office), ed. *Nihon kindaishi jiten* 日本近代史辞典 (Dictionary of Modern Japanese History).

13th printing. Tokyo: Tōyō Keizai Shinpōsha, 1974.

Tolischus, Otto D. *Tokyo Record*. New York: Reynal and Hitchcock, 1943.

Tomioka Sadatoshi 富岡定俊. "Taiheiyō sensō Nihon kaigun senshi" 太平洋戦争日本海軍戦史 (The Japanese Navy in the Pacific War). 14 vols., mimeographed. Tokyo: Maritime Self-Defense Force, 1950s.

Tomita Kenji 富田健治. *Haisen Nihon no uchigawa: Konoe kō no omoide* 敗戦日本の内側・近衛公の想い出 (Inside Defeated Japan: Recollections of Prince Konoe). Tokyo: Kokon Shoin, 1962.

Tōyama Shigeki 遠山茂樹 and Adachi Yoshiko 安達淑子. *Kindai Nihon seiji hikkei* 近代日本政治必携 (Manual of Modern Japanese Politics). Tokyo: Iwanami Shoten, 1961.

Toyoda Soemu 豊田副武. *Saigo no teikoku kaigun* 最後の帝国海軍 (The Last Imperial Navy). Edited by Yanagisawa Takeshi 柳沢健. Tokyo: Sekai no Nihonsha, 1950.

U.S. Congress, Joint Committee on the Investigation of the Pearl Harbor Attack. *Hearings before the Joint Committee on the Investigation of the Pearl Harbor Attack*. 39 parts in 15 vols. Washington D.C.: U.S. Government printing Office, 1946. Cited as *Pearl Harbor Hearings*.

———. *Investigation of the Pearl Harbor Attack: Report*. Senate Document No. 244, Washington, D.C.: U.S. Government Printing Office, 1946. Cited as *Pearl Harbor Hearings, Investigation of the Pearl Harbor Attack: Report*.

U.S., Department of State. *Documents on German Foreign Policy, 1918–1945, from the Archives of the German Foreiqn Ministry*, Series D (1937–1945), Vols. 11 (1960), 12 (1962). Washington D.C.: U.S. Government Printing Office. Cited as *DGFP*.

———. *Foreign Relations of the United States: Diplomatic Papers, 1940*, Vol. 4: *The Far East*. Washington D.C.: U.S. Government Printing Office, 1955. Cited as *FR, 1940*.

———. *Foreign Relations of the United States: Diplomatic Papers, 1941*. Vol. 1: *General, The Soviet Union*; vols. 4–5: *The Far East*. Washington D.C.: U.S. Government Printing Office, 1958, 1956. Cited as *FR, 1941*.

———. *Papers Relating to the Foreign Relations of the United States: Japan, 1931–1941*. 2 vols. Washington D.C.: U.S. Government Printing Office, 1943. Cited as *FR*, Japan.

———. *Peace and War: United States Foreign Policy, 1931–1941*. Washington D.C.: U.S. Government Printing Office, 1943.

U.S., Office of Naval Intelligence, trans. *The Fuehrer Conferences on Matters Dealing with the German Navy, 1939–1945*. Washington D.C., 1947; A Microfilm Project by Scholarly Resources, Inc., Wilmington, DE, 1983.

Wakatsuki Reijirō 若槻礼次郎. *Kofūan kaikoroku* 古風庵回顧録 (Reminiscences from a Moss-Grown Hermitage). Tokyo: Yomiuri Shimbunsha, 1950.

Woodward, Ernest L. *British Foreign Policy in the Second World War*. London: HMSO, 1962.

Yabe Teiji 矢部貞治, ed. *Konoe Fumimaro* 近衛文麿. 2 vols. Tokyo: Kōbundō, 1952.

Index

Abe Nobuyuki, 238, 239
Akamatsu Sadao, 247
Amano Masakazu, 316
Anami Korechika, 19
Anti-Commintern Pact (November 1936), 65, 154
Arima Yoriyasu, 30
Arita Declaration (December 1938), 220
Army, Japan; banking on German victories, 121, 124–25, 141, 147, 153, 156–57, 167, 169, 171–72, 220; "mentality" of, xxx–xxxi; and the Tripartite Pact, 124, 152–53, 154; and war with the Soviet Union, 124, 125, 127–28, 129, 131–33, 154–57, 199; and war with the United States (Britain, Holland), 116–122, 163–67, 173, 199, 296; see also Draft Japanese-American Understanding; Hirohito; Ishii; Iwakuro; Konoe; Mutō; Navy, Japan; Nomura Kichisaburō; Ōno; Sanada; Satō; Sugiyama; Tanaka; Tōjō; Toyoda Teijirō; Tsukada
Army General Staff, xxxvi, 61; and army ministry, 212; fears that negotiations with the United States will succeed, 315–17, 320; ignores Suzuki's three conditions, 296–301; preparations for Imperial Conference of September 6, 1941, xxxvi, 170–72; pro-Axis position of, 89; pro-war group in, 207; and reexamination of state policy, 248–49, 251–52; resolves on war with the

United States, 220, 251–52; *see also* Sugiyama; War Guidance Office, Army General Staff
Asada Sadao, xxxiv
Assassination of Japanese leaders, xxiv, xxxvii, 30, 37
Atlantic, battle of, 115–116, 283–84, 344
Atlantic Conference, 182, 183–84, 284, 301–2, 339
Australia, policy toward Japan, 311–13; *see also* Bruce; Casey; Curtin; Evatt; Menzies

Balfour, Harold, 302–3
Ballantine, Joseph W., 33, 36, 37, 70
Beard, Charles, 318
Britain, 44, 45, 80, 86; German invasion of (victory over), 1, 2, 10, 11, 12, 14, 85, 116, 117, 141–42, 172, 282–83; inseparability from the United States, 121–22, 213, 215, 248; and the Soviet Union, 140; and United States policy toward Japan, 51, 311; *see also* Atlantic, battle of; Atlantic Conference; Balfour; Brooke-Popham; Churchill; Craigie; Cranborne; destroyers-for-bases deal; Draft Japanese-American Understanding; Germany; Halifax; Hitler; Lothian; Nagano; United States, convoying; United States, neutrality
Brooke-Popham, Robert, 342
Bruce, Stanley, 342
Byas, Hugh, xxx

STUDIES OF THE EAST ASIAN INSTITUTE
Selected Titles

Embassy at War, by Harold Joyce Noble. Edited with an introduction by Frank Baldwin, Jr. Seattle: University of Washington Press, 1975.

Tanaka Giichi and Japan's China Policy, by William F. Morton. Folkestone, England: Dawson, 1980; New York: St. Martin's Press, 1980.

State and Diplomacy in Early Modern Japan, by Ronald Toby. Princeton: Princeton University Press, 1983 (hc); Stanford: Stanford University Press, 1991 (pb).

Japan's Modern Myths: Ideology in the Late Meiji Period, by Carol Gluck. Princeton University Press, 1985.

Remaking Japan: The American Occupation as New Deal, by Theodore Cohen, edited by Herbert Passin. New York: The Pree Press, 1987.

Japan and the World, 1853–1952: A Bibliographic Guide to Recent Scholarship in Japanese Foreign Relations, by Sadao Asada. New York: Columbia University Press, 1988.

Aftermath of War: Americans and the Remaking of Japan, 1945–1952, by Howard B. Schonberger. Kent, OH: Kent State University Press, 1989.

Social Mobility in Contemporary Japan, by Hiroshi Ishida. Stanford: Stanford University Press, 1993.

Japan's Foreign Policy after the Cold War: Coping with Change, Gerald L. Curtis, ed. Armonk, NY: M.E. Sharpe, 1993.

Japan's Road to the Pacific War, selected translation of the *Taiheiyo senso e no michi* in five volumes, James W. Morley, ed. New York: Columbia University Press, 1976–94.

Volume I: *Japan Erupts: The London Naval Conference and the Manchurian Incident*, (1984)

Volume II: *The China Quagmire: Japan's Expansion on the Asian Continent, 1933–1941*, (1983)

Volume III: *Deterrent Diplomacy*, (1976)

Volume IV: *The Fateful Choice: Japan's Advance into Southeast Asia*, (1980)

Volume V: *The Final Confrontation: Japan's Negotiations with the United States, 1941*, (1994)